STEEL CHAIR TO THE HEAD

The Pleasure and Pain of

Professional Wrestling

EDITED BY NICHOLAS SAMMOND

DUKE UNIVERSITY PRESS

DURHAM AND LONDON 2005

Designed by Rebecca M. Giménez.
Typeset in Adobe Minion by
Tseng Information Systems.
Republication information and
Library of Congress Cataloging-in-
Publication Data appear on the
last two printed pages of this book.
Research and work for this volume
were supported by the Andrew W.
Mellon Foundation and Washington
University, Saint Louis.

For Sputnik Monroe, who
took the color bar to the mat

CONTENT

ACK-
NOW-
LEDG-
MENTS

Doug Battema and Philip Sewell: The authors thank Nic Sammond, editor of this anthology, for his rigorous and insightful critiques of their essay. The authors also thank Kim Bjarkman for her scholarly input and support in formulating this project.

Laurence de Garis: I would like to thank everybody who ever took a bump for me. I appreciate it and hope to someday return the favor.

Heather Levi: Heather Levi would like to thank the following people: My generous and patient teacher, Professor Luis Jaramillo; Víctor Martínez of Deportes Martínez; and Anne Rubenstein, Verenice Naranjo, and Isabel Pinedo for their ongoing assistance and support with this project.

Sharon Mazer: I must thank Johnny Rodz and the wrestlers at Gleason's Gym for their generosity; in particular, Larry Brisco, with his academic alterego, and Laurence de Garis, who has looked over my shoulder throughout this research. Thanks also to Donna Heiland and Peter Falkenberg for keeping me on point. All errors of fact and analysis are evermore my own.

Lucia Rahilly: Many thanks to Chris Straayer, Chair of the Cinema Studies Department at NYU, and to my colleagues Carla Marcantonio and Arash Hoda for their invaluable insights and support in the early stages of formulating this essay.

Nicholas Sammond: The editor would like to thank Henry Jenkins III, Anna McCarthy, Margaret Garb, Timothy Parsons, Cynthia Chris, Kevin Dunn, Anna Creadick, Chandra Mukerji, and Eric Smoodin for their invaluable feedback. Thanks also to Ken Wissoker and the editorial staff at Duke University Press for their support and encouragement. Special thanks to Emma Bianchi and Neon Weiss for their immoral support. Finally, my thanks to Amy Greenstadt, U.S.A., who patiently abided when I changed the channel to do research — and read and reread — my undying devotion.

Phillip Serrato: My thanks go to Laura E. Ramirez-Diaz, Dr. Mike Lano, Brian Bukantis, and Arena Publishing.

NICHOLAS SAMMOND

Introduction: A Brief and Unnecessary

Defense of Professional Wrestling

It is . . . in the body of the wrestler that we find the first key to the contest. . . . The physique of the wrestlers . . . constitutes a basic sign, which like the seed contains the whole fight. But this seed proliferates, for it is at every turn during the fight, in each new situation, that the body of the wrestler casts to the public the magical entertainment of a temperament which finds its natural expression in a gesture.
—Roland Barthes, "The World of Wrestling"

Since this volume examines a provocative subject (for some), let's begin with a provocative statement: Professional wrestling is a substantial American popular art form, the latest in a long line that includes burlesque, vaudeville, jazz, rock 'n' roll, and punk. If Roland Barthes (in this volume) can trace French professional wrestling back through Racine and Molière, all the way to classical Greece, we can at least trace our own lineage back to Tony Pastor, Edward Albee, the Marx Brothers, the Nicholas Brothers, Fannie Brice, Josephine Baker, Milton Berle, Elvis Presley, James Brown, Little Richard, and the Ramones.

If we were to attempt the same sort of genealogy as Barthes, we would find it easier to trace a line from professional wrestling's ribald American ancestors back to Greek comedy. It's not a stretch to see in burlesque, vaudeville, and so on, the priapic excesses of *Lysistrata*, with its links between the body politic and the sexual body clearly marked by gigantic swollen phalluses dragging their bearers toward acquiescence. But what is there in the neon spandex, leather masks, pounding heavy metal and rap of wrestling that recalls Euripides or Sophocles—the horrible grief of Agave, the literal and metaphorical blindness of Oedipus? Very little, if we limit ourselves to the view that these works are great because they transcend culture and history, offering universal truths that ennoble those wise enough to perceive them. While that may be true, it doesn't exhaust the meanings available to us. The theater of classical Athens was more than entertainment; it was also a forum for arguing about *social* relations—the very immediate question of how its citizens were to live with each other, and within a political and religious order that was very concerned with questions of property, of inheritance, of oppression, and of power.

As such, the stories it told were often bloody or lubricious—filled with murder, rape, incest, suicide, and wanton sexuality. And, like the Parents Television Council or the National Institute on the Media and the Family today, the social critics of the day, such as Plato or Aristotle, warned against the theater (particularly comedy) as a force for corrupting young boys (but not girls, who would never be citizens), and for undermining Athenian society.

While this comparison should make the William Bennetts of our age proud, it is worth noting that Plato, for instance, considered the question of whether young boys should have sex with older men a matter worth debating, rather than simply one requiring condemnation (Plato [n.d.] 1951: 92–103). *O tempora, o mores!*[1] Arguments for the effect of entertainment on culture and society have been with us for millennia, yet no one today would argue that Aristophanes was responsible for the downfall of classical Athenian society. Yet that is the claim often laid at the booted feet of professional wrestling today: that it is both cause and symptom of the breakdown of American social and cultural life.

The same warning cries were made about burlesque in its heyday in the middle of the nineteenth century, about vaudeville at the turn of the twentieth century, and about jazz and rock 'n' roll in their first proud incarnations. What all of these forms share with professional wrestling, and what is lost in viewing Greek (or French, or Shakespearean . . .) drama as simply a literature, is the very carnality they expressed, their celebration and contestation of people and ideas as *embodied*. American popular performance has never been about transcending the moment or passion and emotion; it has always been about the lived experience of social, political, and cultural life. It is about bodies marked by race, ethnicity, gender, class, and sexuality operating in a democratic capitalist national culture that lacks a robust language for speaking about concrete, lived experience.

Professional wrestling is no exception. It shares with burlesque a celebration of public (hetero)sexuality and a complex and imperfect expression of gendered power relations (Allen 1991). It shares with vaudeville a reveling in physical and verbal virtuosity, in excess and immediacy, in the explicit expression of ethnic and racial stereotypes and of common class subjugation (Jenkins 1992). It shares with rock 'n' roll the blurring of lines of class, race, and gender. And like all of these antecedent forms, since it has become a mass phenomenon it has incurred the wrath of moralists and social reformers for whom the messy and often incoherent bodily expression of violence, struggle, and sexuality represents an assault on the public good. Given that this assault has continued unabated for almost 150 years, it's a wonder that the nation still stands.

Certainly, however, movies and other types of television (for though wrestling happens live, it only causes so much vexation when it appears on the living-room screen) feature violence and sexuality as well. What was *Erin Brockovich* (Steven Soderbergh, 2000) but a celebration of the politically transformative power of Julia Roberts's breasts? Does anyone believe that Arnold Schwarzenegger makes box office because of his nuanced line readings? Could we imagine *Temptation Island* set in Greenland? Yet while movies and television sometimes earn the wrath of a Joe Lieberman or Jerry Falwell, they spare themselves much of the righteous indignation reserved for wrestling by hewing to a set of moral frames established some seventy-five years ago during the heyday of the Production Code, a set of norms laid out by the movie industry to avoid censorship. In these frames, representations of violence or sexuality, or racial intolerance, or criminal behavior are acceptable as long as they are redeemed by demonstrating the ultimate wisdom and victory of moral virtue. In short, you can show violence as long as it serves to defeat a greater evil. You can show crime as long as in the end it doesn't pay. You can show sexuality as long as it ultimately serves the greater virtues of love and marriage. Good characters may fall from grace, becoming addicted, promiscuous, violent, and so forth, as long as in the end they (or we) learn from their moral failings. Wrestling, of course, offers no such moral comfort. Week after week, it seems, no one learns anything from its excesses of violence, sexuality, and general moral turpitude. It has become, at the dawn of the twenty-first century, utterly, intentionally, and exuberantly gratuitous.

Nor is the expression of physicality in professional wrestling (or "sports entertainment," a term coined by Vince McMahon to avoid gaming fees) the same as it is in more conventional sports such as football, baseball, soccer, or basketball. In conventional commercial sports (and in their amateur counterparts), the body is first and foremost a vehicle for the skills of the individual, an expression of talent, drive, training, and ability. The athlete's body is that which overcomes the physical, mental, and emotional constraints placed upon it by the demands of the individual sport; it is a tool wielded by the athlete her- or himself, and by the coach who deploys it on the field of play. Secondarily, it is thus subjugated to the will and needs of a larger body, that of the team. It is a body abstracted, and that abstraction is constantly reframed by the commentary of sportscasters, newspaper sports columnists, and fans.

With its gestures toward being a sport, professional wrestling occasionally calls upon all of these meanings in referring to the wrestler's body, but it also consistently violates and undermines them. While ringside announcers may make much of a male wrestler's strength, size, and agility, for instance, the wrestler himself undermines that abstraction, falling prey to strong emotional impulses — anger, jealousy, love, fear — that loosen the grip of discipline over that body. Are those emotions the stuff of the body itself, or the demons of a tormented mind? The male wrestler constantly struggles to control the powerful beast that is his body, and constantly fails in that attempt.

The bodies of female wrestlers suffer a different fate. While the ringside patter may sometimes refer to their strength and agility, announcers rarely forget to mention the female wrestler's body as a sexual object, a formidable assembly of tits and ass that also happens to be able to kick butt. Female wrestlers struggle within and against their own object status, and the emotions that overwhelm them have often to do with that sexuality; while male wrestlers are more likely to grapple over issues of honor and dominance, female wrestlers often engage in cat fights over possession of (or the right to be possessed by) a man. While female fans might sexualize the male wrestler's body, the only time that ringside announcers do so is when his heterosexuality is called into question.

Nor do wrestlers subjugate their bodies to the will of the team. Tag team partnerships are evanescent, rent asunder by the passions that eddy around and through the wrestlers. Either one partner betrays the other, or the team is torn apart by conflicting loyalties (see Salmon and Clerc in this volume). And it is just as likely that a tag team partnership will be forced on two wrestlers by the management, which maliciously and capriciously brings together grapplers who are in competition for the same title, or who bear some grudge against each other. Not only do fierce passions constantly overwhelm the wrestler's control over his/her strength and agility, so does the boss. While the same sort of alienation becomes painfully apparent in conventional sports during contract negotiations and strikes, the cultural convention of the athlete's regulation by a unified self, and by the greater unity of the team, is always quickly restored by the resolution of the labor conflict and by framing commentary which decries labor conflict as unsportsmanlike (i.e., disrupting the illusion that professional sports are not businesses).

Professional wrestling has no such illusions: it's a business, and wrestlers are workers. As Sharon Mazer and Laurence de Garis point out in this volume, the traditional terminology of wrestling acknowledges this, calling wrestlers *workers* and those elements of a wrestling match (or interview) that are planned by management or the wrestlers themselves a *work*. The idea that the wrestler controls his or her body, or the persona that sits uneasily on that body (a wrestler may go through several personae during the course of a career), is disrupted by the conventions of the form, in which the will and freedom of the wrestler are constantly undermined by the whims of the back office. (Retired wrestler Mick Foley, at the height of his career in the [then] World Wrestling Federation [wwf, now the wwe, or World Wrestling Entertainment, Inc.], brought this situation into even starker relief, performing several personae — Cactus Jack, Dude Love, and Mankind — simultaneously, sometimes even within one match or interview.) It bears repeating: wrestlers are workers, and as such they simultaneously reveal the production of their personae, their embodiment of characters of their own making, and their ultimate lack of control over the conditions of that making and over the disposition of the products of their labor. They are twice alienated from the control of their bodies, both by their inability to regulate the passions that drive them, and by a management that plays on that lack of self-control, to enact a transparent appropriation of their labor.

This violation of the cultural convention of the performer's control over her/his character has been further disrupted since the wwe gained monopoly control over televised professional wrestling in the United States in 2001. When work on this volume began, there were two major wrestling venues—the WWF and World Championship Wrestling (WCW)—and one smaller but still substantial venue, Extreme Championship Wrestling (ECW). Since then, the ECW has folded and the WWE has bought out WCW's stable of wrestlers. To capitalize on this smackdown, and to appeal to WCW fans, the WWE has built a number of storylines around the uneasy integration of the two operations, particularly around "interoffice" struggles to streamline the two management systems, and around the troubles of wrestlers (workers) in attempts to accommodate consolidation. Performers in more mainstream narrative forms disappear into their characters and into the narrative; athletes, never characters, perform the control of their bodies by themselves and by the team. Their participation in a capitalist enterprise constantly disappears into the fiction of self-control. Not so for the wrestler, who is worker and product and character, always out of control, always struggling to control self and others, and always failing in that enterprise.

This, then, is what makes professional wrestling so disruptive, so transgressive, so upsetting to its social critics on both the left and right. Focused on the struggle between wrestlers' bodies—oiled, shaved, sweating, pierced, tattooed, and pharmaceutically and surgically enhanced—wrestling resolutely refuses to ground that struggle in a moral order, to subject those bodies to a consistent discipline that would make sense of its excesses of violence and sexuality. It offers absolutely no narrative of redemption. Wrestlers never learn from their mistakes, never see the error of their ways in retrospective regret, nor conquer the external forces that oppress them. Instead, the cycle repeats, over and over: the same mistakes, the same betrayals, the same evanescent victories and defeats.

For Barthes, this was indicative of the wrestler's status as a signifier for basic passions: not fully a character or a player, the wrestler was but a "basic sign." But this reading underplays the levels of signification present in every wrestler today. (Stone Cold) Steve Austin is at once the beer-swilling, redneck good ole boy, the exploited worker caught up in internecine management struggles, and the freelance entertainer playing those factions against each other. Vince McMahon is simultaneously the actual chairman of World Wrestling Enterprises (a savvy businessman), the fictional chairman of the WWE (an irrational, violent, and manipulative exploiter of his workers), an actually loving husband and father to his wife, Linda, and children, Shane and Stephanie, and a fictionally abusive husband and father to the televised versions of those same family members. Chuck and Billy play gay tag team partners on *Smackdown!* and then Chuck Palumbo and Monty Sopp assert their heterosexuality in interviews on *Howard Stern* and *The Today Show*, then Billy and Chuck disavow their homosexuality moments before getting married on *Smackdown*. The circuit of signification flickers uncertainly between the ring and the wider world, and between worker and persona, playing off the obvious homoeroticism of wrestling, raising it and diffusing it. Which passion speaks, desire or fear? Which is genuine? Both? Neither?

Wrestling is brutal and it is carnal. It is awash in blood, sweat, and spit, and for all of its emphasis these days on soap-operatic storylines and backstage intrigue, it still depends on the match—the violent and sensual meeting of human flesh in the ring. Yet that flesh—far from being the seed of meaning from which springs the signifying force of the wrestler, or the match, or wrestling itself—is but a node in a circuit of signification. The most popular wrestlers today aren't simply individuals; they are part of larger commodity packages. Before wrestlers appear at the top of the ramp leading to the ring, they are heralded by their personal entrance video on the Titantron. The soundtrack (available on CD . . .) roars, the images roll, and the fans know from the first few chords/beats which wrestler it announces. Proportionate in scale to their own collectible action figures, the wrestlers pose, dwarfed by their video representations, at the top of a ramp suggestive of a fashion model's runway. Every inch of exposed flesh below the neck is usually shaved clean and often oiled to a sheen. Most bodies are sharply defined through intensive workouts, surgical augmentation, and/or steroids (a fact denied by promoters and widely discussed by fans). Hair is carefully coiffed, tattoos and piercings feature prominently, and any other accessories that might accompany the action figure—from brass knuckles, to a folding table, to a Harley—are likely to make their appearance on the ramp. Particularly popular wrestlers—Triple H, Steve Austin, The Rock—take their time, striking their signature poses as the video shifts from canned intro to live feed.

In a short circuit of signification that moves from the hard plastic body of the toy, through the hard flesh of the performer, to the massive, processed image above them, the presence of the wrestler is consumed, fragmented, and multiplied in the flow of its commodity status.[2] Simultaneously larger and smaller than life, the wrestler's body becomes available in that moment, registering both its power and its submission to the system that articulates it. Seemingly different from the clothed middle-class body that is ostensibly autonomous, yet yoked to disciplinary regimes in which appearance and behavior are regulated according to acceptable norms, the wrestler's body also suggests rebellion contained. If tattoos and piercings (now so commonplace as to be mundane) signal a refusal to adhere to the polite interchangeability of middle-class social signification — the tedious Polo corporate casual uniform — if the brass knuckles, steel pipes, and Harleys signal roadhouse brawling, if the fetishistic posing of sculpted abs, glutes, and pecs signal the body as object, this is a regulated and posable rebellion. (As The Rock used to say, "Know Your Role and Shut Your Mouth.") It is a celebration of oppression freely chosen — of the object mobilizing his, her, or its commodity status with a willful disregard for its effect on his, her, or its body or self. The autonomous sense of self and of relations between free individuals so essential to the middle-class narrative of personal and social progress is a fiction laid waste by the wrestler's body, and it is that celebration of subjection or objectification that undergirds the objections of critics of televised professional wrestling.

One recent example of this confusion between being a subject and an object is the recently retired female wrestler Joanie Laurer, who worked for the WWF as Chyna, "The Ninth Wonder of the World." When Laurer came to the WWF, she had the lean physique of a female bodybuilder. Breast augmentation, facial reconstruction, and a costume that recalled Xena the Warrior Princess transformed her into a straight fourteen-year-old boy's wet dream — a hard-bodied, leather-clad, large-breasted cyborg who sometimes fired a hand-held rocket launcher over the crowd. Chyna embodied adolescent straight male desire and fear: she often allied herself with male characters (such as playing "Mamacita" to Eddie Guerrero, the Latino Heat), flirting and coyly suggesting assignation. But eventually she turned on them and moved on to another partner, and her trash talk against her male counterparts often focused on their lack of masculinity or implied genital inadequacy. Hers was a capricious femininity that confirmed masculinity's inability to control female desire and strength. As a commodity, Chyna circulated widely and wildly. After her appearance in *Playboy* in November 2000, her standing with her fans increased, she drew further wrath from the Parents Television Council, and she was rebuked by the WWF's facetious response to the council, Right To Censor (which included "reformed" male porn star Val Venis).

Like the emblematic performances of her male superstar counterparts—who enacted class resentment or fascist-tinged populism—Chyna's femininity offered a point of contestation and desire constructed around its willfully inappropriate excess. As a woman who could kick men's asses, she offered a delightful counterpoint to the powder-puff "managers" who parade T and A as they accompany their boys to the ring. At the same time, however, she often enacted a slavish subjection to her male love-interests, a struggle to tame herself in response to their insecurity. The walking overdetermination that was Chyna was available equally to critiques of her objectification as a symbol of immature heteromasculine desire, and to celebrations of her mobilization of the anxiety behind that desire as a location of female subjectivity and power.

For example, the 18 November 1999 *Smackdown* featured a replay of a moment from the previous week's RAW, in which Chyna taunted her then-nemesis, Chris Jericho. She had recently beaten Jericho in a match, before which he had promised that if he lost he would have a sex change operation. Chyna appeared ready to collect. Joined by her sidekick, the hyper-femme and diminutive Kat, Chyna held up a pair of bolt cutters and offered to begin the procedure. Kat, dressed in a nurse's uniform, interrupted, suggesting that perhaps a nail scissors would be a more appropriate tool. Then, as Jericho began to wrestle his opponent, the two women circled the stage, pelting them with tampons. Jericho eventually lost. Enraged, he took his revenge sometime later by kidnapping Chyna, duct-taping her to a chair, and breaking her thumb with a hammer.

What are we to make of this storyline? The butch and powerful Chyna, having defeated Jericho in the ring, returns with a threat of castration, which her femme partner couples with mockery of his size and potency. Then, with relish and abandon, the two women pelt the arrogant and self-aggrandizing Jericho with tampons—impolite references to female fertility and to his future as a woman. Is hers an act of feminine empowerment? In revenge, Jericho brutalizes Chyna via an act of symbolic castration (crushing her thumb). Is Jericho's response the erasure and containment of that power, or a satire of threatened and anxious masculinity? Does one act cancel the other? Does the very explicit nature of the drama—representing castration, masculine phallic anxiety, menstruation, and violence against women — qualify it as resistant, a rupture of the rules by which real social anxieties and problems may be properly represented on television? Or does the (never fully) final outcome, the violent and cruel torture of Chyna, mark it as reactionary, the vicious containment of women's power?

WRESTLING AS PLAY, WRESTLING AS SEX

As Sharon Mazer suggests in her ethnographic account of wrestlers and their fans, wrestling's play with the real and the fake, the shoot and the work, engages wrestling's fans and exasperates its critics. For fans, this play of signification offers the opportunity to read wrestling closely and to establish one's self against *marks*, that is, those who can't distinguish between the real — the danger and drama of the unintended — and the ruse. For social critics of wrestling, its blurring of the clear boundaries of reality confuse the young and weak-minded, encouraging violence and cultural relativism; lose the clear line between true and false, they warn, and you lose your moral center. Reality, Mazer suggests, is not something denied to young fans by duplicitous wrestlers and promoters. Rather, play with reality is at the core of wrestling as practice and as performance. And this performance is not confined to the ring: when fans debate the authenticity of various wrestling scenarios and moves, they are engaged in critical analysis, both of the "texts" they discuss and of each other's readings of that material. Far from a deracinating process, the play with the fake and the real in wrestling, in Mazer's view, is a form of semiotic engagement amongst complex communities of practice.

Catherine Salmon and Susan Clerc also find in wrestling a play with signification, but for them it lies not only in the performance of the wrestlers but also in that of their online female fans. These fans reappropriate the masculinity of wrestlers — their brash, unapologetic violence, their bodies sculpted to signify masculine power — and convert it from an object of adolescent male identification into one of female desire and sexual power. For some fans, this involves photo galleries that capture what those women find desirable in the faces, gestures, and bodies of wrestlers, or fiction that imagines them in romantic situations. Some of these romances involve the fans themselves; others play upon the homoerotic tension that Chuck and Billy called up and disavowed, imagining the wrestlers lost in the passion of same-sex romance, sweeping each other off their feet both inside and out of the ring. Like other *slash* fan fiction, this reappropriation of ostensibly straight male bodies and personas plays on narratives of male bonding in dangerous and violent situations. Unlike most other slash, though, it blends the wrestlers' personae with their actual lives, combining elements from their character storylines with those of their personal lives, blurring the line between performer and character, playing with professional wrestling's own coy refusal to delineate the real and the fake, and with the rare public spectacle of nearly naked men consumed in passion and locked in fierce embraces.

For Lucia Rahilly, the expression of that passion is more than just potentially homoerotic; it is also often sadomasochistic. For the embraces that wrestlers bestow upon each other aren't romantic in the conventional sense of the term. Although professional wrestling in the United States has increasingly incorporated the high-flying acrobatic style of Mexican *lucha libre*, its bread and butter is still the delivery and receipt of pain, a dance of dominance and submission. Ostensibly stripped of its overtly sexual connotations, s/m in wrestling emerges in submission holds that test the endurance of wrestlers, and in the work of hardcore legends such as Mick Foley, who earn renown for their ability and willingness to "take bumps," to absorb as much pain as they can. This celebration of pain is further fetishized through lingering close-ups on faces twisted in anguish or masked in blood, of hands wavering on the edge of tapping out, of yielding to domination. Yet, as Rahilly points out, wrestling distances itself from these hints of sadomasochistic sexual practice through the enactment of normative heterosexual tropes and counterbalancing family narratives, and in desexualized struggles for social and economic power. Only in Paul Jay's documentary *Hitman Hart: Wrestling with Shadows* (1998) is wrestling obliquely approached as an overtly sadomasochistic practice, in the depiction of the basement dungeon of Stu Hart—the father of Bret Hart and the late Owen Hart—in which he gleefully trains young wrestlers in the art of taking pain. Yet even this moment is countered by the depiction of Bret's own family life as devoid of domestic pain practices, which he limits to the ring, and only in the name of claiming the title belt. Even as the wrestlers themselves, and their promoters, blur the line between performer and persona, they also sharpen that line in depicting normal family lives that offset the potentially sexually aberrant nature of their work lives.

Yet this business of control—of self and others—is not limited to the disruption and regulation of sexual and familial norms. Before the McMahon monopoly, before the ratings rivalry between wcw and the wwf, before the Nitro Girls and *Hulk Hogan's Rock 'N Wrestling*—before wrestling became a horizontally integrated industry—wrestlers exercised more control over their performance. Sure, they were still often exploited by promoters, but they still retained control over the nuances of their characters and over the structuring of individual matches. Now, plotlines are scripted by writers from the television industry, and many of the particulars of characterization are directed by marketing departments. Matches are planned around story arcs that can last weeks or even months, designed to increase viewership for the pay-per-view events that form the financial backbone of the industry.

For Laurence de Garis, this mainstreaming signals the decline of the form as craft and the disempowerment of wrestlers as workers. Although professional wrestling has been on television since the medium's inception (and helped establish its prime-time presence), until the 1980s its practices were rooted in a territory system which divided the country into local markets. In that system, wrestlers spent much of their time on the road, traveling from one show to the next in much the same way that vaudeville entertainers worked their circuits in the early twentieth century.[3] Sometimes matches were televised; sometimes they weren't. Sometimes they happened in arenas, sometimes in high-school gymnasiums. The work of wrestling—the refinement of moves, the development of animosities and alliances, the creation of characters—happened in motel rooms and locker rooms, not in front offices. New wrestlers learned from old-timers, and often skills were handed down from generation to generation within families. Now, claims de Garis, wrestlers are less and less skilled workers and more products, commodities who play workers on television.

For Douglas Battema and Philip Sewell, Vince McMahon's monopoly consolidation of professional wrestling is itself a performance, one that has taken place not only in the ring and on television, but in the financial press and on the Web—and which includes not only the McMahon family (all of whom are corporate officers in the wwe and performers in its offerings), but also the popular press and business pages in particular. Battema and Sewell suggest that the wwe's aggressive consolidation of the wrestling industry, its failed attempt to encroach on the NFL (National Football League) with its "smash-mouth" XFL (Extreme Football League), and its decision to become a publicly traded company in 1999 are a useful lens through which to read discourses of market populism that arose during the heyday of the now-collapsed bubble economy of the late 1990s. Just as the WWE's male wrestlers perform a populist masculinity which celebrates the resistance of the individual worker against an oppressive and emasculating social and managerial system (see Henry Jenkins in this volume), both the WWE and members of the business press presented the company's initial public offering (as well as participation in the market in general) as a chance for the little guy to escape the bonds of wage slavery. The reciprocity between the masculinity performed in the ring and claims for stock ownership as a form of new populism, they argue, demonstrate that tropes of aggressiveness and of self-interest that so vex social critics of wrestling are part of larger sociocultural formations that oppose an active and productive masculinity to a passive and consuming femininity, and which by extension position collective social action as emasculating.

As the detumescence of the bubble economy revealed that the main beneficiaries of the masculine ethos of market populism were male CEOs from the Viagra set, exposing the fallacy of the 401(k) as a tool for personal empowerment, so the masculinity portrayed in professional wrestling suffers from its own anxieties and logical inconsistencies. Yet where this sudden collapse of the "new economy" has undermined its masculinist discourses, it has in no way limited the play of gender ambivalence and anxiety in professional wrestling. For all its bravado, professional wrestling has often exposed the vulnerable and uncertain construction of masculinity.

WRESTLING AND THE POLITICS OF MASCULINITY

Chyna's romantic pairing with Eddie Guerrero, as his "mamacita," is equally instructive of the interplay of anxiety around masculinity in wrestling. Presented as ridiculous and outrageous to fans, the romance made Guerrero appear diminutive next to the statuesque Chyna, and he played his role as her paramour as a mixture of Latino machismo and blustery anxiety over his inability to contain her sexuality (which came to a head when she appeared in *Playboy*). For Phillip Serrato, this type of situation is typical of professional wrestling's racializing of masculinity, one which organizes masculine power, placing large, white (or hybrid and racially ambiguous, in the case of The Rock) wrestlers at the top of the social order, consigning Latinos to subordinate roles. This has not always been the case, Serrato points out. Prior to the 1980s, Latino wrestlers such as Pepper Gomez or Tito Santana not only vied for championship belts, but spoke in support of *la raza*, sometimes code switching to deliver one message to English-speaking fans and another to Spanish-speaking fans. Lately, Serrato argues, professional wrestling has represented the masculinity of Latinos as inferior to that of many of their white counterparts. Not only are Latino wrestlers consistently barred from major titles, but their characters stereotype Latino masculinity as craven and cowardly (as in the case of Eddie Guerrero) or as animalistic and unstable (as in the recent case of Batista). Serrato's reading of professional wrestling during the last decade suggests that masculinity in professional wrestling expresses intersecting anxieties about both gender and race worthy of more careful consideration.

If such investigation of American professional wrestling reveals hesitations, anxieties, and domination in its production of masculinity, it does so only through a narrow definition of *American*. While Canada contributes significantly to professional wrestling in the United States — many of the wwe's biggest stars are Canadian — there is another North American form, Mexican lucha libre, that maintains its own distinct performative and cultural idioms. Lucha libre is best known in the United States for its acrobatic style and for its masked *luchadores*, and plastic figurines of Mexican wrestlers and cheap knockoffs of their masks are kitsch collectibles in novelty toy stores. In Mexico, however, lucha libre is a vibrant popular tradition with complicated political, cultural, and racial overtones that distinguish it from the relatively incoherent populism of its northern cousins. The mask, Heather Levi argues, is far more than a gimmick: it is a staple of Mexican political culture and a marker for tensions between social and cultural groups that identify with indigenous populations or with Spanish colonizers. Tracing some of the meanings behind masked performance in Mexico — from indigenous traditions, through the ritual *destapado* of revealing new political candidates for office, through rites of masking and unmasking in the wrestling ring — Levi offers a compelling explanation for why lucha libre has on occasion crossed over into the political arena, with luchadores standing up for dispossessed and oppressed groups. When Superbarrio came forward to defend the housing rights of poor Mexicans in 1985, or when Ecologista Universal rose up in defense of the environment not long afterward, these activists chose the mask of the *luchador* as a rallying point because lucha libre had long been associated with social justice, both in the ring and in Mexican cinema. Made popular by El Santo (celebrated here by Carlos Monsiváis, translated by Levi), the figure of the luchador as a crusader for justice resonated in Mexican popular culture; *lucha*, Levi reminds us, translates both as wrestling and as struggle. In addition, Levi suggests, the masked social reformer formed an ironic counterpoint to the ritual "unmasking" of new political candidates, a procedure that merely revealed decisions already made privately by elites. If Mexican men are reduced to macho clowns and surly animals in rings north of the border, in Mexico they stand in as Everyman crusaders for social justice. As with Subcomandante Marcos of the Zapatistas, Superbarrio's identity was never revealed, and it was never clear whether there was just one of him, or many.

WRESTLING AND THE POLITICS OF CULTURE

Whether we are speaking of a populism undermined or contradicted by dominant fantasies of individualism and anxieties around masculine power in the United States, or of an occasionally effective populism circulating between the ring and the streets in Mexico, professional wrestling is neither merely sport nor entertainment. It is a popular entertainment form, but, like its antecedents, it is also a hotly contested site for working out social, cultural, political, and economic ideals and desires. While wrestlers grapple with each other, the signs that flit so uneasily across their straining bodies — whether projected by promoters, fans, or social critics of the form — represent an unequal and uneasy negotiation of social meanings, a struggle to name what proper and just social relations are in a capitalist mass society. Writing in the late 1990s in "Never Trust a Snake," Henry Jenkins described professional wrestling as a "masculine melodrama" in which issues of social justice became personalized in the ring. That particularization of large-scale forces and issues in the struggle between two bodies, he argued, had both expansive and limiting aspects. For (male) wrestling fans, it provided an avenue for a strong emotional response to social inequalities and injustices — particularly class oppression — that polite society usually did not permit. However, at the same time it reduced those injustices and their resolution to a struggle between individuals, and Jenkins saw in Barthes's glorious struggle between primal signs the diffusion of collective impulses.

Returning to the topic some six years later (in the afterword to this volume, cowritten with wrestling fan Henry Jenkins IV)—and drawing upon his experience as a cultural critic and educator caught in the crossfire of the culture wars—Jenkins has taken a step back from the topic to consider how arguments about the effect of professional wrestling on society attempt to impose moral legibility on a performance form, rather than on the social, political, and economic order within which it operates. Whether it is taking heat from the Left—for its violence, homophobia, misogyny, or racism—or from the Right—for excessive violence or moral relativism—the WWE (basically the only game in town, thanks to a national embrace of monopoly practices) has become an easy target for moral and critical vilification. Unlike the motion picture industry in the 1920s and 1930s, the WWE is not overly concerned about such criticism; it feeds on it. With each outcry against the company for its corrupting influence on American youth, the company gains credibility with its core audience, which is disaffected from the usual avenues for social and political expression provided it.

In his contribution to the afterword of this volume, Henry Jenkins IV provides the perspective of a long-time fan who has grown up with the form, and who has grown somewhat alienated from some of the WWE's recent choices. Straddling the line between a fan and a student of media, Jenkins suggests that many of wrestling's fans, having followed wrestling from childhood, remain committed to it because of the important role that it has played in their creative and intellectual development, and because the business has made bank on responding quickly and decisively to perceived changes in their attitudes and preferences. Unlike other media and performance forms, wrestling today offers multiple avenues for fans to aggressively intercede in the narrative and aesthetic choices that producers make. Whether through chanting at live events, chat-room discussions on the Internet, or fan Web sites and zines, wrestling fans speak (if not shout) their preferences, and they discuss in detail what they like and don't like about details and trends in wrestling. Thus, Jenkins suggests, it is sometimes difficult to definitively argue whether the producers lead the fans or the fans lead the producers. While by sheer economic and instrumental bulk, the WWE has a distinct edge over its fans in dictating wrestling's direction, it has built that strength, in part, on learning to respond quickly to the reactions of its fans, building on what works and jettisoning what doesn't.

Taken together, the two halves of this afterword seem to suggest that the problem is not simply that the WWE is encouraging moral relativism or anti-identitarian hostility. Rather, it is that we are unwilling to consider the degree to which the company is playing on currents of discontent and moral incoherence that suffuse our cultural and social fabric. While the willingness to condemn excesses of the form becomes a litmus test for political correctness on the Left or Right — a sign of moral rectitude which candidates from the two major political parties perform for their particular audiences — a disaffected population signals its disinterest in this morality play through apathy or the embrace of "political incorrectness." Conventional wisdom places the blame for this lack of political and moral clarity alternately at the feet of "relativist" academics, or on the decline of clear-cut values in entertainment, or says it is because the children of the middle class have been coddled into a narcissism that has left them without a sense of responsible citizenship. In short, apathy and political incorrectness are the symptoms of the improper stewardship of an infantilized majority.

CONCLUSION: WRESTLING AS CHILD'S PLAY

This attitude, as well meaning as it might be, replaces healthy discussion about the possibility of informed public debate and dissent with an empty rhetoric about the need to regulate impolitic, immoral, or disruptive private representations. It is premised on the notion that citizenship is formed in (mass) consumption, and that certain sectors of the population are susceptible to moral and behavioral degradation through consumption choices foisted on them by unscrupulous marketers. And, in the process, it discounts the possibility that the consumption of improper popular entertainments — and the behaviors, attitudes, and practices that surround that consumption — may express a discontent with the rigid regulation of expression in public life (see Sammond in this volume). The very choice to treat such choices as merely symptomatic forecloses the possibility of seeing them as legitimate (if imperfect) expressions of dissent, or of desire circumscribed by dominant moral regulation. And this choice promotes the fallacy that the regulation of images in any way stands in for more aggressive public action that addresses sexual and economic inequity, institutional and governmental racism, or sexual identity constructed around simple hetero- or homonormative binaries.[4]

For historians of popular culture, however, this reformist rhetoric is more than a bit frayed around the edges, stretching well back into the nineteenth century. It has always targeted one disenfranchised group or another — immigrants, the working poor, African Americans, women — and suggested that because they lacked the requisite amount of reason, they were susceptible to and in need of protection from improper performance forms. In the twentieth century, as each of these groups was either assimilated into mainstream discourse or asserted its rights to full citizenship, this rhetoric has increasingly focused on children and youth and has used minors as a means of attempting to regulate cultural, social, and political expression and identity. In the 1920s and 1930s, for example, calls for the censorship of motion pictures often veiled anti-Semitic attacks on motion picture producers. In the 1950s, public outcry over rock 'n' roll contained no small amount of anxiety over the inclusion of African Americans in U.S. social, political, and cultural life.

Does opposition to the regulation of popular entertainment because it entails the suppression of others' rights of expression indicate an indifference to the well-being of children? Hardly. Rather, it signals a set of priorities which questions the logic of regulating expression based on unproven but durable popular assumptions that the consumption of popular media has a negative psychological effect on children (Freedman 2002; see also Gauntlett 1998). Yet this does not mean supporting calls by media industries for parental responsibility. As Ellen Seiter (1993) pointed out some time ago, that response places the burden for controlling children's consumption on "parents," which inevitably is a code word for mothers. Quite simply, this opposition is based on the more reasonable assumption that there are far more important social, economic, and political determinants — disparities in child-care burdens, housing, schooling, access to health care — that affect children's psychological and physical well-being.

Does this leave us with no basis for criticizing racism, homophobia, and misogyny in professional wrestling? Again, hardly. The mistake is in seeing professional wrestling — or a number of other popular entertainments — as a determinate cause of oppression or intolerance. Whether one sees wrestling as a sport, a dramatic form, or an odd hybrid of the two, it is a playful, irreverent, aggressive commentary on the politics of signification. The WWE's ironic satires of class oppression, of the objectification of women and its criticism, or of gay marriage suggest that for its fans and consumers those issues are important, but that the avenues for meaningful participation in their negotiation are inadequate. The WWE (now the only game in town) performs oppression, subjugation, and objectification as the acts of violence that they truly are, and it performs liberal or conservative responses to that violence as blinkered by a fantasy that oppression can be willed away through the regulation of speech and representation.

This does not mean, however, that one has to accept the oppression represented in the acts that the WWE performs as somehow justified. Heroic efforts by social activists over (at least) the last fifty years have expanded the rights of social groups entirely or partially excluded from meaningful participation in social, cultural, and political life in the United States, and, to be sure, part of that work has involved a critical analysis of representational regimes that supported oppressive practices, as well as the production of oppositional narratives and representations. That work is far from over. Yet to consider the "politically incorrect" narratives and representations of professional wrestling as a potentially legitimate expression of social and political discontent is not equivalent to accepting the acts portrayed as legitimate, or to condoning a return to repression and disenfranchisement. Rather, it is to acknowledge that resistance and reaction to changing understandings of identity and social practice may reveal as yet unconsidered contradictions in those understandings.[5] It is, in a sense, to suggest that one never fully arrives at rectitude, to say that through examining the play of the signifiers that flit across wrestlers' bodies, we may perhaps playfully address some unfinished business.

Yet although one can read in professional wrestling both resistance to the dominant order *and* the enactment of its repressive force, the signifiers traced across wrestlers' bodies are no freer than the wrestlers themselves. At the end of the day, white men tend to win out over women and people of color; bosses manipulate, use, and harass their workers; and gay men, lesbians, and feminists are ridiculed and physically assaulted. Complex markers of identity are stripped of the contextual noise of home, community, and family and set against each other in a raw, emotional struggle for supremacy. Workers become the commodities they produce (as Marx would have it, the crystallization of complex social and material relations), action figures battling in an arena of desire and fear, coming soon to your city, coming into your living room, your child's playroom. The professional wrestler enacts and undermines our fantasy that identity is the same as action, that representing the social order is the same as producing it — the ultimate perversion of the personal as political. Professional wrestling is not a threat to the social order; it is the social order writ both large and small.

NOTES

1. Oh, the times! Oh, the morals!
2. The live spectators' experience of this event is both different and similar, as they are often so far from the performer that the performer's physical body is minuscule, and they watch the action on the Titantron with the added attraction of scurrying camera operators and tiny performers.
3. World Wrestling Enterprises wrestlers still travel extensively. But whereas before they worked a local territory, in venues as large as arenas and as small as high-school gyms, they now play almost exclusively in large, corporate-branded metropolitan sports complexes.
4. See, for instance, Wendy Brown (1995) or Judith Butler (1997).
5. For a discussion of this issue in relation to misogyny in hardcore rap music, see Kimberle Crenshaw (1993).

REFERENCES

Allen, Robert C. 1991. *Horrible Prettiness: Burlesque and American Culture*. Chapel Hill: University of North Carolina Press.

Barthes, Roland. 1972 [1957]. "The World of Wrestling." In *Mythologies*. Trans. Annette Lavers. New York: Farrar, Straus and Giroux.

Brown, Wendy. 1995. *States of Injury: Power and Freedom in Late Modernity*. Princeton, N.J.: Princeton University Press.

Butler, Judith. 1997. *Excitable Speech: A Politics of the Performative*. New York: Routledge.

Crenshaw, Kimberle. 1993. "Beyond Racism and Misogyny: Black Feminism and 2 Live Crew." In *Words That Wound: Critical Race Theory, Assaultive Speech, and the First Amendment*, ed. Mari J. Matsuda. Boulder, Colo.: Westview Press.

Freedman, Jonathan L. 2002. *Media Violence and Its Affect on Aggression: Assessing the Scientific Evidence*. Toronto: University of Toronto Press.

Gauntlett, David. 1998. "Ten Things Wrong with the 'Effects Model.'" In *Approaches to Audiences—A Reader*, ed. Roger Dickinson, Ramaswani Harindranath, and Olga Linné. London: Arnold.

Jenkins, Henry. 1992. *What Made Pistachio Nuts?: Early Sound Comedy and the Vaude-ville Aesthetic*. New York: Columbia University Press.

Plato. [n.d.] 1951. *Symposium*. Trans. Walter Hamilton. New York: Penguin.

Seiter, Ellen. 1993. *Sold Separately: Parents and Children in Consumer Culture*. New Brunswick, N.J.: Rutgers University Press.

ROLAND BARTHES

The World of Wrestling

**The grandiloquent truth of gestures on
life's great occasions.—Baudelaire**

The virtue of all-in wrestling is that it is the spectacle of excess. Here we
find a grandiloquence which must have been that of ancient theaters.
And in fact wrestling is an open-air spectacle, for what makes the circus or the arena what they are is not the sky (a romantic value suited
rather to fashionable occasions), it is the drenching and vertical quality of the
flood of light. Even hidden in the most squalid Parisian halls, wrestling par-
takes of the nature of the great solar spectacles, Greek drama and bullfights:
in both, a light without shadow generates an emotion without reserve.

There are people who think that wrestling is an ignoble sport. Wrestling
is not a sport, it is a spectacle, and it is no more ignoble to attend a wrestled
performance of Suffering than a performance of the sorrows of Arnolphe or
Andromaque.[1] Of course, there exists a false wrestling, in which the participants unnecessarily go to great lengths to make a show of a fair fight; this
is of no interest. True wrestling, wrongly called amateur wrestling, is performed in second-rate halls, where the public spontaneously attunes itself to
the spectacular nature of the contest, like the audience at a suburban cinema.
Then these same people wax indignant because wrestling is a stage-managed
sport (which ought, by the way, to mitigate its ignominy). The public is completely uninterested in knowing whether the contest is rigged or not, and
rightly so; it abandons itself to the primary virtue of the spectacle, which
is to abolish all motives and all consequences: what matters is not what it
thinks but what it sees.

This public knows very well the distinction between wrestling and boxing; it knows that boxing is a Jansenist sport, based on a demonstration of excellence. One can bet on the outcome of a boxing-match: with wrestling, it would make no sense. A boxing-match is a story which is constructed before the eyes of the spectator; in wrestling, on the contrary, it is each moment which is intelligible, not the passage of time. The spectator is not interested in the rise and fall of fortunes; he expects the transient image of certain passions. Wrestling therefore demands an immediate reading of the juxtaposed meanings, so that there is no need to connect them. The logical conclusion of the contest does not interest the wrestling-fan, while on the contrary a boxing-match always implies a science of the future. In other words, wrestling is a sum of spectacles, of which no single one is a function: each moment imposes the total knowledge of a passion which rises erect and alone, without ever extending to the crowning moment of a result.

Thus the function of the wrestler is not to win; it is to go exactly through the motions which are expected of him. It is said that judo contains a hidden symbolic aspect; even in the midst of efficiency, its gestures are measured, precise but restricted, drawn accurately but by a stroke without volume. Wrestling, on the contrary, offers excessive gestures, exploited to the limit of their meaning. In judo, a man who is down is hardly down at all, he rolls over, he draws back, he eludes defeat, or, if the latter is obvious, he immediately disappears; in wrestling, a man who is down is exaggeratedly so, and completely fills the eyes of the spectators with the intolerable spectacle of his powerlessness.

This function of grandiloquence is indeed the same as that of ancient theater, whose principle, language, and props (masks and buskins) concurred in the exaggeratedly visible explanation of a Necessity. The gesture of the vanquished wrestler signifying to the world a defeat which, far from disguising, he emphasizes and holds like a pause in music, corresponds to the mask of antiquity meant to signify the tragic mode of the spectacle. In wrestling, as on the stage in antiquity, one is not ashamed of one's suffering, one knows how to cry, one has a liking for tears.

Each sign in wrestling is therefore endowed with an absolute clarity, since one must always understand everything on the spot. As soon as the adversaries are in the ring, the public is overwhelmed with the obviousness of the roles. As in the theater, each physical type expresses to excess the part which has been assigned to the contestant. Thauvin, a fifty-year-old with an obese and sagging body, whose type of asexual hideousness always inspires feminine nicknames, displays in his flesh the characters of baseness, for his part is to represent what, in the classical concept of the *salaud*, the "bastard" (the key-concept of any wrestling-match), appears as organically repugnant. The nausea voluntarily provoked by Thauvin shows therefore a very extended use of signs: not only is ugliness used here in order to signify baseness, but in addition ugliness is wholly gathered into a particularly repulsive quality of matter: the pallid collapse of dead flesh (the public calls Thauvin *la barbaque*, "stinking meat"), so that the passionate condemnation of the crowd no longer stems from its judgment, but instead from the very depth of its humours. It will thereafter let itself be frenetically embroiled in an idea of Thauvin, which will conform entirely with this physical origin: his actions will perfectly correspond to the essential viscosity of his personage.

It is therefore in the body of the wrestler that we find the first key to the contest. I know from the start that all of Thauvin's actions, his treacheries, cruelties, and acts of cowardice, will not fail to measure up to the first image of ignobility he gave me; I can trust him to carry out intelligently and to the last detail all the gestures of a kind of amorphous baseness, and thus fill to the brim the image of the most repugnant bastard there is: the bastard-octopus. Wrestlers therefore have a physique as peremptory as those of the characters of the *Commedia dell'Arte*, who display in advance, in their costumes and attitudes, the future contents of their parts: just as Pantaloon can never be anything but a ridiculous cuckold, Harlequin an astute servant, and the Doctor a stupid pedant, in the same way Thauvin will never be anything but an ignoble traitor, Reinierès (a tall blond fellow with a limp body and unkempt hair) the moving image of passivity, Mazaud (short and arrogant like a cock) that of grotesque conceit, and Orsano (an effeminate teddy-boy first seen in a blue-and-pink dressing gown) that, doubly humorous, of a vindictive *salope*, or bitch (for I do not think that the public of the Elyseé-Montmartre, like Littre, believes the word *salope* to be masculine).

The physique of the wrestlers therefore constitutes a basic sign, which like a seed contains the whole fight. But this seed proliferates, for it is at every turn during the fight, in each new situation, that the body of the wrestler casts to the public the magical entertainment of a temperament which finds its natural expression in a gesture. The different strata of meaning throw light on each other, and form the most intelligible of spectacles. Wrestling is like a diacritic writing: above the fundamental meaning of his body, the wrestler arranges comments which are episodic but always opportune, and constantly help the reading of the fight by means of gestures, attitudes, and mimicry, which make the intention utterly obvious. Sometimes the wrestler triumphs with a repulsive sneer while kneeling on the good sportsman; sometimes he gives the crowd a conceited smile which forebodes an early revenge; sometimes, pinned to the ground, he hits the floor ostentatiously to make evident to all the intolerable nature of his situation; and sometimes he erects a complicated set of signs meant to make the public understand that he legitimately personifies the ever-entertaining image of the grumbler, endlessly confabulating about his displeasure.

We are therefore dealing with a real Human Comedy, where the most socially-inspired nuances of passion (conceit, rightfulness, refined cruelty, a sense of "paying one's debts") always felicitously find the clearest sign which can receive them, express them, and triumphantly carry them to the confines of the hall. It is obvious that at such a pitch, it no longer matters whether the passion is genuine or not. What the public wants is the image of passion, not passion itself. There is no more a problem of truth in wrestling than in the theater. In both, what is expected is the intelligible representation of moral situations which are usually private. This emptying out of interiority to the benefit of its exterior signs, this exhaustion of the content by the form, is the very principle of triumphant classical art. Wrestling is an immediate pantomime, infinitely more efficient than the dramatic pantomime, for the wrestler's gesture needs no anecdote, no decor, in short no transference in order to appear true.

Each moment in wrestling is therefore like an algebra which instanta- neously unveils the relationship between a cause and its represented effect. Wrestling fans certainly experience a kind of intellectual pleasure in *seeing* the moral mechanism function so perfectly. Some wrestlers, who are great comedians, entertain as much as a Molière character, because they succeed in imposing an immediate reading of their inner nature: Armand Mazaud, a wrestler of an arrogant and ridiculous character (as one says that Harpagon is a character),[2] always delights the audience by the mathematical rigor of his transcriptions, carrying the form of his gestures to the furthest reaches of their meaning, and giving to his manner of fighting the kind of vehemence and precision found in a great scholastic disputation, in which what is at stake is at once the triumph of pride and the formal concern with truth.

What is thus displayed for the public is the great spectacle of Suffering,

Defeat, and Justice. Wrestling presents man's suffering with all the amplification of tragic masks. The wrestler who suffers in a hold which is reputedly cruel (an arm-lock, a twisted leg) offers an excessive portrayal of Suffering; like a primitive Pietà, he exhibits for all to see his face, exaggeratedly contorted by an intolerable affliction. It is obvious, of course, that in wrestling reserve would be out of place, since it is opposed to the voluntary ostentation of the spectacle, to this Exhibition of Suffering which is the very aim of the fight. This is why all the actions which produce suffering are particularly spectacular, like the gesture of a conjuror who holds out his cards clearly to the public. Suffering which appeared without intelligible cause would not be understood; a concealed action that was actually cruel would transgress the unwritten rules of wrestling and would have no more sociological efficacy than a mad or parasitic gesture. On the contrary suffering appears as inflicted with emphasis and conviction, for everyone must not only see that the man suffers, but also and above all understand why he suffers. What wrestlers call a hold, that is, any figure which allows one to immobilize the adversary indefinitely and to have him at one's mercy, has precisely the function of preparing in a conventional, therefore intelligible, fashion the spectacle of suffering, of methodically establishing the conditions of suffering. The inertia of the vanquished allows the (temporary) victor to settle in his cruelty and to convey to the public this terrifying slowness of the torturer who is certain about the outcome of his actions; to grind the face of one's powerless adversary or to scrape his spine with one's fist with a deep and regular movement, or at least to produce the superficial appearance of such gestures: wrestling is the only sport which gives such an externalized image of torture. But here again, only the image is involved in the game, and the spectator does not wish for the actual suffering of the contestant; he only enjoys the perfection of an iconography. It is not true that wrestling is a sadistic spectacle: it is only an intelligible spectacle.

There is another figure, more spectacular still than a hold; it is the forearm smash, this loud slap of the forearm, this embryonic punch with which one clouts the chest of one's adversary, and which is accompanied by a dull noise and the exaggerated sagging of a vanquished body. In the forearm smash, catastrophe is brought to the point of maximum obviousness, so much so that ultimately the gesture appears as no more than a symbol; this is going too far, this is transgressing the moral rules of wrestling, where all signs must be excessively clear, but must not let the intention of clarity be seen. The public then shouts, "He's laying it on!" not because it regrets the absence of real suffering, but because it condemns artifice: as in the theater, one fails to put the part across as much by an excess of sincerity as by an excess of formalism.

We have already seen to what extent wrestlers exploit the resources of a given physical style, developed and put to use in order to unfold before the eyes of the public a total image of Defeat. The flaccidity of tall white bodies which collapse with one blow or crash into the ropes with arms flailing, the inertia of massive wrestlers rebounding pitiably off all the elastic surfaces of the ring, nothing can signify more clearly and more passionately the exemplary abasement of the vanquished. Deprived of all resilience, the wrestler's flesh is no longer anything but an unspeakable heap spread out on the floor, where it solicits relentless reviling and jubilation. There is here a paroxysm of meaning in the style of antiquity, which can only recall the heavily underlined intentions in Roman triumphs. At other times, there is another ancient posture which appears in the coupling of the wrestlers, that of the suppliant who, at the mercy of his opponent, on bended knees, his arms raised above his head, is slowly brought down by the vertical pressure of the victor. In wrestling, unlike judo, Defeat is not a conventional sign, abandoned as soon as it is understood; it is not an outcome, but quite the contrary, it is a duration, a display, it takes up the ancient myths of public Suffering and Humiliation: the cross and the pillory. It is as if the wrestler is crucified in broad daylight and in the sight of all. I have heard it said of a wrestler stretched on the ground: "He is dead, little Jesus, there, on the cross," and these ironic words revealed the hidden roots of a spectacle which enacts the exact gestures of the most ancient purifications.

But what wrestling is above all meant to portray is a purely moral concept: that of justice. The idea of "paying" is essential to wrestling, and the crowd's "Give it to him" means above all else "Make him pay." This is therefore, needless to say, an immanent justice. The baser the action of the "bastard," the more delighted the public is by the blow which he justly receives in return. If the villain—who is of course a coward—takes refuge behind the ropes, claiming unfairly to have a right to do so by a brazen mimicry, he is inexorably pursued there and caught, and the crowd is jubilant at seeing the rules broken for the sake of a deserved punishment. Wrestlers know very well how to play up to the capacity for indignation of the public by presenting the very limit of the concept of Justice, this outermost zone of confrontation where it is enough to infringe the rules a little more to open the gates of a world without restraints. For a wrestling-fan, nothing is finer than the revengeful fury of a betrayed fighter who throws himself vehemently not on a successful opponent but on the smarting image of foul play. Naturally, it is the pattern of Justice which matters here, much more than its content: wrestling is above all a quantitative sequence of compensations (an eye for an eye, a tooth for a tooth). This explains why sudden changes of circumstances have in the eyes of wrestling habitués a sort of moral beauty: they enjoy them as they would enjoy an inspired episode in a novel, and the greater the contrast between the success of a move and the reversal of fortune, the nearer the good luck of a contestant to his downfall, the more satisfying the dramatic mime is felt to be. Justice is therefore the embodiment of a possible transgression; it is from the fact that there is a Law that the spectacle of the passions which infringe it derives its value.

It is therefore easy to understand why out of five wrestling-matches, only about one is fair. One must realize, let it be repeated, that "fairness" here is a role or a genre, as in the theater: the rules do not at all constitute a real constraint; they are the conventional appearance of fairness. So that in actual fact a fair fight is nothing but an exaggeratedly polite one: the contestants confront each other with zeal, not rage; they can remain in control of their passions, they do not punish their beaten opponent relentlessly, they stop fighting as soon as they are ordered to do so, and congratulate each other at the end of a particularly arduous episode, during which, however, they have not ceased to be fair. One must of course understand here that all these polite actions are brought to the notice of the public by the most conventional gestures of fairness: shaking hands, raising the arms, ostensibly avoiding a fruitless hold which would detract from the perfection of the contest.

Conversely, foul play exists only in its excessive signs: administering a big kick to one's beaten opponent, taking refuge behind the ropes while ostensibly invoking a purely formal right, refusing to shake hands with one's opponent before or after the fight, taking advantage of the end of the round to rush treacherously at the adversary from behind, fouling him while the referee is not looking (a move which obviously only has any value or function because in fact half the audience can see it and get indignant about it). Since Evil is the natural climate of wrestling, a fair fight has chiefly the value of being an exception. It surprises the aficionado, who greets it when he sees it as an anachronism and a rather sentimental throwback to the sporting tradition ("Aren't they playing fair, those two"); he feels suddenly moved at the sight of the general kindness of the world, but would probably die of boredom and indifference if wrestlers did not quickly return to the orgy of evil which alone makes good wrestling.

Extrapolated, fair wrestling could lead only to boxing or judo, whereas true wrestling derives its originality from all the excesses which make it a spectacle and not a sport. The ending of a boxing-match or a judo-contest is abrupt, like the full stop which closes a demonstration. The rhythm of wrestling is quite different, for its natural meaning is that of rhetorical amplification: the emotional magniloquence, the repeated paroxysms, the exasperation of the retorts can only find their natural outcome in the most baroque confusion. Some fights, among the most successful kind, are crowned by a final charivari, a sort of unrestrained fantasia where the rules, the laws of the genre, the referee's censuring and the limits of the ring are abolished, swept away by a triumphant disorder which overflows into the hall and carries off pell-mell wrestlers, seconds, referee, and spectators.

It has already been noted that in America wrestling represents a sort of mythological fight between Good and Evil (of a quasi-political nature, the "bad" wrestler always being supposed to be a Red). The process of creating heroes in French wrestling is very different, being based on ethics and not on politics. What the public is looking for here is the gradual construction of a highly moral image: that of the perfect "bastard." One comes to wrestling in order to attend the continuing adventures of a single major leading character, permanent and multiform like Punch or Scapino, inventive in unexpected figures and yet always faithful to his role. The "bastard" is here revealed as a Molière character or a "portrait" by La Bruyère, that is to say, as a classical entity, an essence, whose acts are only significant epiphenomena arranged in time. This stylized character does not belong to any particular nation or party, and whether the wrestler is called Kuzchenko (nicknamed Moustache after Stalin), Yerpazian, Gaspardi, Jo Vignola, or Nollières, the aficionado does not attribute to him any country except "fairness" — observing the rules.

What then is a "bastard" for this audience composed in part, we are told, of people who are themselves outside the rules of society? Essentially someone unstable, who accepts the rules only when they are useful to him and transgresses the formal continuity of attitudes. He is unpredictable, therefore asocial. He takes refuge behind the law when he considers that it is in his favour, and breaks it when he finds it useful to do so. Sometimes he rejects the formal boundaries of the ring and goes on hitting an adversary legally protected by the ropes, sometimes he reestablishes these boundaries and claims the protection of what he did not respect a few minutes earlier. This inconsistency, far more than treachery or cruelty, sends the audience beside itself with rage: offended not in its morality but in its logic, it considers the contradiction of arguments as the basest of crimes. The forbidden move becomes dirty only when it destroys a quantitative equilibrium and disturbs the rigorous reckoning of compensations; what is condemned by the audience is not at all the transgression of insipid official rules, it is the lack of revenge, the absence of a punishment. So that there is nothing more exciting for a crowd than the grandiloquent kick given to a vanquished "bastard"; the joy of punishing is at its climax when it is supported by a mathematical justification; contempt is then unrestrained. One is no longer dealing with a *salaud* but with a *salope*—the verbal gesture of the ultimate degradation.

Such a precise finality demands that wrestling should be exactly what the public expects of it. Wrestlers, who are very experienced, know perfectly how to direct the spontaneous episodes of the fight so as to make them conform to the image which the public has of the great legendary themes of its mythology. A wrestler can irritate or disgust, he never disappoints, for he always accomplishes completely, by a progressive solidification of signs, what the public expects of him. In wrestling, nothing exists except in the absolute, there is no symbol, no allusion, everything is presented exhaustively. Leaving nothing in the shade, each action discards all parasitic meanings and ceremonially offers to the public a pure and full signification, rounded like Nature. This grandiloquence is nothing but the popular and age-old image of the perfect intelligibility of reality. What is portrayed by wrestling is therefore an ideal understanding of things; it is the euphoria of men raised for a while above the constitutive ambiguity of everyday situations and placed before the panoramic view of a univocal Nature, in which signs at last correspond to causes, without obstacle, without evasion, without contradiction.

When the hero or the villain of the drama, the man who was seen a few minutes earlier possessed by moral rage, magnified into a sort of metaphysical sign, leaves the wrestling hall, impassive, anonymous, carrying a small suitcase and arm-in-arm with his wife, no one can doubt that wrestling holds that power of transmutation which is common to the Spectacle and to Religious Worship. In the ring, and even in the depths of their voluntary ignominy, wrestlers remain gods because they are, for a few moments, the key which opens Nature, the pure gesture which separates Good from Evil, and unveils the form of a Justice which is at last intelligible.

Originally published in 1957.

NOTES

1. In Molière's *L'École des femmes* (1972 [1662]) and Jean Racine's *Andromaque* (1990 [1667]).

2. In Molière's *L'Avare* (1950 [1668]).

REFERENCES

Molière. 1972 [1662]. *L'École des femmes.* Trans. Richard Wilbur. New York: Harcourt Brace Jovanovich.

———. 1950 [1668]. *L'Avare.* Paris: Hachette.

Racine, Jean. 1990 [1667]. *Andromaque.* Trans. Douglas Dunn. Boston: Faber and Faber.

HENRY JENKINS III

"Never Trust a Snake":

WWF Wrestling as Masculine Melodrama

See, your problem is that you're looking at this as a
wrestling battle—two guys getting into the ring together to
see who's the better athlete. But it goes so much deeper
than that. Yes, wrestling's involved. Yes, we're going to pound
each other's flesh, slam each other's bodies and hurt each other
really bad. But there's more at stake than just wrestling, my
man. There's a morality play. Randy Savage thinks he represents
the light of righteousness. But you know, it takes an awful
lot of light to illuminate a dark kingdom.—Jake "The Snake"
Roberts, Interview in *WWF Magazine*

There are people who think that wrestling is an ignoble sport.
Wrestling is not a sport, it is a spectacle, and it is no more
ignoble to attend a wrestled performance of Suffering than a
performance of the sorrows of Arnolphe or Andromaque.
—Roland Barthes, "The World of Wrestling"

Like World Wrestling Federation superstar Jake "The Snake" Roberts, Roland Barthes saw wrestling as a "morality play," a curious hybrid of sports and theater. For Barthes, wrestling was at once a "spectacle of excess," evoking the pleasure of grandiloquent gestures and violent contact, and a lower form of tragedy, where issues of morality, ethics, and politics were staged. Wrestling enthusiasts have no interest in seeing a fair fight but rather hope for a satisfying restaging of the ageless struggle between the "perfect bastard" and the suffering hero (Barthes 1982: 25). What wrestling offers its spectators, Barthes tells us, is a story of treachery and revenge, "the intolerable spectacle of powerlessness" and the exhilaration of the hero's victorious return from near-collapse. Wrestling, like conventional melodrama, externalizes emotion, mapping it onto the combatant's bodies and transforming their physical competition into a search for moral order. Restraint or subtlety has little place in such a world. Everything that matters must be displayed, publicly, unambiguously, and unmercilessly.

Barthes's account focuses entirely upon the one-on-one match as isolated event within which each gesture must be instantly legible apart from any larger context of expectations and associations: "One must always understand everything on the spot" (Barthes 1982: 29). Barthes could not have predicted how this focus upon the discrete event or the isolated gesture would be transformed through the narrative mechanisms of television. On television, where wrestling comes with a cast of continuing characters, no single match is self-enclosed; rather, personal conflicts unfold across a number of fights, interviews, and enacted encounters. Television wrestling offers its viewers complexly plotted, ongoing narratives of professional ambition, personal suffering, friendship and alliance, betrayal and reversal of fortune. Matches still offer their share of acrobatic spectacle, snake handling, fire eating, and colorful costumes. They are, as such, immediately accessible to the casual viewer, yet they reward the informed spectator for whom each body slam and double-arm *suplex* bears specific narrative consequences. A demand for closure is satisfied at the level of individual events, but those matches are always contained within a larger narrative trajectory which is itself fluid and open.

The wwf broadcast provides us with multiple sources of identification, multiple protagonists locked in their own moral struggles against the forces of evil. The proliferation of champion titles—the wwf World Champion belt, the Million Dollar belt, the Tag Team champion belt, the Intercontinental champion belt—allows for multiple lines of narrative development, each centering around its own cluster of affiliations and antagonisms. The resolution of one title competition at a major event does little to stabilize the program universe, since there are always more belts to be won and lost, and in any case, each match can always be followed by a rematch which reopens old issues. Outcomes may be inconclusive because of count-outs or disqualifications, requiring future rematches. Accidents may result in surprising shifts in moral and paradigmatic alignment. Good guys betray their comrades and form uneasy alliances with the forces of evil; rule-breakers undergo redemption after suffering crushing defeats.

The economic rationale for this constant "buildup" and deferral of narrative interests is obvious. The World Wrestling Federation (wwf) knows how to use its five weekly television series and its glossy monthly magazine to ensure subscription to its four annual pay-per-view events and occasional pay-per-view specials.[1] Enigmas are raised during the free broadcasts which will be resolved only for a paying audience. Much of the weekly broadcast consists of interviews with the wrestlers about their forthcoming bouts, staged scenes providing background on their antagonisms, and in-the-ring encounters between wwf stars and sparring partners which provide a backdrop for speculations about forthcoming plot developments. Read cynically, the broadcast consists purely of commercial exploitation. Yet this promotion also has important aesthetic consequences, heightening the melodramatic dimensions of the staged fights and transforming televised wrestling into a form of serial fiction for men.

Recent scholarship has focused on serial fiction as a particularly feminine form (Fiske 1987; Modeleski 1982; Feuer 1984: 4–16). Television wrestling runs counter to such a sharply drawn distinction: its characteristic subject matter (the homosocial relations between men, the professional sphere rather than the domestic sphere, the focus on physical means to resolve conflicts) draws on generic traditions which critics have identified as characteristically masculine; its mode of presentation (its seriality, its appeal to viewer speculation and gossip) suggests genres often labeled feminine. These contradictions may reflect wrestling's uneasy status as masculine melodrama. Critics often restrict their discussion of melodrama to the domestic melodrama, a form particularly associated with feminine interests and targeted at female audiences.[2] Such a definition ignores the influence of melodrama on a broader range of genres, including some, such as the western or the social-problem drama, which focus on a masculine sphere of public action. Our inability to talk meaningfully about masculine melodrama stems from contemporary cultural taboos against masculine emotion. Men within our culture tend to avoid self-examination and to hide from sentiment, expressing disdain for the melodramatic. After all, we are told, "real men don't cry." Yet masculine avoidance of public display of emotion does not mean that men lack feelings or that they do not need some outlet for expressing them. Patriarchy consequently constructs alternative means of releasing and managing masculine emotion while preserving the myth of the stoic male. A first step toward reconsidering the place of male affective experience may be to account for the persistence of melodramatic conventions within those forms of entertainment that "real men" do embrace—horror films, westerns, country songs, tabloid newspapers, television wrestling, and the like. By looking more closely at these forms of sanctioned emotional release for men, we may be able to locate some of the central contradictions within our contemporary constructions of masculinity.

This essay will thus consider wwF wrestling as a melodramatic form addressed to a working-class male audience. In focusing on this particular audience here, I do not mean to suggest that this is the only audience interested in such programming. The wwF's multifocused narrative creates space for multiple audience segments—children, young and older women, gays, etc.—who take their own pleasures in its narrative. Nor does my focus on the melodramatic imply that televised wrestling is not readable in terms of other generic traditions, such as the carnivalesque tradition John Fiske (1989: chap. 4) locates. My subtitle, "wwF Wrestling as Masculine Melodrama," signals my focus on one of a number of possible readings of the program. As Peter Rabinowitz has suggested, "Reading is always 'reading as,'" and our decision about a generic frame shapes subsequent aspects of our interpretations (1985: 421). This essay, thus, reads wrestling *as* masculine melodrama, placing particular emphasis upon its relationship to a masculine audience and a melodramatic tradition. Such a focus invites an inquiry into the complex interplay of affect, masculinity, and class, issues which surface in both the formal and the thematic features of televised wrestling, in its characteristic narrative structure(s), its audience address, its treatment of male bonding, and its appeal to populist imagery.

PLAYING WITH OUR FEELINGS

Norbert Elias's and Eric Dunning's path-breaking study *The Quest for Excitement: Sport and Leisure in the Civilizing Process* (1986) invites us to reconsider the affective dimensions of athletic competition. According to their account, modern civilization demands restraint on instinctive and affective experience, a process of repression and sublimation which they call the "civilizing process." Elias has spent much of his intellectual life tracing the gradual process by which Western civilization has intensified its demands for bodily and emotional control, rejecting the emotional volatility and bodily abandon that characterized Europe during the Middle Ages: "Social survival and success in these [contemporary] societies depend . . . on a reliable armour, not too strong and not too weak, of individual self-restraint. In such societies, there is only a comparatively limited scope for the show of strong feelings, of strong antipathies towards and dislike of other people, let alone of hot anger, wild hatred or the urge to hit someone over the head" (Elias and Dunning 1986: 41). Such feelings do not disappear, but they are contained by social expectations: "To see grown-up men and women shaken by tears and abandon themselves to their bitter sorrow in public . . . or beat each other savagely under the impact of their violent excitement [experiences more common during the Middle Ages] has ceased to be regarded as normal. It is usually a matter of embarrassment for the onlooker and often a matter of shame or regret for those who have allowed themselves to be carried away by their excitement" (Elias and Dunning 1986: 64–65). What is at stake here is not the intensity of feeling but our discomfort about its spectacular display. Emotion may be strongly felt, but it must be rendered invisible, private, personal; emotion must not be allowed to have a decisive impact upon social interactions. Emotional openness is read as a sign of vulnerability, while emotional restraint is the marker of social integration. Leaders are to master emotions rather than to be mastered by them. Yet, as Elias writes, "We do not stop feeling. We only prevent or delay our acting in accordance with it" (111). Elias traces the process by which this emotional control has moved from being outwardly imposed by rules of conduct to an internalized and largely unconscious aspect of our personalities. The totality of this restraint exacts its own social costs, creating psychic tensions which somehow must be redirected and released within socially approved limitations.

Sports, he argues, constitute one of many institutions which society creates for the production and expression of affective excitement (Elias and Dunning 1986: 49). Sports must somehow reconcile two contradictory functions — "the pleasurable de-controlling of human feelings, the full evocation of an enjoyable excitement on the one hand and on the other the maintenance of a set of checks to keep the pleasantly de-controlled emotions under control" (49). These two functions are never fully resolved, resulting in the occasional hooliganism as excitement outstrips social control. Yet the conventionality of sports and the removal of the real-world consequences of physical combat (in short, sport's status as adult play) facilitate a controlled and sanctioned release from ordinary affective restraints. The ability to resolve conflicts through a prespecified moment of arbitrary closure delimits the spectator's emotional experience. Perhaps most important, sports offer a shared emotional experience, one which reasserts the desirability of belonging to a community.

Elias and Dunning are sensitive to the class implications in this argument: the "civilizing process" began at the center of "court society" with the aristocracy and spread outward to merchants wishing access to the realms of social and economic power and to the servants who must become unintrusive participants in their masters' lives. Elias and Dunning argue that these class distinctions still surface in the very different forms of emotional display tolerated at the legitimate theater (which provides an emotional outlet for bourgeois spectators) and the sports arena (which provides a space for working-class excitement): the theater audience is to "be moved without moving," to restrain emotional display until the conclusion, when it may be indicated through their applause; while for the sports audience, "motion and emotion are intimately linked," and emotional display is immediate and uncensored (Elias and Dunning 1986: 50). The same distinctions separate upper-class sports (tennis, polo, golf), which allow minimal emotional expression, from lower-class sports (boxing, wrestling, soccer), which demand more overt affective display. Of course, such spectacles also allow the possibility for upper- or middle-class patrons to "slum it," to adopt working-class attitudes and sensibilities while engaging with the earthy spectacle of the wrestling match. They can play at being working-class (with working class norms experienced as a remasculinization of yuppie minds and bodies), can imagine themselves as down to earth, with the people, safe in the knowledge that they can go back to the office the next morning without too much embarrassment at what is a ritualized release of repressed emotions.

Oddly absent from their account is any acknowledgment of the gender-specificity of the rules governing emotional display. Social conventions have traditionally restricted the public expression of sorrow or affection by men and of anger or laughter by women. Men stereotypically learn to translate their softer feelings into physical aggressiveness, while women convert their rage into the shedding of tears. Such a culture provides gender-specific spaces for emotional release which are consistent with dominant constructions of masculinity and femininity — melodrama (and its various manifestations in soap opera or romance) for women, sports for men. Elias's and Dunning's emphasis upon the affective dimensions of sports allows us to more accurately (albeit schematically) map the similarities and differences between sports and melodrama. Melodrama links female affect to domesticity, sentimentality, and vulnerability, while sports links male affect to physical prowess, competition, and mastery. Melodrama explores the concerns of the private sphere, sports those of the public. Melodrama announces its fictional status, while sports claims for itself the status of reality. Melodrama allows for the shedding of tears, while sports solicits shouts, cheers, and boos. Crying, a characteristically feminine form of emotional display, embodies internalized emotion; tears are quiet and passive. Shouting, the preferred outlet for male affect, embodies externalized emotion; it is aggressive and noisy. Women cry from a position of emotional (and often social) vulnerability; men shout from a position of physical and social strength (however illusory).

WWF wrestling, as a form which bridges the gap between sport and melodrama, allows for the spectacle of male physical prowess (a display which is greeted by shouts and boos) but also for the exploration of the emotional and moral life of its combatants. WWF wrestling focuses on both the public and the private, links nonfictional forms with fictional content, and embeds the competitive dimensions of sports within a larger narrative framework which emphasizes the personal consequences of that competition. The "sports entertainment" of WWF wrestling adopts the narrative and thematic structures implicit within traditional sports and heightens them to ensure the maximum emotional impact. At the same time, WWF wrestling adopts the personal, social, and moral conflicts that characterized nineteenth-century theatrical melodrama and enacts them in terms of physical combat between male athletes. In doing so, it foregrounds aspects of masculine mythology which have a particular significance for its predominantly working-class male audience — the experience of vulnerability, the possibilities of male trust and intimacy, and the populist myth of the national community.

Elias and Dunning offer a vivid description of the dramaturgy of the ideal soccer match: "a prolonged battle on the football field between teams which are well matched in skill and strength . . . a game which sways to and fro, in which the teams are so evenly matched that first one, then the other scores" (1986). The emotional consequences of the close and heated action are viscerally felt by the spectators. Each subsequent play intensifies their response, "until the tension reaches a point where it can just be borne and contained without getting out of hand." A decisive climax rewards this active engagement with "the happiness of triumph and jubilation" (Elias and Dunning 1986: 86–87). The writers emphasize many traits which football shares with melodrama — the clear opposition between characters, the sharp alignment of audience identification, abrupt shifts in fortune, and an emotionally satisfying resolution. Yet there is an important difference. While melodrama guarantees emotional release through its conformity to tried and true generic structures, actual athletic competition, unlike staged wrestling, is unrehearsed and unscripted. Matches such as the ones Elias and Dunning describe are relatively rare, since so much is left to chance. Where the actual competition lacks narrative interest, that gap must be filled by sports commentary which evokes and intensifies the audience's investment. However, as Barthes notes, wrestling is not a sport but rather a form of popular theater, and, as such, the events are staged to ensure maximum emotional impact, structured around a consistent reversal of fortunes and a satisfying climax. There is something at stake in every match — something more than who possesses the title belts.

As a consequence, wrestling heightens the emotional experience offered by traditional sports and directs it toward a more specific vision of the social and moral order. Peter Brooks (1976) argues that melodrama provides a post-sacred society with a means of mapping its basic moral and ethical beliefs, of making the world morally legible. Similarly, wrestling, Barthes argues, takes as its central problematic the restoration of moral order, the creation of a just society from a world where the powerful rule. Within the World Wrestling Federation, this battle for a higher justice is staged through a contest for the title belts. Like traditional melodrama, wrestling operates within a dualistic universe: each participant is either a good guy or a villain, a "fan favorite" or a "rule breaker." Good guys rarely fight good guys; bad guys rarely fight bad guys. Championship is sometimes unjustly granted to rule-breakers but ultimately belongs to the virtuous. wwf wrestling offers its viewers a story of justice perverted and restored, innocence misrecognized and recognized, strength used and abused.

MIGHT MAKES RIGHT

Within traditional sports, competition is impersonal, the product of prescribed rules which assign competitors on the basis of their standings or on some prespecified form of rotation. Rivalries do, of course, arise within this system and are the stuff of the daily sports page, but many games do not carry this added affective significance. Within the wwf, however, all competition depends upon intense rivalry. Each fight requires the creation of a social and moral opposition and often stems from a personal grievance. Irwin R. Schyster (irs) falsely accuses the Big Boss Man's mother of tax evasion and threatens to throw her in jail. Sid Justice betrays Hulk Hogan's friendship, turning his back on his tag team partner in the middle of a major match and allowing him to be beaten to a pulp by his opponents, Ric Flair and the Undertaker. Fisticuffs break out between Bret Hart and his brother, "Rocket," during a special "Family Feud" match which awakens long-simmering sibling rivalries. Such offenses require retribution within a world which sees trial by combat as the preferred means of resolving all disputes. Someone has to "pay" for these outrages, and the exacting of payment will occur in the squared ring.

The core myth of wwf wrestling is a fascistic one: ultimately, might makes right; moral authority is linked directly to the possession of physical strength, while evil operates through stealth and craftiness (mental rather than physical sources of power). The appeal of such a myth to a working-class audience should be obvious. In the realm of their everyday experience, strength often gets subordinated into alienated labor. Powerful bodies become the means of their economic exploitation rather than a resource for bettering their lot. In wwf wrestling, physical strength reemerges as a tool for personal empowerment, a means of striking back against personal and moral injustices. Valerie Walkerdine argues that the *Rocky* films, which display a similar appeal, offer "fantasies of omnipotence, heroism, and salvation . . . a counterpoint to the experience of oppression and powerlessness" (Walkerdine 1986: 172–74). Images of fighting, Walkerdine argues, "embody a class-specific and gendered use of the body," which ennobles the physical skills possessed by the working-class spectator: "Physical violence is presented as the only open to those whose lot is manual and not intellectual labor. . . . The fantasy of the fighter is the fantasy of a working-class male omnipotence over the forces of humiliating oppression which mutilate and break the body in manual labor" (173).

A central concern within wrestling, then, is how physical strength can ensure triumph over one's abusers, how one can rise from defeat and regain dignity through hand-to-hand combat. Bad guys cheat to win. They manipulate the system and step outside the rules. They use deception, misdirection, subterfuge, and trickery. Rarely do they win fairly. They smuggle weapons into the ring to attack their opponents while their managers distract the referees. They unwrap the turnbuckle pads and slam their foes heads into metal posts. They adopt choke holds to suffocate them or zap them with cattle prods. Million Dollar Man purposefully focuses his force upon Roddy Piper's wounded knee, doing everything he can to injure him permanently. Such atrocities require rematches to ensure justice; the underdog heroes return next month and, through sheer determination and willpower, battle their protagonists into submission.

Such plots allow for the sterilization of the wwf narrative, forestalling its resolution, intensifying its emotional impact. Yet at the same time, the individual match must be made narratively satisfying on its own terms, and so, in practice, such injustices do not stand. Even though the match is over and its official outcome determined, the hero shoves the referee aside and, with renewed energy, bests his opponent in a fair (if nonbinding) fight. Whatever the outcome, most fights end with the protagonist standing proudly in the center of the ring, while his badly beaten antagonist retreats shamefully to his dressing room. Justice triumphs both in the long run and in the short run. For the casual viewer, it is the immediate presentation of triumphant innocence that matters, that satisfactorily resolves the drama. Yet for the wwf fan, what matters is the ultimate pursuit of justice as it unfolds through the complexly intertwined stories of the many different wrestlers.

BODY DOUBLES

Melodramatic wrestling allows working-class men to confront their own feelings of vulnerability, their own frustrations at a world which promises them patriarchal authority but which is experienced through relations of economic subordination. Gender identities are most rigidly policed in working-class male culture, since unable to act *as* men, they are forced to act *like* men, with a failure to assume the proper role the source of added humiliation. WWF wrestling offers a utopian alternative to the situation, allowing a movement from victimization toward mastery. Such a scenario requires both the creation and the constant rearticulation of moral distinctions. Morality is defined, first and foremost, through personal antagonisms. As Christine Gledhill has written of traditional melodrama, "Innocence and villainy construct each other: while the villain is necessary to the production and revelation of innocence, innocence defines the boundaries of the forbidden which that villain breaks" (1987: 21). In the most aesthetically pleasing and emotionally gripping matches, these personal antagonisms reflect much deeper mythological oppositions — the struggles between rich and poor, black and white, urban and rural, America and the world. Each character stands for something, draws symbolic meaning by borrowing stereotypes already in broader circulation. An important role played by color commentary is to inscribe and reinscribe the basic mythic oppositions at play within a given match. Here, the moral dualisms of masculine melodrama finds its voice through exchanges between two announcers, one (Mean Gene Okerlund) articulating the protagonist's virtues, the other (Bobby "the brain" Heenan) justifying the rule-breaker's transgressions.

Wrestlers are often cast as doppelgängers, similar yet morally opposite figures. Consider, for example, how *WWF Magazine* characterizes a contest between the evil Mountie and the heroic Big Boss Man: "In the conflict are Big Boss Man's and the Mountie's personal philosophies: the enforcement of the law vs. taking the law into one's own hands, the nightstick vs. the cattle prod, weakening a foe with the spike slam vs. disabling him with the nerve-crushing carotid control technique." (Greenberg 1991a: 40). The Canadian Mountie stands on one page, dressed in his bright red uniform, clutching his cattle prod and snarling. The former Georgia prison guard, Big Boss Man, stands on the other, dressed in his pale blue uniform, clutching an open pair of handcuffs, with a look of quiet earnestness. At this moment the two opponents seem to be made for each other, as if no other possible contest could bear so much meaning, though the Big Boss Man and the Mountie will pair off against other challengers in the next major event.

The most successful wrestlers are those who provoke immediate emotional commitments (either positive or negative) and are open to constant rearticulation, who can be fit into a number of different conflicts and retain semiotic value. Hulk Hogan may stand as the defender of freedom in his feud with Sgt. Slaughter, as innocence betrayed by an ambitious friend in his contest against Sid Justice, and as an aging athlete confronting and overcoming the threat of death in his battle with the Undertaker. Big Boss Man may defend the interests of the economically depressed against the Repo Man, make the streets safe from the Nasty Boys, and assert honest law enforcement in the face of the Mountie's bad example.

The introduction of new characters requires their careful integration into the WWF's moral universe before their first match can be fought. We need to know where they will stand in relation to the other protagonists and antagonists. The arrival of Tatanka on the WWF roster was preceded by a series of segments showing the Native American hero visiting the tribal elders, undergoing rites of initiation, explaining the meaning of his haircut, makeup, costume, and war shout. His ridicule by the fashion-minded Rick "the Model" Martel introduced his first antagonism and ensured the viewer's recognition of his essential goodness.

Much of the weekly broadcasts centers on the manufacturing of these moral distinctions and the creation of these basic antagonisms. A classic example might be the breakup of the Rockers. A series of accidents and minor disagreements sparked a public showdown on Brutus "the Barber" Beefcake's Barber Shop, a special program segment. Shawn Michaels appeared at the interview, dressed in black leather and wearing sunglasses (already adopting iconography signaling his shift toward the dark side). After a pretense of reconciliation and a series of clips reviewing their past together, Michaels shoved his partner, Marty Jannetty, through the barbershop window, amid Brutus's impotent protests.[3] The decision to feature the two team members as independent combatants required the creation of moral difference, while the disintegration of their partnership fit perfectly within the program's familiar doppelgänger structure. WWF Magazine portrayed the events in terms of the biblical story of Cain and Abel, as the rivalry of "two brothers": "[The Rockers] were as close as brothers. They did everything together, in and out of the ring. But Michaels grew jealous of Jannetty and became impatient to succeed. While Jannetty was content to bide his time, work steadily to improve with the knowledge that championships don't come easily in the wwf, Michaels decided he wanted it all now—and all for himself" ("Mark of Cain" 1992: 41).

If an earlier profile had questioned whether the two had "separate identities," this reporter has no trouble making moral distinctions between the patient Jannetty and the impatient Michaels. Subsequent broadcasts would link Michaels professionally and romantically with Sensational Sherri, a woman whose seductive charms have been the downfall of many wwf champs. As a manager, Sherri is noted for her habit of smuggling foreign objects to ringside in her purse and interfering in the matches to ensure her man's victory. Sherri, who had previously been involved with Million Dollar Man Ted Dibiase, announced that she would use her "Teddy Bear's" money to back Michaels's solo career, linking his betrayal of his partner to her own greedy and adulterous impulses. All of these plot twists differentiate Jannetty and Michaels, aligning spectator identification with the morally superior partner. Michaels's paramount moral failing is his all-consuming ambition, his desire to dominate rather than work alongside his long-time partner.

The Rockers' story points to the contradictory status of personal advancement within the wwf narrative: these stories hinge upon fantasies of upward mobility, yet ambition is just as often regarded in negative terms, as ultimately corrupting. Such a view of ambition reflects the experience of people who have worked hard all of their lives without much advancement and therefore remain profoundly suspicious of those on top. Wrestling speaks to those who recognize that upward mobility often has little to do with personal merit and a lot to do with a willingness to stomp on those who get in your way. Virtue, in the wwf moral universe, is often defined by a willingness to temper ambition through personal loyalties, through affiliation with others, while vice comes from putting self-interest ahead of everything else. This distrust of self-gain was vividly illustrated during a bout between Rowdy Roddy Piper and Bret "the Hitman" Hart at the 1992 *Wrestlemania*. This competition uncharacteristically centered on two good guys. As a result, most viewers suspected that one fighter would ultimately be driven to base conduct by personal desire for the Intercontinental Championship belt. Such speculations were encouraged by ambiguous signs from the combatants during "buildup" interviews and exploited during the match through a number of gestures which indicate moral indecision: Rowdy stood ready to club Hart with an illegal foreign object; the camera cut repeatedly to close-ups of his face as he struggled with his conscience before casting the object aside and continuing a fair fight. In the end, however, the two long-time friends embraced each other as Piper congratulated Hart on a more or less fairly won fight. The program situated this bout as a sharp contrast to the feud between Hulk Hogan and Sid Justice, the major attraction at this pay-per-view event. Their budding friendship had been totally destroyed by Justice's overriding desire to dominate the wwf: "I'm gonna crack the head of somebody big in the wwf. . . . No longer is this Farmboy from Arkansas gonna take a back seat to anybody" ("wwf Superstars" 1992: 18). Rowdy and Hart value their friendship over their ambition; Justice lets nothing stand in the way of his quest for power.

PERFECT BASTARDS

wwf wrestlers are not rounded characters; the spectacle has little room for the novelistic, and here the form may push the melodramatic imagination to its logical extremes. wwf wrestlers experience no internal conflicts which might blur their moral distinctiveness. Rather, they often display the "undividedness" that Robert Heilman sees as a defining aspect of nineteenth-century melodramatic characters: "[The melodramatic character displays] oneness of feeling as competitor, crusader, aggressor; as defender counter-attacker, fighter for survival; he may be assertive or compelled, questing or resistant, obsessed or desperate; he may triumph or lose, be victor or victim, exert pressure or be pressed. Always he is undivided, unperplexed by alternatives, untorn by divergent impulses; all of his strength or weakness faces in one direction" (1973: 53).

The wwf athletes sketch their moral failings in broad profile: the Mountie pounds on his chest and roars, "I am the Mountie," convinced that no one can contest his superiority, yet as soon as the match gets rough, he slides under the ropes and tries to hide behind his scrawny manager. The Million Dollar Man shoves hundred-dollar bills into the mouths of his defeated opponents, while Sherri paints her face with gilded dollar signs to mark her possession by the highest bidder. Ravishing Rick Rude wears pictures of his opponents on his arse, relishing his own vulgarity. Virtue similarly displays itself without fear of misrecognition. Hacksaw Jim Duggan clutches an American flag in one hand and a two-by-four in the other.

(*top*) "Everyone Has a Price": The Million Dollar Man laughs
at human corruptibility. (*bottom*) Painted Woman: Sensational
Sherri gilds her face with dollar signs to suggest her possession
by the Million Dollar Man.

The need for a constant recombination of a fixed number of characters requires occasional shifts in moral allegiances (as occurred with the breakup of
the Rockers). Characters may undergo redemption or seduction, but these
shifts typically occur quickly and without much ambiguity. There is rarely
any lingering doubt or moral fence-straddling. Such characters are good one
week and evil the next. Jake "the Snake" Roberts, a long-time hero — albeit
one who enjoys his distance from the other protagonists — uncharacteristically offered to help the Ultimate Warrior prepare for his fight against the
Undertaker. Their grim preparations unfolded over several weeks, with Jake

forcing the Warrior to undergo progressively more twisted rituals—locking him into a coffin, burying him alive—until finally Jake shoved him into a room full of venomous snakes. Bitten by Jake's cobra, Lucifer, the Ultimate Warrior staggered toward his friend, who simply brushed him aside. As the camera pulled back to show the Undertaker standing side by side with Jake, the turncoat, laughed, "Never trust a snake." From that moment forward, Jake was portrayed as totally evil, Barthes's perfect bastard. Jake attacks Macho man Randy Savage's bride, Elizabeth, on their wedding day and terrorizes the couple every chance he gets.

The program provides no motivation for such outrages, though commentary both in the broadcasts and in the pages of the wrestling magazines constantly invites such speculation: "What makes Jake hate Savage and his bride so fiercely? Why does he get his jollies—as he admits—from tormenting her?" What Peter Brooks said about villains of traditional melodrama holds equally well here: "Evil in the world of melodrama does not need justification; it exists, simply. . . . And the less it is adequately motivated, the more this evil appears simply volitional, the product of pure will" (1976: 34). Jake is evil because he is a snake; it's in his character and nothing can change him, even though in this case, less than a year ago, Jake was as essentially good as he is now totally demented. We know Jake is evil and without redemption, because he tells us so, over and over:

> I'm not really sure I have any soul at all. . . . Once I get involved in something—no matter how demented, no matter how treacherous, no matter how far off the mark it is from normal standards—I never back down. I just keep on going, deeper and deeper into blackness, far past the point where any sensible person would venture. You see, a person with a conscience—a person with a soul—would be frightened by the sordid world I frequent. But Jake the Snake isn't scared at all. To tell you the truth, I can't get enough of it. ("WWF Interview" 1992: 17)

Jake recognizes and acknowledges his villainy; he names it publicly and unrepentantly.

Peter Brooks sees such a process of "self-nomination" as an essential feature of the melodramatic imagination: "Nothing is spared because nothing is left unsaid; the characters stand on stage and utter the unspeakable, give voice to their deepest feelings, dramatize through their heightened and polarized words and gestures the whole lesson of their relationship" (1976:

"Never Trust a Snake":
Jake "The Snake" Roberts
contemplates the nature
of his own evil.

4). The soliloquy, that stock device of traditional melodrama, is alive and well in WWF wrestling. Wrestlers look directly into the audience and shove their fists toward the camera; they proclaim their personal credos and describe their sufferings. Tag team partners repeat their dedication to each other and their plans to dominate their challengers. Villains profess their evil intentions and vow to perform various forms of mayhem upon their opponents. Their rhetoric is excessively metaphoric, transforming every fight into a life-and-death struggle. Much as nineteenth-century theatrical melodrama used denotative music to define the characters' moral stances, the wrestlers' entry into the arena is preceded by theme songs which encapsulate their personalities. Hulk's song describes him as "a real American hero" who "fights for the rights of every man." The Million Dollar Man's jingle proclaims his compelling interest in "money, money, money," while Jake's song repeats "trust me, trust me, trust me."

This public declaration ensures the constant moral legibility of the WWF narrative and thereby maximizes the audience's own emotional response. Spectators come to the arena or turn on the program to express intense emotion—to cheer the hero, to boo and jeer the villain—without moral ambiguity or emotional complexity. (Wrestling fans sometimes choose to root for the villains, taking pleasure in their inversion of the WWF's moral universe, yet even this perverse pleasure requires moral legibility.) Operating within a world of absolutes, WWF wrestlers wear their hearts on their sleeves (or, in Ravishing Rick Rude's case, on the seat of their pants) and project their emotions from every inch of their bodies. Much as in classic melodrama, external actions reveal internal states; moral disagreements demand physical expressions. As Brooks writes, "Emotions are given a full acting-out, a full representation before our eyes. . . . Nothing is *under*stated, all is *over*stated" (1976: 41). The Million Dollar Man cowers, covering his face and retreating, crawling on hands and knees backward across the ring. Sherri shouts at the top of her lungs and pounds the floor with her high-heel shoe. Rowdy Roddy Piper gets his dander up and charges into the ring. With a burst of furious energy, he swings madly at his opponents, forcing them to scatter right and left. Roddy spits in the Million Dollar Man's eyes, flings his sweaty shirt in his face, or grabs Sherri, rips off her dress, throws her over his knee, and spanks her. Such characters embody the shameful spectacle of emotional display, acting as focal points for the audience's own expression of otherwise repressed affect.

INVINCIBLE VICTIMS

Fans eagerly anticipate these excessive gestures as the most appropriate means of conveying the characters' moral attitudes. Through a process of simplification, the wrestler's body has been reduced to a series of iconic surfaces and stock attitudes. We know not only how the performer is apt to respond to a given situation but what bodily means will be adopted to express that response. Wrestlers perform less with their eyes and hands than with their arms and legs and with their deep, resounding voices. Earthquake's bass rumble and Roddy's fiery outbursts, Ric Flair's vicious laughter and Macho Man's red-faced indignation are "too much" for the small screen, yet they articulate feelings that are too intense to be contained.

This process of simplification and exaggeration transforms the wrestlers into cartoonish figures who may slam each other's heads into iron steps, throw each other onto wooden floors, smash each other with steel chairs, land with their full weight on the other's prone stomach, and emerge without a scratch, ready to fight again. Moral conflict will continue unabated; no defeat can be final within a world where the characters are omnipotent. If traditional melodrama foregrounded long-suffering women's endurance of whatever injustices the world might throw against them, wwf wrestling centers around male victims who ultimately refuse to accept any more abuse and fight back against the aggressors.

Such a scenario allows men to acknowledge their own vulnerability, safe in the knowledge that their masculine potency will ultimately be restored and that they will be strong enough to overcome the forces which subordinate them. Hulk Hogan has perfected the image of the martyred hero who somehow captures victory from the closing jaws of defeat. Badly beaten in a fight, Hulk lies in a crumpled heap. The referee lifts his limp arms up, once, twice, ready to call the fight, when the crowd begins to clap and stomp. The mighty hero rises slowly, painfully to his feet, rejuvenated by the crowd's response. Blood streams through his blond hair and drips across his face, but he whips it aside with a broad swing of his mighty arms. Hulk turns to face his now-terrified assailant.

"SEEING IS BELIEVING"

Such broad theatricality cuts against wrestling's tradition of pseudorealism; the programs' formats mimic the structures and visual styles of nonfiction television, of sports coverage, news broadcasts, and talk shows. The fiction is, of course, that all of this fighting is authentic, spontaneous, unscripted. The WWF narrative preserves the illusion at all costs. There is no stepping outside the fiction, no acknowledgment of the production process or the act of authorship. When the performers are featured in *WWF Magazine*, they are profiled in character. Story segments are told in the form of late-breaking news reports or framed as interviews. The commentators are taken by surprise, interrupted by seemingly unplanned occurrences. During one broadcast, Jake the Snake captured Macho Man, dragging him into the ring. Jake tied him to the ropes and menaced him with a cobra which sprang and bit him on the forearm. The camera was jostled from side to side by people racing to Macho's assistance and panned abruptly trying to follow his hysterical wife as she ran in horror to ringside. A reaction shot shows a child in the audience reduced to tears by this brutal spectacle. Yet, at the same time, the camera refused to show us an image "too shocking" for broadcast. Macho Man's arm and the snake's gaping mouth were censored, blocked by white bars, not unlike the blue dot that covered the witness's face at the William Kennedy Smith rape trial that same week. (A few weeks later, the "uncensored" footage was at last shown, during a prime-time broadcast, so that viewers could see "what really happened.") The plot lines are thus told through public moments where a camera could plausibly be present, though such moments allow us insight into the characters' pri-

"Seeing is Believing": Jake "The Snake" Roberts's deadly cobra bites into "Macho Man" Randy Savage's arm.

vate motivations. Such campy self-acknowledgment may be part of what makes male spectators' affective engagement with this melodramatic form safe and acceptable within a traditionally masculine culture which otherwise backs away from overt emotional display. Whenever the emotions become too intense, there is always a way of pulling back, laughing at what might otherwise provoke tears. WWF wrestling, at another level, provokes authentic pain and rage, particularly when it embraces populist myths of economic exploitation and class solidarity, feeds a hunger for homosocial bonding, or speaks to utopian fantasies of empowerment. The gap between the campy and the earnest reception of wrestling may reflect the double role which Elias and Dunning ascribe to traditional sports: the need to allow for the de-controlling of powerful affects while at the same time regulating their expression and ensuring their ultimate containment. The melodramatic aspects are what trigger emotional release, while the campy aspects contain it within safe bounds. The plots of wrestling cut close to the bone, inciting racial and class antagonisms that rarely surface this overtly elsewhere in popular culture, while comic exaggeration ensures that such images can never fully be taken seriously.

ROMANCE IN THE RING

WWF's plots center on the classic materials of melodrama: "false accusation. . . . innocence beleaguered, virtue triumphant, eternal fidelity, mysterious identity, lovers reconciled, fraudulence revealed, threats survived, enemies foiled" (Heilman 1968: 76). The ongoing romance of Macho and Elizabeth bears all of the classic traces of the sentimental novel. The virginal Miss Elizabeth, who almost always dresses in lacy white, stands as the embodiment of womanly virtues. WWF fans were fascinated by her struggle to civilize her impassioned and often uncontrollable Macho Man, withstanding constant bouts of unreasoning jealousy, tempering his dirty tactics. As a profile of Miss Elizabeth explained, "She embodies the spirit of a grassroots American wife. She cares for her man. She provides him with comfort in the midst of chaos. She provides him with a sense of unity when his world seems to be disintegrating. Elizabeth calmly handles these difficult situations with grace and tact" ("Elizabeth Balancing" 1992). WWF fans watched the course of their romance for years, as Macho rejected her, taking up with the sensuous and anything-but-virtuous Sherri, but he was reunited with Elizabeth following a devastating defeat in a career-ending match against the Ultimate Warrior. They followed her efforts to rebuild her Macho Man's self-confidence, his fumbling attempts to propose to her, and their spectacular pay-per-view wedding. They watched as the beloved couple were attacked during their wedding party by Jake and the Undertaker, as Macho begged the WWF management to reinstate him so that he could avenge himself and his wife against this outrage, and as he finally returned to the ring and defeated the heartless Snake during a specially scheduled event. No sooner was this conflict resolved than Ric Flair produced incriminating photographs which he claimed show that Elizabeth was his former lover. In a locker-room interview, Ric and Mr. Perfect revealed the photographs as evidence that Miss Elizabeth is "damaged goods," while the fumbling announcer struggled to protect Elizabeth's previously unquestioned virtue. Once again, this domestic crisis motivated a forthcoming bout, creating narrative interest as the all but inarticulate Macho defended his wife with his muscles.

The Macho Man–Elizabeth romance is unusual in its heavy focus on domestic relations, though not unique: Sherri's romantic entanglements with the Million Dollar Man and Shawn Michaels offer a similar (albeit morally opposite) narrative, while the complex family drama of the Hart family (whose patriarch, Stu, was a long-time wrestler and whose four sons have all enjoyed WWF careers) has motivated images of both fraternal solidarity and sibling rivalry. More often, however, the masculine melodrama of WWF wrestling centers on the relationships between men, occupying a homosocial space which has little room for female intrusions. There are, after all, only two women in the WWF universe—the domestic angel, Elizabeth, and the scheming whore, Sherri. A more typical story involved Virgil, the black bodyguard of the Million Dollar Man, who, after years of being subjected to his boss's humiliating whims, decided to strike back, to challenge his one-time master to a fight for possession of his "Million Dollar Belt." Virgil was befriended by the feisty Scotsman Rowdy Roddy Piper, who taught him to stand tall and broad. The two men fought side by side to ensure the black man's dignity. The antagonism between Virgil and the Million Dollar Man provoked class warfare, while the friendship between Virgil and Roddy marked the uneasy courtship between men.

Here and elsewhere, WWF wrestling operates along the gap that separates our cultural ideal of male autonomy and the reality of alienation, themes that emerge most vividly within tag team competition. The fighter, that omnipotent muscle machine, steps alone, with complete confidence, into the ring, ready to do battle with his opponent. As the fight progresses, he is beaten down, unable to manage without assistance. Struggling to the ropes, he must admit that he needs another man. His partner reaches out to him while he crawls along the floor, inching toward that embrace. The image of the two hands, barely touching, and the two men, working together to overcome their problems, seems rich with what Eve Sedgwick calls "male homosocial desire" (Sedgwick 1985). That such a fantasy is played out involving men whose physical appearance exaggerates all of the secondary masculine characteristics frees male spectators from social taboos which prohibit the open exploration of male intimacy. In their own brutish language, the men express what it is like to need (and desire?) another man. Consider, for example, how WWF *Magazine* characterizes the growing friendship between Jake the Snake and Andre the Giant: "At a glance, Andre gives the impression of granite—unshakable, immutable and omnipotent. Inside, there is a different Andre. His massive size and power belie the fact that his spirit is as fragile as anyone's. And that spirit was more bruised than was his body. Like Andre, Jake projects a sense of detachment from the world of the average guy. Like Andre, Jake has an inner self that is more vulnerable than his outer shell" ("Meeting of the Minds" 1991: 52).

The story describes their first tentative overtures, their attempts to overcome old animosities, and their growing dependency on each other for physical and emotional support. As Jake explains: "Andre was afraid of serpents. I was afraid of people—not of confronting people, but of getting close to them. We began to talk. Slow talk. Nothing talk. Getting to know one another. The talk got deeper. . . . I never asked for help from anybody. I never will. But Andre decided to help me; I won't turn him down. I guess we help one another. You might call it a meeting of the minds" ("Meeting of the Minds" 1991: 52). Jake's language carefully, hesitantly negotiates between male ideals of individual autonomy ("I never asked for help") and an end to the isolation and loneliness such independence creates. Will Jake find this ideal friendship with a man who was once his bitter enemy, or does he simply lay himself open to new injuries? These images of powerful men whose hulking bodies mask hidden pains speak to longings which the entire structure of patriarchy desperately denies.

Such a narrative explores the links that bind and the barriers that separate men. Yet, at the same time, its recurring images of betrayed friendship and violated trust rationalize the refusal to let down barriers. Texas Tornado describes his relationship to his former tag team partner: "I know the Warrior as well as any man in the World Wrestling Federation. . . . Of course, in wrestling, you never get too close with anybody because one day you might be facing him on the other side of the ring. Still, Warrior and I have traveled and trained together. We've shared things" (Greenberg 1991b: 52). Wrestling operates within a carefully policed zone, a squared ring, that allows for the representation of intense homosocial desire but also erects strong barriers against too much risk and intimacy. The wrestlers "share things," but they are not allowed to get "too close."

Consider what happened when the Beverly Brothers met the Bushwhackers at a live WWF event at the Boston Gardens. The two brothers, clad in lavender tights, hugged each other before the match, and their down-under opponents, in their big boots and work clothes, turned upon them in a flash, "queer baiting" and then "gay bashing" the Beverly Brothers. I sat there with fear and loathing as I heard thousands of men, women, and children shouting, "Faggot, faggot, faggot." I was perplexed at how such a representation could push so far and spark such an intense response. The chanting continued for five, ten minutes, as the Bushwhackers stomped their feet and waved their khaki caps with glee, determined to drive their "effeminate" opponents from the ring. The Beverly Brothers protested, pouted, and finally submitted, unable to stand firm against their tormentors. What may have necessitated this homophobic spectacle was the need of both performers and spectators to control potential readings of the Bushwhackers' own physically intimate relationship. The Bushwhackers, Butch and Luke, are constantly defined as polymorphously perverse and indiscriminately oral, licking the faces of innocent spectators or engaging in mutual face-wetting as a symbolic gesture of their mutual commitment. By defining the Beverly "Sisters" as "faggots," as outside of acceptable masculinity, the Bushwhackers created a space where homosocial desire could be more freely expressed without danger of its calling into question their gender identity or sexual preference. This moment seems emblematic of the way wrestling more generally operates — creating a realm of male action which is primarily an excuse for the display of masculine emotion (and even for homoerotic contact) while ensuring that nothing which occurs there can raise any questions about the participant's "manhood."[4]

POPULIST PLEASURES

One key way that wrestling contains this homoerotic potential is through the displacement of issues of homosocial bonding onto a broader political and economic terrain. If, as feminism has historically claimed, the personal is the political, traditional masculinity has often acknowledged its personal vulnerabilities only through evolving more abstract political categories. Populist politics, no less than sports, has been a space of male emotional expression, where personal pains and sufferings can be openly acknowledged only through allegorical rhetoric and passionate oratory. Melodramatic wrestling's focus on the professional rather than the personal sphere facilitates this shift from the friendship ties between individual males to the political ties between all working men. The erotics of male homosocial desire is sublimated into a hunger for the populist community, while images of economic exploitation are often charged with a male dread of penetration and submission.

Although rarely described in these terms, populism offers a melodramatic vision of political and economic relationships. Bruce Palmer argues that populism is characterized by its focus on a tangible reality of immediate experience rather than political abstraction, its emphasis on personal rather than impersonal causation, and its appeal to sentimentality rather than rationality (all traits commonly associated with the melodramatic). As he summarizes the basic axioms of the southern populist movement, "what is most real and most important in the world was that which was most tangible, that which could be seen and touched. . . . People made things move and if some people were moved more than movers, it was because others, more powerful, moved them" (Palmer 1980: 3). American populism sees virtue as originating through physical labor, as a trait possessed by those who are closest to the moment of production (and therefore embodied through manual strength), while moral transgression, particularly greed and ruthlessness, reflects alienation from the production process (often embodied as physical frailty and sniveling cowardice). Populism understands politics through the social relations between individuals rather than groups, though individuals are understood in larger allegorical categories — the simple farmer vs. the slick Wall Street lawyer, the factory worker vs. the scheming boss, the small businessman vs. the Washington bureaucrat, the American voter vs. the party bosses. Social changes come, within this model, through personal redemption rather than systemic change. A populist utopia would be a community within which individuals recognized their common interests and respected their mutual responsibilities. As Palmer explains, "The only decent society was one in which each person looked out for every other one, a society in which *all* people enjoyed equal rights and the benefits of their labor" (1980: 5). Such a movement made common cause between workers and farmers (and its most progressive forms, between whites and blacks) in their mutual struggle for survival against the forces of capitalist expansion and technological change.

If populism draws on melodramatic rhetoric, populism has also provided the core myths by which the masculine melodrama has historically operated. French melodrama might concern itself with the struggles of the aristocracy and the bourgeois; American faith in a classless society translated these same conventions into narratives about scheming bankers and virtuous yeomen, stock figures within the populist vision. American melodrama, David Grimsted tells us, imagines a democratic universe which rewards a commitment to fraternity and hard work and demonizes appeals to privilege (1968). Michael Denning argues that the sentimental fiction provided by turn-of-the-century dime novels similarly interpreted the economic relations between labor and capital within essentially melodramatic terms (Denning 1987: 80). While such visions of American democracy were not automatically populist and often lent themselves to middle-class social reform, melodrama was always available as a vehicle for populist allegory, especially within masculine forms which displace melodrama's characteristic interest in the domestic into the public sphere.

In that sense, melodramatic wrestling fits squarely within the larger tradition of masculine melodrama and populist politics. What is striking about the mythology of wwf wrestling is how explicitly its central conflicts evoke class antagonisms. Its villains offer vivid images of capitalist greed and conspicuous consumption. The Million Dollar Man wears a gold belt studded with diamonds and waves a huge wad of hundred-dollar bills. Magazine photographs and program segments have shown him driving expensive cars, eating in high-class restaurants, living in a penthouse apartment, or vacationing in his summer house at Palm Beach. What he can't grab with brute force, he buys: "Everybody has a price." In one notorious episode, he bribed Andre the Giant to turn over to him the sacred wwf championship belt; another time, he plotted the hostile takeover of the wwf. Similarly, Ric Flair brags constantly about his wealth and influence: "I'll pull up [to the match] in my stretch limousine with a bottle of Dom Perignon in one hand and a fine-looking woman holding the other. The only thing I'll be worried about is if the champagne stays cold enough" ("wwf Superstars" 1992: 18). Mean Gene Okerlund interviews him on his yacht, *Gypsy*, as he chuckles over his sexual humiliation of the Macho Man and brags about his wild parties. The Model enjoys a jet-setting lifestyle, displays the "finest in clothing," and tries to market his new line of male perfumes, "the scent of the 90s, Arrogance." Irwin R. Schyster constantly threatens to audit his opponents, while Repo Man promises to foreclose on their possessions: "What's mine is mine. What's yours is mine too! . . . I've got no mercy at all for cheats. Tough luck if you've lost your job. If you can't make the payment, I'll get your car. Walk to work, Sucker" ("Personality Profile" 1992: 11).

The patriotic laborer (Hacksaw Jim Duggan), the virtuous farm boy (Hillbilly Jim), the small-town boy made good (Big Boss Man), the Horatio Alger character (Virgil, Rowdy Roddy Piper, Tito Santana) are stock figures within this morality play, much as they have been basic tropes in populist discourse for more than a century. wwf heroes hail from humble origins and can therefore act as appropriate champions within fantasies of economic empowerment and social justice. A profile introducing Sid Justice to *wwf Magazine* readers stressed his rural origins: "Sid Justice comes from the land. . . . Born and raised on a farm in Arkansas, imbued with the hard-working values of people who rise before dawn to till the earth and milk the cows. . . . A lifestyle that is the backbone of this country" ("Salt of the Earth" 1991: 47–48). Justice developed his muscles tossing bales of hay into his grandfather's truck, and his integrity reflects the simplicity of an agrarian upbringing: "Don't confuse simplicity with stupidity. A man who learned to make the land produce its fruits has smarts." Sid Justice understands the meaning of personal commitments and the value of simple virtues in a way that would be alien to "people who get their dinner out of a cellophane package from the supermarket."

Pride in where one comes from extends as well to a recognition of racial or ethnic identities. Tito Santana returns to Mexico to rediscover his roots and takes lessons from a famous bullfighter, changing his name to El Matador. Tatanka emerges as the "leader of the New Indian Nation," demonstrating his pride in his "Native American heritage." He explains, "the tribes of all nations are embodied in me" ("Tatanka" 1992: 55). The creation of tag teams and other alliances cuts across traditional antagonisms to bring together diverse groups behind a common cause. Tag team partners Texas Tornado and El Matador, the Anglo and the Mexicano, join forces in their shared struggle against economic injustice and brute power. "Rule-breakers" are often linked to racial prejudice. The "Brain" releases a steady stream of racial slurs and epithets; the Million Dollar Man visits the "neighborhoods" to make fun of the ramshackle shack where El Matador was raised or to ridicule the crime-ridden streets where Virgil spent his youth. What wwf wrestling enacts, then, are both contemporary class antagonisms (the working man against the Million Dollar Man, the boy from the barrio against the repo man, the farmer against the IRS) and the possibilities of a class solidarity that cuts across racial boundaries, a common community of the oppressed and the marginal.

The rule-breaker's willingness to jeer at honest values and humble ancestry, to hit the proletarian protagonists with economic threats and to shove their own ill-gotten goods in their faces, intensifies the emotions surrounding their confrontations. These men are fighting for all of our dignity against these forces which keep us down, which profit from others' suffering and prosper in times of increased hardship. Big Boss Man defends his mother against false allegations leveled against her by the IRS: "My mama never had a job in her life. All she did was take care of her children and raise food on the farm down in Georgia" ("Talk with Big Boss Man" 1991: 18). Virgil strikes back not only against the man who forced him to wipe the perspiration from his brow and pick the dirt from between his toes, but also against the conditions of economic subordination which made him dependent on that monster.

COMING TO BLOWS

Such evil must be isolated from the populist community; its origins must be identified and condemned because it represents a threat to mutual survival. This attempt to name and isolate corruption emerges in a particularly vivid fashion when Sgt. Slaughter discusses the Nasty Boys' delinquency:

> The Nasty Boys are un-American trash. You know, their hometown of Allentown is a very patriotic town. Its people have worked in the steel mills for years. Their hard work is evident in every skyscraper and building from coast to coast. Allentown's people have worked in the coal mines for years. Their hard work has kept America warm in the dead of winter. But the Nasty Boys don't come from the same Allentown I know. . . . They spit on hard-working Americans. They spit on Patriotic people. And they spit on the symbol of this great land, Old Glory herself. ("American Pride" 1992: 52)

Slaughter's rhetoric is classic populism, linking virtue and patriotism with labor, treating evil as a threat originating outside of the community which must be contained and vanquished.

This process of defining the great American community involves defining outsiders as well as insiders, and it is not simply the rich and the powerful who are excluded. There is a strong strand of nativism in the wwf's populist vision. When we move from national to international politics, the basic moral opposition shifts from the powerless against the powerful to America and its allies (the United Kingdom, Australia, and New Zealand, Canada) against its enemies (especially the Arabs and the Communists, often the Japanese). The central match at the 1993 Survivor Series, for example, pitted the "All-Americans" against the "Foreign Fanatics" (a mix that involved not only predictable villains such as Japan's massive Yokozuna but also less predictable ones, such as Finland's Ludwig and the Montrealers). The appeal to racial stereotyping, which had its progressive dimensions in the creation of champions for various oppressed minorities, resurfaces here in a profound

xenophobia. Arab wrestlers are ruthless, Asian wrestlers are fiendishly in-
scrutable or massive and immovable. While America is defined through its
acceptance of diversity, foreign cultures are defined through their sameness,
their conformity to a common image. This is true for sympathetic foreigners,
such as the Bushwhackers, as it is for less sympathetic foreigners, such as
Col. Mustafa and Gen. Adnan. At this level, Hulk's long-time possession of
the wwf title becomes an issue of national sovereignty, with threats coming
from outside not only the populist community but the American nation-
state as well; "Foreign Fanatics" are trying to take what belongs always in
American hands, and they must be taught that they can't mess with Uncle
Sam.

America's foreign relations can be mapped through the changing alliances within the wwf: Nikolai Volkov, one of the two Bolsheviks, retired
from view when the Cold War seemed on the verge of resolution, but reemerged as a spokesman for the new Eastern Europe, redefined as a citizen
of Lithuania. The wwf restaged the Gulf War through a series of "Body-
bag" bouts between Hulk Hogan and Sgt. Slaughter. Slaughter, a former
Marine drill sergeant, was brainwashed by Iraqi operatives Col. Mustafa
and Gen. Adnan. Under their sinister tutelage, he seized the wwf championship belt through brutal means and vowed to turn the entire federation and its followers into "pows." In a series of staged incidents, Slaughter burned an American flag and ridiculed basic national institutions. The
turncoat leatherneck smugly pounded his chest while his turbaned sidekick
babbled incessantly in something resembling Arabic. Hulk Hogan, the all-
American hero, vowed that his muscles were more powerful than patriot
missiles and that he could reclaim the belt in the name of God, family, and
the country. He dedicated his strength to protect the "Little Hulkamaniacs"
whose mothers and fathers were serving in the Gulf. The blond-haired, blue-
eyed Hulkster looked into the camera, flexing his pythons and biceps, and
roared, "What ya gonna do, Sarge Slaughter, when the Red, White and Blue
runs wild on you?" Hulk and Hacksaw Jim Duggan incited the crowd to
chant "usa" and to jeer at the Iraqi national anthem. Here, the working-class
heroes emerge as flag-waving patriots, fighting against "un-Americanism"
at home and tyranny abroad.

Yet however jingoistic this enactment became, wwf's melodramatic conventions exercised a counterpressure, bridging the gap between otherwise
sharply delimited ideological categories. Humiliated by a crushing defeat,

Restaging the Gulf War: Hulk Hogan and Sgt. Slaughter (accompanied by his attaché, Gen. Adnan) "draw a line in the sand."

Slaughter pulled back from his foreign allies and began a pilgrimage to various national monuments, pleading with the audience, "I want my country back." Ultimately, in a moment of reconciliation with Hacksaw Jim Duggan, the audience was asked to forgive him for his transgressions and to accept him back into the community. Sarge kneeled and kissed an American flag, Hacksaw embraced him, and the two men walked away together, arm in arm. That moment when one tired and physically wounded man accepted the embrace and assistance of another tired and psychically wounded man contained tremendous emotional intensity. Here, male homosocial desire and populist rhetoric work together to rein in the nationalistic logic of the

Gulf War narrative, to create a time and space where male vulnerability and mutual need may be publicly expressed. Here, the personal concerns which had been displaced onto populist politics reassert their powerful demands upon the male combatants and spectators to ensure an emotional resolution to a story which in the real world refused satisfying closure. The story of a soul-less turncoat and a ruthless tyrant evolved into the story of a fallen man's search for redemption and reunion, an autonomous male's hunger for companionship, and an invincible victim's quest for higher justice.

Such a moment can be described only as melodramatic, but what it offers is a peculiarly masculine form of melodrama. If traditional melodrama centers upon the moral struggle between the powerful and the vulnerable, masculine melodrama confronts the painful paradox that working-class men are powerful by virtue of their gender and vulnerable by virtue of their economic status. If traditional melodrama involves a play with affect, masculine melodrama confronts the barriers which traditional masculinity erects around the overt expression of emotion. If traditional melodrama centers on the personal consequences of social change, masculine melodrama must confront traditional masculinity's tendency to displace personal needs and desires onto the public sphere. The populist imagery of melodramatic wrestling can be understood as one way of negotiating within these competing expectations, separating economic vulnerability from any permanent threat to male potency, translating emotional expression into rage against political injustice, turning tears into shouts, and displacing homosocial desire onto the larger social community. Populism may be what makes this powerful mixture of the masculine and the melodramatic popularly accessible and what allows wrestling to become such a powerful release of repressed male emotion.

Laura Kipnis's thoughtful essay, "Reading *Hustler*" cautions us against reading popular culture (or working-class ideology) in black-and-white, either-or terms, imposing upon it our own political fantasies: "There is no guarantee that counter-hegemonic or even specifically anti-bourgeois cultural forms are necessarily also going to be progressive" (1992: 388). Kipnis finds that *Hustler* "powerfully articulates class resentments" but does so in terms which are "often only incoherent and banal when it means to be alarming and confrontational." Kipnis does not deny the profound "anti-liberalism, anti-feminism, anti-communism, and anti-progressivism" which characterizes the magazine's contents; she does not attempt to rescue Larry

Flynt for progressive politics. She does, however, see *Hustler* as speaking to an authentic discontent with middle-class values and lifestyles, as a voice that challenges entrenched authority. Kipnis's essay is controversial because it neither condemns nor romanticizes *Hustler* and because its writer struggles in print with her own conflicted feelings about pornography.

WWF wrestling poses this same problematic mixture of the antihegemonic and the reactionary. It is a fascist spectacle of male power, depicting a world where might makes right and moral authority is exercised by brute force. It engages in the worst sort of jingoistic nationalism. It evokes racial and ethnic stereotypes that demean groups even when they are intended to provide positive role models. It provokes homophobic disgust and patriarchal outrage against any and all incursions beyond heterosexual male dominance. But, as Jake the Snake reminds us, "it goes much deeper than that. . . . There's more at stake than just wrestling, man." WWF wrestling is also a form of masculine melodrama which, like its nineteenth-century precedents, lends its voice to the voiceless and champions the powerless. Wrestling allows a sanctioned space of male emotional release and offers utopian visions of the possibility of trust and intimacy within male friendship. It celebrates and encourages working-class resistance to economic injustice and political abuse. It recognizes and values the diversity of American society and imagines a world where mutual cooperation can exist between the races. In short, wrestling embodies the fundamental contradictions of the American populist tradition. The politics of WWF wrestling is punchdrunk and rambunctious, yet it builds upon authentic anger and frustrations which we cannot ignore if we want to understand the state of contemporary American culture. Wrestling makes you want to shout, and perhaps we have had too much silence.

Originally published in 1997.

NOTES

1. For useful background on the historical development of television wrestling, as well as for an alternative reading of its narrative structures, see Michael Ball (1990). For a performance-centered account of WWF Wrestling, see Sharon Mazer (1990: 96–122).

2. Christine Gledhill (1987:12–13). David Thorburn similarly finds melodramatic conventions underlying much of prime-time television programming. See Thorburn (1987: 7).

3. Brutus was injured in a motorcycle accident several years ago and had his skull reconstructed; he is no longer able to fight but has come to represent the voice of aged wisdom within the wwf universe. Brutus constantly articulates the values of fairness and loyalty in the face of their abuse by the rule-breaking characters, pushing for reconciliations that might resolve old feuds, and watching as these disputes erupt and destroy his barbershop.

4. This incident could also be read as a response to a series of rumors and tabloid stories centering on the sexuality of wwf athletes. The Ultimate Warrior was "outed" by one tabloid newspaper, while charges of sexual harassment surfaced on an episode of the *Phil Donahue Show*. Complicating an easy reading of this incident is the strong popularity of wrestling within the gay male community and the existence of gay fanzines publishing sexual fantasies involving wrestlers.

REFERENCES

"American Pride: Sarge and Duggan Protect Old Glory from the Nastys." 1992. *wwf Magazine*, March, p. 52.

Barthes, Roland. 1982. "The World of Wrestling." In *A Barthes Reader*, ed. Susan Sontag. New York: Hill and Wang. (Original English publication in "The World of Wrestling," *Mythologies*, trans. Annette Lavers [New York: Farrar, Straus and Giroux, 1972 (1957)]).

Ball, Michael R. 1990. *Professional Wrestling as Ritual Drama in American Popular Culture*. Lewiston: Edwin Mellen Press.

Brooks, Peter. 1976. *The Melodramatic Imagination: Balzac, Henry James, Melodrama and the Mode of Excess*. New Haven, Conn.: Yale University Press.

Denning, Michael. 1987. *Mechanic Accents: Dime Novels and Working-Class Culture in America*. London: Verso, 1987.

Elias, Norbert, and Eric Dunning. 1986. *The Quest for Excitement: Sport and Leisure in the Civilizing Process*. New York: Basil Blackwell.

"Elizabeth Balancing Family with Business." 1992. *wwf Wrestling Spotlight*, March.

Feuer, Jane. 1984. "Melodrama, Serial Form and Television Today." *Screen* 25: 4–16.

Fiske, John. 1987. *Television Culture*. London: Methuen.

———. 1989. *Understanding Popular Culture*. Boston: Unwin Hyman.

Gledhill, Christine. 1987. "The Melodramatic Field: An Investigation." In *Home Is Where the Heart Is: Studies in Melodrama and the Woman's Film*, ed. Christine Gledhill. London: BFI.

Greenberg, Keith Elliot. 1991a. "One Step Too Far: Boss Man and Mountie Clash over Meaning of Justice." *wwf Magazine*, May, p. 40.

Greenberg, Keith Elliot. 1991b. "The Darkness Is in Me Forever . . . ." *wwf Magazine*, August, p. 52.

Grimsted, David. 1968. *Melodrama Unveiled: American Thought and Culture, 1800–1850*. Chicago: University of Chicago Press.

Heilman, Robert Bechtold. 1968. *Tragedy and Melodrama: Versions of Experience*. Seattle: University of Washington Press, 1968.

————. 1973. *The Iceman, the Arsonist and the Troubled Agent: Tragedy and Melodrama on the Modern Stage*. Seattle: University of Washington Press.

Kipnis, Laura. 1992. "Reading *Hustler*." In *Cultural Studies*, ed. Lawrence Grossberg, Cary Nelson, and Paula Treichler. New York: Routledge, Chapman, and Hall.

"The Mark of Cain: Shawn Michaels Betrays His Tag Team Brother." 1992. wwf *Magazine*, March, p. 41.

Mazer, Sharon. 1990. "The Doggie Doggie World of Professional Wrestling." *Drama Review* (winter): 96–122.

"Meeting of the Minds: Jake and Andre—Psychological Interplay." 1991. wwf *Magazine*, August, p. 52.

Modeleski, Tania. 1982. *Loving with a Vengeance: Mass Produced Fantasies for Women*. London: Methuen.

Palmer, Bruce. 1980. *"Man over Money": The Southern Populist Critique of American Capitalism*. Chapel Hill: University of North Carolina Press.

"Personality Profile: Repo Man." 1992. wwf *Magazine*, February, p. 11.

Rabinowitz, Peter J. 1985. "The Turn of the Glass Key: Popular Fiction as Reading Strategy." *Critical Inquiry* 12, no. 2: 421.

"Salt of the Earth: Sid Justice Comes from the Land," 1991. wwf *Magazine*, November, pp. 47–48.

Sedgwick, Eve Kosofsky. 1985. *Between Men: English Literature and Male Homosocial Desire*. New York: Columbia University Press.

"A Talk with Big Boss Man." 1991. wwf *Magazine*, November, p. 18.

"Tatanka: Leader of the New Indian Nation." 1992, wwf *Magazine*, April, p. 55.

Thorburn, David. 1987. "Television Melodrama." In *Television: The Critical Eye*, ed. Horace Newcomb. 4th ed. New York: Oxford University Press.

Walkerdine, Valerie. 1986. "Video Replay: Families, Film and Fantasy." In *Formations of Fantasy*, Victor Burgin, James Donald, and Cora Kaplan. London: Methuen.

"wwf Interview: A Talk with Jake 'The Snake' Roberts." 1992. wwf *Magazine*, February, p. 17.

"wwf Superstars Talk about Wrestlemania." 1992. wwf *Magazine*, March, p. 18.

SHARON MAZER

"Real" Wrestling / "Real" Life

I'll ask you the standard question . . .—John Stossel, *20/20*

Why do people believe in a bunch of actors that get
together and play fight? These guys are nothing but actors
that act mad at each other and call each other names and
then pretend to beat each others [*sic*] heads in. Then after the
so-called match they go to the bar together and drink beer
and laugh at all the money that they made off a bunch of fools
that believed they were actually fighting. Beats me. Get it?
—Anonymous RSPW poster

I don't care if it's real or not. Kill him! Kill him!—A fan, any fan

The fans believe—and the 'rasslers do too. But you
don't want to know about that. All you want is the answer
to one question: Is 'rassling real? Did he really hit
you? And the answer is: I know, but you don't know. The
answer is: What do you mean by real?—Clifton Jolley

The question of the real permeates any discussion, academic or popular, of professional wrestling—along with its correlate, the problem
of the fake, which is considered at once as a moral judgment and as a
sign of knowledge. The fake is what distinguishes professional wrestling from "real" sport (i.e., football, basketball, baseball) and underlies the
conventional wisdom that professional wrestling, unlike "real" (i.e., amateur) wrestling, is a kind of theatrical enterprise; wrestlers are actors, and

anyone who watches is a dupe of a corrupt, exploitative system personified by Vince McMahon, owner of the World Wrestling Federation. The fake is what binds fans to wrestlers, and to each other, creating a performance of denial and complicity that in its ambivalence and ambiguities eludes moral and academic authority.

Professional wrestling presents a totalizing worldview in which any representation of the real is reflexively suspect. Wrestlers are not merely bad actors, taking on outrageous characters and talking trash, any more than fans—at least those over the age of ten—are simply blind to the pretense of violent conflict, of hitting and stomping, of antagonism and turnabout. What wrestlers perform, what fans cheer or jeer, are amplifications of the social roles according to the rules of a traditional performance practice which has antecedents that can be traced historically through the nineteenth-century carnivals to medieval contests and ancient rituals. Life, like professional wrestling, is a performative game. Success is more a matter of style than of sincerity, determined more by dramaturgical conventions and social conservatism than by the actual skill and force of the players.

The interplay between the real and the fake is what generates much of the heat in wrestling. The pleasure for wrestlers and spectators alike may be found in the expressive tension between the spontaneous and the rehearsed, in the anticipation of, and acute desire for, the moment when the real breaks through the pretended. Just as in theatrical performances—or for that matter, in jazz—wrestling's spectators and performers alike are in a position to enjoy the distancing effect that comes with knowing the formal aspects of the performance at the same time as they look for the moment when knowledge (or consciousness) is suspended, penetrated by the rush of something far more urgent and demanding than artifice.

Gleason's Gym, 2 April 1993.[1] I'm being tested once again while watching the wrestlers work out. "So. What do you think? You think wrestling's fake?" This time it's Rubio (Rubio 1993), who has been practicing *lucha libre* (Mexican freestyle wrestling), although almost every wrestler has thrown the question at me in some way. I answer him as I've answered the others: "If by 'fake' you mean do I think the game is fixed, and 'real' means that it's supposed to be a *contest*, then wrestling's a fake. But if you're asking me if I think you guys are really strong, really skilled, really athletic, then it's real. That makes it real to me. And I also think you guys have to be very smart, really know what you're doing, or you'll kill each other and yourselves." Satisfied, he goes back to working out. Relieved, I go back to watching, and taking photographs and notes.

A couple of months later, when I arrive at Gleason's the first thing I see is Rubio in the ring "wrestling" with a young boy, who appears to be the son of one of the boxers and, at about 3 1/2-feet tall, looks about nine or ten years old. Standing somewhat shyly in the ring and cheerfully encouraged by Rubio and Frankie, the boy pushes Rubio with a finger, causing Rubio to perform an extraordinary series of pratfalls, landing prone and panting at the boy's feet in an exaggerated display of submission. At the end of the display, Rubio issues the first of what were to be regular invitations to me: I, too, can get into the ring with him and win a few rounds.

But I don't get in the ring. And I don't tell the wrestlers that what they do is fake. No boxed ears for me. I'm not John Stossel, the *20/20* reporter who in his relentless "exposé" of pro wrestling was senseless enough, even after what must have been at least a few weeks of researching and filming wrestlers, to pose the "standard question" to an obviously hostile David "Dr. D." Schultz outside the ring, and who suffered a very real beating as a result.

STOSSEL: I'll ask you the standard question.
SCHULTZ: Standard question?
STOSSEL: I think it's fake . . .
SCHULTZ: You think it's fake, huh? (Slaps Stossel on each ear with an open hand, then as Stossel falls, kicks and taunts the fleeing reporter.)

No, indeed. If nothing else, I'm well aware of the wrestlers' potential for actual violence when confronted with an outsider's skepticism. By the time I'm being asked the wrestler's version of the "standard question," I'm more like Clifton Jolley, who comes to be "in on the game" — or at least to sound as though he's "in on the game" — in his PBS (Public Broadcasting Service) special on professional wrestling, *I Remember Gorgeous George*. Like Jolley, I have come "inside" insofar as this is possible given that, unlike Jolley, I resist entering the ring myself. Like Jolley, I have come to recognize what many fans accept: that what they watch when they watch professional wrestling is not what they watch when they watch other sporting events and, consequently, that the question of real versus fake is not quite the point.

WHILE THE POPULAR press almost invariably focuses on and criticizes professional wrestling's fakery, scholarly writing almost always reduces the meanings produced by wrestling to its morality play aspects. What must be recognized, however, is these two perspectives are complementary. In order to control and shape the play of virtue and vice to a moral end, the game *must* be fixed. How, then, are we to reconcile the clichés of childhood sportsmanship — "It's not whether you win or lose. It's how you play the game" — with the transparent unfairness of wrestling: that it's not a fair fight on any level, that if it's not that the bad guy has cheated, then it's that the promoter has fixed the finish? Roland Barthes closes his seminal essay with a paean to an idea of professional wrestling's moral certainties, in which he exults:

> A wrestler can irritate or disgust, he never disappoints, for he always accomplishes completely, by a progressive solidification of signs, what the public expects of him. In wrestling, nothing exists except in the absolute, there is no symbol, no allusion, everything is presented exhaustively. Leaving nothing in the shade, each action discards all parasitic meanings and ceremonially offers to the public a pure and full signification, rounded like Nature. This grandiloquence is nothing but the popular and age-old image of the perfect intelligibility of reality. What is portrayed by wrestling is therefore an ideal understanding of things; it is the euphoria of men raised for a while above the constitutive ambiguity of everyday situations and placed before the panoramic view of a univocal Nature, in which signs at last correspond to causes, without obstacle, without evasion, without contradiction. (Barthes 1972 [1957]: 25)

Yet, the apparent moral clarity of wrestling is not so clear after all. Professional wrestling's moral universe is, in fact, imbued with essential contradictions within and between the fiction of the play and the fact of the business. What fans come to recognize and interact with as they come inside the game is the play outside the play: first the signs of a hero or villain, then the inevitable failure of the representatives of authority in the ring to assure a fair fight and a just end, and finally that the true power lies not in the ring at all but rather in the hands of the promoter whose contract with a wrestler includes the right to dictate his success or failure.

What is certain is not a "Justice which is at last intelligible" (Barthes 1972 [1957]: 25), but an *injustice* which is visible both in the dramaturgy of the performance and in the structure of the game itself, in the ongoing failure of authority to assert itself for the hero in the ring and in the success of the authority outside the ring, the promoter, as he dictates an outcome that negates the possibility of any genuine contest between men. It is not a fair fight, neither for the wrestlers in the ring, nor for the wrestlers and the fans in relation to those in power. The microcosm of the squared circle reflects first the largely unseen conditions of the game and then the world outside. As in the game that is wrestling, the game of life, at least its finish, is almost certainly fixed.

But if what fans are being told by the performance is that they don't stand a chance against those who are more economically and hierarchically powerful in the culture — the owners, the bosses, the lawyers, the politicians — why is professional wrestling so popular? Why would the fans return to arenas and their televisions with such devotion if what they are being sold is simply the representation of futility, of their own potential losses and actual disempowerment as workers and as consumers? Where is the satisfaction in witnessing repeated demonstrations of the failure of those who represent truth, justice, and the American way — the hero, the rules, the referee, the ropes — to prevail against lies, unfairness, and more than a few corrupt foreign bodies?

As with everything else in professional wrestling, the truth lies somehow with the cheat. When I first started this research in 1989, in my naïveté, before I'd read Barthes or consulted the relatively small body of scholarly writing on wrestling, I did three things: I watched television, went to matches, and found my way to the Unpredictable Johnny Rodz School of Professional Wrestling at Gleason's Gym (Brooklyn, New York). What astonished me then, what amazes me still, is the enthusiasm with which fans actively claim their knowledge and authority, their rightness and righteousness as participants in the professional wrestling event, even as they rail against this wrestler or that promoter. They don't simply cheer or jeer, celebrate or lament as their favorites win or lose. They narrate the event, anticipate a turn or a finish, evaluate the performance as a performance. They tell each other, and anyone who will listen, the background of each wrestler: his current storyline, his wrestling history, and the details of his "real" life — his name, his marital status, his original occupation, his wrestling patrilineage, and so on. They wax nostalgic for the good years of wrestling — the fifties and sixties for some, the eighties now for others — and complain about the cynicism of the promoters, the way in which the event we are witnessing is no longer real wrestling but ersatz, a cheap counterfeit. They wouldn't buy the ticket, the pay-per-view, the magazine, the souvenir, if it were not for liking this particular wrestler or wanting to see that particular angle played out.

At Madison Square Garden, at Gleason's Arena, at countless arenas and venues around the United States and the world. . . . The action slows in the ring for a moment, becomes repetitive, static. The fans stand together and take up the chant: "Bor-ring!" In response, the wrestlers immediately accelerate: a wrestler body-slams his opponent and then catapults from the top rope, and/or they take it out of the ring and into the front rows, and/or a couple of stars race from the locker room to mix things up in the ring. Satisfied that they've been heard, the fans settle back into their seats. Everything about the event, from the advance publicity — the development of grudges into angles and storylines culminating in the announcement of the evening's card — to the action in the ring, has explicitly catered directly to them. The promoter promises he's going to give them what they want: "real" wrestling. If it happens that what the promoter presents fails to fulfill their expectations, the fans have ways of telling him and his wrestlers so. It is a consumer's paradise, no deception here. They've been promised their money's worth, and if they are rarely fully satisfied, they remain optimistic enough to return on a regular basis — in the tens of thousands to live matches, in the millions to weekly programs and pay-per-views — for more of the same. Asked if they think it's real or fake, most fans prevaricate as much as the wrestlers. Even the neophytes, except for the youngest children, will acknowledge at least having heard that the game is fixed, that wrestlers don't really land all those punches, that the moves are choreographed. . . .

JOHN STOSSEL BEGINS his now infamous *20/20* report (21 February 1985) on the perfidy of pro wrestling by recognizing that "Apparently, *this* is what the public wants." He displays his moral outrage: "This stuff kind of makes me mad, because this isn't really wrestling. This is *'rassling.'*" He goes on: "I was a high school wrestler. *That's* wrestling. *I* appreciate it, but that's because *I* understand the sport." With this he establishes his credentials; he is a wrestling connoisseur who knows the difference between the fake and the real. Doing "what any journalist would do" in pursuit of the truth, he takes an "exit poll," talking to fans under the EXIT sign after a WWF match at Madison Square Garden where he gets the predictable range of responses: "I think it's all fake, you know. It's a form of entertainment," one man declares. "Well, it's fun, but it's fake," a boy says, adding "I mean, they don't hit 'em in the head and everything and make 'em bleed and everything." The women in Stossel's poll seem more gullible: "I don't think a lot of people are gonna pay their money to come see a play fight out there," one asserts. Another simply states, "No, I don't think it's fixed. No, baby." Still trawling for an answer, he goes "backstage," and "the Iron Sheik" (Ali Vazari), a ring veteran, gives the same challenge-in-response I've heard from Johnny and the others: "Come in the ring. I can take your head off. Or anybody else's. My sport is not phony. Come in the ring. I show you. Anything else?"[2] Then, Stossel announces in all (apparent) seriousness: "But, fans, I'm afraid I have to tell you. (Pause.) It *is* fake."

He continues his pursuit of the inside scoop, exposing Vince McMahon ("the man in the vest") with all the expressive earnestness of a contemporary Dorothy seeing the real Wizard of Oz behind the curtain for the first time. He uncovers and shows us the tricks, the way wrestlers work with rather than against each other, by stepping into the ring with a disgruntled ex-wrestler. He listens attentively to another ex-wrestler who claims he quit because of homosexual coercion and to a female promoter who has been squeezed out of the Atlanta market. Stossel's ultimate targets are not the hard-working wrestlers, but the promoters, who are revealed to abuse their wrestlers and create monopolies, implicitly implicating Vince McMahon in particular. His report closes with the confrontation with David Schultz and the danger that fake violence can become real. In a coda Barbara Walters commiserates with Stossel, who (it appears) has suffered serious permanent damage to his ears, and tells the viewing audience: "I hope that nobody thinks that this was part of your story. You really *were* beaten by this man." Ruefully, he tells her of his journalistic prowess, pursuing all kinds of crooks and fakers, but "the one time I get hit is when it's obvious that it's a fake." Walters recaps Stossel's story, calling it "amazing": "It started out being funny and entertaining, then became very real . . . *too* real, in your case."

What becomes apparent in this exposé is the convergence of two not dissimilar narratives. The *20/20* program can be read as a morality play that is no less codified and reductive than that of professional wrestling as presented within the program. Characters and action conform to the dramaturgical conventions of investigative journalism, and like wrestling its presentation of a contest between virtue and vice even includes a high degree of gender stereotyping—the "smart" male fans in contrast to the "mark"

female fans — as well as archetypal characterizations: the noble and beleaguered underdogs versus the imperious bosses. In the end, the assumption
of a patriotic, masculine ideal remains unquestioned and the outcome is as
expected: Wrestling is a fake, and its economics pose a danger to the American ethos. It even has a final twist — a bit of genuine heat, real violence, and
real blood — in its last minutes. The intrepid reporter, call him "Little John,"
self-consciously presents himself to his audience as virtuous if a bit naive
in his faith in the rules of sportsmanlike conduct. He even talks directly to
his audience, assuming their collusion in his quest, before he boldly (and
literally) steps into the ring to do battle with a threat to the American community's ethical foundations. Everyone knows that it's his job to ask these
questions. He's the one who gets to throw the (verbal) punches. He's the
American journalist standing for freedom of the press and the American
way. The renegade wrestler — "most are just hard-working guys who know
it's a fake" — transgresses the boundaries of proper interviewee behavior. As
he attacks the hero "for real," outside the ring, in the context of the interview,
David Schultz then stands in for and becomes a symbol of the corruption
that the wrestling audience doesn't necessarily see and wouldn't necessarily
recognize if actual blood were not drawn as proof.

The moral of the 20/20 story is that the "fake" violence of the performance
not only leads to "real" violence but more importantly is symptomatic of
the "real" dangers of wrestling's dishonesty. The cheat of the wrestling performance and the promoters' corruption, it is implied, may overflow the
boundaries and infect American society for real. Implicit in Walters's attempt to assert the reality of what happened to Stossel is a fear that, with
the exposure of wrestling's fraudulent representational ethos, the viewer's
perception of authenticity of the 20/20 program will itself be destabilized.
That is, as Walters insists that Stossel's narrative is not "part of [the] story"
she (I assume inadvertently) points toward her own anxiety. Paradoxically,
the notion that fake violence might become real and leak from the wrestling
event into life implies the possibility of another kind of leakage. One revelation of simulation implies the probability of others, even by those who are
doing the revealing. If wrestling is fake, a contrived performance scripted in
order to manipulate gullible spectators and thereby increase the promoters'
profits, as Stossel demonstrates, then what is to prevent the 20/20 audience
from viewing Stossel's confrontation with Schultz as staged on the same
terms and for the same reasons? What Walters and Stossel tiptoe around in

the end is what many hardcore wrestling fans would see as the point: everything—wrestling, life, the whole shooting match—might really be a work.

FOR THE FANS, not only are the stories that are told to them in the ongoing professional wrestling narratives drawn from life; life itself can be read through the structures and understandings that professional wrestling provides. Current events become material for characters and stories, as one fan announces to the RSPW [rec.sport.pro-wrestling] newsgroup, presumably with irony intended: "Harry Helmsley, who was husband of the target of satire [Leona] for Vince [McMahon], died yesterday. There has been no word from Titan as to whether they will make an angle out of his death" (Richard S. 1997). Conversely, a recent discussion on RSPW quickly moves beyond why current WWF champion Bret Hart cannot be a Republican (he's Canadian) to reconstituting the current political scene as a wrestling angle. The original poster begins the shift with "Anyway, I apologize for bringing this political BS into this NG and I won't mention it again unless Gingrich signs to meet Clinton in a cage at Wrestlemania 13" (Paul S. 1996). Another puns: "What about mad dog dornan against bill clinton in a falls count anywhere match at the next starcade :-)" (Timothy H. 1997). Another implies that political events are generally contrived much as wrestling events and that the plots are not dissimilar: "After Dornan gave that shoot interview about the Evil Mexicans taking over Southern California, I don't think he'll ever be hired by a major US promotion again" (Ryan G. 1997). Pointing to the power of negative heat, another proposes an angle: "The heat-generating power of the 'B-1 Bob' gimmick cannot be denied, so there's ALWAYS going to be a place for him in a major promotion, in spite of the difficulties. Consider the possibilities of bitter war veteran B-1 Bob teaming with Mr. Bob Backlund to instill respect and morality in America's youth. Better yet, imagine B-1 being seconded at Wrestlemania or Starrcade [sic] by his old friend, the 'Monster from Missouri,' [popular neoconservative talk-radio host] Rush H. Limbaugh III" (Unsigned 1997b).

To know the rules by which the game of wrestling is played, not just the names of the moves, but the way the wrestling event is constructed by promoters, is to know how the game of life is played. Whether in the arena or in the magazines and on the Internet, fans love to display their expertise. They are "smarts," not "marks." As what Henry Jenkins has termed "textual poachers," they not only compete against one another in spotting the fix and predicting the angle; they construct narratives of their own, from conceiving of politics as wrestling to fantasy wrestling networks. Jenkins notes the sophistication of fan culture, calling it "an institution of theory and criticism, a semistructured space where competing interpretations and evaluations of common texts are proposed, debated, and negotiated and where readers speculate about the nature of the mass media and their own relationship to it" (1992: 86). Against the assumption that theoretical and critical activity is the exclusive domain of the academic, Jenkins declares that fans are the "true experts" of popular culture, constituting "a competing educational elite, albeit one without official recognition or social power" (86). What is important and empowering to wrestling fans, then, what they repeatedly seek to display and prove is their hard-won knowledge of the game, their facility with its vocabulary and dramaturgy, and their position in the exchange.

Professional wrestling's fan culture is extraordinarily rich and complex, with many regular spectators also distributing their own newsletters (on paper and on the Internet) as well as getting involved at least peripherally in staging matches. One such fan/participant is Ben Lagerstrom, aka "Big Daddy Money Bucks" and "the Shoeshine Boy." In our first conversation Ben told me of his obsessive love of the game: "Ever since I was six years old it's been my dream to be in the wrestling business" (Lagerstrom 1994). When we met in person, what I saw was a tall, soft-appearing (although not overweight) fifteen-year-old, wearing glasses, with wisps of beard and mustache matched by a ponytail. He told me of his wrestling archives — more than six hundred videotapes, newsletters, and magazines — and that he was also publishing his own newsletter (*The Squared Circle*) and managing a couple of wrestlers in a small local promotion (20 July 1994). Ben was full of ambition. His plans included a two-week excursion to Seattle, Washington, where, he said, he had a friend with a connection who might find him wrestling work. He also talked of a possible trip to Japan and of hustling tours to Puerto Rico and London. Most of all, he was proud of an appearance on the WWF's *Monday Night RAW*, in which he shined shoes for the Million Dollar Man, Ted DiBiase, and which had earned him the name Shoeshine Boy. He was riding on this moment of fame in his local gigs, where he would appear as heel manager Big Daddy Money Bucks and dare the audience to call him Shoeshine Boy, which of course, he said, they did with great glee.

Clearly intelligent and obviously privileged — in particular, being "home-

Macho Fans at *Monday Night RAW* in the early 1990s. Photo by the author.

schooled" gave him room to pursue his dream — Ben considered himself no longer a fan or a mark, but an insider: "I can give you Vince McMahon's phone number, but don't tell him it was me." Eager to set himself apart from the fans, he talked about working as a ring boy for the ECW in Philadelphia where he blamed unruly fans for creating an uncontrolled situation. Eager to demonstrate his "smarts," he displayed his vocabulary and taught me a few new words, described the day-to-day existence of most wrestlers, and shared gossip about drug use in the big leagues, telling me that most promoters won't tolerate steroids because they cause wrestlers to "fuck up their spots" but that many wrestlers (whose names he was pleased to share with me) are on other drugs. Eager to legitimize himself as a manager, he showed me his promotional materials. And eager to distinguish himself and claim his authority over my other sources, he pooh-poohed the training at Gleason's, telling me that the ring wasn't authentic ("a boxer's ring with no spring"), that Johnny "teaches a few bumps" but not wrestling, and that his wrestlers don't work at all ("don't get a payday"). While at the time I found myself surprisingly defensive on Johnny's behalf — the ring is a real wrestler's ring, the wrestlers do work — in retrospect, Ben's performance was an astonishing display of desire, of genuine fanaticism: nine years of watching at ringside, dreaming of being in on the game with just enough of a toehold (and little enough parental restraint) to sustain his urgency.

Everyone who comes into contact with wrestling—from the first-time spectator to the most experienced wrestler or promoter, even the occasional academic—is engaged in a process of coming inside. Beyond knowing that the finish is fixed, the more hardcore the fan, the more he or she is knowledgeable about the way in which matches are constructed and promoted. Like the wrestlers, they insist on respect for, and the integrity of, the game: "Just because the finishes of wrestling are predetermined and have been since the beginning of this century doesn't mean that laws and ethics do not apply to those involved in this business."[3] With a knowledge and ferocity that would impress any theater producer or teacher, they argue about the believability of characters and evaluate storylines, talking back to promoters in the arena as well as in their own networks: "Hey Eric [Bischoff, wcw promoter] . . . psssst . . . I've got a word for you . . . It's called CATHARSIS. That basically means that all your angles should have an ENDING! Try it sometime. At least McMahon [wwf promoter], with his limited roster and gimmicks for 12-year-olds, knows when to end a story" (Unsigned 1996).

They note the shifts in dramaturgical practice, for example, from clarity to ambiguity in the positioning of wrestlers, weighing the pros and cons. One RSPW fan begins with a question: "Someone please help me out with this Michaels/Hart angle [wwf]. Bret is supposed to be the face, right? And Michaels is supposed to be the tweener/heel right? So why do they have Bret making excuses and whining and Michaels coming right out and admitting that he was beaten even though he is the one who has the excuse?" He then goes on to evaluate the theatrical implications for himself:

> I'm not saying this is bad, for too long the lines between faces and heels have been too clear cut in the wwf. Now, thank goodness all the faces don't have to be friends, and all the heels don't have to be friends, moreover, whether a lot of guys are heel or face (Michaels, Bulldog, Hart, Goldust, Bret etc. etc.) is unclear, which is an excellent step in the right direction, to increasing the realism. Having Bret behaving true to [heel commentator] Lawler's "Excellence of Excuses" [a pun on Bret's "Excellence of Execution" refrain] label, is going to put Michaels even more over than he is, which is great, because he's a superb talent and deserves it. But at the expense of the Hitman? Why? (Mustafa M. 1997)

Ultimately, the real contest from the fans' perspective is not between wrestlers, with whom they identify, but rather between themselves as competing experts and, most important, between the fans as consumers and the promoters who produce and market the wrestling product. They complain when certain wrestlers are "pushed" and others repeatedly used as "jobbers," and they evaluate the heat generated by a particular wrestler, gimmick, angle, or match, often proving their points by describing the "pop" from the other fans as they try to second-guess the promoters. The basis for the contract between promoter and spectator is economic, a promise that fans will get their money's worth. It is perhaps ironic that the fans who might be considered fanatic addicts, those who spend the most time and money on wrestling, are the least passive purchasers. Rather, they actively engage in recouping their investment in the ticket, the pay-per-view, the magazine and souvenir, often regarding their efforts as part of a natural struggle to win against the promoter, whose sole desire is, as one RSPW poster put it, to create "an empty void in your pockets!" (Councell 1997).

More than skeptical of the wrestling event as an elaborate con game, many fans are openly antagonistic toward promoters and proud of their facility for retrieving pleasure regardless of what is offered to them. For one fan, who calls himself "superfan," the point is to remain autonomous, a "real" wrestling fan, unsold and unmarked by the promoter's guile:

[B]oth [the WWF and the WCW] cheat their fans. That's the way of the promoter. At least the WCW gives us some great mid-card matches, while the WWF fills it full of Hog Farmers battling imposters from another promotion. I'm no WCW fan, I'm no WWF fan, I'm no ECW fan, I'm no international fan, I'm a wrestling fan. I take bits and pieces of all the promotions, and put together a wrestling reality that suits my interests best. I think that is what we all should do instead of saying on[e] is better than the other, although this is wrestling and that is the nature of the beast. (Superfans 1997)

For this fan, as for many others, knowing that wrestling is fixed is liberating rather than constraining, a form of imaginative empowerment. To be in on the game as a fan offers the fan the potential for constructing and enjoying the wrestling performance on highly individualistic terms.

Hardcore fans are explicitly obsessed with reading live and televised wrestling performances for the signs of the real and the fake. But rather than looking for proof of the fix, what they seek is twofold: opportunities to demonstrate their expertise in reading (and explaining) performances and moments when the display of violence becomes, or at least appears to have become, actual. That is, the fans operate in a tension between wanting to appear "smart" and wanting the experience of the "mark," of what they call "marking out." In what might be considered an informed discussion of suspension of disbelief in which belief is never fully suspended, they debate, in their terms and on the basis of their knowledge of a wrestler's "true" history or their close observation of the event: "Was it a work, or a shoot?" The sign that the game has crossed from simulation to actuality is generally tied to the revelation of injury, for which blood is the most vivid sign. The knowledge that wrestlers blade their foreheads does not necessarily diminish the impact of seeing blood stream down a wrestler's face, and, in any case, the fact that the bleeding may be self-induced does not make the blood itself less real, regardless. Aware of the actual risks involved in wrestling — the hazards of slamming, hitting, and leaping at another man — the fans are driven to look more closely, to look again, and to come back for another chance to look.

When Billy Gunn of the Smoking Gunns (wwf) is carried from the ring after being slammed by his "brother" Bart, one fan worries: "I couldn't sleep last night thinking that Billy could be seriously injured" (Mike M. 1996). Another responds: "The only way he's hurt is if the dopes carrying the stretcher dropped him on the way out. Compared to Shawn's collapse (which had me fooled for the duration of the show at least), this was blatantly obvious. If they hadn't had one of their wives say 'How can you do this to your brother?' (even marks who've seen them before the wwf know they aren't even related), it might have worked a little bit. That line killed what little cred[ibility] that work had for me though" (Joseph T. 1996).

This thread peters out with an insult — "It's a work and if you can't see that you're more of a mark then [sic] I am" (Slugger 1996). But it leads directly into an extended debate over the facts of Shawn Michaels's injury. One fan asks: "I have a co-worker who thinks that the Shawn Michaels collapsed [sic] last year due to head injuries was real. However, I felt it was a work. As a matter of fact I'm 100% sure it was a fake. So can anyone tell us once and for all if it was a for real or a fake" (Richard C. 1996). He is told: "The head injuries (among others) were real, he was attacked, while out with Davey Boy Smith and 1-2-3 Kid Sean Waltman. The collapse on Raw was

100% staged, and the best work in wrestling history. Period" (Timothy M. 1996). This leads to further explanation:

> Let me take it one step further and explain to Richard that, from what I could find out, the RAW collapse was faked BECAUSE of the real injuries sustained during the Syracuse attack. Because of very real injuries they created the angle in order to give Shawn a break. This fact alone makes the angle, in my opinion, more remarkable. It's amasing [*sic*] to me that they could come up with and execute such a realistic and believable angle in such a short time. I for one had already become rather jaded as far as angles go and for at least the moment that it was occurring, I was a believer. (Powerhug 1996)

To which is added: "And it proves to everyone that the Michaels collapse was incredibly realistic, because it was based on resalistic [*sic*] events. I personally marked out huge, I was sweating bullets afterwards, and I was wondering where the hell I could find info on the collapse after. This was before RSPW. Tyson's opponents should have been taking notes" (Milan G. 1996). Clearly, from the perspective of at least one wrestling fan, boxers such as Peter MacNeeley [McNeeley] would do well to learn how to perform a showstopping injury from the real pros.[4] While the fans' concern for the well-being of wrestlers is evident, what is striking is the way in which their desire to know the *truth* about injuries is constantly balanced against their evaluation of the *performance* of injuries.

Even fan behavior is suspect and comes under scrutiny, as when someone attempted to attack Rowdy Roddy Piper and Hulk Hogan in the ring during the main event at WCW's 1996 *Starcade*: "Well the guy who charged the ring /had/ to be a shoot. I mean, did you see how strong the ref became when he started going after the fan? No wimpy pushover any more! I also notice that when a fan gets stomped at the edge of the ring (like at Bash at the Beach during Hogan's heel turn) the stomps are quieter since they're putting more weight on the stomping foot and less on the noisemaker foot" (David L. 1996). This display of knowledge and observational skills leads to the ultimate put-down: "What marks! The fan at the Bash was a work and so was the one at Starcade. If a real fan rushed the ring, the wrestlers would probably run like heeck [*sic*] from him because the guy could have a gun! Ask any professional athlete what happens when a fan runs onto the field or into the ring. They usually let security handle it because they don't know what the guy has on him. This was so obviously a work that anybody who believed it was real probably thought the guy who got up in the ring and took a picture of Hogan with an exploding camera while he was in the wwf was also real" (Johnson 1996). This, in turn, leads to an argument based on dramaturgy and business: "Don't be a moron. Are you telling me that [a]fter a month of non-stop barrage of ads for the 'match of the decade' that during the ending sequence, featuring Piper getting out of the chokeslam and slapping the sleeper on Hogan, that wcw would send in a plant to confuse the ending, distract the audience, and overall accomplish absolutely nothing. As for waiting for security, it was a good 6 or 7 seconds before the guards made it to the mark. Hogan would have been dead whether he intervened or not" (Charles H. 1996). The definitive answer seems to come from the eyewitness, who tells the others: "Well after Starrcade [sic] all of the hardcore fans went outside and cheered the fan as he went away in the paddy wagon. His face was real bloody and he was drunk off his ass. However, he was glad to hear our cheers. . . . He may be a lowly loner with nothing else but wrestling, but hey, it was brave of him to do what he did. LONG LIVE THE DRUNK FAN!" (Unsigned 1997a).

The more insistent fans become in their exposés of wrestling's fakery, the more they look to experience the real. As they expose the con artistry of the game, they revel in it and, on some level, seek to be conned, at least momentarily. They "see through" the fiction of the wrestling event to its facts, to distinguish between what is improvised and what is staged, between the real and the not-so-real event, and in so doing attempt to shatter any illusions others might have. Yet they also appear to yearn for the illusion to be real regardless. That is, they disbelieve what they see as they look to believe. Just as they are often nostalgic for the good old days of wrestling, they seem nostalgic for the time when they still believed the fictions presented. They revel in their own deception, and they discuss, sometimes rapturously, the moments when they "marked out," when they were fooled into believing that the wrestler was injured for real, that the fan rushed the ring for real, that the blood was not from a blade but was for real, that the promoter's grip over the wrestlers and the matches will slip, that the fight will be more than play, and that they will see the violence for real. This phantom of the real is at the heart of professional wrestling's appeal. It keeps the fans coming back for another look, keeps them reading into and through performances and predicting future events for each other.

Paradoxically, what is fervently desired — the moment of real impact, the display of real blood — is also secretly dreaded. At a match at Gleason's Arena in 1989 the action slammed to a halt when a wrestler, one of the "Twin Towers," was thrown from the ring onto the concrete. What had been a fast and furious tag team match accompanied by raucous shouts from the audience went silent. The wrestlers, good guys and bad alike, froze. Spectators rushed to look over shoulders while the referee and judges checked out the nearly unconscious man. Everyone waited until he arose and reentered the ring. The match resumed, with the Twin Towers winning the NCW [National Championship Wrestling] tag team title to the loud cheers of the crowd. But the blood on the concrete and the man's damp, matted hair remained vivid reminders of the very real risks to the game. The spectacle had collapsed into reality.[5] And yet, as we left the arena, I overheard some debating about whether or not the moment had been staged.

More recently, in 1999, the threshold between dangerous display and danger was irrevocably ruptured when the harness worn by WWF superstar Owen Hart failed, and instead of flying into the ring from the ceiling fifty feet above, he fell to his death in front of 14,000 spectators at Kemper Arena (Kansas City, Missouri). Coming from a large wrestling family, Hart was a graceful acrobat in the ring and played the game with remarkable élan. Although Jim Ross, the announcer, repeatedly advised the audience that the fall had not been scripted, he did not indicate the extent of Hart's injuries, and after the wrestler was taken away by paramedics, the matches continued. At the same time, the video images of Hart's fall and the failed effort to revive him were not broadcast to the tens of thousands watching on closed circuit and pay-per-view; however, that audience was informed more directly. As a result, there was symmetrical discrepancy between those who saw the fall but did not know what had happened, and those who did not see the actual event but were informed. For both audiences, however, the ambivalence of the wrestling event was preserved, and in retrospect a narrative which moved from denial to eulogy was constructed. A number of Web sites currently carry descriptions of the accident and tributes from fans and other wrestlers.[6]

Given that most wrestlers begin as fans, it is not surprising that the wrestlers at Gleason's are also captivated by the convergence of the real and the fake both in performances that they see and in their own workouts. In fact, on the day I began this research in 1989, I watched as one wrestler,

Gino, was hurt when his opponent, a novice, shied away from a dropkick. The shift in the atmosphere was electric. The other wrestlers pushed Gino's sparring partner away and kept him at a distance for a good ten minutes while they examined Gino's injury and offered advice. Only after Gino had reassured the others that he would be okay was the other man allowed to approach and apologize. At the same time, one of the others confronted me with "Game, huh?!"

What is "real" wrestling? Even as they disparage the critics who say that professional wrestling isn't real wrestling, the wrestlers at Gleason's, the performers in the big leagues, and the fans don't simply defend their sport. Rather everyone who is in on the game actively works to promote his or her definition of real wrestling. As I was nearing the end of my research at Gleason's, I sat for a while at ringside with Mohammed (23 July 1994). We watched Rubio and Frankie work out. I was admiring their acrobatics, the balletic grace with which they performed their exchanges, when Mohammed interrupted my reverie to tell me why he doesn't like lucha libre. "It's too fake," he judged. I asked him if by fake he means that it's too visibly choreographed for his taste. He answered yes and continued: "American wrestling is more violent and aggressive. It's more real." Taking a breather, Rubio and Frankie then came to sit with us. Rubio, still perched on the apron of the ring, motioned to me, inviting me in: "Come on. Come wrestle with me. I'll let you throw me. You can be the tough guy. Promise." I declined, and a month later I moved to New Zealand.

Professional wrestling is at once like life and like a lot of other things, theater and academia included: real and fake, spontaneous and rehearsed, genuinely felt and staged for effect, prodigious and reductive, profoundly transgressive and essentially conservative . . . Like Barthes, I frequently find the ecstasy of wrestling's rhetorical and metaphoric possibilities irresistible. (Indeed, I am often tempted to produce a self-help book entitled something like "The Tao of Wrestling" or perhaps "The Wrestler's Way of Being and Doing.") Unlike Barthes, however, I have come to believe that what professional wrestling is most like is professional wrestling. It is a discrete genre of performance, with a long history as a ritual and cultural practice that intersects with many others, and with its own explanatory narratives. I admit my current position may be the result of too many years ringside, but at the moment, I am more inclined to marvel at how many other cultural activities—including many of those in my own daily life—are like professional wrestling.

In particular, the lessons I learned ringside have served me well in the academic arena. The University of Canterbury (Christchurch, New Zealand) is a remarkably masculine, and masculinist, environment. Only 18 percent of the academic staff are female; most are at the lower levels, few as visible as I am. Formal meetings are held in the Council Room, which features an enormous, brightly lit oblong table, with two elevated "spectator" rows on either side. I spent my first years on the sidelines, observing men display their status and prowess in a series of poses and feints. Now, as a head of department I am often pushed by someone who, with a veneer of irony that reminds me of Rubio, grins, holds the door and a chair for me, and urges me to take a place at the table myself. To me, the give-and-take at an Academic Board meeting is as much a work as what happens in the squared circle, and I have tried to school myself to perform accordingly. Who are the real players (as opposed to the posers)? Where is the fix? How am I expected to perform? How can I put myself over?

The questions I ask are not necessarily very different from those I ask when I consider the public arena as a Stanislavskian acting exercise—in which I am to act "as if" in a given situation. But theatrical realism, with its suspension of disbelief, forecloses on critical awareness, whereas the most successful academic performances I have observed have been those which effectively balance sincerity against irony, originality against conventionality. In the academy, the players resist the idea of the fix, even as they evade real risk and collude in a largely status quo game. Challenges are proffered and deflected, histories are recounted and remade, someone appears to take a fall, but the outcome is generally determined well in advance, and any transgressions in the performance seem in the end to serve, rather than displace, the basic power structure. At times it occurs to me, as it used to in Broadway theaters, that the real freedom would be to stand up and shout "Borrrrring," to have others around me join in, and to have the action shift, accelerate, or stop entirely—if only for an illusory moment. But having moved from the sidelines to the center, I'm often too busy these days giving the performance of my life to keep score.

Originally published in 1998.

NOTES

1. During the original part of my research, in 1989, the Unpredictable Johnny Rodz School of Professional Wrestling operated out of Gleason's Arena, down the street from the gym. Early in the 1990s the arena was shut down, and the school returned to the gym. References to Gleason's, unless otherwise specified, indicate activities at the gym.

2. This incident is discussed from the fanzine perspective in "The Renegades of the Ring" (*Wrestling World*) by Jerry Prater who explains: "Ali is a superb athlete, a former Olympic competitor and coach; but having once been a bodyguard for the Shah of Iran, he isn't too anxious to get deported back to his home country for punching out a reporter." And he adds: "I have personally seen the Iron Sheik dispose of several irate, chair-wielding fans who went after him outside the ring, so there can hardly be any doubt as to the damge [*sic*] he could inflict on one wise-cracking reporter" (1990: 35–36).

3. A parenthetical comment under the heading "It's Only Wrestling, Right?" in "News and Analysis" (1992: 2).

4. McNeeley was Tyson's first postprison opponent and lost as a result of a rather preemptive disqualification.

5. This passage was originally written years before the events of September 11, 2001. It stands as an accidental, albeit eerie, provocative, and oddly macrocosmic point of contact between playing and reality.

6. See, for example, http://www.angelfire.com/oh3/owenhart02/, which provides both the news account and a series of tributes, as well as a sampling of the audio record.

REFERENCES

Primary Sources

Interviews
Lagerstrom, Benjamin (aka Big Daddy Money Bucks and the Shoeshine Boy). 1994a.
    Phone conversation with author, 20 July.
———. 1994b. Conversation with author, Joe Bar. New York, N.Y., 2 August.
Rubio. 1993. Conversation with author, Gleason's Gym, Brooklyn, N.Y., 2 April.

Postings on RSPW: Rec.sport.pro-wrestling
Charles H. 1996. "Re: What was the fan thinking?!?!" 30 December.
Councell. 1997. "Re: What if Vince had thought up the NWO." 6 January.
David L. 1996. "Re: What was the fan thinking?!?!" 30 December.
Johnson. 1996. 30 December.
Joseph T. 1996. "Re: Update on Billy's condition?" 18 December.
Mattie C. 1996a. "Re: [WCW] Would you like a Frosty Beverage, Mr. Bischoff?"
    12 December.
———. 1996b. "Re: WWF vs. WCW vs. ECW vs. Stampede Wrestling." 12 December.
———. 1996c. "Re: WWF vs. WCW vs. ECW vs. Stampede Wrestling." 13 December.

Mike M. 1996. "Re: Update on Billy's Condition?" 18 December.

Milan G. 1996. "Re: Micheals [sic] collapse last year, work or shoot?" 22 December.

Mustafa M. 1997. "Michaels/Bret angle—I'm confused." 6 January.

Paul S. 1996. "Re: [Raw] Bret a Republican?" 31 December.

Powerhug. 1996. "Re: "Micheals [sic] collapse last year, work or shoot?" 22 December.

Richard C. 1996. "Re: Micheals [sic] collapse last year, work or shoot?" 20 December.

Richard S. 1997. "(RIP) Harry Helmsley Dead at 87." 6 January.

Ryan G. 1997. "Re: [Raw] Bret a Republican?" 3 January.

Slugger. 1996. "Re: Billy Gunn Injury." 18 December.

Superfans. 1997. "Re: Who has better Pay-Per-Views–WWF or WCW? It's a no brainer!" 1 January.

Timothy H. 1997. "Re: [Raw] Bret a Republican?" 3 January.

Timothy M. 1996. "Re: Micheals [sic] collapse last year, work or shoot?" 20 December.

Unsigned. n.d. As quoted by Chris Ariens. 1996. "Re: WHY DO PEOPLE BELIEVE IN FAKE FIGHTING?" 19 December.

————. 1996. "Bishoff [sic] the Bore." 31 December.

————. 1997. "Re: What was the fan thinking?!?!" 1 January.

————. 1997. "Re: [Raw] Bret a Republican?" 3 January.

Television Broadcasts and Videos

20/20. 1985. ABC/TV. 21 February.

I Remember Gorgeous George. n.d. PBS Special. Produced and directed by Clifton Jolley.

Secondary Sources

Barthes, Roland. 1972 [1957]. "The World of Wrestling." In *Mythologies.* Selected and translated from the French by Annette Lavers. New York: Hill and Wang.

Jenkins, Henry. 1992. *Textual Poachers: Television Fans and Participatory Culture.* New York: Routledge.

"News and Analysis" of the World Wrestling Federation. 1992. *Pro Wrestling Torch*, no. 207 (28 December).

Prater, Jerry. 1990. "Renegades of the Ring." *Wrestling World* 30, no. 5 (March): 32–36.

CARLOS MONSIVÁIS

The Hour of the Mask as Protagonist: El Santo

versus the Skeptics on the Subject of Myth

odolfo Guzmán Huerta, El Santo, is born on 23 September 1915 in Tulancingo, Hidalgo, and dies in 1984 in Mexico City. In 1920, his family
moves to the capital, to the neighborhood of El Carmen, and there
Rodolfo opts for the great option of all children without options: athletic triumph. He plays soccer and baseball, learns Olympic wrestling, and
finally (economic necessity being the most personal calling), Rudy and his
brothers dedicate themselves to professional wrestling in the small arenas:
Roma Mérida, Escandón, Libertad. . . . What active tedium! For less than
symbolic pay, and credit lost in torn and badly painted posters, they fight
three times a day in tumbledown locales, where the lighting only allows one
to intuit his adversary, and the only motivation comes from the promoters'
lies and the insults and objects pitched by the crowd with deadly intent. "Hit
'em with a rotten tomato, it'll hurt 'em more than the insults do."

Rudy Guzmán is a name without a "hook," proclaiming neither merit nor
style. With adoring prose, El Santo's biographer Eduardo Canto recounts his
change of appeal. One fine day, the referee and matchmaker Jesús Lomelín
observed the talented Rudy and his lack of an image. To triumph, he tells
Guzmán, a wrestler needs a spectacular character. Persuaded, Rodolfo puts
on a mask, and appears as Murciélago (Bat) II (in honor of Jesús el Murciélago Velázquez, who would release a bag full of bats onstage to the delight of the spectators in the upper balconies). Without the influence of exis-
tential philosophy, Lomelín persuades Rodolfo once more: "you have to be
yourself, and to do that you must be something else," and he reminds him
of Simon Templar, El Santo, hero and maker of justice of the thrillers of

Leslie Charteris, and of a cinematographic series. Rodolfo accepts, and El Santo appears in the universe of wrestling and catch-as-catch-can, in Arena Nacional, Arena México, Arena Coliseo in the capital, Arena Anáhuac in Acapulco, Arena Canada Dry in Guadalajara, Arena Monterrey, Palacio de los Deportes in Torreón.

Professional wrestling in Mexico, forty or fifty years ago: a popular preserve where unconcealable passions are ignited and allowed to bloom; idols who exist as such because many pay to see them; brawls in the ring where the temperaments are even more colorful than the costumes; guttural and visceral passion for the *rudos* and doubtful admiration for the *técnicos*; spectators who rise to their feet to shout, "we want to see blood!" perhaps imagining the sacrifices of the Templo Mayor; names that evoke snarls of theatrical rage, and the symphony of the thunderclaps of falling bodies. Remember, remember them: Tarzan López, La Tonina Jackson, Sugi Sito, Black Shadow, Blue Demon, El Cavernario Galindo, El Médico Asesino, Enrique Llanes, Gori Guerrero, Jack O'Brian, Bobby Canales, Firpo Seguro, El Lobo Humano, El Lobo Negro. . . . For two or three hours and several times a week, these local celebrities amassed combative followers, imitators, fake and real adversaries, inside and outside the ring.

Gala opening! Don't miss the grand finale in Arena Coliseo in Peru Street: Tarzan López, champion of the world versus El Santo, challenger, national middle and welterweight champion. In a long interview, El Santo relates the tale:

It was April 2, 1943. I remember it perfectly. For the first time in the history of boxing, the sport of kings, and of professional wrestling, a colossus of concrete and steel with room for several thousand fans would serve the public. The lights of the monster shone intensely, and like insects swarming around a flame, thousands of people fought to get into the wrestling event that would inaugurate the Coliseo. I had been chosen along with Tarzan López to fight in the star event. The responsibility was enormous, but I was considered to have enough merit to occupy that privileged spot, because at the time I held the welter- and middleweight championships of the Republic of Mexico. I was the first wrestler to hold two crowns, and my ambition carried me to try to reach the third—but this one was a world title. On that night I would fight to wear it proudly. The whistle blew to announce the first round, and I threw myself on my opponent with a blind will to eliminate him quickly, but all my efforts crashed into an immovable wall: that was Tarzan López. In those days I doubt that any man in his weight class could have been able to defeat him.

Tarzan was a real champion, and for that reason I'm not ashamed to say, in my own opinion, that it was the best match we had ever fought. I fought hard for long minutes that seemed to me interminable centuries. The encounter went back and forth, but at last the serenity of my adversary, his better preparation, his longer experience, in sum, his greater ability had to impose itself. So under the pressure of a powerful lock, I surrendered, and went to my corner to chew on my spite and my defeat. I went out with the same fury for the second round: history repeated itself. I used my best weapons. Even when I knew that I had hurt him, the champion's pride did not decrease, and that let him rise above the pain. And if all that wasn't enough, the multitude that had, unexpectedly, filled the arena to its farthest corners, was against me. My *rudo* style of wrestling had won me great dislike, and even though at the moment, in accordance with the respective rules, I was wrestling a clean match, the mocking and disdainful shouts followed me. My opponent, on the other hand, was pampered the whole time. Naturally, that has a direct influence on anyone's spirits, and gives him courage to keep fighting. I don't want to remember it, but I lost the second round too, and the third was cancelled, and even though I have suffered terrible defeats since then, I never suffered so much humiliation, for which I consider that night to have been the roughest that I have ever had in the ring.

At the time, El Santo was still a villain, the Bad Guy who boasts of being a swine, and gives eye pokes or sharp kicks to the Fallen Hero, while the referee asks for moderation, and those present at the circus of Aztec Roma howl with indignant pleasure. Their perversity makes for record ticket sales, furies in the ring, instant poetry: "Every wrestling match of El Santo is a page full of drama. A tragedy of Aeschylus or a Homeric poem" (J. Valero Mere in *100 años de lucha libre en Mexico* [One hundred years of wrestling in Mexico]).

Debut: 26 July 1942. El Santo defeats Ciclón Veloz, without the least pity for his place in the history of professional wrestling. Benefit: dozens of titles and a plethora of belts since 1946; more than fifteen masks and twenty haircuts to his credit. Data for the legend: El Santo forms the Atomic Partners with Gori Guerrero, and is also partnered with Cavernario Galindo, Blue Demon, Black Shadow, Mil Mascaras, Rayo de Jalisco. Farewell: in fact, there will never be one: in 1984 El Santo is still in the ring, even if it was in the Teatro Blanquita. (From there he will leave, after a debilitating routine, to the hospital to die.)

In the endurance of El Santo, his merits play a part, as does, in a notable way, the contributions of the mask (which does not hide but creates his identity), and of his "pseudonym," which implies religiosity and mystery, otherworldly forces, and self-defense techniques which, incidentally, protect Humanity. There are wrestlers of his quality, and perhaps even better, but El Santo is a rite of poverty, of the rough consolations in the Great-Disconsolation-that-is-life, the exact mix of classical tragedy, circus, Olympic sport, comedy, variety, and catharsis at work.

CHOREOGRAPHIES AND FLYING KICKS

The public goes mad for a moment. Right away it goes dumb. There's no guessing which side it's on, who it will support, but suddenly the cry goes up of "Santo! . . . Santo!" which is prolonged to delirium when El Santo wins the second round to tie the match. He locks both ankles and an arm, and, in response to the pain, Black Shadow gives up. The two colossi retire to their corners, pushed by the referee, and both masks are flooded with sweat, with a sweat so intense that it drips to the muscles of their chests.

EDUARDO CANTO, EL SANTO,
EL ENMASCARADO DE PLATA

What merciless hatred does not long for the relief of a few flying kicks? What need to punish does not wish to embrace the enemy in a "bear hug?" In the arena, the recently shorn mane of the rival is a war trophy, and it is the war itself, the unmasking is the loss of the face, and the world and national scepters are dreams of glory that the Bronze Race can recognize. Without stopping their barrage of beer cans and almost liquid howls, the public ages, is rejuvenated, and stays fixed in one of the dates of its beloved anachronism. And El Santo, Antaeus outside of his Hellenic stage, metaphor in search of his mythology, recovers his impetus if the public implores the primordial forces (their throats, the effect of violence on theatricality) for the unleashing of the ass kicking. Evil boasts. Good despairs. Evil sends Good outside of their roped-off reality. Good returns with a serenity exempt from compassion. Man, short of days and sick of troubles, is exasperated: "Kill him! Finish him off! Fuck him up! Destroy him! Tear the bastard's eyes out!"

After hearing so many philanthropic orders, El Santo accepts the beatitude of his name, and changes over to the defense of the noble causes as a *técnico* on 22 June 1962.

EL SANTO'S COSMOLOGICAL ROLE

In 1948, El Santo rents his effigy to the producer and comic book author José G. Cruz, for his unreal mixtures of *fotonovela* (graphic novel) and comic. There El Santo defeats and combats (in this order) diabolical zombies, female vampires from the third century BC, mad scientists, lost tribes. . . . Success demands the following step: the movies. If in the first wrestling movie (*El Enmascarado de Plata* [The Man in the Silver Mask], by Ray Cardona, 1952), the stellar figure—surprisingly—is Médico Asesino (Doctor Assassin), El Santo soon dominates the subgenre ("Neanderthal style") aided— says Jorge Ayala Blanco in *La búsqueda del cine mexicano* (In search of Mexican cinema)—by the impact of the comic and the television broadcasts of professional wrestling. In the filmic arena, El Santo presides, surrounded by Neutron, Blue Demon, Mil Mascaras, Doctor Satan, La Sombra Vengadora, Las Tigresas. . . .

What an enviable repertory is this "Neanderthal cinema"! Criminals, anxious to increase the number of widows and orphans (or, failing that, eager to commit genocide), stage sets that boast of their humble carpenter origin, dangers all the more diabolical because the script never makes clear their nature, somber castles reduced by the budget to poor university cubicles, frightful combats for the salvation of the beautiful young woman, of the good scientist, of the human race, of the galaxy.

In the El Santo series, the titles are fundamental. They seduce the spectator and summarize the plot, to prevent any distraction caused by complications in the script. Thus, for example, in the 1960s, El Santo wrestles (with the film as his adversary) against Capulina, the Evil Brain, the Specter, the Strangler, the King of Crime, the Invasion of the Martians, the Infernal Men, the Villains of the Ring, and the Zombies, and he stays in the Hotel of Death, in the Wax Museum, and in the Treasure of Dracula. He is the perennial victor in the labyrinth of headlocks and figure eights, arm bars and scissor locks and Irish whips, and kicks à la Filomena and *tapatías* and *quebradoras* and *cruceros* and half nelsons. Thanks to the lucha libre sequences, the healthy irreality filters and absolved the delirious stage sets, hilarious makeup, non-existent performances. . . . — "Fuck'em Santo!" — and in the neighborhood cinemas, the public protects El Santo with a fence of insults and whistles that immobilize the dark science and its ineffective allies, the sad powers from beyond the tomb. What Beyond would allow itself to be kicked out of the ring with one blow?

In 1962, Alfonso Corona Blake directs *El Santo versus the Vampire Women*. The film, an international kitsch classic, affirms the profitability of the sub-genre and explains, in its own manner, the richness of the ethical punches on the stage. In the dance of the "locks," the primordial values of the universe let themselves be translated by masks, morbid gazes, eye pokes, quebradoras, punches that reverberate in the soul, defiant steps, minimal ambitions. The screenwriters stop at nothing, and the director, the scenographer, and the actors refuse nothing, as they mass-produce the glances of José G. Cruz: zombies, living corpses, priests of antiquity, wells of snakes, smoking sar-cophagi. And, if anyone's interested, if the national censors eliminate every-thing "daring" from *El Santo versus the Vampire Women*, the producers re-store the scenes of esoteric and cosmic lesbianism in the copies that circulate outside of Mexico.

What is the plot (so to speak) of *El Santo versus the Vampire Women*? In the cemetery that infuses life into a prop castle, a moonbeam resuscitates the vampire women, whose high priestess, Tundra, sends her demonic con-tingent in pursuit of blood. Only this divine liquid will do for Zorina, the despot of the reign with no geography attached, who must be replaced by her descendant, the young heroine Nora. Nora's father, Professor Orlak, Egyp-tologist of tremendous prestige, solicits the aid of El Santo. The vampire women begin a crime wave and send a slave to destroy El Santo in the ring. He wins, rescues Tundra, and sees the flames return the Amazons to hell.

In each film, El Santo risks his life and, more important, his mask. He saves and protects, is the warrior El Cid in his laboratory; he's the Torso of the Good at the juncture of the shadow of death; he's the unreal and convincing hero of the hundreds of thousands who accept, in solidarity, the scenes and situations that he proposes. The fans of El Santo, used to laughing at jokes that have not yet been told, add an involuntary humor to their conditioned reflexes. "Kick that vampire woman's ass, Santo!"

THE SOBRIETY OF THE EXCESSES

Roland Barthes dedicated one of his mythologies to professional wrestling, "the spectacle of excess, the grandiloquence which must be that of ancient theater" (Barthes 1972 [1957]). And at the *luchas*, which take place in the open air of marginalization, one attends a genuine Human Comedy, where the hues of the passions (dissimulation, refined cruelty, Pharisaism, the sensation of "I owe nothing to nobody") find the sign to carry them, express them, and carry them in triumph. In this sense, according to Barthes, what matters is not the genuineness of the passion but its imagery, and in professional wrestling, or in theater, to explain the representation of morality lessens the truth of the spectacle. Interiority is emptied in favor of exterior signs, and extenuation of the content by the form is the very principle of classical art triumphant. Professional wrestling is a more effective pantomime than dramatic pantomime because, to show themselves to be authentic, the gestures of the wrestler need no plotlines, scenery, or any kind of explanation.

It makes sense to add to Barthes's words that which occurs in Latin American countries, where vitality redeems the dilapidation of the scenery (miserable arenas, odors that cannot be the work of one generation alone, seating that speaks to the low wages of the audience, fatigue of the actors and performers). The idols are usually sixty-year-olds (or even seventy-year-olds) — El Santo, Blue Demon, Huracán Ramírez — because the legend transcends agility. In the voluptuous order ("we want to see blood!"), the least important is the age and condition of the wrestlers and the thousand patched-up areas in the arena. What matters is the eternal youth of credulity. A wrestler doesn't age as long as the public recognizes itself in him.

EL SANTO VERSUS THE CRITICS OF POPULAR CULTURE

El Santo: a realist fable of our urban culture; a professional life whose first raison d'être was the lack of a face; a fame without facial features to adhere to.

The proclamation of the fans persists: "Santoooo! Santoooo!" In the street, plastic figurines are for sale.

Translated by Heather Levi

REFERENCES

Ayala Blanco, Jorge. 1986. *La búsqueda del cine mexicano*. Mexico City: Posada.
Barthes, Roland. 1972 [1957]. "The World of Wrestling." In *Mythologies*. Trans. Annette Lavers. New York: Farrar, Straus and Giroux.

HEATHER LEVI

The Mask of the Luchador: Wrestling,

Politics, and Identity in Mexico

Old or young, creole or mestizo, general or laborer
or lawyer, the Mexican seems to me to be a person who
shuts himself away to protect himself. His face is a
mask and so is his smile.—Octavio Paz, *The Labyrinth*
of Solitude and the Other Mexico

O n 3 February 1984, El Santo, the most popular professional wrestler in the history of the sport in Mexico, was interviewed on national television by journalist Jacobo Zabludovsky. He was invited, along with his long-time colleagues Wolf Ruvinski, "Mocho" Cota, and Blue Demon to discuss the eternal question of the nature of professional wrestling: whether it was a "sport" or merely "circus, tumbling and theater." The sixty-three-year-old wrestler had retired the year before, ending a career that spanned four decades as a pop culture hero, and had been working occasionally as an escape artist, against his doctor's advice. During his career, he had starred in fifty-six movies, and won more championships and captured more masks than any wrestler before or since, but he had never exposed his own face to the world . . . until the prerecorded interview was broadcast that night.

That night, in front of what must have been millions of viewers, El Santo removed his mask. For the first time since 1942, he revealed his face to his public, and let them know his "real" name: Rodolfo Guzmán Huerta. Two days later, while doing his escape act in the Teatro Blanquita, he suffered a fatal heart attack. Hijo del Santo (Son of El Santo), his youngest son and heir to his mask, was wrestling in Acapulco when it happened, and wasn't told of his father's death until he stepped out of the ring. El Santo, in accordance with the terms of his will, was waked and buried with his mask in place (Morales 1998).

Ten years later, a small army of ski-mask clad Mayan peasants occupied San Cristóbal de Las Casas, the capital of the southern state of Chiapas. Within hours, one figure emerged as the representative of the new Ejército Zapatista de Liberación Nacional (EZLN), an articulate and evidently educated man, his face (like the faces of the rest of the Zapatistas) obscured by a balaclava, calling himself Subcomandante "Marcos." In February of the following year, near the anniversary of El Santo's passing, the Mexican government launched a new offensive against the Zapatistas. As part of that offensive the attorney general's office released a photograph of a man they claimed (rightly or wrongly) to be the movement's charismatic leader, the ski-masked figure known only as Subcomandante Marcos. Metaphorically ripping off his mask, they revealed him to be nothing more than Rafael Sebastián Guillén Vicente, former university professor and son of a furniture dealer in Tampico, Tamaulipas. Government officials claimed that the photograph's circulation in and of itself was an important victory. The next day's *New York Times* quoted an unnamed official who insisted (rather prematurely) that "the moment that Marcos was identified and his photo was shown and everyone saw who he was, much of his importance as a symbol vanished. . . . Whether he is captured or not is incidental" (Golden 1995: 1). On the face of it, the statement was absurd. Although Guillén was clearly not indigenous (a fact that officials used to undermine the EZLN's claim to represent the indigenous Maya of Chiapas), there had never been any pretense to the contrary. His identity was revealed to be what everyone more or less expected, although journalist Alma Guillermoprieto observed that the unmasking temporarily lessened his sex appeal. As a politicomilitary gesture, however, it did make sense if it was seen as a familiar trope from *lucha libre*, Mexico's version of professional wrestling.

The history of professional wrestling in Mexico goes back to 1933, when a promoter named Salvador Lutteroth brought a group of wrestlers from Texas to Mexico City for a series of matches. Lucha libre soon became among the most popular and culturally resonant forms of entertainment in urban

Mexico. From the mid-1930s on, it has been a fixture in working- and lower-class neighborhoods of the capital and many other cities in the center and north of the country. While broadly similar to professional wrestling as it is practiced in the United States, lucha libre has its own rules and its own aesthetic practices. In common with other national variants of professional wrestling, the wrestlers (called *luchadores*) are divided into good guys and bad guys: in Mexico, ethically upright *técnicos* and nefarious *rudos*. Lucha libre is faster and more acrobatic than U.S. professional wrestling, and it uses fewer "power moves." The size of the wrestlers' bodies per se is less important to the spectacle than their agility. And, unlike other versions of professional wrestling, lucha libre has developed a complex set of practices around the use of masks.

In this context, Marcos's response seemed to echo an incident involving Hijo del Santo during his divorce some years before. In the middle of their divorce, the wrestler's soon-to-be-ex-wife sent photographs of his unmasked face (she claimed) to the press. The son of El Santo responded by denying that he was the man in the photographs. Since there was no way to know unless he unmasked himself, her claim was impossible to prove (Rugos 1994: 24). That was precisely the reaction of Marcos to the government's ploy. Within days he relayed a message to the Mexico City press in his familiar epistolary style:

> *P.S. that rapidly applauds this new "success" of the government police*: I heard they've found another "Marcos," and that he's from Tampico. That doesn't sound bad, the port is nice. . . .

> *P.S. that despite the circumstances does not abandon its narcissism*: "So . . . Is this new Subcomandante Marcos good-looking? Because lately they've been assigning me really ugly ones, and my feminine correspondence gets ruined. . . . [signed] The Sup, rearranging his ski mask with macabre flirtatiousness" (quoted in Guillermoprieto 1995: 44, italics in original).

Like the son of El Santo he was able, through simple denial, to reestablish his imperiled sex appeal, his revolutionary credentials, and, most important, the charisma of his mask.

Masks, masking, and unmasking are themes that pervade not only lucha libre, but Mexican culture as a whole. This essay is an exploration of the power of the mask in lucha libre and in the broader Mexican context. My aim is to draw out connections between lucha libre and the national culture in which it is embedded and to which it contributes through the medium of the mask.

Masks have been a part of lucha libre since the 1930s. By the 1950s the wrestling mask had come to symbolize the sport itself. The mask is a metonym for lucha libre, worn by perhaps half to two-thirds of Mexico's wrestlers. Although masks have been used by a few wrestlers in the United States, they have never come to be used very much, let alone come to represent the very essence of the performance genre. Yet in Mexico the mask, and play with the mask, is very important to the genre, for the mask is more than just an element of costume. The mask "matters" in lucha libre: both by its capacity to shift the rules of performance and by its capacity to align wrestling performances with other discourses about culture and nation.

THE WRESTLER'S MASK

The use of wrestling masks in the United States predates their use in Mexico. In 1915, a wrestler calling himself "the Masked Marvel" debuted in Manhattan. The wrestler (later revealed to be Mort Henderson) set up a series of escalating challenges until he was unmasked by Ed "Strangler" Lewis. After that, several different U.S. wrestlers played the role of the Masked Marvel for short periods. The Masked Marvel "himself" was never really a character, but a gimmick (Jares 1974).

The Mexican wrestling mask, however, was designed by a shoemaker in Mexico City in 1934. Antonio H. Martínez moved from León, Guanajuato, to Mexico City in the late 1920s, where he became one of lucha libre's earliest fans. According to his son, Víctor (the current proprietor of his shop, Deportes Martínez), Antonio Martínez was a special fan of the wrestler Charro Aguayo. The two eventually met, and when Aguayo found out he was a shoemaker, he asked to design a boot for luchadores who, until then, had been using boxing shoes.[1] Martínez soon became known among wrestlers as a source for wrestling boots. Later that year, he was approached by a North American wrestler, who fought under the name Cyclone MacKay, and who used the Masked Marvel gimmick in Mexico. MacKay asked Martínez if he could make him a hood. As Víctor Martínez recounts, when his father asked MacKay what he meant, he replied that he wanted "a hood, some-

Víctor Martínez, Mexico's premiere maker of wrestling
masks, at work in the shop founded by his father.

thing you can put on, tie on, like the Ku Klux Klan or something like that"
(Martínez 1997).

The first Martínez mask was made of two pieces of suede. It didn't fit well,
and was uncomfortable to wrestle in, so he refined the design. Today a "classical" mask, based on the Martínez design, is made from four pieces of solid
color cotton-Lycra blend that are sewn together to cover the entire head except for the eyes, nose, and mouth. In the back there is an opening, with a
tongue, that is laced like a tennis shoe to hold the mask in place. There can be
contrasting trim around the eye, nose, and mouth holes, and/or some type of
insignia or pattern. The form of the wrestling mask changed little for several
decades after its invention. Before the 1990s, the most radical change in design was a trend in the 1970s toward leaving the lower jaw uncovered. Since
lucha libre returned to television in the early 1990s, however, more elaborate

variations—with horns, beaks, fringe, and other projections—have become more common.

Masked Marvel was the only wrestler to use a mask until 1936, when a Mexican wrestler, Jesús Velásquez, started performing as El Murciélago (the Bat) Velásquez. Wearing a leather mask and an elaborate cape, he would carry a bag into the ring from which he would release a swirl of bats. In the wake of his success (and a wave of popularity of masked comic book heroes), more luchadores put on masks.[2] Rodolfo Guzmán Huerta took up the mask in 1942. Born in Tulancingo, Hidalgo, but raised in Mexico City, he followed two of his older brothers into professional wrestling in 1932. He wrestled as a *rudo* (bad guy) under his own name (Rudy Guzmán) without much success, until his promoter suggested that he wear a mask. Newly masked, Guzmán billed himself as El Murciélago II, but when the original threatened to sue him, he changed character. In 1942, still a rudo, he covered his face with a silver lamé mask, and entered the ring as "El Santo, el enmascarado de plata" (The Saint, the man in the silver mask, after the comic book character Simon Templar). With that, his wrestling career took off. In 1958 he starred in his first movie, and in 1962, he changed his role from *rudo* to *técnico* (good guy). Then he spent the rest of his life as a professional symbol of the triumph of good over evil.

By 1955, dozens of wrestlers wore masks, prompting *Box y Lucha* to publish a two-part photographic feature on "mask mania" (*Box y Lucha* 1955a:17–18, 1955b:18–19). When Mexican wrestlers took up the mask, they transformed it from an occasional gimmick to an important part of the performance. The spread of the use of masks in the late 1940s and 1950s coincided with the advent and growth of the wrestling movie: low-budget films turned out by the dozen after the end of "golden age" of Mexican cinema in the 1940s. The most famous masked wrestlers were recruited to the film industry, which in turn bolstered and widened their fame. Certain masks, that of El Santo, that of Blue Demon, that of Huracán Ramírez (among many others) gained iconic status, and an etiquette developed around protecting the honor and anonymity of the lucha libre mask. El Santo was known for his exemplary care of his mask and his secret identity. He wouldn't even let his guard down during his work in the movies. Moreover, in his cinematic career, El Santo did not actually speak his lines. The director would tell him how many seconds his line would last, he would count them aloud, and his voice would be dubbed by an actor in postproduction.[3] The effect was to conceal not only his face, but his voice as well. He was, in a sense, a body double of himself. "El Santo" *was* the mask and the torso. He both was and was not Rodolfo Guzmán, for the mask transformed the wrestler and the performance. The mask transformed lucha libre.

LA MÁSCARA AND LO MEXICANO

One of the ways that the mask transformed lucha libre was by associating wrestling performance with a key symbol of Mexican national culture, rooted in a pre-Hispanic past. Many people, both in and outside of the subculture of wrestlers, referees, promoters, and reporters that make up the "wrestling family," have called attention to the connection between the use of masks in lucha libre, and their ritual use by indigenous peoples in Mexico. By connecting lucha libre to the indigenous world, the mask is seen as central to the Mexicanization of the genre, in the words of the artist Sergio Arau: "In the United States, wrestlers started to use masks, but it didn't stick, and they stopped, using makeup instead, because it's more normal, more Hollywoodesque. But in Mexico, I say and as I suppose the anthropologists say, it seems more logical that we use masks, because all our ethnic groups . . . employ masks in their rituals" (quoted in Alipi 1994: 25).

The use of masks in traditional rituals or dramas is indeed widespread in rural, indigenous Mexico. In calling these practices "traditional" or "indigenous," I do not mean that they are timeless and unchanging. But as products of complex historical processes of syncretization, such practices function as signifiers of tradition (whether understood as indigenous or mestizo) and make statements about communal identities and rights, whether by signifying difference from the national or urban culture, or signifying participation in an underlying "deep" culture common to all Mexicans.

In the ethnographic literature, traditional masked performances are reported to take place across a large geographic and cultural range in Mexico. Most uses of masking in Mexican ritual appear to fall into two categories of performance: satirical or parodic genres (or roles), and what Francis Gilmore (1983) calls "combat plays." One of the former performance types is the role of sacred clown. The performance of sacred clowns — such as the Yaqui *p'askola*, the Mayo *pariseiro*, or the Mayan *k'ohetik* — is usually interpreted as an inversion ritual in which the clowns deliberately violate community (and natural) norms in order to make them explicit, or as a way to criticize the powerful without risking retaliation.[4] It is confined to communities that are considered unambiguously indigenous — remote, rural communities where most people speak a language other than Spanish, and where Catholic religious practices and beliefs are heavily mixed with local, heterodox ones. Another parodic use of masks, however, is widespread in both indigenous and mestizo contexts: the *pastorela*. *Pastorelas* are performed all over Mexico during the month before Christmas.[5] Although the pastorela originated in Mexico as a religious pageant portraying the Journey of the Magi (Sánchez Hernández 1997), its most common contemporary form is that of a satirical play that couches social critique in burlesque parody. Pastorelas can (in theory) be performed by anyone, are composed for the occasion, and allow for a great deal of improvisation on the actor's part. Thus pastorelas include everything from small-town productions that mock the local power structure, to professional productions that critique key figures in the national government. Although masking is not essential to the genre, at least some actors in most pastorelas wear masks.

Combat plays are also associated with masking in much of Mexico. The most widespread of these, a ritual dance/drama called Moros y Cristianos (Moors and Christians), is performed all over Latin America (as well as Spain), and celebrates the Catholic "reconquest" of the Iberian Peninsula. Some variants portray the Spanish conquest of the Aztecs instead, or conflate the two events. Participants in these rituals are divided into two morally marked "sides," one side representing the Christians, led by Santiago, and the other representing the Moors or Indians. Although the Christians always vanquish their enemies by the end of the ritual, Nájera-Ramírez (1997) argues that (at least in the case of a variant called Los Tastoanes), the Christian victory represents incorporation, rather than defeat of the other side.[6] In most variants, the participants who play the role of non-Christians wear masks of some kind. In *Moors and Christians*, the mask may be as simple as a bandana and sunglasses, or a fake beard (Gilmore 1983). In Los Tastoanes, some individual characters (such as a morally ambivalent character Cireneo) and the masses of "tastoanes" wear masks specific to their roles.

Another masked combat play performed in Nahuatl-speaking communities in the state of Guerrero, a fertility ritual called the *danza del tigre* (tiger dance). A petition for rain that takes place in May, the danza is performed by young men of the community who dress as jaguars, wearing painted clothing and heavy wooden or leather masks that resemble lucha libre costumes.

The youths fight each other with rope whips in order to shed one another's blood as a sacrifice, so "that by shedding human blood, the jaguar deity will release his own blood in the form of rain which then fertilizes the maize crop" (Saunders 1998: 38–39).

Masks are thus most likely to be used in two kinds of performances in traditional contexts in Mexico: those in which participants mock powerful figures or violate community norms, and those in which participants engage in ritual combat (or both). In this sense, they resemble lucha libre both in its melodramatic-agonistic and its ludic aspects. When used by those who violate community norms—sacred clowns, Moors, Tastoanes—the mask helps to perform a necessary separation of the community member from the morally problematic actions of his or her character. But the mask empowers performance on a more profound level as well.

Early (but persistent) anthropological theories of the mask held that masking was a universal phenomenon originally rooted in the inability (or unwillingness) of the masker's audience (and to some extent of the masker) to distinguish between the entity represented by the mask and the masker representing the entity. This position, rooted in the (Lucien) Levy-Bruhlian notion of an ontological difference between the perceptual orientation of "primitive" and modern societies, has come under attack for both theoretical and empirical reasons (Crumrine and Halpin 1983; Pernet 1992). More recent work suggests that the relationship of masking and identity is far more nuanced and complex. There are different ways in which masks can be inhabited by maskers (and maskers inhabited by masks), even within the same dramatic tradition, including trance visitation, mimicry of visitation, and interpretation based on visitation.[7]

Although I have found no reference to a tradition of trance possession and masked ritual per se in Mexico, there does seem to be a variety of ideas about the relationship between the masker and the mask. In some masked performances, the mask may be seen as an instrument of empowerment. Stephen Lute (1983) writes that commitment to the p'askola clown role facilitates the acquisition of spiritual power for the masker. The mask is considered to have a kind of life of its own, but the p'askola spirits do not possess the initiate during performance. Instead, through contact with the spirits, the masker gains (healing and other) powers that can be used outside of performance. In this case, the masks themselves empower performance by facilitating the spiritual powers or the performer. On the other hand, the masks used in Moors-and-Christians style combat plays are not treated as loci of the supernatural; nor do people pretend that they don't know who the dancers "really" are. The same is, of course, true of the more conventionally theatrical pastorela. In all cases, however, the mask allows the masker a moral authority or moral immunity, freeing him or her to take on or embody the role of social critic.

The first wrestling mask used in Mexico was not carried from the villages of Jalisco or Guerrero to Mexico City. It was invented by an urban, mestizo shoemaker at the behest of a North American performing in a genre recently imported from the United States. It alluded not to the ritual practices of indigenous Mexican communities, but to the Ku Klux Klan. Nevertheless, the presence of the mask associates lucha libre with indigenous ritual practices. Moreover, that association simultaneously aligns lucha libre with an important trope in the discourse of national culture in Mexico. The revolution of 1910–17 stimulated a shift in thinking about the Mexican national subject. As part of the postrevolutionary nationalist project, the ideal Mexican came to be imagined as mestizo—the product of racial and cultural mixture between Spanish and Indian—rather than as Creole. The conceptualization of the mestizo subject was, moreover, explicitly gendered, as the mestizo was imagined as the son of the Spanish father and Indian mother. The indigenous thus became identified as the locus of "México profundo," the ground of Mexico's irreducible cultural identity. Yet the indigenous were not identified as the Mexican national subject per se. Claudio Lomnitz Adler has written, rather, that the dominant discourse constituted "an argument about the individuality of the Mexican process: the soul of Mexican culture is Indian and its political body is destined to be ruled by mestizos against the Europeanizing process of the lackeys of foreign imperialism" (Lomnitz Adler 1992: 2). To link the urban practice of lucha libre to indigenous ritual, then, can have the effect of legitimating it as a *nationalist* practice.

MASKED PERFORMANCE

The mask allows professional wrestling, an imported entertainment genre, to seem more Mexican, but that is not the only thing that the mask accomplishes. The use of masks allows luchadores to foreground some elements of performance and mute others; for although there is no unambiguous tradition of "visitation" in traditional Mexican masquerades, the presence of a mask changes the dynamic of the relationship between the character (en)acted, the actor, and the "script" of the actions. As John Emigh notes:

> In working up a role, the unmediated self of the actor, the mask (persona) that is to be acted and the text that is to be spoken within the flow of action form a triad. The tendency in most Western theater today is to begin with the confrontation of actor and text and to work towards the persona—a term which in common usage has come to mean character as well as mask. [In masked theatrical forms] this process begins, instead, with the confrontation of actor and mask. . . . The text and *mise-en-scène* . . . will be shaped by this encounter and will often be improvised within the boundaries established by aesthetic form and social occasion. (Emigh 1996:xviii–xix)

In lucha libre, then, the mask changes the relationship between the wrestler, the wrestler's "script," and the wrestler's character, first of all, by objectifying the wrestler's character in a material and visual form. This is one way that lucha libre has tended to privilege the visual and gestural over the verbal. The pre- and postmatch interview and hyperbolic exchange of insults, so important to narrative development of U.S. professional wrestling, are rarely used. The identification of the wrestler with his or her role, *even for wrestlers who do not mask* seldom depends on what they say or how they say it. In lucha libre, the body and mask signify. The voice seldom does. Moreover, the transformation of the wrestler-actor into the character happens whenever he or she puts on the mask whether or not the individual changes his/her behavior.

In addition, the use of masks opens up the possibility of a set of rules of play that are about masks. These include rules regarding actions in the ring, and a set of "metarules": who can be masked, what mask they can use, and the etiquette that protects a wrestler's anonymity. The rules that govern or are supposed to govern lucha libre performance include both rules of play, and the metarules that determine the context within which play can take place. These include both formal mandates (the size of the ring, the rules for disqualification, and rules for different types of matches) and tacit conventions (e.g., that there should usually be a rudo side and a técnico side).

This section will lay out the formal and informal rules of masking, and their implications for wrestlers who wear the mask.

METARULES

1. A wrestler who wants to wear a mask must be specifically licensed to do so by the Comisión de Lucha Libre (hereafter, the Commission).[8] The Commission is said to hold masked wrestlers to a higher standard on the licensing exam, because a masked wrestler is protected from humiliation if he or she wrestles badly.

2. A masked wrestler must never publicly expose his or her unmasked face, or disclose his or her identity. On the one hand, this means enlisting the collusion of people who must know the wrestler's secret (family, close friends, business associates, and so on). On the other, it means complying with a set of rituals for negotiating the border between wrestling space and quotidian space.[9] A masked wrestler should don (and remove) the mask in a space where his or her face will not be noticed and associated with the mask. The mask should be off when wrestlers leave their homes, but in place when they arrive at the arena. It's not a problem for wrestlers who can afford a car, but most wrestlers do not own cars. They must arrive at and leave the arena in taxis or public transportation, and so they have to negotiate the masking in a taxi, or a couple of blocks away from the arena. To pull it off, to achieve the transformation, requires a sense of timing, and a faith in the anonymity of most interactions in the city—a sense that taxi drivers don't notice the faces of their fares, nor bystanders and bartenders the face of the guy who came in to use the bathroom. Or, perhaps it depends on their collusion— that they understand the importance of the wrestler's anonymity and will respect his or her responsibility to maintain it.[10]

PERFORMANCE RULES

Inside the ring, the mask is treated as a fetishized object that represents the wrestler's honor. Masked wrestlers cannot let their faces be seen under any circumstances. This opens up a range of possibilities of play, since in lucha libre (especially for the rudos) it's often as good to humiliate an opponent as to defeat one. A wrestler can humiliate an opponent by exposing the opponent's face, but to do so is grounds for disqualification. Thus, a wrestler

A masked wrestler must never reveal his or her unmasked face. Outdoor fair, Mexico City.

can pursue dominance through victory, or exploit the fetishistic value of the mask and pursue it through humiliation. Between those two extremes, wrestlers can tear each other's masks without actually removing them. While that doesn't mean disqualification or exposure for either wrestler, it does cost one wrestler an expensive, custom-made mask.

An unmasked wrestler is disempowered. Until the mask is returned, the wrestler can't fight, but can only clutch his or her face and wait—either for a partner to retrieve it or be led to the dressing room to put on a fresh one. The unmasking trope, then, can be played in several different ways to build the narrative of a given match. Here I will give three examples:

1. A torn or stolen mask in the second round is a set up for revindication in the third. I saw one dramatic instance of this in a match which featured the técnico Solar II, teamed up with two other técnicos against a group of three rudos led by Solar's rival Scorpio. In round 2, Scorpio managed to unmask Solar, who rolled himself out of the ring, covered his face, and crouched miserably in the corner. His teammates were unable to recover the mask, so he stayed there until a small boy led him away to the dressing rooms. The referee declared the técnicos the winners of round 2 by disqualification. As soon as round 3 started (while Solar was still absent), the rudos ganged up on the remaining técnicos, two of them kicking and punching one, while the third

kept his partner at bay. Then, just when it looked hopeless for the técnicos, Solar reappeared with a sparkly new mask, leapt into the ring and energetically took on all three of the bad guys. Revitalized, his partners joined in and quickly pinned the rudos to win the match.

2. Another example is when the rudo unmasks himself. This is another tactic used by rudos, where the bad guy spontaneously clutches his groin and drops moaning to the ground, hoping that the referee will disqualify his opponent for fouling him. In the mask version, when the referee is ostentatiously otherwise engaged, the rudo undoes his own mask and thrusts it into the hands of a puzzled técnico. Then he writhes around clutching his face, just as the referee turns, sees them, and disqualifies the técnico.

3. In the *lucha de apuesta* (betting match), a wrestler will bet his or her mask or hair on the outcome of the match, against the opponent's mask or hair. Some hair, long trademark manes that are identified with particular wrestlers, is relatively valuable, but since it grows back, hair can never have the value of a mask. Losing a mask causes the wrestler to lose anonymity. His or her face, name, and birthplace are publicly revealed, first in the arena, and later in wrestling fanzines and the sports section of some newspapers. Even more important, the wrestler loses the right to use a mask thereafter. In the metarules of lucha libre, to change from one character to another, from one mask to another, is not considered dishonest, but to cover a face (and an identity) once it has been uncovered is fraud.

The wrestler who has agreed to lose a lucha de apuesta is paid a bonus by the event's promoter, since it usually draws a large audience. Sometimes a lucha de apuesta takes place because the *empresa* (league) wishes to promote the career of the winner.[11] Sometimes it takes place because the loser either needs money, is planning to switch empresas anyway (where he or she will fight under another name chosen by the new empresa), or has tired of the responsibility of remaining incognito. Luchas de apuesta take place after a period of several months of heightened rivalry between two wrestlers (called a *pique*), during which time they exchange threats and escalating challenges. During the fight itself there is no real risk to mask or hair, since victory and defeat have been agreed to in advance. However, that does *not* mean that nothing is at stake for the wrestlers. Masked wrestlers take a genuine risk when they agree to lose, for loss of a mask might mean loss of charisma, and loss of the ability to move the public. The moment of revelation clarifies the relationship of a particular wrestler to a particular mask.

A wrestler who takes up the mask has to confront the problem of how to inhabit it, how to make another's face his or her own. As in other forms of masked theater, "the unworn mask begins as something clearly set apart: an inert and disembodied other. The actor confronting the mask is nakedly and pathetically himself (or, increasingly, herself). For the actor, the otherness of the mask becomes both the obstacle and the goal. He or she must redefine the sense of self in order to wear the other's face and be true to it in spirit, thought and action" (Emigh 1996:xviii).

At the moment of unmasking, the wrestler faces a new task: that of transferring the charisma that the mask had accrued to pure bodily gesture. He or she loses the illusion of being more than human, beyond the everyday obligation of having a name and a history. The wrestler must transfer the redefinition of self that he or she developed to wear the mask, to his or her human body. In that moment, the wrestler's future becomes a matter of speculation, and the wrestler's career is put at serious risk. The ritual of unmasking might reveal that the mask was the key to his or her success. On the other hand, the wrestler might be able to transcend the unmasking and prove (in the words of the wrestler Conan the Barbarian) that "the mask doesn't make the wrestler, the wrestler makes the mask" (Quoted in Fascinetto 1992: 27).

Meanwhile, the mask of the winner is invested with the charisma of the mask of the loser. A wrestler's official career history always includes a list of masks and hair as well as championships won, and everyone knows that the masks (depending on whose mask) are worth far more than a championship. Really big stars (especially masked ones) have to be able to claim several masks on their shelves as evidence of prowess and a willingness to risk the irretrievable. But, since the matches are fixed, the conquered masks really represent a decision made at some earlier time by the empresa to advance the winner's career. They are thus a testament to the wrestler's position in the empresa.[12]

The fact that anonymity and the charisma of mystery can be irrecoverably lost gives wrestling masks a heightened value. Even though many careers continue after an unmasking, it is widely believed that many more do not. In the words of one reporter: "In the moment in which wrestler takes off the mask, people fall like a plague on the ring. All want to know the unmasked, but with the passage of time, people cool down and forget about the fallen. Oh tragedy! He loses his anonymity and loses his public" (Valentino 1993: 4). The lucha de apuesta is therefore a mechanism by which the mask is in-

(*top*) Mil Mascaras and
Dr. Wagner engaging
with the public. Arena
Coliseo, Acapulco.

(*right*) Rudo attempting
to unmask his técnico
rival. Arena Caracol,
State of México.

vested with significance. To unmask a wrestler increases the value attributed to the mask of the winner. The very possibility of unmasking, and its irrevocability, makes all masks "worth something." The care with which the rules around masking are observed empowers the mask to both conceal and to transcend. It allows the mask to be the vehicle for other meanings, which I will now examine.

One of the ways in which the mask helps wrestling to "signify" is in foregrounding linked discourses of kinship, nation, mortality, and permanence. As stated above, when a wrestler is unmasked, his or her name and place of birth are published the following week in magazines such as *Box y Lucha* and *Superluchas*, as well as the sports section of newspapers such as *L'Afición* or *Ovaciones*. By extension, the wrestler's personal history and genealogy become definitely knowable. Unmasking reveals the wrestler's embeddedness in the social world. Yet the relationship of masking to kinship is not only one of concealment. It can also be one of display, or selective revelation.

Lucha libre characters are often inherited, passed from parent to child, uncle or aunt to nephew or niece, godparent to godchild, teacher to student. Of all characters, masked characters are the most likely to be passed down. If a parent is or was a successful masked wrestler, one of his or her children may inherit the mask, inheriting, in a sense, the parent's social identity. The original wrestler has the right to decide who will use the mask, even if he or she was unmasked and made unable to use the mask during the rest of his or her career.[13] One effect of this is a kind of hypercontinuity: El Santo, Rayo de Jalisco, Dr. Wagner, Blue Demon, and others whose careers started in the 1940s still appear to be with us, still wrestling at the same arenas.

In practice, the transmission of masks from parent to child is gender specific — I know only of masks that passed from father to son, uncle to nephew, or godfather to godson. Women are less likely to mask at all, and I know of no woman's mask that has been passed to a second generation. The person who dons a classic mask may not, in fact, be the son or nephew of the original, but it is conventionally expected that he will be. If the father's mask was very prestigious, taking up the mask may be a heavy burden. Heirs may worry about failing to preserve its prestige and charisma. Hijo del Santo, for example, did not put on his father's mask until he had proved himself a good wrestler under another nom de guerre. Although there are many wrestling families, those who do not wear masks seldom refer to themselves as legends. They can't. Aside from rare exceptions, only by masking are wrestlers able to convert themselves into national or regional symbols, and *only* through masking can they appear to efface time.

A QUESTION OF HONOR

A dramatic example of the importance of the mask in embodying continuity was a lucha de apuesta for the mask of Hijo del Santo against the hair of Negro Casas that took place on 19 September 1997. Both Hijo del Santo and Negro Casas are heirs of wrestling lineages, men who were (according to the announcer when the match finally took place) "formed genetically for the *lucha profesional.*" Negro Casas is the son of Pepe Casas, a técnico of the same generation as El Santo, then working as a referee. Negro Casas has uncles in the business, and a brother who wrestles as the masked Felino. He used to be a rudo, but had fought as a técnico for some years prior to the lucha de apuesta. His rudo past notwithstanding, Negro was wonderful as a técnico: elegant, acrobatic, and expressive, with a trademark mane of lush black hair.

Hijo del Santo, on the other hand, had been fighting as a rudo since the previous December, a switch that had angered his public. According to the wrestling journals, one of the ostensible reasons for his going over to the dark side was his long-standing hatred of Negro Casas. The two wrestlers had engaged in an escalating series of attacks and counterattacks, challenges and counterchallenges since the New Year. This lucha de apuesta, which the EMLL press release titled "A Question of Honor," was to settle accounts once and for all. Instead of following lucha libre's usual format, in which the winner must win two pins out of three, this was to be decided with only one pin. The match was to be the final event of a gala celebration of the sixty-fourth anniversary of lucha libre's arrival in Mexico.[14]

It had not been a good year for live lucha libre. Ticket sales had been low, and many matches took place in arenas that were half full at best. The EMLL had closed down the smallest of its three arenas in Mexico City that June, and there were rumors that they were going to close the Acapulco arena as well. This match, however, was different. Tickets to the 18,000-seat arena sold out by 1:30 in the afternoon. By 6:30 the streets were full of fans and scalpers seeking each other out and bargaining over tickets. Many of those who could not buy tickets stood outside all evening waiting to learn the outcome of the final match.

Wrestling events in Mexico usually consist of five matches in ascending importance. This one was no exception, as each match heightened the sense of drama and anticipation. The preliminary match between *minis* was elegantly paced, climaxing with a beautiful corkscrewing "suicide leap" out of the ring by Cicloncito Ramírez onto Damiancito.[15] The next match was equally dramatic, and risky. In the third, Lola González (who had announced her intention to retire some weeks before) won the last match of her twenty-two-year career against her Japanese rival, Bull Nakano. She was escorted into the ring by a pair of muscular young men with copies of Aztec stone masks covering their faces. After the match, she was sent off with gifts and tributes from her colleagues. Bull Nakano gave her a porcelain doll, and wiped away tears as the others made speeches. In the next match, when Rayo de Jalisco made his entrance accompanied by mariachis, his rival Cien Caras grabbed a guitar and broke it over Rayo's head. As they usually do, the matches moved from relatively orderly preliminaries to increasingly chaotic, violent, and prestigious later ones until the time came for the final.

Because Hijo del Santo had been fighting as a rudo, the moral coding, the symbolic importance of the event, was unclear to me. Although I knew that Hijo del Santo, no matter what, still "signified" as the son of his illustrious father, I also knew that Negro Casas was going in as the técnico, as the representative of decent folk. I had also read in *Superluchas* that Hijo del Santo was going to star in his own television series.[16] Each of the two had threatened to retire if he lost, so (although I knew about the scandalous retirement match between Konan and Perro Aguayo, after which neither retired), I wondered if it wasn't Hijo del Santo's way of moving on to an acting career. But any doubts I might have had vanished as we waited for the match to begin.

Suddenly, on the screen above the ring, we could all see the silver mask, the shoulders covered by the matching cape. It was hard to make out where he was standing—a dark space with metal beams in the background. And then he spoke:

> Today will be the fiftieth defense of this mask. El Santo and Hijo del Santo are *united*. And I will show you why I carry this mask with pride—Because *I am the son of El Santo*.[17]

After he finished his speech, he entered the ring, lowered on cables from the rafters of the arena. The silver lamé covered his head as always, but instead of his usual cape, he wore one that, while still of silver lamé, had three vertical strips, one each of green, silver (standing in for white), and red (the colors of the Mexican flag). In the silver space, instead of the flag's eagle insignia, he wore an image of the Virgin of Guadalupe.[18] As he waited in the ring, Negro Casas's theme song, Juan Luis Guerra's anti-imperialist merengue "El costo de la vida," came over the loudspeakers, and Negro's face appeared on the overhead screen. He spoke from the dressing room, responding to Hijo del Santo's challenge:

> Santo, your hour has come. Tonight the threats will end, the challenges will end, and you too will end. I will show your face. Arena Mexico and all the world will know who is your master — I, sir. Tonight the legend ends.

But by then it was clear that Negro Casas didn't have a chance. The symbolic weight that Hijo del Santo carried into the ring was too great: aligned verbally and iconically with his late father and the spiritual mother of the Mexican nation, descending like the holy spirit.

For the first few minutes the two men stayed near the center of the canvas, engaged in an intense and focused exchange of holds. Negro Casas grabbed Hijo del Santo and dragged him toward the corner ropes as the arena started to echo with whistles and cheers, cries of "Santo, Santo," and a few of "Negro, Negro." He hung Hijo del Santo by his feet from the corner ropes, backed up, then slid feetfirst across the canvas into Santo's chest. Then he took the abject wrestler down, dragged him to another corner, and slid into him again. He repeated the whole thing once more, but, then, on the fourth attempt, Hijo del Santo was ready. He ducked to the side at the last second, and Negro slid all the way out of the ring. Hijo del Santo righted himself on the ropes, then leapt through the air onto his opponent. They got up from the ground, both a little groggy, and reentered the ring. From then, it went back and forth for a while. Hijo del Santo tried to put Negro Casas into the *de a caballo* (camel clutch) hold (his late father's signature move), but Casas escaped. Negro managed to hang him from the ropes again, but Hijo del Santo pulled himself up to sit on the corner, and then leapt onto Negro. He tried to apply the de a caballo again, but couldn't pull it off, so he shifted his body until he held Negro's arm between his legs and, using his body as a fulcrum, pulled the arm downward to apply a painful shoulder lock. Negro immediately spread his fingers and wiggled his hands in the conventional gesture of surrender, and the referee declared Hijo del Santo the victor. Negro Casas stood up, grabbed a microphone, and complained that El Santo had cheated by taking advantage of his recent broken clavicle, but to no avail. The official barber came out, wearing his official jacket — a blazer with a big pair of scissors in a blue circle printed on the back. Negro Casas grabbed his scissors and started to cut his own hair, throwing the locks contemptuously out of the ring. The barber started to shave the sides of his head, the lights went up, and it was over.

Negro Casas's defeat was overdetermined because it was only *his* defeat. It was not the end of a legend, as Hijo del Santo's would have been. The pre-match speeches (which are not the norm in lucha libre) accomplished the identification of the mask of El Santo with such powerful national symbols as the flag and the Virgin of Guadalupe. Negro Casas could be the son of Pepe Casas, but he could not *be* Pepe Casas, and Pepe Casas was not El Santo. Hijo del Santo, in contrast, proclaimed his unity with his dead father. Only masked wrestlers can truly inherit a parent's very identity at his retirement or death, and only they must carry the full burden of the parent's image.

In this respect, the wrestling mask is an inalienable possession in the sense put forth by Annette Weiner: possessions "imbued with the identities of their owners which are not easy to give away . . . certain things assume a subjective value that places them above exchange value" (1993: 6). The mask makes possible a transfer of charisma and power from the older generation to the younger, an instance, perhaps, of "cosmological authentication" (6). The dynamic by which masks pass through generations portrays "the need to secure permanence in a serial world that is always subject to loss and decay" (7). The mask in this sense, effaces time, effaces generations, and effaces mortality.

THE MASK AND ITS CIRCULATION

Whether the mask can or should be considered the inalienable property of the wrestler, the fact is that masks circulate. They circulate as concrete objects and as symbols. This section will trace the paths of circulation of masks and of "the mask."

If you walk down Doctor La Vista Street or Peru Street during a weekday, Arenas México and Coliseo are not hard to find. But if you walk there when the arenas are open, they are impossible to miss, for as you approach the arena you hear melodious cries of "*máscara, máscara*, get you favorite wrestleeeer." Lining the sidewalk along the block are women and men

Masks for sale in Deportes Martínez.

standing next to blankets on the ground. These are covered with brightly
colored wrestling masks, copies of the designs worn by the thirty or so most
popular wrestlers of the moment. They range in style from the minimal-
ism of El Santo's plain silver covering to the elaborate beaks and horns of
Mosco de la Merced or Violencia. They come in all sizes, from key chain
ornaments to full-sized masks to fit an adult. The mask makers have shops
in the old neighborhoods of the city, such as Tepito, or in peripheral areas,
such as Nezahualcóyotl or Pantitlán. While the fabric is very different from
that used in professional-quality masks (usually a heavyweight, sometimes
padded synthetic instead of lightweight cotton and Lycra), the method by
which they are made is not that different. They aren't custom made, but the
souvenir masks are handmade by home workers who sell them for anywhere
from about US$1.00 for a key chain ornament to US$4 or US$5 for a full-sized
mask. Inside the arena, another mask vendor circulates with racks of masks
for sale. Most are bought for children, who wear them in the arena, so star
wrestlers' faces are echoed in miniature during the program. They are ubiq-
uitous in Mexico City—sold in public markets as well as the arenas. Worn
by children at play, collected by adults, the souvenir masks represent one
instance of the wrestling mask's circulation.

In a second instance of circulation, the wrestling masks are purchased by young men in rural Guerrero to use as liners to protect their faces from the rough wooden or leather jaguar masks that they use when they perform the danza del tigre (Moebius 1997). The wrestling mask is often regarded as the extension of pre-Columbian cultural forms into the modern city. In this instance, however, it exemplifies the selective adoption of modern technologies into indigenous cultural performance forms.

In addition to its circulation as an object, the wrestling mask also circulates as an icon, and the drama of unmasking as a trope. In the culture of what Martin Needler (1998) has labeled the "classical Mexican political system," which collapsed or which was at least transformed with the victory of the PAN (Partido Acción Nacional) candidate Vicente Fox in July 2000, unmasking constituted a very powerful positive or negative act. As Needler and others have described it, the system itself could be described as an elaborate masquerade: a one-party state, set up as if it were a multiparty democracy. While competing political parties are legal under the postrevolutionary constitution, the PRI (Partido Revolucionario Institucional) and its precursors contrived to exclude other parties from political power through a complex combination of tactics including monopoly on or manipulation of national and popular symbols, patronage, co-optation of dissent, sponsoring ineffectual "opposition" parties, electoral fraud, and violence.[19]

Under the Mexican system, the presidency carries nearly unlimited power, but since the constitution forbids reelection, the power of individual presidents is limited to one six-year term. Until 1999, the selection of the PRI's candidate was the prerogative of the president himself, and since the PRI's candidate was guaranteed the election, the process gave the president the right to appoint his successor. The party has, however, always been made up of various factions which would maneuver for position in advance of an election (at the local as well as national level). The identity of the PRI candidate was a matter of secrecy and speculation until the president announced his decision, an act called the *dedazo* (the big finger) or *destapa* (unveiling, or *unmasking*). In the act of revelation, the president's successor would be invested with the prestige of the president himself. The destapa would come, however, only after a series of behind-the-scenes maneuvers by different factions and political tendencies within the party. Once the candidate's identity was revealed, all factions would be expected to give him unconditional support. The electoral campaign itself consisted of a series of presentations of the candidate to the public (a public which was ritually constructed through such presentations—Lomnitz and Adler 1993). Since it was not possible for any other party to win it, the election itself was not a ritual of selection, but the ratification or manifestation of a decision that had already been made.

This aspect of the political system, then, strongly resembled a lucha libre match. In lucha libre and in presidential elections, much is at stake. Different factions struggle for dominance; different wrestlers maneuver for position within their empresa; decisions are made about who will be brought into the spotlight and who will have to wait their turn (or be satisfied with having taken their turn). The match is performed for its own sake, not as a means of determining winners or losers. As in the elections, the outcome of the match is predetermined, and the result is the manifestation of decisions that had already been made at another level of the system. But even though the ending is predetermined, *how* the match is played out, how grace or force is displayed (whether by wrestlers, or by party members mobilizing blocs of voters and suppressing the opposition in support of the *destapado*, the unmasked or unveiled one), makes a difference for future matches.

Lucha libre came to Mexico when the classical political system was consolidated under Plutarco Elías Calles and Lázaro Cárdenas, presidents from 1924 to 1928 and 1932 to 1940, respectively. Its development paralleled that of the PRI's hegemony, during which time Mexican citizens voted in elections in which their performance as voters, but not the election's outcome, was at stake. I do not believe that lucha libre was organized as a deliberate critique of the PRI. The sport was integrated into the bureaucracy of the Mexican state through the Commission and the unions early in its history, and the EMLL demonstrated its commitment to the PRI over the years. The empresa has arranged benefit wrestling performances for PRI candidates, and it has organized its wrestlers to march in May Day parades until the PRI lost the Mexico City mayoral election in 1997. The present trainer in the empresa, El Faisán, identified himself to me as a PRI militant. In short, the promoters who worked in Mexico City's dominant empresa were not likely to have been critical of the hegemony of the PRI. The resemblance between the genres of performance was not formally articulated by wrestlers, or even by Mexican social commentators who have written about lucha libre. Nevertheless, the parallels invested lucha libre with an implicit, and potentially subversive, political significance.

On 19 September 1985 an earthquake devastated Mexico City. Confronted with a slow and inadequate response by the government, the city experienced a unique moment of unity and common purpose as citizen brigades organized to dig survivors out of the rubble. Some of the deadliest damage was sustained by housing complexes and hospitals built by firms under government contract. It was soon revealed that many of the collapsed buildings had not been built to code. Over the next year, groups of grassroots activists organized to protest the government's inadequate response, and demand housing for those left homeless (whether by the earthquake or by economic circumstance). In 1986, a number of them formed a coalition, the Asamblea de Barrios, that emerged as an independent political force in its own right.

During the election of 1988, for the first time since the early 1940s, the PRI faced a serious challenge for the presidency, not from the right-wing Partido de Acción Nacional, but from a breakaway coalition from the left wing of the PRI itself. In 1987, unwilling to risk division in its ranks, and jealous of its autonomy, the Asamblea decided not to endorse any of the candidates, but to run its own instead. Thus on 17 November, the Asamblea unveiled its presidential candidate in front of the Monument to Benito Juárez in Alameda Park: Superbarrio. Resplendent in his red and yellow mask, wrestling tights, boots, and cape, the candidate promised to struggle for a "superpolitics of Superbarrio for housing, employment, schools and land." (Quoted in Cuéllar Vásquez 1993: 128). Unlike the PRI's candidate, he was not, strictly speaking, a destapado. His trademark mask stayed in place. But since the first formal act of a destapado was, traditionally, to offer his resignation to the ministry where he worked, Superbarrio went to Arena Coliseo a few days later and asked to enter the ring before the first match. There he asked the lucha libre public to accept his resignation from his position as luchador.

Superbarrio is both a real figure and a piece of political theater. He debuted in June 1987, several months before he announced his candidacy. According to Marcos Rascón Bandas (now a PRD [Partido Revolucionario Democratica] representative, and generally credited as Superbarrio's "intellectual author"), the wrestler was never intended to be a permanent fixture in the movement, just a gimmick to use in a couple of demonstrations (1997). Yet nearly fifteen years later, Superbarrio remains a fixture on the Mexican

Left. Moreover, when Superbarrio began his struggle for housing rights in Mexico City, another wrestler in a bright green mask appeared to march in protests against the proposed Laguna Verde nuclear reactor in the state of Veracruz. Ecologista Universal and Superbarrio were the first two "social wrestlers"—people (perhaps wrestlers, perhaps not) who take up noms de guerre and wrestling masks to represent social causes. Mujer Maravilla, SuperAnimal, SuperGay, and Superniño all emerged in the 1990s to fight, respectively, for the rights of women, animals, gays, and street children.

The Superbarrio figure was inspired by a theatrical intervention organized by a group of housing activists in the early 1980s. It was, as Rascón Bandas (Rascón Bandas 1997) recounts, "a typical accident."

I was a fan when I was a little boy in Ciudad Juárez, and . . . it's one of those things that gets interrupted, no? Your fandom, as a boy, changes and stops. But in 1983, we started political work in the center of the city, and the first place we started to organize was a building that was right behind Arena Coliseo. . . . The landlord was one of the classic rich men out of a cartoon. He was a Lebanese man, a Mr. Atala, who would arrive in a black Buick, like those of the 1950s, with a bowler derby, and an ascot, a real ascot, and full of rings, with a most proper black suit, with a bow tie. And he would get out of the car and go into the building to collect the rent himself, and he arrived with his assistant or secretary who was like "el licenciado" [a title used by university graduates generally and attorneys in particular] with his briefcase. So he would start to knock on doors, and he was the boogie man, he was the horror . . . the first lucha that we had to fight was to end people's fear of Mr. Atala.

So you had Mr. Atala and El Licenciado. And El Licenciado was like . . . not only economic power was going to fall on you, but also the law. So it was horrible. And it was a *vecindad* [apartment building with a common patio] full of balconies, with many places to hide. You would enter by 19 Chile Street and leave by 20 León Rubio, no? So you could cross, entering by the little entrance on 19 Chile, and the moment you enter, there were three patios full of apartments, eight hundred apartments, and it was filthy. And since you could leave through the other side, obviously, it was full of gangs of kids who were robbing people in the center, and the police would chase them, and they would duck in there, and leave by the other side. It was like the Casbah.

And in the middle of all that violence and tension, Mr. Atala would come to collect the rent. He was so tough that he dared to do it. And then it was common for him to perform his own evictions. He would arrive and "chun!" he would gave them the "get out!" and they practically went and threw the people's stuff into the patio, and nobody interfered. It was shocking, but nobody interfered.

So it was a little bit remembering [his childhood] and a little bit of it being in the lucha libre environment, where a lot of people attended the luchas or were fans of the luchadores. It coincided with the fact that in July of 1983, El Santo died, and this was a reason to resuscitate him.[20] So the older women, I said to them, "Why not, when Mr. Atala comes to collect and evict, have El Santo suddenly appear on the balconies. Let's buy the whole uniform and have El Santo appear saying 'halt right there!'"

Four years later, the Asamblea de Barrios membership decided to create their own wrestler, to represent them in the fight for housing. One of the Asamblea's tactics was to organize physical interventions to prevent evictions. The idea for Superbarrio emerged after one such demonstration, in which a large group of people prevented an eviction in the neighborhood of La Merced. After the demonstration, some of the Asamblea membership met, Rascón recalls, and "remembered what we wanted to do in 1983. We began to talk, and the Superbarrio thing came out. And from there, with the ladies who came to the meetings, some went to get the tights, others the trunks, others to find the mask" (Rascón Bandas 1997).[21] Like the "El Santo versus Mr. Atala" action, Superbarrio was supposed to be a short-term tactic, meant to add a ludic element to the Asamblea's organizing efforts. He became a permanent fixture, however, once the Asamblea discovered the effect that he had on politicians, who were unnerved by the presence of a masked man. As Rascón explains:

A very common way that demonstrators arrive at public offices is to send a commission. Now, in this transition, where the commission enters the office of the functionary, there's a change of attitude. They start ready to do battle and . . . as soon as four or five enter, there's a guy behind a desk, who says, "What is your problem?" You arrive and everything is a sanctuary, with photographs of the president . . . and someone suddenly wants to know "What do you want?" You have to express yourself well. . . . In that terrain, in that little parcel, many movements are left humiliated, we might say, no? But when suddenly Superbarrio enters the struggle (lucha), and Superbarrio appears in the office, the functionary behind his desk feels absolutely disoriented, out of order. He's the one who starts to stutter, who stumbles and knocks things over. . . . Because he knew by the presence of Superbarrio that we were mocking him.

Why did social wrestlers make sense in Mexico? The answer lies in the complex layers of signification that were already at play in lucha libre by the late 1980s. First, lucha libre had come to stand as a synecdoche for the culture of the urban popular classes and a set of claims valorizing that culture as a site of Mexican authenticity. Second, the meanings attached to lucha libre in the ring were supplemented by the meanings attached to the luchadores of the cinema.[22] The wrestler could thus symbolize the triumph of justice over corruption. But in addition to the wrestler's symbolic weight as the hero and representative of the poor (or of civil society in general), the social wrestler could articulate the interpretation of the Mexican political system that was latent in the live performance, and rework it as an explicit critique of the PRI. Superbarrio, Ecologista Universal, and the other social wrestlers used the wrestling mask as a Brechtian device: not merely a means of calling attention to the artifice of theater, but as a way to call attention to the artifice and alienation of the dominant system, and to enable the oppressed to understand it, and thus work for its overthrow. Lucha libre's potential as political theater even lay in the name of the genre: lucha, glossed as wrestling, also means struggle. Social wrestlers merely shifted the ground of struggle from the arena to the *lucha social.*

Lucha libre performance inverted the trope of masking as it was used in the political ritual of the Mexican state. Where the presidential candidate was ritually empowered through unmasking (in a gesture that implied both the generative power of the president and the heretofore hidden powers inherent in the person of the candidate) lucha libre locates power in the mask itself. In lucha libre, masking implies the assumption and maintenance of an empowered identity, and unmasking signifies divestment and humiliation. Transposed to the context of Mexican opposition parties, the lucha libre mask empowered figures such as Superbarrio.

Superbarrio created two problems for party functionaries and for the state. First, his presence at meetings changed the key (in Erving Goffman's sense) of the event, and made it difficult for politicians dealing with the

Asamblea to dominate the meeting. But in addition, Superbarrio created a problem in terms of the PRI's post-1968 strategy of neutralizing dissent by co-opting and assimilating the leadership of potential opposition.[23] In order to be co-opted, however, one must have an identity that is embedded (or can be embedded) in personal relationships. Superbarrio's "real" identity is still not a matter of public record. Some say there are many Superbarrios; some claim that Marcos Rascón Bandas is Superbarrio, some say he's really the essayist Carlos Monsiváis. He is also said to be a former wrestler, forced into retirement by chronic injuries some years before. But in another sense, Superbarrio doesn't exist as an individual at all, and since in order to be co-opted, one must have an identity, the mask granted Superbarrio the power of incorruptibility.

Whereas Superbarrio was born of collective effort, the wrestler who embodies Ecologista Universal invented the character himself, because he wanted to contribute to the struggle against the Laguna Verde nuclear reactor. Before his transformation in 1987, he was a wrestler, struggling with problems with alcoholism and depression. His life changed when he saw a television documentary on the monarch butterfly. As he explained to me (January 1997), seeing the butterfly's long migration motivated him "to reflect, to take a moral inventory. What had I done? Like the insect, I fought for life." Inspired, he decided to develop a wrestling character who could leave the ring and to participate in the struggle for the environment. To find a name, he looked in the dictionary. "I went to the dictionary and found *ecología, ecologismo . . . ecologista.* Since the lucha for the defense of nature is universal, I needed a universal vision, so I chose Ecologista Universal." His costume was designed to symbolize his new commitment: a green cape bordered with yellow flowers and lined with white ("the flowers represent hope, because they become fruit; green and yellow represent nature and the sun; white represents the purity of the sky"), and a single black glove ("the costume represents the cycle of life, so the black glove represents death").

Ecologista Universal's approach to political activity has been less playful than that of Superbarrio's. His actions have made use of forms of protest traditionally associated with Catholic religious ritual: pilgrimage and fasting. For example, he fasted against NAFTA (North American Free Trade Agreement) in 1991 and again in 1993. After the 1992 gas explosion in Guadalajara, he walked across Jalisco, Michoacán, Hidalgo, Querétaro, México, Tlaxcala, and other states to inform people about the explosion and connect it to the movement against nuclear power. He also carried a wooden cross from Jalapa, Veracruz (his home) to Laguna Verde, Veracruz, to protest the power plant itself. He toured for clean elections in 1994, and walked from the monument Angel de la Independencia in Mexico City to San Miguel Chiapas for peace. However, he also participated in more theatrical forms of ritual protest, fighting lucha libre matches against his enemy El Depredador (The Despoiler), and (along with SuperAnimal), performing a "destapa" of a Green Party candidate by pulling a pillowcase off his head in 1997. As a result of his very visible political activities, he has been beaten up several times during his campaigns. Thus, he says that his visibility makes him vulnerable; his mask makes it easier for thugs to identify him. But the mask also helps him gain supporters. "It makes it easier to present the struggle as universal, to say, 'I am the people, I exist, and I do not agree with what is going on.'"

CONCLUSION

The lucha libre mask is not simply a gimmick, not simply an element of costume. On the contrary, the mask has been of crucial importance in the construction of lucha libre as a signifying practice. The presence of the mask has several interrelated effects. First, it has an impact on performance itself by serving as the motor for a range of narrative tropes. Symbolizing the masked wrestler's honor, it provides the pretext for attacks on that honor and for its defense. Because it is so central to the performance, and because it is beautiful, the mask serves as a metonym for the genre itself. And because of its centrality, the mask connects lucha libre with other discourses of nation, class, and culture in which masks (whether actual or metaphoric) are important.

Many writers and artists have asserted that the masks of lucha libre demonstrate a continuity between indigenous Mexico (whether pre-Hispanic or contemporary) and the urban present. The lucha libre mask is not, however, a direct continuation of rural tradition. Its history is rooted in the urban, modernizing environment of Mexico City in the 1930s, and its link with indigenous practice is filtered through the nationalist discourse of the postrevolutionary state. Nevertheless, the association of masks with the civilizations of the pre-Columbian past, the "México profundo" of the indigenous present, and the modern, urban practice of lucha libre empowers the latter with a complex set of symbolic, affective associations. It allows lucha libre to represent a new model of national culture that transcends the hackneyed division between the modern and the indigenous.

But the mask has a symbolic function beyond that of unifying the urban and the Indian. The centrality of masking in lucha libre allows the elaboration of a primarily visual, corporeal conversation about myth and secrecy and about the relationship between personhood, individuality, and role. Insofar as lucha libre is a conversation about social agency, the mask provides a symbolic means of communicating a series of propositions about mid- to late-twentieth-century Mexican political culture. For over sixty years lucha libre set up a mise-en-scène in which the battle between good and evil was always arbitrated by corrupt authorities. It provided a space for a playful commentary about the political system as a whole. The mask allowed it to add a crucial element—it portrayed the struggle for power as a dialectic of concealment and disclosure. The act of hiding a wrestler's face with a mask both personalizes and depersonalizes. It allows the male wrestler to become a transcendent, mythic figure, even as it may mark him as the heir to his father's or uncle's very identity. It portrays masking as an empowering act and unmasking as a disaster. The discourse of the lucha libre mask thus provided a parodic contrast with some of the central metaphors of the twentieth-century Mexican state. In a system in which "unmasking" was used to empower the presidential candidate, lucha libre insisted on recognizing that power was found behind the scenes and before the matches— behind the mask, but also *in* the fact of the mask itself.

Originally published in 1995.

NOTES

Unless otherwise noted, all translations are my own.
1. As I learned in practicing lucha libre, the acrobatic moves place an enormous strain on the feet and ankles. When the feet land at the end of a lucha libre–style forward roll, there is a shock, and the foot absorbing the impact slides toward the inside. To protect the wrestler, the boot needs to provide a lot of shock absorption, a lot of ankle support, and extra reinforcement on the arch side of the toe box. The elder Martínez designed a boot, still used by wrestlers, that is nearly knee high, with a heavy rubber sole, built in arch support, and a reinforced toe box.

2. Andy Coe (1992), in fact, attributes the craze for masked wrestlers to the popularity of the Phantom comics.

3. A friend whose uncle worked for the Churubusco film studios in the 1960s told me the following story about El Santo's protection of his anonymity. When the man, now in his forties, was a boy, his uncle would often invite him to visit the studio with his cousin while they were filming. One of those times, they went to watch them film an El Santo movie. The wrestler would arrive at the studio every morning with his mask in place, and would keep it on throughout the day, even during meals. The uncle tried to convince El Santo that it was safe to come without his mask until it was time to shoot — after all, hundreds of people worked in the studio, and no one would associate an anonymous worker with the great El Santo. The wrestler finally agreed, and one day left the mask off as he went to lunch.

The uncle, however, had noticed that El Santo always ate the same thing for lunch, and so when lunchtime arrived he looked for a bulky man eating *chilaquiles* with chicken and cream. He then bribed his son and nephew to go up to the stranger eating the chilaquiles, and say to him: "Santo, we really admire you." They did, and to their surprise and bewilderment, the man jumped, clasped his face, and ran off "shrieking like a showgirl."

But even more puzzling to my informant (who did not know about the dubbing) was what happened when the cameras started to roll and El Santo (now recognizable in his mask) stood facing the other actors, and, when it came time for his lines began to gesticulate and intone "one, two, three, four. . . ."

4. Variations on the role of "sacred clown" have been reported in indigenous communities from Chiapas to Sonora. Examples include the Yaqui p'askola (Lutes 1983) in Sonora, who dance at a variety of saint's festivals; the Mayo pariseiro in southern Sonora and northern Sinoloa, who crucify Christ in the Passion play (Crumrine and Halpin 1983); and the k'ohetik in Chiapas, who appear during the festival of Carnival to parody the municipal officials (Bricker 1973).

5. The pastorela originated in the sixteenth century as a tool of Catholic missionization. In older versions, the play portrays the Journey of the Magi. The Three Magi are set upon by demons, who try to keep them from their goal and are defended by angels, who assist them on their way (Sánchez Hernández 1997).

6. *La fiesta de los tastoanes*, a combat play performed in Jocotán, Jalisco, and studied by Nájera-Ramírez, portrays the Spanish conquest of the Indians, but it mixes in elements of the Easter Passion Play.

7. John Emigh (1996), for example, discovers a continuum of sorts, in the masking practices of several genres of Hindu drama (in Orissa, India, and in Bali). In some genres, masks are understood to facilitate "visitation" by the sometimes dangerous divine beings that the masks are believed to contain (in both senses of the word). During performance, a performer might or might not enter a trance state, which would allow the supernatural entity to act directly, using the dancer's masked body. That need not happen for the performance to take place — if the entity does not take over, the performer can follow the script. In other genres, masks represent characters (rather than divinities), which dancers inhabit by "referencing the aesthetics of ancestral visitation" (Emigh 1996: 125).

8. Lucha libre is overseen by an office of the Federal District by the Commission (originally Comisión de Box y Lucha Libre). The Commission was founded in the late 1930s as a branch of the Oficina de Espectáculos Públicos (Office of Public Spectacles), itself a division of the Departamento del Distrito Federal (DDF — the government of the Federal District). The commission is supposed to regulate all aspects of the spectacle, from setting the basic rules and determining what activities would be permitted in performance, to licensing wrestlers and referees, to registration of characters.

9. When wrestlers go on tour outside of Mexico, the problems of border crossings can be literalized. Several people told me that El Santo had an agreement with U.S. customs that he would be taken to an office to remove his mask, so that only one or two customs agents would see his face or his passport.

10. Although most masked wrestlers struggle to keep their faces hidden, others are sometimes less careful. For example, anyone can visit a sandwich shop in the Historic Center which is owned and run by Super Astro, a wrestling star who has worked in three different leagues over the course of about twenty years. The walls are covered with lucha libre paraphernalia, including photographs of Super Astro, defying gravity as he launches himself off of the ropes and onto his opponent. At times a video of his career history runs on the television monitor. It is not hard, then, to recognize the unmistakable body (his nickname is "grape body"), busily pulling espressos below a round, unmasked, and balding head.

11. *Lucha libre* is organized by empresas, private enterprises minimally consisting of a promoter and a stable of wrestlers. An empresa might or might not own its own arena(s). A "promoter" may be the owner of an empresa, an agent for individual wrestlers, or the owner of an arena. The stability of any of these entities depends on their overlap. An empresa without an arena is in an inherently unstable position, as is an arena owner without wrestlers. The only empresa in Mexico City to succeed in maintaining both elements over a long period of time is the EMLL (Empresa Méxicano de la Lucha Libre). The first and oldest empresa in Mexico, the EMLL owns both of the main arenas in the Federal District. In addition to the EMLL, many smaller empresas have operated in and around Mexico City. At the time of my research, the EMLL's main competition came from two large-scale empresas that operated without permanent access to any particular arena. The first, the AAA (its name was later changed to PAPSA), was owned by the mass media conglomerate Televisa. The second, Promo Azteca, was owned by rival television station TV Azteca. For further discussion of the politics of mediation, see Levi (2001).

12. The very biggest stars, such as Hijo del Santo or Mil Mascaras, are independent agents. Their mask collection reflects not only their position within whatever leagues they have worked in, but their position in lucha libre as a whole.

13. The thing inherited is not the physical object, but the design. Masks can get torn, can wear out, and at minimum can get very sweaty, so a masked wrestler actually owns several copies of the same mask. Sometimes the mask can come in different colors or in different materials. The design, however, is usually stable and is passed on.

14. Eerily, although the date fell near the sixty-fourth anniversary of the debut of lucha libre in Mexico (21 September), it fell directly on the twelfth anniversary of the 1985 earthquake that devastated Mexico City.

15. Minis are small wrestlers (some are dwarves, and some are just men approximately under five feet tall), who usually enter the ring as "mini" versions of full-size stars.

16. As far as I can tell, the series fell through. I never saw it listed or otherwise mentioned again.

17. Speeches of Hijo del Santo and Negro Casas are from a transcript of Televisa broadcast of the match.

18. This was, incidentally, in violation of a Commission regulation which prohibits bringing national or religious symbols into the ring.

19. For analyses of the political system under the PRI, see M. C. Needler (1998), Peter Smith (1979), and Ilya Adler and Claudio Lomnitz (1993). For a historical account of the PRI's electoral tactics (among other things), see Agustín (1994 [1990]). The remarkably resilient system faced its first serious challenge in 1988.

20. Actually, El Santo retired in 1983, but didn't die until February of 1984. I learned of the date after my last contact with Rascón Bandas, so I don't know whether he misremembered the date of the action, or the reasoning behind it.

21. Superbarrio's costume references a number of pop culture icons. In addition to his association with lucha libre and El Santo, and the allusion to Superman, the costume's colors allude to a television character called El Chapulín Colorado (the Red Grasshopper). The Chapulín, a creation of the comedian Chespirito, is a comic antihero. He fights crime and protects the innocent, but his triumphs are always due to the unintended consequences of his clumsiness. The Superbarrio figure thus simultaneously references the "cultural imperialism" of the North American comic book and the Mexican mass-mediated figure of the sympathetic incompetent, as well as the cinematic and live incarnations of lucha libre.

Superbarrio himself gives a different account of his own origins, which further separates his quotidian identity to his function as Superbarrio:

> I was evicted for the first time when I was eight years old, and the second time when I was eleven. I have felt the unfairness of the landlords, the abuse of police—those I have lived. Afterward, when the earthquake happened, I was one of the damaged, and I participated in the neighborhood organizations of the Center. Now I'm a street vendor. One day, 12 June 1987, at about 7:30 in the morning, when I opened the door of the house to go to work, a red light blew into my room and whirled everything around in my room. When it calmed down, when the light disappeared and the wind stopped blowing, I had on the mask and clothing of Superbarrio, and a voice said to me: You are Superbarrio, defender of the poor tenants and evictor of the voracious landlords. With all the concern that I had over the evictions and for the people who came to complain that they had been evicted, it was the response to that mortification that had happened to me so many times. (Cuéllar-Vásquez 1993: 103)

22. I address these issues in chap. 7 of Levi (2001).

23. For examples of how such co-optation is carried out with ambulant vendors, squatter settlements, and right-wing cultural activists, see Cross (1998), Vélez-Ibáñez (1983), and Rubenstein (1998) respectively.

REFERENCES

Agustín, José. 1994 [1990]. *Tragicomedia mexicana*. Vol. 1. Mexico City: Editorial Planeta.

Alipi, Dario. 1994. "Entrevista con Sergio Arau: La lucha en el Art-Nacco." *Colosos de la Lucha Libre*, no. 41.

Box y Lucha. 1955a. *Mascaramania* 1. 1 May.

———. 1955b. *Mascaramania II*. 15 May.

Bricker, Victoria. 1973. *Ritual Humor in Highland Chiapas*. Austin: University of Texas Press.

Coe, Andrew. 1992. "La mascara! La mascara!" *Icarus* 8:157–70.

Cuéllar Vásquez, Angélica. 1993. *La noche es de ustedes, el amanecer es nuestro: Asamblea de Barrios y Superbarrio Gómez*. Mexico City: Universidad Nacional Autónoma de México.

Cross, James. 1998. *Informal Politics*. Palo Alto, Calif.: Stanford University Press.

Crumrine, N. Ross, and Marjorie Halpin, eds. 1983. *The Power of Symbols: Masks and Masquerade in the Americas*. Vancouver, B.C.: University of British Columbia Press.

El Santo. 1984. Interview with Jacobo Zabludovsky. Televisa Channel 8. Mexico City, 3 February.

Emigh, John. 1996. *Masked Performance: The Play of Self and Other in Ritual and Theater*. Philadelphia: University of Pennsylvania Press.

Fascinetto, Lola Miranda. 1992. *Sin máscara ni caballera: La lucha libre en México hoy*. Mexico City: Marc Ediciones.

Gilmore, Frances. 1983. "Symbolic Representations in Mexican Combat Plays." In *The Power of Symbols: Masks and Masquerade in the Americas*, ed. N. Ross Crumrine and Marjorie Halpin. Vancouver, B.C.: University of British Columbia Press.

Golden, Tim. 1995. "Mexico's New Offensive: Erasing Rebel's Mystique." *New York Times*, 11 February, 1.

Guillermoprieto, Alma. 1995. "The Unmasking." *New Yorker*, 13 March, 40–47.

Interview with wrestler from Promo Azteca. 1996. *En Caliente*. Channel 13, 13 October.

Jares, Joe. 1974. *What Ever Happened to Gorgeous George?* Englewood, N.J.: Prentice Hall.

Levi, Heather. 2001. "Masked Media: The Adventures of Lucha Libre on the Small Screen." In *Fragments of a Golden Age: The Politics of Culture in Mexico Since 1940*, ed. Gilbert Joseph, Anne Rubenstein, and Eric Zolov. Durham, N.C.: Duke University Press.

Lomnitz Adler, Claudio. 1992. *Exits from the Labyrinth: Culture and Ideology in Mexican National Space*. Berkeley: University of California Press.

Lomnitz, Claudio, and Ilya Adler. 1993. "The Function of the Form." In *Constructing Culture and Power in Latin America*, ed. Daniel Levine. Anne Arbor, Mich.: University of Michigan Press.

Lucha Libre. 1954. No Title. 1 April.

Lutes, Steven V. 1983. "The Mask and Magic of Yaqui Paskola Clowns." In *The Power of Symbols: Masks and Masquerade in the Americas*, ed. N. Ross Crumrine and Marjorie Halpin. Vancouver, B.C.: University of British Columbia Press.

Martínez, Víctor. 1997. Interview with author.

Moebius, Janna. 1997. Personal communication. June.

Morales, Alfonso. 1998. "La máscara rota." *Luna Córnea* 14 (Centro de Imagen): 88–97.

Nájera-Ramírez, Olga. 1997. *La Fiesta de los Tastoanes*. Albuquerque: University of New Mexico Press.

Needler, M. C. 1998. *Mexican Politics: The Containment of Conflict*. Westport, Conn.: Praeger Publishers.

Paz, Octavio. 1985 [1961]. *The Labyrinth of Solitude and the Other Mexico, Return to the Labyrinth of Solitude, Mexico and the United States, The Philanthropic Ogre*. Trans. Lysander Kemp, Yara Milos, and Rachel Phillips Belash. New York: Grove Weidenfeld.

Pernet, Henry. 1992. *Ritual Masks: Deceptions and Revelations*. Columbia: University of South Carolina Press.

Rascón Bandas, Marcos. 1997. Interview with author, September.

Rubenstein, Anne. 1998. *Bad Language, Naked Ladies, and Other Threats to the Nation*. Durham, N.C.: Duke University Press.

Rugos, Ralph. 1994. "Q: What's the Difference Between Superman and Superbarrio? A: Superbarrio exists!" *LA Weekly*, 14–20 January.

Sánchez Hernández, Carlos Alfonso. 1997. *Máscara y danzas tradicionales*. Toluca, Mexico: Universidad Autónoma.

Saunders, Neil. 1998. *Icons of Power: Feline Symbolism in the Americas*. New York: Routledge.

Smith, Peter H. 1979. *Labyrinths of Power: Political Recruitment in Twentieth Century Mexico*. Princeton, N.J.: Princeton University Press.

Valentino. 1993. La Máscara. *Diario de Yucatán*, 9 May.

Vélez-Ibáñez, Carlos. 1983. *Rituals of Marginality: Politics, Process, and Culture Change in Central Urban Mexico*. Berkeley: University of California Press.

Weiner, Annette. 1993. *Inalienable Possessions*. Berkeley: University of California.

NICHOLAS SAMMOND

Squaring the Family Circle:

WWF *Smackdown* Assaults

the Social Body

I t is Thanksgiving night, 1999, and the TV is tuned to WWF *Smackdown!*
on the United Paramount Network (UPN). The World Wrestling Federation (WWF, since 2002 the WWE) has only recently come to prime-time
broadcast television, and is an overnight sensation, drawing upwards of
5 million viewers a night.[1] This evening's program was taped before a live
audience in Rochester, New York. As is the case with the WWF's hit cable
show, RAW, the program moves between matches on the main floor of the
arena and backstage, where soap-operatic tales of intrigue and double-
dealing play out between wrestlers, partners, and the upper management of
the WWF (owner Vince McMahon, wife Linda, daughter Stephanie, and son
Shane). Each program follows a pattern. The opening matches usually feature less popular wrestlers from the WWF roster or promising newcomers
brought up for a national tryout. The program builds toward 9 PM and a
bout between mid- or top-card wrestlers, then settles in for smaller bouts
and backstage drama until about 9:45, when the final match, around which
the evening's storylines have been building, will (hopefully) close out the
show with a bang.

Tonight, The Rock, at this point the most popular WWF wrestler ("the
most electrifying man in sports-entertainment") is on the microphone ringside, admiring a huge Thanksgiving meal set up alongside the announcers'
table. Dressed in calf-length leather boots and bikini briefs, his hairless body
oiled and shining, he extols the merits of each dish, including one dessert
labeled "poontang pie" (the pleasures of which, he suggests, the ringside

announcers have never known). Soon after The Rock and Mankind make short work of the Holly Brothers, the action moves backstage, where Hunter Hearst Helmsley—commonly known as Triple H and rapidly becoming the most popular heel in the w w F—is plotting revenge against Vince McMahon for having robbed him of the championship belt. Triple H has invited home-less men backstage for a charitable Thanksgiving dinner. While the suspi-ciously well-dressed "bums" wait for permission to eat, Triple H and his henchmen, Degeneration X, whisper among themselves; apparently this act of charity is not as generous as it seems. In the end, the homeless are cast out unfed, the gambit an effort to discredit McMahon. By 9:45, the poontang pie has ended up in Jerry "King" Lawler's face, Degeneration X is beating Shane McMahon senseless, and Vince calls for reinforcements. Within minutes the ring fills with wrestlers pummeling each other randomly and violently. In-evitably, the brawl becomes a food fight, and soon wrestlers are beating foes over the head with whole turkeys, flinging mashed potatoes into the audi-ence, slipping on slicks of cranberry sauce and destroying the announcers' table . . . as announcer Michael Cole wishes the home audience a Happy Thanksgiving. . . .

What does the troubling, incoherent, exuberant excess of the w w f's version of Thanksgiving mean? Triple H's backhanded gesture—offering charity to the homeless and then withdrawing it—seems a perfect repre-sentation of working-class contempt for the apparent refusal of the able-bodied poor to work for their food and shelter. Yet the character Hunter Hearst Helmsley began as a spoiled rich kid from Greenwich, Connecticut, slumming in the world of wrestling. Is his gesture, then, a representation of working-class resentment or an example of the baser motives behind the largesse of the rich, to keep the poor weak and dependent on charity? And what of the final melee, in which the bounty of the Thanksgiving meal—the essential celebration of American family togetherness—is purposely wasted in an orgy of riotous violence? Is it biting satire that points out celebrations of abundance in the midst of want, or merely a gratuitous festival of excess? Or is it, as L. Brent Bozell III, the head of the Parents Television Council, has described professional wrestling: "pornography propaganda" and "gar-bage . . . aimed directly at children . . . at the start of the Family Hour" (Bozell 1999; Bozell 2000)?

Whether professional wrestling is progressive, transgressive, or regressive (or all of these at different moments) depends on how it serves the social goals of its producers, performers, audiences, and critics — not just what it *means*, but who shapes that meaning and to what expected ends. Therefore, to make sense of *Smackdown*, one must move beyond the performances themselves to consider the social and cultural circumstances in which that sense is made — by wrestling's fans, performers, and critics. In this essay, I will argue that it is especially important to understand the WWF as both an entertainment vehicle and a marketing tool. While it is crucial to notice the class, race, and gender antagonisms that surround *Smackdown*, it is equally necessary to see its version of social disruption as a response to the history of network broadcasting. Wrestling first appeared on TV in the postwar years, but disappeared from prime time when the networks and advertisers directed the medium toward an idealized middle-class family. For decades, network television has claimed to represent and serve such families, addressing mothers in particular as the focal point of domestic moral regulation and consumption. That model has broken down in recent decades, however, and at the same time wrestling has reemerged, but in a different form. What was once a popular entertainment that spanned class lines, like vaudeville and variety television, has come back as a representation of working-class rebellion specifically tied to youth culture: a fantasy of impropriety that adolescent boys are meant to use to thumb their noses at the imagined descendants of June Cleaver. The WWF is the antifamily to television's ideal family.

Here I examine not only the rhetoric used by social critics of televised professional wrestling (journalists, columnists, and media-reform groups) and responses to that criticism by the WWF, its sponsors, and advertisers, but also the consequences of staging social conflict in terms of family dysfunction. In the extratextual smackdown that takes place between the two sides in the press, each side needs the other as heel to its face, and both benefit from the heat they produce. Wrestling's critics loudly and publicly decry its impropriety in order to elicit funds and to move their constituents to pressure legislators, advertisers, and broadcasters to police the form. The WWF welcomes and repudiates this rhetoric of reform, gaining credibility with its audiences by portraying its critics as prudish, "politically correct," and ignorant about the fluidity of identity or the difference between representation and reality.

Of particular importance in this mutually constitutive discourse are the meanings assigned to the family and to adolescence. In terms both implicit and explicit, wrestling's critics argue that the consumption of WWF products (along with rap, heavy metal, and video games) encourages white, middle-class children and adolescents to imitate the behaviors of members of the white and nonwhite underclass, making those children hostile to middle-class values and resistant to parental authority. Mobilizing this criticism on its own behalf, the WWF revels in its impropriety, creating storylines that portray social reformers as self-interested hypocrites and the nouveau riche McMahons (real-life officers of the company) as a parody of TV's model family, one engaged in an intergenerational battle for corporate control and willing to use violence, sex, and class and racial animus to achieve their goals. *Smackdown* (and RAW, the WWF's more "adult" cable offering) draws a great deal of its vitality—if not the premise behind many of its storylines—from that opposition: it is designed to mobilize criticism in the service of its sneering alterity, to counter any easy narrative containment through its trash-talking, beer-swilling, tit-jiggling affront to the polite liberal mores that make prime-time American television generally so safe, so predictable, so utterly unwilling to offend or misspeak (cf. DuttaAhmed 1998). *Smackdown* joins wrestling's working-class roots to commodified adolescent nihilism in its trademarked "Attitude": it aestheticizes and packages unruliness, a refusal to behave and to internalize discipline.

Yet an emphasis on adolescence constrained by and resisting family dynamics limits our understanding of viewership: not only adolescent boys watch *Smackdown*, even though the show and its advertisers seem to address themselves to that imagined viewer. Ads that play during and within the program, and cross-promotions (WWF theme-song collections, action figures, T-shirts, etc.) pitch video games, music, clothing, snack food, and action movies. The audience for *Smackdown* (as for many of these other products) extends well beyond this demographic, faring best with men aged eighteen to forty-nine, garnering an enthusiastic following on college campuses, and drawing significant numbers of women.[2]

In what way, then, are differences of gender, sexuality, race, ethnicity, and class highlighted by this address? If the show reaches far more than children, why are they its imagined audience? What the WWF offers in *Smackdown* is a representational fantasy of "adolescent" impropriety—the abandonment of the political rectitude deemed necessary for civil society in favor of the unabashed expression of uncivil relations of power and pleasure—that is attractive to adolescents, and to a significant number of nonadolescents as well. What its critics fear is that children and adolescents watching the WWF will fail to understand it as a fantasy, will treat its often racist, homophobic, and misogynist social relations as real, and model their lives after it.

THE GREAT IRONY behind the WWF's sudden popularity is that it *is* modeling reality: the return of professional wrestling to prime-time broadcast television after a fifty-year hiatus is the return of a suppressed class conflict. In the postwar era, performances of sexuality, ethnic and racial identity, and improper social decorum associated with the working class were pushed to the margins of the airwaves in favor of a propriety represented by the middle-class family. In the trajectory of the American Dream, behaviors associated with the working class have always marked an imagined social adolescence on the evolutionary path of upward mobility into the more mature middle class. The excitement and outrage that have attended the WWF's entry into prime time have made clearer that link between adolescent rebellion or resistance and underclass impropriety, bringing class conflict into the private sphere of the home. Creating a fantasy of empowerment through that impropriety, the WWF has evoked and called into question the consuming middle-class family as the symbolic center of the social order, and the ways in which TV's "focus on the family" places an impossible burden on this ideal unit as the governor of social and moral order.

Because the excitement and moral panic that erupted around professional wrestling arose when *Smackdown* burst onto broadcast television, I will discuss the historical role of TV in linking regimes of consumption, social action, and family life (and wrestling's exclusion from that process).[3] Then, because this contestation is framed in terms of the *consumption* of proper and improper representations, I will examine how popular conceptions of people as consuming subjects both permit and constrain social action in American society, and why children and youth — who are imagined as enthusiastic and vulnerable consumers — become focal points in arguments about the power of representations to shape social life. Finally, having provided a frame for understanding the WWF's assault on "family values," I will return to a close reading of the battle between the company and its critics, and how wrestling (a performance form centered on struggle and contestation) is constituted as a location where certain forms of speech and behavior become stereotypically "adolescent" — a demographic category both feared for its seeming lack of social responsibility and desired for its economic power.

Punch-drunk palooka Mountain McClintock (Jack Palance) listens as his manager, Maish Renick (Keenan Wynn, right), tries to convince him to become a professional wrestler. McClintock's trainer, Army (Ed Wynn, left), looks on sadly, regretting what both men are becoming. *Wisconsin Center for Film and Theater Research*

TELEVISED WRESTLING: CLASS CONTACT
(SPORTS) IN HISTORICAL CONTEXT

Although professional wrestling was a mainstay of prime-time network television's early years, by 1956 and Rod Serling's dramatic portrayal of wrestling, *Requiem for a Heavyweight*, it no longer appeared during television's family-viewing period. In *Requiem*, a live television drama, a failing, punch-drunk boxer is cajoled by his manager into playing a hillbilly on a regional wrestling circuit in order to pay off the manager's gambling debts. Serling's version of wrestling is a seedy underworld populated by derelicts, freaks, failed athletes, and parasitic bookers. The trajectory of the story is one of a collective fall from grace, from the nobility of true sport to the sham of tawdry fixed performances in an irredeemable backwater of the human spirit populated by lonely, broken individuals.[4] Creating a revisionist hierarchy, this story positioned wrestling as outside of a mainstream, progressive history of American culture and of the dream world then taking shape in its new suburbs.[5] Like its cousins, vaudeville and burlesque, wrestling belonged to a past the postwar United States was leaving behind.

Requiem attested to wrestling's marginalization in the medium it helped to establish. From 1948 to 1954 (first on NBC, then on newcomer ABC), it occupied the late edge of prime-time programming, showing for an hour at 9:30 or 10 PM.[6] After 1954, it vanished from evening programming and increasingly appeared locally, not nationally. Along with live TV and variety television (the last remnant of burlesque and vaudeville, it had generally occupied the dinner hour), wrestling was edged aside by sitcoms, which were growing in popularity, and by prerecorded crime dramas and westerns.[7] Responding to a variety of institutional pressures — from critics who saw television as an ideal vehicle for improving American culture, to advertisers who wanted the medium to more closely model the world in which their products would appear, to reform groups fearful that TV engendered violence, sexuality, and antisocial behaviors in children, to audiences that wanted to be entertained — broadcast networks in the 1950s struggled to create a representational environment that balanced entertainment and social relevance (Boddy 1990; Taylor 1989; Baughman 1992; Brook 1999; Lipsitz 1990).

To claim, however, that wrestling's exclusion from prime-time television was simply the outcome of the consolidation and standardization of the industry is to oversimplify the matter somewhat. Wrestling arrived on national television during the emergence of what was called the *mass middle class*, the rapid upward mobility of U.S. workers during the postwar economic boom. As American industries capitalized on the boom, the J. Walter Thompson advertising agency asked potential clients, "And what of America's great *new middle class* . . . the millions of families who have moved up several notches in income without changing their habits to match? Are you sure you are getting your share of that *new* sales potential?" (J. Walter Thompson 1949; italics in original). The very middle class that was meant to set an example for European immigrants and the working classes in the previous generation was suddenly swelling with newly prosperous members of those groups, and old cultural and social markers of proper class behavior seemed threatened by the insufficiently assimilated. At the same time, though, those social boundaries were also barriers to a new market, and the appeal that advertisers such as Thompson pitched to the members of this new "mass class" was not based on catering to the tastes and prejudices of their working-class roots, but on a fantasy of what proper middle-class life should look like—one based on consumption as class behavior. Rank with the imagined smell of sweat, raucous with the wrangling of wrestlers and the catcalls of its audience, wrestling represented contact between the old working-class culture and a new middle-class culture as a vector of infection, the introduction of improper and destabilizing behaviors into middle-American culture (cf. Dell 1998). Given its necessary impropriety and its low-budget appeal, wrestling was a poor fit for an emerging middle-class domestic fantasy (see, e.g., Spigel 1992: 65).

Even before the arrival of television, marketers had identified women—particularly wives and mothers—as the primary decision makers in domestic consumption patterns (Hilmes 1999). Furthermore, they recognized that in middle-class and upwardly mobile homes, women were more likely to view domestic purchases as an outward expression of the social and cultural status of their families (see, for instance, Katz and Lazarsfeld 1955; see also Lears 1994 and Strasser 1989). As managers of domestic space, women were also the ones encouraged to regulate the role that TV would play in the social and cultural life of the family (Spigel 1992: 36–73). These assumptions were replicated in popular depictions of television and other modern conveniences, as well as in TV advertising and programming. Live television drama in the late 1940s and 1950s, for instance, often held as its central theme the tensions surrounding difficult negotiations of instant assimilation into the new (white) mass middle class, and the shedding of traces of ethnicity and old-world culture, with women usually cast as the primary advocates for modernization. While markers of ethnicity or class were assigned to a receding past in live drama, the increasingly popular situation comedies that were gradually edging out those shows tended to feature an ideal present.[8] In sitcoms, the social reality represented on television screens most often featured white, middle-class families in new suburban homes, using the very products that were pitched during commercial breaks, their lives devoid of the complex social problems dramatized in live programming. Thus, fantasies of both the disruption and stabilization of middle-class decorum were inscribed within a system of consumption in an attempt to create a mirror-world of ideal American living centered on the suburban family (see Spigel 1992; Schudson 1984; Barnouw 1978; Brook 1999).[9] The prime-time family of the 1950s, operating in a recursive loop between the two sides of the screen, circulated as a fantasy of a middle-class matriarchal unit based around consumption (see Taylor 1989). Against this model, which accommodated the sociology of domestic relations to the institutional needs of sponsors and advertisers (i.e., demographics), wrestling's regressive address to working-class sensibilities made it a poor candidate for prime time. Although wrestling's modular nature (its segmentation into discrete bouts) made it ideal for commercial interruption, its extreme dislocation from the narrative of modernization made it hard to integrate into a fantasy of suburban uplift.[10]

The homogenization of prime-time television in the late 1950s and early 1960s was more than simply the stabilization of institutional practices in the broadcast industry. It was an effort by institutional actors—broadcasters, advertisers, producers—to isolate domestic viewers as members of an ideal family, to determine when and how each member watched, and to present entertainment that naturalized that representation of domestic social life while maintaining an emphasis on consumption. This demographic address was (and is) a reflexive practice, one that required constant adjustment and refinement. It is important to remember that the seamless, white-bread world of the Cleavers, Nelsons, and Andersons was relatively short lived, giving way to a (somewhat) more nuanced prime-time "America" by the mid-1960s.[11] Over the next two decades, prime-time broadcast television accommodated—in a cautious, limited, liberal fashion—"women's liberation," the "youth movement," integration, an increasing divorce rate, and single parenthood. More Black faces appeared after the dinner hour, women made it out of the kitchen and into the workplace, and social issues such as racial bigotry and sexual discrimination were more often addressed. In short, significant demographic, political, and cultural shifts in American society registered on the screen, but without significantly challenging the middle-class family as the organizing principle underpinning consumption.[12]

FAMILY VALUES AND THE DECREASING
VALUE OF THE FAMILY

By the mid-1980s, however, several factors converged to undermine this arrangement. The children of the baby boom, subjects of this domestic address from birth, were producing their own families in the midst of their own economic boom, one that left them—and by extension their children—

flush with cash. Children born after the baby boom were coming of age, but were staying single longer than the previous generation. At the same time, consumer cable television was becoming economically viable and popular, servicing emerging markets less interested in standard broadcast fare. Prime-time television in the 1980s was witnessing a significant shift in demographics, and in the means marketers used to reach out to different consumers. The era of the mass class was over, and the era of the niche market was in full swing (see Slater 1997). A unified idea of the "family" was giving way to one in which individual family members appeared to have greater autonomy in their tastes and decisions, and in which youth in particular were understood as increasingly independent consumers. Although the middle-class family continued to be central to prime time (particularly in comedies), it had to make room for alternative representations — from the ultrarich and vicious clans of evening soap-opera parodies, the Ewings and Carringtons, to the affectionately dysfunctional working-class families such as those in FOX's *Married . . . with Children* (1987–97) and *The Simpsons* (1989–present), and in ABC's *Roseanne* (1988–97) — as well as for audiences increasingly uninterested in the tidy morality that prime time had to offer.[13]

Perhaps the most significant indication of the diminishing value of the middle-class family as a touchstone linking regimes of representation to those of consumption was Vice President Dan Quayle's attack on *Murphy Brown* (NBC, 1988–98) during the 1992 presidential election. When the title character, a successful TV news anchor, chose to have and raise a child by herself, Quayle singled out the program as an example of the decline in "family values" in the United States. Although the attack played well with the Christian Right, the public in general was underwhelmed, and Quayle was widely ridiculed for his attempt to instigate moral outrage against broadcasters and their fictional employees.

In a sense, though, Quayle was right. The value of the family as a unified social unit of consumers was declining, and the three major networks knew it. In addition to cable's fragmenting demographic address, with the arrival of FOX in 1986 and the WB and UPN in 1995 (and their success in capturing teen, young adult, and nonwhite audiences), ABC, CBS, and NBC watched their audiences shrink.[14] Yet even as the older networks attempted to accommodate these new demographic realities, they clung to the family, either implicit or explicit, as the predominant social unit for prime-time broadcast television. And the WWF's *Smackdown*, returning wrestling to prime time after a fifty-year absence (and a successful run on cable), was no exception, building its address around the antifamily of the McMahons and their unruly children/workers. This is key to understanding the popularity of the WWF's arrival during prime time in 1998: *Smackdown* was consciously designed to appeal to a demographic segment of the population excluded from (or hostile to) the tidy and accommodating living-room and workplace life of most prime-time narratives. The family that occupied both sides of the prime-time television screen provided a perfect maternalized foil against which the WWF could fling its "adolescent" impropriety. As a cover story in *Newsweek* put it, "at a time when television has lost the ability to seduce young male viewers with sex and violence, [WWF owner Vince] McMahon has crafted a luridly compelling new delivery system" (Leland 2000: 48). *Smackdown* was more than simply sexual and violent; it was intentionally hostile to family values.

WRESTLING AND THE METAPHYSICS OF CONSUMPTION

This depiction of television as a "delivery system" in a popular periodical points to a shared awareness of television as a device for entertainment, for providing consumers with access to goods, *and* for delivering its audiences to advertisers (Smyth 1977). It also bespeaks a common understanding that television production and consumption constitute social interaction at the level of consumer demographics. Perhaps most important, though, it reiterates anxieties about television as an uncontrollable aperture through which potentially unwelcome intrusions arrive into well-ordered and private family relations. Thus, discussing the negative social effects of consuming wrestling and rap music on white, suburban children, popular-culture critic R. J. Smith declared in the *New York Times Magazine* that "professional wrestling is about family excess" without ever really explaining what "family excess" was (Smith 2000: 40). How could one have an excess of the family? The phrase suggests, perhaps, that when it brought *Smackdown* to broadcast TV, the WWF introduced an excess of meaning around the term *family* that required containment and regulation. It also points to a performance of family life that is excessive in the same way that working-class and racial subjects are excessive in the eyes of middle-class, middle-American propriety—in behaviors and attitudes that are vulgar, impolite, and resentful of moralizing authority. The meaning becomes clearer when Smith continues, "It's an old working-class entertainment that has only gotten more violent and cheesy, and through that has sucked every social class into its audience" (40).

So, a working-class entertainment polluted the middle-class family life of prime-time broadcast television, bringing its excess meanings and social relations into middle-class homes and threatening to disrupt proper American life and culture. But note the logic of this sentiment. It was *because* professional wrestling had become more violent and cheesy that it attracted viewers from outside of its demographic proper. For some reason, professional wrestling's excesses were exactly what attracted other demographics. Reporting on the immense popularity of the WWF and WCW (since bought out by the WWE) with "blue-chip marketers" of products targeted at mainstream audiences (such as soft drinks and fast food), *Advertising Age* cited a marketing executive with Turner Broadcasting, who stated, "The demographics have evolved. Wrestling fans are better educated, more affluent, and very loyal" (Jensen 1998: 3).

The damage that wrestling wreaks, then, is not so much to the actual social fabric as it is to its representation in the more sedate prime-time television that *Smackdown* opposes. Even at its most "issue-oriented," mainstream broadcast fare tends to reduce complex relationships between people to simpler markers: programming targets women of certain ages, or men — or, for FOX or UPN during certain time slots, African American middle-class audiences — or takes up race as a problem specifically between African Americans and whites, while other forms of difference are suppressed in the service of accessibility and coherence. In public discussions of this address, such as the 1999–2000 NAACP (National Association for the Advancement of Colored People) boycott of the major networks, which called for more faces of color in front of and behind the camera, we acknowledge simultaneously the construction of those categories and their potent social reality. This boycott was a noble effort to mobilize a demographic in its own service by encouraging its members to deploy what was perhaps their most effective weapon: withholding themselves as consumers. It also allowed those outside of the target group sympathetic to the cause of economic and representational equity to join in concerted demographic resistance.

The power of such practices derives in part from the widely held belief that consumption constitutes durable social action. From the generic (and often misinformed) notion of "buying American," to more specific, targeted campaigns and boycotts ("socially responsible" investing, spending "gay dollars," the Southern Baptists' campaign against Disney/ABC for being gay-friendly, etc.), moral and political action in the United States are regularly (though not exclusively) constituted through individual acts of consumption collectivized via membership in organizations built around demographic categories. Viewed as *positive* social acts, these economic campaigns are usually linked to other efforts, such as public-interest advertising and letter-writing campaigns. The assumption in these instances is of enlightened self-interest: the pursuit of a group's goals also benefits the larger society through increased tolerance, moral rectitude, inclusion, and so on. The marketplace of ideas and the marketplace of products meet in the realization of truly democratic capitalism, the competition of consumption-based "interest groups."

This type of purposeful social consumption is not the same as choosing whether to watch programs that feature Black casts (or Latino or Asian casts, if such existed on a regular basis), because the target demographic for those shows (which are almost always sitcoms) is not exclusively a Black audience; they are intended to appeal across a racial spectrum to a middle-class-oriented audience (see Jhally and Lewis 1992). As such, in their representations and in the advertising that supports them, they do nothing to directly challenge the status quo. For that type of imagined resistance, one must return to cable — to some BET programming, or hip-hop and rap on MTV, which is designed not only for Black audiences, but also for demographic "crossovers," particularly teens . . . but with a difference (see Wojcik 1993). In the case of gangsta rap programming in particular, it is designed to appeal to white youth for whom a certain version of Black culture — violent, misogynistic, fatalistic, angry — appears as an alternative to the tidy, middle-class narratives that dominate broadcast TV. As *negative* social action, this sort of consumption is imagined (and marketed) as resistance to stultifying cultural norms, a refusal to behave properly. Likewise, audiences who cross demographic boundaries by consuming professional wrestling appear to disrupt social harmony by importing working-class and racialized behaviors into an inherently middle-class mainstream. But this trend, so egregious to moralizing social reformers who patrol popular culture's precincts, is exactly what makes wrestling attractive to its audiences and to marketers.[15] In this struggle between proper and improper consumption as social action, being "working class" or "Black" is positioned as inherently adolescent — loud, irreverent, iconoclastic, excessively and chaotically sexual, and so forth

—in relation to a middle-class propriety that is white, maternal, and disapproving.

WHO ARE THESE adolescents? Far from innocent bystanders and potential victims in this contestation over the social power of popular representations, children and youth are essential to its operation. They form the vital metaphysical link in the circuit from the representation of social relations to their enactment as social reality. Adults are understood to know the difference between fact and fiction; children do not, and it is commonly assumed (in the absence of any substantial evidence) that what they see today they will do tomorrow as adults. This understanding is not simply the creation of right-wing political opportunists interested in making hay out of the decline of "family values." It is shared by a wide range of groups, including Media Watch, Children Now, the American Medical Association, and the American Psychological Association, all of which decry excesses of sex and violence on television, and all of which describe family television viewing as a primary location for the beneficial or detrimental production of persons and citizens.[16] Generally speaking, these groups base their arguments around media-effects research that attempts to isolate detrimental behavioral changes in children and youth—such as an increase in aggression or premature sexual activity—and to ascribe those changes to television viewing. Linking this research to anecdotal reports of child-on-child violence or teen sexuality, these popular advocacy groups then warn of broader social consequences—the breakdown of social norms as a direct result of unregulated media production and consumption. Inevitably, though, the anecdotal reports are shown to have no meaningful relationship to the trends they represent. Likewise, studies that link media to violence by necessity ignore so many other variables to make their case that they are soon countered by reasoned professional critique (Freedman 2002; Huesmann et al. 2003). This refutation, though, doesn't circulate as broadly as did the research it corrects, and the "fact" that media consumption can cause antisocial behavior lives on. What persists, in spite of evidence and argument to the contrary, is a widely and stubbornly held popular belief that children's consumption of media has significant and long-lasting positive or negative effects not only on individuals, but on society as a whole. Joining a belief in consumption as social action to the fear that through unregulated viewing children form antisocial behavioral constitutions, this rhetoric naturalizes socially and culturally specific qualities such as aggression or sexuality as indices of proper and improper socialization.

Whether conservative or liberal, this type of regulation serves to demonize behaviors associated with certain race and class positions and naturalize others, creating a powerful and productive fantasy of contagion and prophylaxis. From the admonitions of the openly hostile Parents Television Council (PTC), to warnings by concerned members of the Television Critics Association, to journalistic accounts in popular and marketing periodicals, a common theme is the possibility—sometimes implicit, sometimes overt—that white, middle-class youth (particularly boys) are mimicking the representations of the racially coded working-class lifestyle products they consume (see Smith 2000; Consoli 1999; Gordon 1999; Jensen 1998).[17] Commenting on a recent lawsuit by the WWF against the PTC, for instance, the *Wall Street Journal* reported on the efforts of prominent PTC board members (which include Senator Joseph Lieberman and comedian Steve Allen) to shame WWF advertisers:

> At an MCI WorldCom shareholders meeting earlier this year, [C. Dolores Tucker, president of the National Political Congress of Black Women] quoted from a monologue delivered by a black *WWF Smackdown* wrestler called the "Godfather": "It's time for everybody to come aboard the 'Ho' Train. Hey, I ain't the only one. Is there any pimps in this house? Well, if you are, you oughta know, the Godfather, the real Godfather, be pimpin' 'hoes' nationwide. Man, I want you to reach in that bag, roll a fatty for this pimp daddy, light that stinky green up and say, 'Pimpin' ain't easy.'" ("Grudge Match" 2000)

Ms. Tucker's concern seemed to be with the perpetuation of an egregious racist stereotype. As one might expect, though, the *Journal* avoided a serious discussion of the long history of the representation of Black men as pimps and drug dealers in film and television, focusing instead on the appeal of that stereotype to the youth market and the implicit disapproval of parents: "Most of us can see how this kind of thing would bring in the teenage boys on Thursday nights. Likewise, most would see why it's also the kind of thing Mr. McMahon is not to eager to have . . . the PTC bring before the WWF's corporate advertisers" (ibid.).

What goes unexamined in this sort of discussion is why undefined "teenage boys" might find the stereotype attractive, or why sponsors for *Smack-*

down might gladly fund its depiction until publicly shamed into threatening to withdraw their support.[18] What is missing is the appropriate narrative frame that would render the representation legible as morally bankrupt.[19] As Anna McCarthy (2001) suggests in her discussion of the use of hip-hop in point-of-sale marketing to teens, figures such as The Godfather and his Hos (a "pimp" and a group of scantily clad women who danced around him before matches) are unimportant to marketers as symbols of redemption or its failure; rather, they are aggregates of desire: "Key terms like *urban* and *suburban* (rather than *black* or *white*) are more than just *euphemisms* for race; they are terms that encourage identification with racially coded market categories—not people. Modeling brand-name styles, video images of black performers help to facilitate a white teen's identification with a consumer *profile* that is mnemonically represented by black consumption's most visible embodiment on the national stage: the hip-hop star" (191–92; italics in original). The common concern of organizations interested in regulating media production and consumption is that through this identification—which provides an affective hook designed to make products more appealing to their target market—teenagers will incorporate inappropriate ideas of social interaction into their behavioral matrix. In doing so, they will damage both the larger social fabric and their own futures: they will translate their *identification* with inappropriate objects into an *identity* that is personally and socially destructive. The explicit sexuality, violence, and racial animosity/stereotyping/bonding of professional wrestling —as well as its appeal to adult audiences—provide fodder for a reformist discourse concerned with a childhood or adolescence polluted by inappropriate adult behaviors that youth are ill equipped to understand as wrong. Understanding adolescents as persons in formation (as opposed to adults, who are ostensibly fully and irrevocably formed), this alarmist discourse collapses complex mechanisms of identification into the relatively simple process of consumption, and the improvement of society into the regulation of the products consumed.

The intersection of race, class, and sexuality in the figures of The Godfather and his Hos was unacceptable, not simply because of the stereotyping of a Black pimp and his victims/workers, but because they (and their fans) *celebrated* their illiberal performance of naked commodity relations rather than performing in a narrative of redemption which rejected those stereotypes in favor of more universal standards of individual uplift and self-improvement (cf. Jhally and Katz 2000).[20] Indeed, the WWF made this rejection all the more explicit when The Godfather (becoming "The Good-father") joined the wrestling collective Right to Censor (RTC), a parody of the Parents Television Council in which "reformed" wrestlers dressed like Mormon missionaries. Covering their formerly exposed bodies with black pants, white button-down shirts, and black neckties, Right to Censor used underhanded tactics to defeat their opponents and to force them to renounce excesses of sexual expression and gratuitous violence. In pre- and postmatch speeches, members of the group mouthed pieties about the positive contributions they were making to society, yet exposed those sentiments as hollow through the use of immoral tactics motivated by pure self-interest. This narrative thread (since abandoned) positioned the excesses of the "unre-pentant" wrestlers battling the RTC as more authentic for their refusal to ground their personal struggles in false, self-serving narratives of a greater social good.

IN SHORT, EFFORTS to regulate or reform performance forms such as professional wrestling are themselves productive, glamorizing the transgressive and oppositional qualities of the cultural Others they oppose. As of this writing, for example, rap star Eminem / Marshall Mathers has used this mainstream finger-wagging to his advantage, situating critiques of his homophobic and misogynistic lyrics as politically regressive assaults on free speech and culturally ignorant misreadings of post-ironic positioning. This is where reform groups such as the Parents Television Council come in, acting as surrogate parents and providing the moral authority against which the WWF can react; the company needs its detractors in order to bolster its image of impropriety. In the wrestling business, this is known as producing "heat." Usually accomplished by a vicious heel turn that victimizes a face (good guy), it is meant to draw an enthusiastic response from the crowd. Whether that response is sympathy for the face, hostility toward the heel, or a celebration of a dastardly turn of events, does not matter. What matters is the response. For instance, in 1999, responding to criticism of Smackdown, Vince McMahon disingenuously claimed that "there's no murder, no attempted murder, no shotgun blasts . . . no robbery, no rapes. When you compare us to some network dramas, we're Sunday school" (Consoli 1999). No, there were no murders or shotgun blasts; there were, however, attempted murders and implied rapes in the program's subplots, and the quote was meant to draw a correction—which would confirm the show's outsider status to its consumer base. Likewise, in the same year, McMahon chose to taunt the highly critical PTC by writing it a letter that soon appeared in the mainstream media. "Thanks for getting on our ass," he wrote after the council issued a report critical of the WWF. "Now I'm getting on yours. . . . Lighten up . . . ! Where's your sense of humor?" (Gordon 1999). The irony was, of course, that the interchange was as good for the face—the PTC—as it was for the heel, McMahon. Each appealed to its constituency; the difference was that the WWF did it with a smirk. Grounding its criticisms on the commonplace that the consumption of inappropriate media fare had a directly negative effect on individuals, and by extension on society as a whole, the PTC made use of the WWF in its efforts to regulate children's television and the viewing practices that constituted family relations in prime time, as well as to solicit funds. Meanwhile, McMahon and the WWF pointed to the PTC as an example of the sort of outdated and priggish moralizing that failed to distinguish between social satire and real social relations.

To put it another way, the WWF played the exasperated and exasperating adolescent to the PTC's indignant mother. Like *Roseanne*, *The Simpsons*, and *Married . . . with Children*, *Smackdown* models its impropriety on more than simply foul language, sexual innuendo, and violent or aggressive behavior. What makes this move so much more offensive to critics such as the PTC is that unlike the Bundys or the Simpsons, who were clearly fictional families (and which the organization also dislikes), the McMahons simply play themselves. While *Newsweek* told its readers that the offscreen McMahons were an incredibly tight-knit family (that, for example, son / wrestler / marketing VP Shane McMahon chose father/wrestler/chairman Vince as his best man when he married), the onscreen McMahons presented family life as utterly performative and completely subordinate to corporate politics and the imperatives of personal gain. In this way, the McMahon saga blends class hostility with a critique of the middle-class fantasy of the family. In one episode, for instance, Vince bellows at his ecstatically booing fans:

I'm Vince McMahon. Hell, I'm a billionaire . . . ! I could buy and sell every one of you in this arena tonight . . . ! I'm the chairman of the World Wrestling Federation! A man like me should be respected by people like you. A man like me—

[Boos. Chants of "Asshole, Asshole, Asshole. . . ."]

A man like me — shut up when I'm talkin'! A man like me should be admired by people like you. Hell, a man like me should be *praised* by people like you for all my accomplishments.

A few moments later, McMahon turns to his wife and CEO, Linda, and, his face red and lips flecked with spittle, announces that he is divorcing her (*Smackdown*, 7 December 2000). As the character Triple H put it in an off-screen interview, "there is no horror now. To the average person, the real-life enemy is their boss" (Leland 2000). McMahon, though, was boss, father, husband, and father-in-law. Triple H was not simply an employee of the WWF; he was until recently also the fictional husband of daughter and VP Stephanie McMahon, and they had repeatedly plotted to wrest control of the company from her father. In this fantasy, then, the family is no longer a private sanctuary from the excesses of a consumer-capitalist culture, but a location where its impersonal power relations became personal and where it became possible to actively link class resentment to the subversion of an imagined middle-class parental authority. This is both the apotheosis of teen marketing and the bane of proponents of "family-oriented" viewing.

As authority and responsibility fade onscreen and in the home, so will they elsewhere. The *Washington Post*, summarizing a recent debate over the proper span of adolescence, noted that some researchers have extended its upper limit to thirty years old (the National Academy of Sciences) and even thirty-four (the MacArthur Foundation Transition to Adulthood project), and glibly suggested that "plenty of Americans who vote, fight wars, buy houses and alcohol and serve in Congress can be branded as adolescents." Within this context, the *Post* noted that "Powerful lobbies are at work to stretch adolescence as far into the third decade of life as they can. . . . One of these groups is retail merchandisers. The number of adolescents in the United States is greater today than ever before, 60 million if you start at age 10 and continue to 24, 80 million if you count all the way to 30. Or should we count higher? Once the different ages wore different styles. Now a 60-year-old can wear the casual clothes of a 20-year-old" (Stepp 2002).[21] Nationwide, it would seem, adulthood is waning, and perpetual adolescence is becoming the norm. Is the family excess of the McMahons a symptom, then, or a cause? To describe an evening of watching wrestling as "family viewing" is to call into question the circuit that operates between the family that watches and the family that is watched. It suggests that the sex and violence, and larger

"Billionaire" promoter Vince McMahon demands a divorce from stunned wife Linda in front of thousands of cheering fans.

problems of racism, misogyny, and class struggle that weave through the family life of the McMahons, are not problems from which the family is a sanctuary. With no proper family on either side of the screen to provide the moral frame within which to make sense of this contestation, is the viewing child doomed to become the adolescent adult, lacking respect for authority and for polite social relations? And does the adolescent adult disrupt the tidy evolutionary order of upward mobility, threatening the social order through its rebellious expression of regressive traits?

Behind this threat of personal and social regression, the specters of race and class are always lurking. Courted as a consumer and represented as a victim of commercial manipulation in social and political discourse, the (white) "adolescent" becomes the poster child for nihilism and the disaffected consumer of commodities that signify a similar disenfranchisement, such as those of the working class and people of color. This is the demographic that Smith's feature story in the *New York Times Magazine* has labeled *mooks*, a generation that is "fast, *white*, and out of control" (Smith 2000; italics added). This group, Smith warns, is the monstrous creation of the entertainment industry: of record companies which push gangsta rap and hardcore music on otherwise healthy young boys, and of the wwf, which encourages middle-class youth to experience an alienated identification with a lower-class and often nonwhite culture which has nothing to do with their actual upbringing.

The inclusion of a racial marker ("white") in the *Times*'s pithy description of a generation going wrong signals not only the policing of the category of American youth — the separation of white, suburban children from disposable "urban youth" — but the belief that the practice of demographic address is at fault for encouraging this willful abandonment of the proper bounds of class and race position. (Apparently it is more acceptable [or understandable] for youth to be fast and out of control if they are nonwhite.) Here at last we can better parse the meaning of *family excess*. The popularity of prime-time professional wrestling — an "old working-class entertainment" — disrupts a tidy moral economy in which the ideal viewing family is inherently white and middle class. If it were only nonwhite and working-class families that were attracted to wrestling, there would be no problem: the boundaries of race and class would remain intact, and with them the system that regulates the production of identity out of identification.

CONCLUSION: BETWEEN THE
CARNIVALESQUE AND THE SHOOT

Social critics of televised professional wrestling (and video games, and rap music, and "mook culture" in general) often argue that its excesses signal the breakdown of polite society. This claim depends on taking a short view of history. Far from unique in its use of shocking and disturbing language, scenarios, and images, televised professional wrestling is part of a long tradition in American popular performance that Robert Allen has described as "grounded in the aesthetics of transgression, inversion, and the grotesque" (Allen 1991: 26). Some of its ancestors include burlesque, minstrelsy, vaudeville, jazz, rock 'n' roll, and punk. Yet even these forms of popular performance, which have so shaped our cultural and political landscape, were themselves inheritors of older forms. Blackface minstrelsy—in which white performers covered their faces in burnt cork and performed "authentic" Black music and dance for white audiences—dates back to the 1840s, and it continued on stage and in film until the 1940s (see Lott 1993 and Rogin 1996). Burlesque began in the 1870s as a slightly risqué form of musical satire; by the 1890s the burlesque show had become much bawdier, a place where (mostly) men could blend class slumming with sexuality by admiring and pursuing "fallen women" and "chorus girls"; by the 1920s it had evolved into the strip-tease (Allen 1991). Beginning in the 1880s, entrepreneurs such as B. F. Keith, Edward Albee, and Tony Pastor presented vaudeville—which featured acts that played on broad ethnic and racial stereotypes—as a more tasteful form of "lower-class" variety entertainment that would appeal to middle-class audiences (particularly women and children) at risk of damage or offense from the overt sexuality of burlesque (Allen 1991; Slide 1988; Snyder 1989; Jenkins 1992).

What these earlier forms share with wrestling is more than a common history of transgressing polite norms, though. Each has, in its turn, acted as a focal point around which the performance of difference—specifically class difference in a complex relationship with racial, ethnic, and sexual or gender difference—was publicly debated and regulated. And this regulation was itself performed—in newspapers, magazines, and through public policy— not just by limiting what entertainers could do onstage, but also by policing how audiences were expected to behave during the show. Since performers generally came from the "lower" social orders, and since audiences (though segregated by race) included patrons of different social classes, popular discussions of these performance forms provided a space for the definition and regulation of the "higher" and "lower" classes, and of the proper performance of their contact (Levine 1996). In simpler terms, while performers might act as if they were from the lower classes, audiences were expected to adhere to norms of middle-class behavior, creating a class boundary between producer and consumer. As Stallybrass and White (1986) point out, this back and forth is absolutely necessary. Without a transgressor to regulate, the dominant class cannot define itself:

> A recurrent pattern emerges: the "top" attempts to reject and eliminate the "bottom" for reasons of prestige and status, only to discover, not only that it is in some way frequently dependent upon that low-Other . . . but also that the top *includes* that low symbolically, as a primary eroticized constituent of its own fantasy life. The result is a mobile, conflictual fusion of power, fear and desire in the construction of subjectivity: a psychological dependence upon precisely those Others which are being rigorously opposed and excluded at the social level. It is for this reason that what is *socially* peripheral is so frequently *symbolically* central. . . . The low-Other is despised and denied at the level of political organization and social being whilst it is instrumentally constitutive of the shared imaginary repertoires of the dominant culture. (5–6)

In the case of televised professional wrestling the opposite is also true: without an oppressive and inherently parental regulating force, transgression loses its definition. As with its forebears, a goodly part of what makes professional wrestling appealing/threatening is its seemingly willful rejection of the values of polite society, and the appeal and the threat are inextricably interwoven. In this case, the "dominant culture" that the WWF claims as its Other (and vice versa) is not America's wealthy elite (whose truly criminal excesses have been quite evident lately), but its middle class, represented by the middle-class family, embodied by the mother as moral center. The WWF truly is a threat to "family values": it politicizes the ostensibly apolitical domestic sphere, denaturing its seemingly well-ordered relations.

This is what makes the struggle between televised wrestling and its critics such a compelling show: it links the markers of race and gender to class more explicitly (and contentiously) than does polite social discourse (see Schudson 1997). More specifically, in attempts to regulate the consumption of wrestling (or "mook" culture in general) by white teens and young adults, class suddenly and significantly emerges as a category in the expression of anxieties about the potential for racialized working-class entertainments and behaviors to undermine the development of individual children, young adults, and the culture and society as a whole. This is not the working class as lived experience but the working class as that which is to be consumed. Nor is this a generic representation of working-class "attitude"; it is one that revels in inappropriate and explicit references to gender and sexuality (poontang and puppies) and race and ethnicity (pimpin' and *pendejos*). It is, to put it in McCarthy's apt term, the "mimetic cultural logic of *white* teenage marketing" (2001: 191; italics in original).

What the interplay between televised professional wrestling and critical attempts to regulate or eliminate it make clear, briefly and potently, are the underlying class dynamics that are inextricably woven into proper or improper expressions of race, gender, or sexuality. Although complaints about wrestling's impropriety generally focus on issues of violence or sexuality, it is the *excessive* nature of that violence and sexuality that is disturbing. As wwf owner Vince McMahon is fond of pointing out, prime-time broadcast television is rife with images and narratives of violence (from *Law and Order* to *csi*) and sexuality (from *Friends* to *Will and Grace*).[22] The difference, of course, is that these images and narratives are always contained within a redemptive system that positions violence (generally, rape and murder) in opposition to a protective legal system, and sexuality within a trajectory that leads inexorably toward, if not heterosexual marriage, at least stable pair bonding. What makes the sex and violence of *Smackdown* and its companion programming transgressive is that it is *pointless*: it suggests no moral or behavioral lesson, no transcendent terminus of self-improvement. It is intentionally gratuitous.

The grounding of generic sex and violence in an imagined working-class aesthetic becomes explicit, not so much in their coding in performance itself as in reformist complaints about its effect on immature viewers, and in its potential to capture those viewers as a demographic for marketers. Here, the "attitude" toward the redemptive quality of middle-class narratives to produce better consuming subjects through moral and behavioral lessons—the refusal to better one's self through consumption—is feared/desired as a demographic consciousness of class and its relation to race, gender, and sexuality that seems both sophisticated in its articulation of those relationships, and naive in its insistence on reducing them to matters of consumption rather than more complex interpersonal social relations.

When it comes to wrestling, then, issues of race, gender, sexuality, and class take shape, not in an environment conducive to the democratic mixing of ethnically marked working-class audiences and their white, middle-class betters (as in vaudeville), or in the pollution of upper-class masculine heterosexuality (as in burlesque), but in discourses of individual consumption — either as that which threatens individual success and social coherence, or as an expression of resistance to socially constraining normative codes. If we understand race, gender, and sexuality as expressed in a struggle on the cusp between a multicultural social formation and a fantasy of complete, social color- or gender-blindness, class finds its expression in demographic consciousness not so much as an expression of solidarity, but of identity. This is true whether we speak of a middle-class white "adolescent" desire to obtain working-class (plus Black/Latino/Asian . . .) authenticity through consumption, or of reformist anxieties around the loss of class position through such illicit consumption.

At the center of this particular social formation resides the ostensible target demographic for professional wrestling: the white adolescent boy. Too often confused with *actual* teenaged boys — whose subjectivity depends very much on their specific social and material situations — the "attitude" of this demographic construct is produced around depoliticized rage, desire, and a fatalistic cynicism usually ascribed to the sociobiological category of adolescence that has been delineated at the boundaries of psychology, sociology, and physiology. It is this figure that *Times* author Smith invokes as the horrific example of a downwardly mobile white, middle-class male youth whose enthusiasm for products such as wrestling and gangsta rap signifies a dangerous and misguided betrayal of the very principles that produce his privilege. These boys, he warns his implicitly sympathetic middle-class audience, have carelessly adopted the rage that their working-class idols (of color) earned through oppression, without considering the personal and social consequences of that stance — generally, the perpetuation of the oppression of women, minorities, and gays and, specifically, the loss of command of polite speech and behavior (the appearance of tolerance), the practice of which lead to personal advancement. For these boys, he argues, the "imperative is 'speak freely': say things you could never say at work or in school. Talk the way guys 'really talk' when women and authority figures aren't watching" (Smith 2000).

The criticism has some merit, but it misses the point . . . several times. First, "women and authority figures" *are* watching, and that vague imagined audience is very important to the performance. But perhaps more significant is the idea of access to some sort of authentic speech and behavior, and of its foreclosure in domains outside of the bounds of gender-, class-, and race-based oppression. The association made here is not unlike those made in nineteenth-century and early twentieth-century discussions of vaudeville and burlesque, in which the moral center of middle-class life (and "American" culture) was described as female and maternal, and working-class and nonwhite performance forms provided relief from that (necessary) emasculating repression that was permissible as long as it was observed and not enacted (Allen 1991; Snyder 1989; Caffin 1914).

It is the potential disruption of this tidy moral center that is so unnerving, as in the case of Smith's dismayed and confused description of the performance of two female "law students," who gleefully participate in wrestling's degradation of women — one of whom even attempts to join the Godfather's Hos onstage (2000: 41). To the horror of its critics and the glee of its promoters and marketers, wrestling's "adolescent" impropriety also appeals to people outside of its target demographic, if not to its victims. The attraction of *Smackdown* and other WWF products to demographics outside its target market argues for the possibility of demographic slumming as an imagined resistance to social and representational regimes that bind individual advancement to the rejection of explicit and improper markers of race, gender, and sexuality (see Jenkins 1997 and in this volume). The experience of empowerment as consumers and disempowerment as social and political actors, considered proper (if annoying or threatening) in adolescent boys (and girls), is perhaps a feeling more widely shared, and which may find its expression in the positive reception of *Smackdown* and other WWF products and performances. What is potentially troubling/interesting about this phenomenon is not so much its imagined disruption of the tidy middle-class representational regime of prime-time television, but how it raises the possibility of inappropriate consumption as a popular criticism of the demographic regulation of consumer citizens.

The study of demographic awareness in fans, viewers, and producers and in critics of professional wrestling may not determine conclusively whether the phenomenon is widely and clearly understood or articulated by its subjects, but it may have the potential to reveal to researchers the positive and productive aspects of demographic address and consciousness, and to give a space for subjects to articulate the benefits and constraints of operating through, or escaping, a demographic position. The point, then, would not be to determine whether positive or negative media effects obtain — or even to lay to rest the fallacy of media effects — but to explore how the underlying metaphysical assumptions and the potentials they point to are made available to and manipulated by the subjects of that discourse. As Henry Jenkins (2002) has aptly pointed out, fans in particular engage in parallel economies of textual construction and analysis that simultaneously resist and submit to larger logics of production and criticism, accepting the limitations of their marginal positions as obstacles that are unavoidable, but not insurmountable. Where this is true in more self-reflexive fan communities, it may also be true in the larger sense for subjects of (always) mediated democratic capitalism. The point, finally, is not to determine whether the inherent imperfection of either resistance or its constraint is fully good or bad, but to take advantage of the self-reflexive nature of cultural production/consumption itself as a site for encouraging dialogue and negotiation.[23] What the production, circulation, consumption, and criticism of professional wrestling (or gangsta rap, or "reality TV," or . . .) offers is a location to critically engage with popular discourses about how people articulate and enact themselves as subjects in conditions of less than absolute (but more than passive) agency (see Ang 2000). For students of media as lived experience, this means treating troubling objects such as professional wrestling, not as *either* resistant or regressive, but as *both* resistant and regressive, constituted not simply in themselves but through the ways people attempt to use them for their own personal, social, and political ends. Perhaps it means reconsidering The Rock's once-popular admonition to his fans and foes — "Know your role and shut your mouth!" — rethinking the relationship between the production of popular speech and the social life of an action figure.

NOTES

1. After a lawsuit by the World Wildlife Federation in 2002, the World Wrestling Federation was forced to change its name to World Wrestling Enterprises, or WWE.

2. Market data suggests that the core audience for WWE products is men aged eighteen to forty-nine. This audience is approximately twice as large as that of the twelve- to seventeen-year-old boys, or of women aged eighteen to forty-nine. These numbers are consistent across race, when looking at White, Black, and Hispanic audiences. The only audience significantly out of step with these trends is that of girls aged twelve to seventeen, which is only one fifth as large as wrestling's core audience. (Statistical information courtesy of Initiative analysis of Nielsen Media Research data.) Anecdotal evidence from student papers and informal discussion suggest that many young women in college begin watching because their boyfriends insist, and then are drawn in as they argue the meaning and import of the programs with their partners and friends. See also Salmon and Clerc in this volume.

3. In teasing out this notion, I intend to build upon Ien Ang and Joke Hermes's (1991) observation that while television viewers bring certain investments to the subject positions they occupy while watching, they also engage in specific social practices around viewing that aid in the ongoing articulation of those subject positions. Yet while Ang's and Hermes's study (which centered on the question of gender articulation in viewing) considers the question largely from the point of view of *stabilizing* one's subject position in the act of viewing, in this essay I am interested in considering the fantasy of the attendant pleasures/dangers of temporarily *destabilizing* subject positions, of escaping a set of preconceptions about proper social behavior linked to demographic and categorical markers such as age, gender, class, and race without incurring the social and economic consequences of that misbehavior. (What are the imagined pleasures and consequences of acting like trailer trash without waking in the trailer?) In doing so, I take seriously Kimberle Crenshaw's (1993) observation that certain individuals experience their subjectivity as an intersection of these different markers, one that is constantly and imperfectly negotiated in their daily lives against those parts of their subjective experience or position that don't fit a given sociological or demographic profile.

4. *Requiem* was later produced as a feature-length movie starring Anthony Quinn.

5. Throughout the twentieth century, social theorists have located the moral and behavioral center of American social and cultural life in that family, which popular media have described as living the American Dream. See, for instance, Robert S. Lynd and Helen M. Lynd (1929); David Riesman, Reuel Denney, and Nathan Glazer (1950), or Arthur Schlesinger (1993); see also Elaine Tyler May (1988), Karal Ann Marling (1994), and George Lipsitz (1990).

6. The ABC network replaced wrestling with boxing, which remained in the 10 PM Wednesday slot for several years. Wrestling also took a hiatus from prime time in the 51/52 season, returning the following year.

7. This may have had as much to do with the fall of the sponsorship system and the rise of network production in 1957/58 as with a change in tastes; see William Boddy (1990) and Erik Barnouw (1978).

8. Historians of television may point out exceptions such as *The Honeymooners* (class) or *I Love Lucy* (class and ethnicity). The *Honeymooners* was actually a segment in Gleason's long-running (1952–56) variety show, and it only ran on its own during the 1955–56 season.

I Love Lucy ended its much longer run not in Manhattan, but in suburban Connecticut, joining the suburban pastoral of other sitcoms.

9. Even as producers and marketers abandoned the more class-based marketing strategies of previous generations, they worked to resegment their market by honing their address to the primary American social unit, the suburban nuclear family. Due to restrictive housing covenants and discriminatory loan practices, the new suburbs were overwhelmingly populated by young, white baby-boom families (Whyte 1956; Riesman, Denney, and Glazer 1950; Lipsitz 1981, 1990, 1995). The consolidation of a national television market as an imaginary mirror attempting to reflect an ideal America—one incredibly varied in its actual makeup (between urban, rural, and suburban; "native," "racialized," and assimilated; poor, working class, middle class, and upwardly mobile)—favored the production of an inoffensively bland location for its realization, which increasingly resembled the burgeoning white suburbs. (The primary exceptions to this were the crime show, which could present nonsuburban spaces people as transgressive threats contained through regulation, and the western, which reinscribed the white family as forming and informing the landscape that would become twentieth-century America.) As with variety and live drama, wrestling troubled the production of this fictional modern America, and was rapidly pushed to the margins.

10. For a discussion of televisual flow and interruption, see Raymond Williams (1974).

11. It is also important to remember that while prime-time entertainment avoided excesses of conflict and extreme value statements, the period also marked the rise of television news programming which increasingly addressed pressing social problems, such as segregation, red baiting, and U.S. imperial expansion.

12. In the midst of these accommodations, however, the audience addressed by prime-time programming, its core demographic, remained relatively unchanged. Depictions of working-class families—whether white (*All in the Family*) or Black (*Good Times*)—displayed a marked liberal condescension, presenting them as Other to the implicitly normal and absent middle-class family that watched (Barker 2000; Bogle 2001). Single-parent families (*The Partridge Family, Alice, The Courtship of Eddie's Father*) marked the absence of the missing parent as the central theme, and often supplied surrogates. Crime dramas continued to depict cities as the Other to normal life in the suburbs, as unpopulated by anyone but the criminal class (Gerbner and Gross 1976). Even nondramatic programming situated in the workplace (*The Mary Tyler Moore Show, Taxi, wkrp in Cincinnati*) replicated the basic structure of the working-class family, with managers and workers taking the roles of mother, father, and children (Bathrick 1984). Advertising followed suit, continually hailing the family, individually and collectively, as the central consuming unit.

13. For example, *Married . . .* creator Ron Leavitt described "the typical family on television" as one that "makes us sick" (quoted in Block 1990). "Us" here included both the producers and the members of their audiences.

14. The cbs network in particular was pegged in trade journals as the "gray" network, appealing to audiences over fifty, which tend to consume less.

15. A contrasting example of this "postmodern" situation is the appearance and disappearance of William on the cbs reality tv show *Big Brother* during its first season. A handsome, articulate Black man, William was chosen (as were the other contestants) for his demographic value. When he began to call into question the racial assumptions and motivations of the other players, William was positioned via editing and voice-over as an extremist and troublemaker and rapidly eliminated from the show by his housemates and the audience. While it was acceptable to *appear* as a Black man—with all the semiotic openness that entails—it was not okay for him to *speak* as a Black man. When William began to speak, neither as a polite middle-class man, nor as an angry, violent, inarticulate working-class man, but as a Black man both articulate and angry, one who called into question racial dynamics in the program and beyond, he violated the terms around which the show's "reality" had been constructed.

There is, however, something very important in this regulation. Television producers and programmers insist that they don't simply impose these schematic representations of identity on their viewers. New shows are subjected to rigorous focus-group testing, which includes eliciting biographical information, electronic feedback during test viewing, postviewing questionnaires, and group discussion. Popular accounts of this process suggest that in some ways, television programmers have a very nuanced understanding of their audiences. For example, according to David Poltrack, CBS head of audience research, when the network requests biographical information from focus-group members, it doesn't ask about income, because "the real defining characteristic is education. The guy who makes $1 million who never graduated from college watches TV like other people who never graduated from college" (quoted in Bunn 2002: 36). In this instance, researchers understand class as active and as based in affiliation, having more to do with social and intellectual bonds to peers than simply with economic status or employment. Of course, audience feedback continues during the life of the program, via the well-known Nielsen rating system, and, increasingly, via systems linked by telephone such as digital cable or TiVo (e.g., Shim 2002). This information is correlated against the reasonably reliable national indicator of class and race, the zip code (McCarthy 2001: 102, 274). Add to this sales data collected by marketers and advertisers, charted against ad slots in programming, and the logic becomes clearer: people don't choose what they watch, demographics do. Here the personal meets the institutional, and on unequal terms. One does not say, "as a straight, white, middle-class male of forty-two, this is what I like." One says, "this is what I like," and a complex institutional matrix correlates those tastes according to a lifestyle profile that relates one's age, race, class, and sexuality to other similar individuals, commodifying compatible desires as a collectivized identity available for consumption via products tailored to that profile.

16. Nor is this understanding solely applied to television. From the dawn of mass media in the United States—beginning with radio and the movies, and continuing with subsequent forms—the notion that the consumption of mass media products entails the absorption and integration of the moral and behavioral makeup of its producers, and its reproduction in the social and cultural life of consuming subjects, has endured, in spite of any persuasive evidence that such "media effects" exist (Jowett, Jarvie, and Fuller 1996; Sammond 1999; Buckingham 2000; Freedman 2002). The persistence of this notion, both in the academic research that continues to attempt (and to fail) to isolate such effects, and in the efforts of reform groups which utilize the results of that highly equivocal research in pursuing their own agendas, indicates more than simple institutional inertia.

17. Eric Bischoff, head of wcw and now working for wwe, at one point attempted to distance his product from that of Vince McMahon's for exactly these reasons, claiming that his promotion was more family friendly (Jensen 1998).

18. The wwf eventually won the suit in question, forcing, among other things, a retraction by the ptc concerning links between wrestling and child-on-child murder, and the purported abandonment of the company by sponsors. In addition, the ptc Web site no longer archives past invectives against the company.

19. This echoes requirements in the 1930s mppda (Motion Picture Producers and Directors Association) Production Code for cinematic representations of crime, in which criminals may never be shown enjoying the fruits of their crime. See Richard Maltby (1995).

20. While here and in their other works criticizing wrestling, Jhally and Katz offer valuable contributions to analyzing relations of domination and oppression in the form, I do not share all of their conclusions.

21. Conversely, in the case of violent crime, adolescents — particularly those who are non-white or poor — are increasingly being charged as adults at a younger age, sometimes as low as fourteen.

22. To be fair, the ptc also takes exception to this programming, as it would prefer that there be no violence, sexuality, or profanity during prime time. However, in its public relations campaigns, it has gone after the wwf much more than it has focused on sitcoms and crime dramas.

23. Similarly, Robert White (2000) has argued that a more Freirean (after Paulo Freire, a Brazilian educator) approach to media research — one that moves beyond the gathering or analysis of data, to one that gives subjects a greater hand in research design and data production — may help to empower fans and viewers to connect their critical and productive skills to explicitly political activity.

REFERENCES

Allen, Robert C. 1991. *Horrible Prettiness: Burlesque and American Culture.* Chapel Hill: University of North Carolina Press.

Ang, Ien. 2000. "Comment on Felski's 'The Doxa of Difference': The Uses of Incommensurability." In *Provoking Feminisms*, ed. Carolyn Allen and Judith A. Howard. Chicago: University of Chicago Press.

Ang, Ien, and Joke Hermes. 1991. "Gender and/in Media Consumption." In *Mass Media and Society*, ed. James Curran and Michael Gurevitch. New York: Routledge.

Barker, David. 2000. "Television Production Techniques as Communication." In *Television: The Critical View*, ed. Horace Newcomb. 6th ed. New York: Oxford University Press.

Barnouw, Erik. 1978. *The Sponsor: Notes on a Modern Potentate.* New York: Oxford University Press.

Barthes, Roland. 1972 [1957]. "The World of Wrestling." In *Mythologies*. Trans. Annette Lavers. New York: Farrar, Straus and Giroux.

Bathrick, Serafina. 1984. "*The Mary Tyler Moore Show*: Women at Home and at Work." In *MTM "Quality Television"*, ed. Jane Feuer et al. London: British Film Institute.

Baughman, James. 1992. *The Republic of Mass Culture: Journalism, Filmmaking, and Broadcasting in America since 1941*. Baltimore: Johns Hopkins University Press.

Block, Alex Ben. 1990. *Outfoxed: Marvin Davis, Barry Diller, Rupert Murdoch, Joan Rivers and the Inside Story of America's Fourth Television Network*. New York: St. Martin's Press.

Boddy, William. 1990. *Fifties Television: The Industry and Its Critics*. Chicago: University of Illinois Press.

Bogle, Donald. 2001. *Primetime Blues: African Americans on Network Television*. New York: Farrar, Strauss and Giroux.

Bozell, L. Brent. 1999. "Statement by Brent Bozell, Chairman of the PTC, On WWF Smackdown's Sponsor Withdrawal." 1 December, www.parentstv.org.

———. 2000. "Veni, Vidi, Vince: McMahon's Manifesto." 17 October, www.parentstv .org

Brook, Vincent. 1999. "The Americanization of Molly: How Mid-fifties TV Homogenized the Goldbergs (and got Berg-larized in the process)." *Cinema Journal* 38, no. 4 (summer).

Buckingham, David. 2000. *After the Death of Childhood*. Cambridge, England: Polity Press.

Bunn, Austin. 2002. "The Wasteland." *New York Times Magazine*, 23 June, 32–37.

Caffin, Caroline. 1914. *Vaudeville*. New York: Mitchell Kennerley.

Consoli, John. 1999. "In the Ring with WWF's McMahon." *Media Week* 9, no. 30 (26 July): 25.

Crenshaw, Kimberle. 1992. "Whose Story Is It Anyway? Feminist and Antiracist Appropriations of Anita Hill." In *Race-ing Justice, En-Gendering Power: Essays on Anita Hill, Clarence Thomas, and the Construction of Social Reality*, ed. Toni Morrison. New York: Pantheon Books.

———. 1993. "Beyond Racism and Misogyny: Black feminism and 2 Live Crew." In *Words that Wound: Critical Race Theory, Assaultive Speech, and the First Amendment*, ed. Mari J. Matsuda. Boulder, Colo.: Westview Press.

Dell, Chad. 1998. " 'Lookit That Hunk of Man!' Subversive Pleasures, Female Fandom, and Professional Wrestling." In *Theorizing Fandom: Fans, Subculture and Identity*, ed. Cheryl Harris and Alison Alexander. Cresskill, N.J.: Hampton Press.

DuttaAhmed, Shantanu. 1998. "Heartbreak Hotel: MTV's the Real World, III, and the Narratives of Containment." *American Studies* 39, no. 2 (summer): 151–71.

Freedman, Jonathan L. 2002. *Media Violence and Its Affect on Aggression: Assessing the Scientific Evidence*. Toronto: University of Toronto Press. Gerbner, George, and Larry Gross. 1976. "Living with Television: The Violence Profile." *Journal of Communication*, 26, no. 2 (spring).

Gordon, Devon. 1999. "wwf Tones Down Its 'Smackdown' Act." Newsweek, 13 December, 74.

"Grudge Match: The World Wrestling Federation Tries to Smack Down Its Critics with a Lawsuit." 2000. *Wall Street Journal*, 26 November.

Hendershot, Heather. 1998. *Saturday Morning Censors*. Durham, N.C.: Duke University Press.

Hilmes, Michele. 1999. "Desired and Feared: Women's Voices in Radio History." In *Television, History, and American Culture: Feminist Critical Essays*, ed. Mary Beth Haralovich and Lauren Rabinovitz. Durham, N.C.: Duke University Press.

Huesmann, L. Rowell, Jessica Moise-Titus, Cheryl-Lynn Podolski, and Leonard D. Eron. 2003. "Longitudinal Relations between Children's Exposure to tv Violence and Their Aggressive and Violent Behavior in Young Adulthood: 1977–1992." *Developmental Psychology* 39, no. 2: 201–21.

Jenkins, Henry. 1992. *What Made Pistachio Nuts?: Early Sound Comedy and the Vaudeville Aesthetic*. New York: Columbia University Press.

———. 1997. " 'Never Trust a Snake': wwf Wrestling as Masculine Melodrama." In *Out of Bounds: Sports, Media, and the Politics of Identity*, ed. Aaron Baker and Todd Boyd. Bloomington, Indiana: Indiana University Press.

———. 2002. "Interactive Audiences? The 'Collective Intelligence' of Media Fans." In *The New Media Book*, ed. Dan Harries. London: British Film Institute.

Jensen, Jeff. 1998. "Wrestling Goes Mainstream, Draws Big Ratings, Sponsors." *Advertising Age* 69, no. 33 (17 August): 3.

Jhally, Sut, and Jackson Katz. 2000. "Manhood on the Mat." *Boston Globe*, 13 February, pp. E1+.

Jhally, Sut, and Justin Lewis. 1992. *The Cosby Show, Audiences, and the Myth of the American Dream*. San Francisco: Westview Press.

Jowett, Garth S., Ian C. Jarvie, and Kathryn H. Fuller. 1996. *Children and the Movies: Media Influence and the Payne Fund Controversy*. New York: Cambridge University Press.

J. Walter Thompson Advertising Agency. 1949. "Advertisement." *Sales Management*, 1 September.

Katz, Elihu, and Paul Lazarsfeld. 1955. *Personal Influence: The Part Played by People in the Flow of Mass Communication*. Glencoe, Illinois: Free Press.

Lears, Jackson. 1994. *Fables of Abundance: A Cultural History of Advertising in America*. New York: BasicBooks.

Leland, John. 1993. "Why America's Hooked on Wrestling." *Newsweek*, December, 46–54.

Levine, Lawrence. 1996. *The Opening of the American Mind: Canons, Culture, and History*. Boston: Beacon Press.

Lipsitz, George. 1981. *Class and Culture in Cold War America*. New York: Praeger Publishers.

———. 1990. "Why Remember Mama? The Changing Face of Women's Narrative." In

Time Passages: Collective Memory and American Culture. Minneapolis: University of Minnesota Press.

————. 1995. "The Possessive Investment in Whiteness: Racialized Social Democracy and the 'White' Problem in American Studies." *American Quarterly* 47, no. 3 (September): 369–427.

Lott, Eric. 1993. *Love and Theft: Blackface Minstrelsy and the American Working Class*. New York: Oxford University Press.

Lynd, Robert S., and Helen M. Lynd. 1929. *Middletown: A Study in American Culture*. New York: Harcourt Brace and Co.

Maltby, Richard. 1995. "The Production Code and the Hays Office." In *Grand Design: Hollywood as a Modern Business Enterprise*, ed. Tino Balio. Berkeley: University of California Press.

Marling, Karal Ann. 1994. *As Seen on TV: The Visual Culture of Everyday Life in the 1950s*. Cambridge, Mass.: Harvard University Press.

McCarthy, Anna. 2001. *Ambient Television: Visual Culture and Public Space*. Durham, N.C.: Duke University Press.

Nasaw, David. 1992. "Children and Commercial Culture: Moving Pictures in the Early Twentieth Century." In *Small Worlds: Children and Adolescents in America, 1850– 1950*, ed. Elliot West and Paula Petrik. Lawrence: University Press of Kansas.

————. 1993. *Going Out: The Rise and Fall of Public Amusements*. New York: Basic Books.

Omi, Michael, and Howard Winant. 1994. *Racial Formation in the United States from the 1960s to the 1990s*. New York: Routledge.

Riesman, David, Reuel Denney, and Nathan Glazer. 1950. *The Lonely Crowd: A Study of the Changing American Character*. New Haven, Conn.: Yale University Press.

Rogin, Michael. 1996. *Blackface, White Noise*. Berkeley: University of California Press.

Sammond, Nicholas. 1999. "Manufacturing the American Child: Child-Rearing and the Rise of Walt Disney." *Continuum* 13, no. 1 (April): 29–55.

Schlesinger, Arthur M. 1993. *The Disuniting of America: Reflections on a Multicultural Society*. New York: Norton.

Schudson, Michael. 1984. "Advertising as Capitalist Realism." In *Advertising: The Uneasy Persuasion*. New York: Basic Books.

————. 1997. "Why Conversation Is Not the Soul of Democracy." *Critical Studies in Mass Communication* 14: 297–309.

Seiter, Ellen. 2000. "Making Distinctions in TV Audience Research: Case Study of a Troubling Interview." In *Television: The Critical View*, ed. Horace Newcomb. 6th ed. New York: Oxford University Press.

Shim, Richard. 2002. "Nielsen Begins Monitoring TiVo Usage." *CNET News*, 6 August.

Slater, Don. *Consumer Culture and Modernity*. Cambridge, Mass.: Polity Press, 1997.

Slide, Anthony, ed. 1988. *Selected Vaudeville Criticism*. Metuchen, N.J.: Scarecrow Press.

Smith, R. J. 2000. "Among the Mooks." *New York Times Magazine*, 6 August, 36–41.

Smyth, Dallas. 1977. "Communications: Blindspot of Western Marxism." *Canadian Journal of Political and Social Theory*.

Snyder, Robert W. 1989. *The Voice of the City: Vaudeville and Popular Culture in New York*. New York: Oxford University Press.

Spigel, Lynn. 1991. "From Domestic Space to Outer Space: The 1960s Fantastic Family Sitcom." In *Close Encounters: Film, Feminism, and Science Fiction*, ed. Constance Penley et al. Minneapolis: University of Minnesota Press.

———. 1992. *Make Room for TV: Television and the Family Ideal in Postwar America*. Chicago: University of Chicago Press.

Stallybrass, Peter, and Allon White. 1986. *The Politics and Poetics of Transgression*. Ithaca, N.Y.: Cornell University Press.

Stepp, Laura Sessions. 2002. "Adolescence: Not Just for Kids." *Washington Post*, 2 January, p. C1.

Strasser, Susan. 1989. *Satisfaction Guaranteed: The Making of the American Mass Market*. New York: Pantheon.

Taylor, Ella. 1989. *Prime Time Families: Television Culture and Postwar America*. Berkeley: University of California Press.

Tyler May, Elaine. 1988. *Homeward Bound: American Families in the Cold-War Era*. New York: Basic Books.

White, Robert. 2000. "The Role of Media in Generating Alternative Political Projects." In *Consuming Audiences? Production and Reception in Media Research*, ed. Ingunn Hagen and Janet Wasko. Cresskill, N.J.: Hampton Press.

Whyte, William, Jr. 1956. *The Organization Man*. New York: Simon and Schuster.

Williams, Raymond. 1974. *Television: Technology and Cultural Form*. London: Fontana.

Wojcik, Rick. 1993. "Pop That Coochie: The Video Jukebox and the Aesthetics of Consumption." *Stanford Humanities Review* 3, no. 2 (autumn): 61–71.

CATHERINE SALMON AND SUSAN CLERC

"Ladies Love Wrestling, Too":

Female Wrestling Fans Online

"Ladies Love Wrestling, Too" is the name of a Web ring (2001), one of dozens that connect Web sites of female wrestling fans.[1] Girls and women are not the audience explicitly hailed by the World Wrestling Federation, the former World Championship Wrestling, or the many small independent promotions around the country. The current metaphor for professional wrestling is "a soap opera for men," a phrase that denies space for female fans while co-opting a traditionally female-centered genre. The emphasis in the ring of manly men doing manly things manfully; the misogynistic, sexist depictions of women; and the attempt to suppress pleasure in the beautiful bodies of the men through camera work and announcers, would seem to prevent a large female audience. Nevertheless, "the wrestling audience is almost equally divided between men and women" (Mazer 1998: 113). Indeed, the most cursory search of the Internet reveals that girls and women take an active, often exuberantly salacious, interest in professional wrestling.

As Chad Dell's (1998) study of post–World War II fandoms reveals, women have always been a vocal part of the professional wrestling audience. We find that many of the attitudes of those earlier generations continue, in particular the intense interest in male bodies on display. Today's female fans, however, have found new ways to express and communicate their pleasure in watching the spectacle in the ring. Our primary interest is in exploring the ways female fans of professional wrestling negotiate the "spectacle of excess" (Barthes 1992: 15) differently from their male counterparts. To accomplish this, we examine the picture galleries they create on the Web and the fan fiction (stories about the wrestlers or their ring personae) they write and share online. Our study is necessarily informed by being fans of sports entertainment and by being women, ourselves, but also by our separate research on media fandom. ("Media fandom" connotes the subculture described by Henry Jenkins [1992] and others, as well as the component fan communities for television programs such as *Star Trek* or *The X Files*. Our work has focused on gender differences within online fandom [Clerc] and erotic fiction [Salmon]).

"FOR THE BENEFIT OF THOSE WITH FLASH PHOTOGRAPHY . . ."

Is professional wrestling strictly entertainment for men? John Fiske (1987: 247) claims that performers with names such as "Beefcake" are a nod to the female demographic, but "pretty boys" and sexual predators enact male psychodramas and are elevated or cast down, turned heel or face, based on the reactions of the male audience. Any joy female fans derive is the result of their unintended interpretations and pleasure at watching big men in small trunks. Dell's examination of female fan populations in the post–World War II era confirms the enduring interest of American women in watching nearly naked men rolling around in the ring. Wrestling was a staple in the Golden Years of television, right along with Milton Berle, *I Love Lucy*, and *Playhouse 90*, and the post–World War II generation of women contributed to its popularity. Their public outbursts of "lookit that hunk of man" (Dell 1998) are echoed by their granddaughters and great-granddaughters at the turn of the twenty-first century. The fan clubs the earlier generation ran and belonged to have been replaced by scores of Internet discussion groups and Web sites run by and for female fans. Wrestling_hunks (2001) is one mailing list that proudly announces its purpose and invites new members: "Hey . . . Yo! Women Wrestling Fans Rejoice, the creation of a list where we talk nothin but the fine, hot sexy men of the WCW, WWF, ECW, et al. I have no real rules, we can be as nasty as we wanna be, just as long as we respect each other — no flamers please!" While women derive much pleasure by looking at "that hunk of man," female fans are also supportive of less aesthetically pleasing performers: Mick Foley, Kane (before the removal of his mask), and Bubba Ray Dudley, who are unlikely to be offered centerfolds in

Playgirl, nevertheless have many female fans. Foley is extremely clever and funny on the microphone as well as a daredevil in the ring, Kane emotes better than many wrestlers who aren't handicapped by wearing a mask, and Bubba Ray. . . . well, we aren't sure about Bubba Ray but there are a startling number of Web sites for him created by female fans.

And those female fans are necessary to a performer's survival; because the wrestling audience is mixed, wrestlers must cultivate a mixed following in order to achieve the level of popularity necessary to rise to the top. Attracting too many female fans, however, can hurt a performer's credibility with male fans: "Kane vs. Jericho feud: Kane cut the best promo of his career. Granted, that isn't saying much, but his character has gained momentum since he started talking more. The storyline that Kane is jealous of Jericho's looks is solid, but the wwf needs to be careful not to turn the male fans against Jericho (a la Shawn Michaels)" (Powell 2001). Like Rick Rude before him, Michaels's "Heart Break Kid" (also called hbk) persona was interpreted as sexually aggressive while he was a heel, and his bad-boy attitude combined with incredible athletic skill and charisma in the ring made him extremely popular among both male and female fans. Because of his popularity, Michaels was elevated to wwf champion and was turned from heel to face, effectively neutering his outsider antiestablishment stance by making him the officially approved poster boy of the wwf. His in-ring skills sustained his popularity for a time, but gradually his pelvic thrusts, swaggering, crowd-mooning performances took on a different meaning for the male audience. The female audience continued to enjoy him as much as it ever had, and in a rare instance of the wwf's acknowledging female fans, Michaels posed for a pictorial layout in *Playgirl* magazine (Cole 1996). Although he was fully or partially clothed in every photo, the *Playgirl* spread seemed to incense male fans. They found a voice in one of Michaels's opponents, Bret Hart, who repeatedly brought up the photos (oddly referring to *Playgirl* as a "girlie" magazine) and questioned its intended audience: "I don't think it is a girlie magazine; I think it's a gay magazine" (Hart 1997). Adding fuel to the fire, the wwf printed a pullout poster in their February 1998 *raw Magazine* ("Nothing Comes between Me and the Title") of Michaels wearing nothing but his strategically placed Heavyweight Title Belt. The resulting chants of "Shawn is gay" and "hbGay", and the widespread booing that filled the air during the champion's matches, finally forced the WWF to respond with interviews and desperate-sounding assurances that Michaels was "a real man's man." They also took the title off him and revamped his character over the next few months.

Too much emphasis on male bodies and too many women in the audience also make it more difficult to suppress the fact that wrestling is sports entertainment, not pure sport, and that the entertainment is all about half-naked, sweaty men pretending to fight while they have their faces and hands in each others' groins. There is danger to the straight male viewers and the performers in allowing the camera to linger in ways that might be read as gay and that, coincidentally, would please straight female viewers.

Given the implicitly straight male look of the camera in most popular media, female fans have had to develop their own strategies for obtaining pleasure from visual media. In comparison to men's publicly sanctioned opportunities to look at women, ways for women to look at men have always been limited. Liesbet Van Zoonen gives the short list as soap operas, posters, and "sports photography," and observes that the ability of women to look has been confined "to the incidental bits and pieces offered in patriarchal culture" (1994: 99, 101). Frame grabbers and the Internet have enhanced women's ability to appropriate images and display them for each other outside the confines of mass media, although the selection is still limited by the camera work used to construct the televised narrative. (This is often a source of consternation for female fans, who are disappointed when the camera quickly shifts from a moment of comfort between tag team partners to a long camera shot of the victors holding aloft their title belts.)

Inadvertent and incidental moments, close-ups of crotches and asses, and looks that lend themselves to subversive interpretations, are available for exploitation by female fans, yet they choose to capture and share images, augmented with words, that temper their voyeurism with affection, romance, and concern for characters and performers. In effect, they attempt to use visual images to reproduce what media fans more often do in conversation—present a summary of the character and analyze his nature. Rather than gathering pictures of the men's bodies, the extensive galleries of frame grabs and photo scans found on almost every female fan's site are filled with dozens of close-ups. Smiles and unguarded emotional moments are particularly popular, the pictorial equivalent of shoot moments in the ring when the performer's guard is down and the real person spontaneously appears. In "The Rhetoric of the Camera in Television Soap Opera," Richard Timberg

(1987) points out that close-ups denote and create intimacy with the character portrayed. David Thorburn also notes the distance between actors and viewers of television is closed by camera work: "the camera . . . can achieve a lover's closeness to the performer" (1987: 639). A desire for intimacy, to know the performer or character by studying him, is evident in the collections of pictures in female fans' Web galleries. Perhaps value is also placed on these moments because the wrestling ring is a joyless place; the emotions deliberately shown to the camera during promos and matches are usually anger, disdain, and aggression, in support of the masculine or sport values of competitiveness and domination. Laughter is always at someone else's expense, and usually the person has it coming. All of this creates difficulties for female fans interested in the emotional life of the performer or character, and frame grabs are attempts to overcome this limitation by extending momentary glimpses of emotion, vulnerability, and happiness.

The contrast between the strength and power emphasized by official photos and the openness and intimacy favored by female fans was illustrated in images from the w w F's official Rock Web site (www.therock.com) and from fan sites such as Hellfire's Rock Gallery (2001d). The official photos showed the wrestler's body from the knees up, emphasizing the muscular development of his torso and thighs. In the first photo, illustrating the days of the character when he was a good-natured face, he was smiling. The overall gist of the display is the evolution of the character played by Duane Johnson from nice guy Rocky Maivia, to egocentric and articulate leader of the heel faction Nation of Domination as The Rock, to member of the heel Corporation, to his emergence as a face and true People's Champ. Only in the first, or weakest, stage of the character's evolution was he smiling. The fan gallery had several smiles and the ironic People's Eyebrow. There are also candid shots of The Rock posing with a fan at an event (w w F 2001), pictures from amusing moments on RAW when he was struggling to keep a straight face or had said something funny (fans can usually identify the referenced scenes), a graduation photo, and a shot of him during the tribute show for Owen Hart on the night after his tragic death. Many of the captured moments hint at the real man beneath the persona, but in keeping with the blend of real life and ring life that dominates wrestling, and with media fan convention of using the actor's face to delve into the character's motives and feelings, it is not always clear whether it's the man or persona under scrutiny. In picture galleries such as the Hellfire one, a female fan can reconstruct the persona or performer as she sees him, and reproduce her gaze by manipulating the images created for a different audience.

Other forms of vulnerability and openness are shown briefly on screen as well, and these also appear in Web galleries, especially in tributes to tag teams. Tag team pages emphasize closeness and homosocial bonding, suggesting that the relationship, the partners' reliance on each other, like buddy cops facing death, is what appeals to some women. X-pac Angel's "Pictures of My Babies Together" (2001) highlighted moments of celebration and cooperation between X-pac and Kane when they were a tag team, including a screen capture of the two of them embracing on the entrance ramp after Kane chose X-pac over Kane's brother, The Undertaker. Many sites dedicated to the Kliq (e.g., JR2sweet 2001), real-life friends Kevin Nash, Scott Hall, Shawn Michaels, Sean Waltman, and HHH (Triple H), display photos of the men as tag teams (Nash and Michaels in the WWF, Nash and Hall in the WCW) rather than singles wrestlers.

Moments grabbed from bootlegged copies of the Madison Square Garden Incident are also extremely popular. At the end of Nash and Hall's last event in the WWF before heading to the WCW, they embraced Michaels and Triple H in the ring, saying good-bye to the crowd and to each other. The story of the Kliq has added emotional value for their fans because it is widely believed the Triple H's career suffered from it. Vince McMahon was unhappy with the performers for breaking *kayfabe* (the illusion that wrestling is real) by revealing their friendship; in the storylines at the time, Michael and Hall were faces and Nash and Triple H were heels, therefore their enemies. Since Michaels was the reigning champion, he was beyond punishment, so Helmsley bore the brunt. His scheduled win at King of the Ring, normally given to performers the WWF believes will join the top ranks at the end of the year, was reassigned to Steve Austin. Triple H won the next year, and in his speech the following night on RAW made reference to the postponement. By that time, the WWF had undergone changes in its storytelling approach to incorporate more quasi-shoot moments.

One aspect of vulnerability and emotion missing from the galleries, although quite evident in fan fiction, is the manifest suffering required by all wrestlers. Although the persona of wrestlers is fierce macho toughness and imperviousness to pain, the hardcore ethic demands both the physical record of pain (bleeding, stitches, broken bones, scars) and the performance of suffering (grimacing and writhing to sell their opponents' moves). A gallery of photos of faces twisted in pain, however, would give quite a different impression from the usual ones of smiles and ironically raised eyebrows or a series of hurt/comfort stories (discussed later in the essay).

Another feature of many female fan Web sites are playful Hunk of the Week or Stud of the Week contests (e.g., Hellfire 2001c), in which frame grabs are accompanied by comments detailing what the voters find attractive. Looks are rarely enough; most female fans place high value on verbal skills and humor, as well as on athletic ability. Few women and girls find the appreciation of the masculine form and these qualities mutually exclusive, as was shown by an anonymous photo of Kanyon smiling and accompanying testimony on Beach Bum Creations' (2001) Hunk of the Week site. "I vote for Kanyon because not only is he gorgeous, but he can wrestle and he's funny. A good sense of humor is so sexy!"

Sites such as Men in Pink and Black (MIPB; see Bobby and Mottola 2001a) use photos to illustrate comments on what they like and don't like about men's bodies. In Posers and Hosers (see Bobby and Mottola 2001c), they displayed a series of "Fashion Dos and Don'ts," modeled on those in magazines, critiquing the fashion faux pas of the wrestlers and valets: the image 04corinodont.jpg was accompanied by "MIPB: Buy a vowel. Get a clue. Don't wear a yellow singlet when you're hung like an acorn." Men in Pink and Black also hosted "Bakery" (see Bobby and Mottola 2001b), where the site creators and visitors commented on whose asses they would have liked to see and whose they'd seen too often or never wanted exposed. Rikishi, for example, could be found in the "Cold, Old and Stale" area, while Bret Hart and The Rock were Hot Cross Buns. The Bakery was not illustrated with evidence that was either revealing or concealing in spite of the many opportunities offered by some of the men named. In spite of the nature of this portion of the Web site, the creators shied away from posting the kind of graphic close-up images prevalent on male-created sites with pictures of female performers.

Other uses of frame grabs include caption contests or ongoing commentary, along the lines of the cable television program *Mystery Science Theater 3000* (USA Network, 1988–99), illustrated with screen shots. The women at Hellfire's Hot Men of Wrestling (2001a) site provided multiple frame grabs with captions for each episode of *RAW* with their favorites from each episode later collected in a "Best of" collection. One photo, for example, of The Rock looking at Stone Cold Steve Austin, who had his back turned, was accompanied by "F/AJ: (3.26.01 RAW) Rock: Ya know I never really noticed before but Stone Cold's got a nice ass" (Hellfire 2001b: "Best of 2").

The absence of ass and crotch shots in galleries built by female fans is a marked contrast to pictures of female performers at male fan sites. When "Nitro" Girl Chae's top slipped during a dance routine and accidentally revealed a breast, it became the nipple seen round the world, thanks to male fans with frame grabbers and Web sites. Frequently, pictures of the women are relegated to a special section of a site devoid of wrestling content. At straight site http://www.pro-wrestling.com/ (2001), which at one point called itself "Your Online Search Engine for Professional Wrestling Websites," the "Wrestling Women" link led to an adults-only site fronted by a photo of Terri Runnels covering her naked breasts with her hands. Crow's Wrestling Babes site (2001) consists of nothing but videos and photos of female performers in revealing costumes and positions. Male fans are aided by the industry's pandering—the WCW and WWF have published videos and photo spreads, as it were, of their female performers. The practice extends to female performers who are athletes and compete in the ring. Lita, probably the most popular female performer with female fans, had to have implants before the WWF would give her a push. The photos in the divas section of the official WWE Web site (WWEDivas.com 2004) emphasize her sexuality— Lita's cleavage is prominently displayed—and are an illuminating comparison to the official Rock photos discussed above.

The gender-based differences in the picture galleries further underscore the impact of wrestling as a conservative narrative with very clear, essentialist, gender lines. Fiske argues that in wrestling, "When the object is pure spectacle it works only on the physical senses, the body of the spectator, not in the construction of a subject. Spectacle liberates from subjectivity" (Fiske 1987: 243). As a spectacle, he claims, wrestling "exaggerates the visible, magnifies and foregrounds the surface appearance, and refuses meaning and depth" (243). This is clearly not the case for female fans who create picture galleries filled with smiles, candid moments, and intense emotion. These fans are romantically interested in their visions of the personae or wrestlers. While obviously attracted by the hypermasculinity of the men's powerful bodies, they seek to temper the hardness of those bodies and the shallowness of characterization by focusing on revelatory moments of emotional vulnerability whether expressed in a smile or an embrace.

Van Zoonen's reading of *Playgirl*, a text created for a female audience rather than being created by the audience for itself, found that the magazine "constructs . . . the *Playgirl* man as a romantic object rather than a sexual one" and further that "obviously, one-dimensional voyeurism in the masculine tradition does not satisfy female desires" (1994: 101–2). The galleries lend themselves to this reading as well. However, the adherence of female fans to the clichés of romance in the visuals they select is offset by the explicitness of their comments and the stories they write. None of this implies that women do not experience as much lust as men do, but their preferred modes of stimulation are typically quite different. The visual world of pornography is a stark illustration of the importance of visual stimulation for men. In contrast, the erotic industry for women is largely a textual one, major examples of which are the romance novel and other erotic writings (Salmon and Symons 2001). Male and female fantasies in general echo these differences, with male sexual fantasies concentrating on physical appearance and variety and female fantasies relying more on a specific object, setting, and emotional context. Wrestling fans online mirror these differences in a male-fan preoccupation with overtly sexual photos of the women of wrestling and the female-fan tendency toward emotional content in their chosen pictures and fictional work. It is the focus on the textual in the products of female wrestling fans that we will concentrate on now.

"ANYTHING CAN HAPPEN IN THE WWF"

Two common, related features of male wrestling sites absent from those created by women and girls are role playing and fantasy booking. In role playing, fans either create their own wrestling personae or take on the persona of a wrestler and have fantasy matches against each other in fantasy leagues. Sometimes the matches are carried out by polling, and the character with the most votes wins. Fantasy booking, like that exemplified by Rick Scaia's Fantasy Universe (2001), involves rewriting episodes of RAW or other televised wrestling programs as the booker wishes they had been, or would be, played out. While males generally role-play, female fans are more likely to write fictional stories about their favorite wrestlers. Posted to discussion lists, message boards, and Web sites, fan fiction provides female fans a way to fill in the empty spots and background in wrestling storylines, giving the characters pasts and futures, exploring issues relevant to them (as opposed to men) in much the same way as female media fans in general appropriate male media characters, rewriting them to suit their own narrative desires.

And *desire* is the operative word. Pleasure in discussing men's physiques on message boards and mailing lists and the interest in knowing the inner character expressed in the close-ups and shoot photos combine in the stories. In fan fiction, the wrestlers' bodies and emotions are both entwined, both objects of desire, as in this story which was posted to wrestlingslashfiction: "He's beautiful when he sleeps. Some people are ugly. Hunter looks like a street bum asleep, but Kev looks like an angel. His long lashes brushing his cheeks, his beautiful lips relaxed into a slight smile that was more than likely anything but angelic. His hair was tumbled across one cheek and I brushed it back to get a good look at him" (Flame 2001).

This image sharply contrasts with Fiske's view that "in wrestling the male body is no object of beauty: it is grotesque" (1987: 247). Clearly not all wrestlers are viewed that way by women, and perhaps there have always been wrestlers female fans have found attractive, not only as a result of their physical appearance but also the nature of their performance. While Fiske focuses on their strength and power (and female fans are obviously attracted to these aspects), female fans add to these features in their online products, transforming them, much as a romance novel does. In fan fiction, their overt hypermasculinity is tempered by descriptions of the softness of their hair, the sweetness of their face while asleep. Female fans create a wealth of character and meaning behind the spectacle.

Jenkins (1992) has suggested the term *textual poachers* be applied to media fans who appropriate television or movie characters and settings and rewrite them in a way that serves their needs as opposed to those they were designed to serve, typically men of twenty to forty years. His work, and that of Michel de Certeau (1984), suggests that fans take away from literary or television products only those things they find useful or pleasurable. Female wrestling fans appropriate a male-oriented product and reshape it or interpret it in a way that is pleasing to them, making inferences and speculations that go beyond the information conveyed to the male fan.

Female wrestling fans are in many ways just like other media fans in their inclinations toward fan fiction and in their collections of emotive photos and artwork. In addition, both share two forms of fan fiction: *Mary Sue* stories and *slash*. We will discuss slash in a moment; as for Mary Sue, she's amazingly beautiful, insightful, and smart, and everyone in the story loves her . . . though most fans detest her. Mary Sue is the generic name for a character that represents the author of the story, allowing her entry into a world of people that she watches on television and fantasizes about. She first came into existence in the days of early *Star Trek* fandom. Melissa Wilson describes her well:

> You already know Mary Sue. Mary Sue is the perky, bright, helpful sixteen-year-old ensign who beams aboard the ship. Everyone on the ship likes Mary Sue, because Mary Sue is good at everything. Mary Sue is an engineer, a doctor in training, a good leader, an excellent cook, and is usually a beautiful singer. Mary Sue often has mental powers that may manifest themselves as telepathy, precognition, or magic. . . . Her name is often the author's name, be it a net.name, a favored nickname, or the author's middle name. . . . By the end of the story, Mary Sue will be in bed with the desired character, will have beamed away amid cheers from all the regulars, or will be dead, usually accompanied by heavy mourning from the cast. The reader, on the other hand, will be celebrating. (2001)

Mary Sue has long been widely detested in media fandom, but with the migration of fandom online she has spread like kudzu among fan fiction writers and can be found in almost every form of media fandom. Wrestling is no exception. Most frequently, she's tied to The Undertaker, though his little brother, Kane, seems to call to her, too. Perhaps the best examples of this are the Brides of The Undertaker (The Brides 2001) and Brides of Kane. As part of the collaborative Web sites described above, the Brides write stories in which they are engaged in romantic and sexual relationships with The Undertaker and (for one of them) with Kane. In her unpublished paper "Too Good to Be True: 150 Years of Mary Sue," Pat Pflieger (2001) points out several of Mary Sue's more endearing characteristics, a number of which are shared by the Brides. In the supernatural tale "The Undertaker's Brides," for instance, this collection of Mary Sues reunites the brothers and helps them to defeat Paul Bearer. The Brides are all described as attractive, most with long dark or auburn hair, much like that of The Undertaker and Kane themselves. All the Brides appear to be able to link telepathically to each other and to The Undertaker and Kane. The Brides are empowered women who go off to face Paul Bearer alone in order to spare their lovers. Tragedy dogs Mary Sue. Kaleigh's dark and painful past is hinted at. One of the Brides, Judy, becomes a vampire. Afraid she is a threat to the safety of the other Brides and The Undertaker, she returns to her home in the Tennessee mountains and stays outside to watch the sun rise one final time.

Mary Sue stories exist for no other reason than to express the writers' own romantic and sexual interest in their objects of desire, whether he is a character in a traditional television series, a singer in a boy band, or a wrestler. The physical beauty of the beloved is extolled in sensual detail: "His green eyes glowed with a fire of their own. His dark auburn hair hung loose past his massive shoulders. Tight black jeans and a leather vest hugged his body like a second skin" (The Brides 2001). Like the romance novels they evoke, the stories dwell on the cycle of a relationship from meeting; to falling in deep, mutual, and complete True Love; to having fabulously fulfilling and perfect sex; to a commitment: "Many hours later after the two lovers had exhausted themselves, Kaliegh [Kaleigh] lay sleeping in his arms. The Undertaker gently propped himself up on an elbow and gazed into her peaceful face. He was once again overcome by how lucky he was to still have her here with him. He was sure that he had finally found the same love that Kane and Storm shared. The Undertaker knew that someday he would take her as his Lady, if she would have him as her Lord" (The Brides).

The contradictory popularity of and loathing for Mary Sue stories pose a dilemma. If Mary Sues are so hated by readers, why are there so many—indeed, an increasing number—of them? Part of the answer lies in the changes in media fandom and fan fiction as a result of the Internet. Media fandom created Mary Sue, as well as the consensus that she is a blight on fan fiction. Fandom is meant to share the characters of favored texts; when Mary Sue shares her fantasy by posting it, she places a claim on the characters on behalf of the writer. Mary Sue is an author who operates on the basic principle of "I want to be liked," and therefore she makes the character likable to the characters in the story. It is her fantasy after all. She expects readers to feel the same, but readers don't want a character to like; they want one to identify with. Media fandom has also put an emphasis on learning to write and tell a story while using shared universes and characters. Media fans often proudly refer to members of the community who have become professional writers. The best stories allow the reader to put themselves in the role of the protagonist, but Mary Sue's have no one but the author in them. Among media fans, Mary Sues have been seen as at a beginning stage of writing, expressing something to get out of your system on your way to becoming a better writer and storyteller. When media fandom was an offline community, a consensus on what was good storytelling and what was to be avoided could more easily be regulated by zine editors. When the community moved online, however, the open-publishing platform of the Web opened the doors to waves of newcomers ignorant of established customs. Exposure on the net also allowed fan fiction as a mode of expression to spread to fans of other texts who have adopted it as their own. Thus, the number of Mary Sues has expanded—in wrestling fiction and beyond—with seemingly less access to a structure or process to move them beyond this initial, embarrassing stage.

While Mary Sue stories are blatantly heterosexual expressions of their authors' fantasies, slash stories remove the author and focus on the homo-erotic features of the narrative. Slash stories refer to romantic or erotic narratives written almost exclusively by and for women, in which both protagonists are expropriated male media characters. In media fandom, the idea of slash (fan-authored stories about same-sex relationships between male characters) is well established. Typically, slash characters are the costars of various police, detective, adventure, spy, and science fiction television series. Popular pairings include Kirk and Spock from the original *Star Trek*, Starsky and Hutch from the eponymous show, Illya and Napoleon from the *Man from U.N.C.L.E.*, and Jim and Blair from *The Sentinel*. (The name *slash* refers to the "/" placed between the initials or names of the pair: *K/S* for Kirk/Spock stories. The "/" is silent in spoken references.) With fandom of all kinds going online, the possibilities of cross-pollination of fan modes of consumption and fan texts, and the spectacle of men in the ring provided by professional wrestling, it was only a matter of time before female wrestling fans adopted slash as their own. Among wrestling fans, slash includes pairings such as Kane/X-pac, Austin/Triple H, Shawn Michaels/Diesel (Kevin Nash), Matt and Jeff Hardy, and The Rock/Triple H. As in most slash stories, the wrestlers are often partners—in this case, tag team partners. Tag teams present a classic hero pair similar to those in the science fiction and police series that provided the genesis of slash. Tag teams ally the strength and power of the men's bodies with emotional vulnerability, as each must rely on and take care of the other. The potential for a homosexual coding of tag teams is probably responsible for the insistence in the wwf and other organizations on presenting unrelated performers as brothers when they form a tag team, as they have with Edge and Christian, among others. This trend has been satirized in the Dudley Boys, a mixed-race tag team who claim to be brothers from different mothers. This fear of unintended readings of the tag team dynamic is probably also responsible for the lack of longevity among unrelated tag team partners. In the last few years, more tag teams seem to be temporary partnerships built to disintegrate when one or both performers are deemed popular enough to pursue a singles career, or to provide a quick boost to the less popular of the partners.

There have also been an increasing number of very brief reluctant partnerships put together for body-sparing main events; four-man main events require less time in the ring for wrestlers returning from injuries. Short-lived partnerships seldom achieve the emotional intensity a slash fan looks for, unless the unwilling partners throw off a lot of sparks, for instance when enemies are forced by a storyline to pair up. The camera work, at least in the wwf, has also changed to take the focus off of slash-friendly poses that used to be standards of the tag team repertoire: the celebratory embrace, the tight focus on the outstretched hand of a partner writhing in pain trying desperately to reach his comrade for the tag, the cradling of one's fallen partner after a devastating win by the enemy (face teams only), the dastardly clasping of hands to increase leverage in a hold (heel teams).

One tag team that radiated "slashiness" in the ring was the unlikely pairing of Kane and X-pac. They were initially united by a common foe, but even the announcers quickly came to make veiled comments about X-pac's heart and how he was teaching Kane that he, too, had a heart. Their partnership was marked by two stints as wwf tag team champions and a lot of angst, as X-pac always had to deal with being responsible when his team lost matches. The typical end of one of their losing matches had X-pac flat on his back, with Kane's hand resting on his partner's chest, or with Kane walking out of the arena with his partner slung over his shoulder The one pinned was always X-pac, and finally he decided that Kane was better off without him, that Kane needed a partner he could rely on. That episode of RAW featured Kane (speaking for almost the first time) calling Sean's (X-pac's) name out as the other man abandoned him. This came right after an angle in which The Undertaker tried to reclaim the allegiance of his brother, Kane, but Kane chose X-pac over him. When X-pac eventually returned to Kane's side, problems with Undertaker dogged them. At one point during an inferno match between Kane and Triple H, Undertaker dragged a broken and bleeding X-pac out to the entrance ramp, dumping him there. Kane abandoned the ring, his arm catching fire in the process, and ran back to his fallen partner. Ignoring his burning hand, he touched his partner with the other, obviously distraught. After the commercial break, we saw Kane in the locker room, X-pac slumped beside him. He reached out to brush his fingers against X-pac's face and hair and then, in frustration, started hitting the wall and rocking back and forth. As we saw above, at least one Web site is devoted to capturing, in pictures, this Kane / X-pac story arc. Slash stories about the pair can elaborate on the emotions and intimacy that seem to be just below the surface:

"I'm sorry, Kane. It's better for you without me." He reached for the door and without thinking, Kane jumped up, hands holding Sean still.

"No." Closing his eyes at the risk he was taking, Kane bent his neck, leaning down to gently press his mask against Sean's cheek, wishing he were able to press a kiss there, to show the other man how much he cared. (Catherine 2001b)

Lacking the support of the camera-constructed narrative for tag team slashiness, many slash fans have turned to the other popular kind of homoerotic pair: hero and villain. Conversations about pairs such as HHH and The Rock focus on the chemistry the two men exhibit in the ring; the sparks they generate are reminiscent of screwball comedy teams where the excessive initial dislike turns to True Love by the end of the film. Although his reading of wrestling sometimes overlooks female fans, Fiske, referring to the alleged ugliness of the performers, aptly points out that "the excessiveness of this strength, in alliance with its ugliness, opens a space for oppositional and contradictory readings of masculinity: the grotesqueness of the bodies may embody the ugliness of patriarchy, an ugliness that is tempered with contradictory elements of attraction" (1987: 247). For slash fans, the hypermasculinity of the performers and the emphasis on aggression and toughness allow space for a more campy and subversive interpretation of their actions. Conflict-based slash discussions also exploit the reality of wrestling for extra piquancy: the love/hate relationship of characters who must cooperate and trust each other in order to give a good performance, yet dislike each other, creates a nice little frisson of UST (unresolved sexual tension) for slash fans. Stories focusing on The Rock and Triple H tend to be that way, with the relationship emerging from their in-ring fights, and from a combination of grudging respect and sexual attraction, as in "The Game" series by

Christina Ortega (2001): "He shouldn't be here, Duane knew. The belt was his. Now was the perfect time to walk away, but he couldn't. The thought of his enemy lying on his bed inside waiting for him sent shivers up his spine."

The proliferation of slash discussion groups and slash story archives on the Web provides ample evidence of women's interest in homoerotic readings of wrestling texts. Slash stories about wrestlers have been posted to such discussion groups as wrestlingslashfiction, shMARTASS (2001), and StevieRichardsandRavenFanfiction (2001). Many other stories are posted to personal Web pages and archives devoted to a particular federation (WWF) or group of pairings (the Kliq).

As in other media slash, the pairings tend to emphasize the differences between the men, in a true romance-style vein, despite the fact that most wrestlers are rather large muscular men. But there are still differences in size and in temperament. Kane is a foot taller and over a hundred pounds heavier than his one-time tag team partner X-pac, while Shawn Michaels is smaller but feistier than his sometimes partner, Diesel: "Diesel gave a sharp gasp and released the captive wrist, reaching instead to wrap long arms round Shawn's shoulders, pulling the smaller man hard against his bigger body. Suddenly, Shawn was surrounded by warm wet strength, a powerful thigh between his legs, pressing against him" (Catherine 2001a). In other forms of media fandom slash, much is also made of the differences between members of a pair: Starsky is darker in coloring than Hutch; and Blair is smaller but emotionally stronger than his partner, Jim. Such differences even extend to the size of sexual "equipment." Blake, of *Blake's 7*, for example, is almost always described as hung like a horse, in comparison to his sometimes sexual partner, Avon. Such a particular size convention appears to a lesser extent in wrestling slash, though much is often made of the large penis size of men such as Kevin Nash, Kane, and The Undertaker, illustrating WCW (now WWE)[2] star Ric Flair's suggestion to "Take a ride on Space Mountain."

As in the emphasis on size difference, wrestling slash resembles media fandom slash in many respects, but not all. Many stories are short in length, often PWPs (plot-what-plot, a story which is really just a sexual interlude lacking a storyline), which may be due to the youth and lack of writing experience of authors and partly to the continuity problems inherent in the fragmented narrative style of the pro-wrestling genre. The incidence of real-people slash stories (between performers rather than characters) is also much greater in wrestling slash (see below). In particular, two kinds of stories common in media fandom are found more often in wrestling than in most types of fandom: *h/c* and AU stories. Both h/c (hurt/comfort stories, in which one or both members of a pair are injured in some way, creating emotional closeness) and AU (alternate universe stories, in which the characters are taken out of the source text and placed in a different time or place) are subgenres in their own right, but are also commonly found as elements in slash, *het* (heterosexual relationship), and *gen* (nonsexual, or general audience) stories.

Fan reading and writing place a great deal of importance on issues concerning the motivations and emotional states of characters. As a result, fans often emphasize moments of crisis, for example, episodes where characters respond emotionally and in a supporting and caring way toward the psychological problems or physical injuries of other characters. When Starsky hugged Hutch after the murder of one of his girlfriends, or when Napoleon tended to Illya's injured back in a *Man from U.N.C.L.E.* episode are but two examples. Wrestling is a rich text for such scenarios: Kane kneeling to press a hand to an injured X-pac's chest, or Owen Hart and the British Bulldog holding onto Bret Hart after he received a beating from Steve Austin. In fact, the emotionally rich tag team storyline of trust and betrayal, and the potential of ring action to lead to hurt/comfort scenes both appeal strongly to women and girl wrestling fans; hence the popularity of the Kane and X-pac pairing to female fans. As previously mentioned, their matches often ended with X-pac injured, protected, and comforted by his larger partner. In slash stories, the comfort continues backstage in a more intimate way.

The hurt/comfort genre of stories focuses on such moments, building on a crisis from an episode or inventing situations in which the characters experience vulnerability. The hurt experienced provides the pretext or opportunity for comfort, and for physical and emotional intimacy. Shared suffering serves to renew the commitment between the partners. Such stories allow macho men to express softer emotions, whether brotherly, romantic or sexual. Fans know that the characters and most likely the performers are straight, but h/c provides a way for buddy to become lover: "His chest was smooth, the nipples small and hard. Sean frowned at the faint bruising developing on the left one. Sean rose and stepped closer. 'Does it hurt?' he whispered, fingers almost touching. . . . Taking a deep breath, Sean rested his hand against Kane's heart, pressing lightly. Kane whimpered and tilted his head back" (Catherine 2001b).

In his article on *Rambo* and the popular pleasures of pain, William Warner (1992) reflects on the vulnerability and sensitivity exhibited during moments of suffering. Such moments are seen every day in the agonized faces of wrestlers caught in various submission moves. They also appear when the wrestling storyline calls for emotional exhibition. Even The Undertaker, not known for his emotional expressiveness, demonstrated intense sorrow and pain when he found out that his brother, Kane, was alive and hated him. The camera angles and strong key lighting used during this part of the Dark Brothers storyline served to emphasize Undertaker's emotions, as did scenes showing him visiting his mother's grave.

Removing the wrestlers from the ring and placing them in a different setting or universe can allow for additional emotional exploration. One method of doing this is a story form again from media fandom, the alternate universe (AU) story. The AUs may change the ending of an episode or series, transform the characters into animals or elves, or transport them to a different place or time period. In many ways, the characters themselves are intact, but the setting changes completely. Alternative universe stories might portray The Undertaker as a warlord's son and X-pac his prize (Glass Tiger 2001: "The Gift"), or Raven as a pirate and Shane McMahon a captive nobleman (Lady Kai 2001: "Raven's Prize"):

> Shane McMahon lifted his spyglass from the hook on the wheel and put it to his eye, turning in the direction the lookout in the crow's nest had indicated. He focused on the flags snapping wildly in the brisk ocean breeze, stiffening as he recognized the colors of a pirate ship. He peered at them, noticing something unusual about them, then cursed in shock and dismay, dropping the glass and shouting orders to his crewmen. It was one thing to be attacked by pirates. It was quite another to be attacked by the most infamous of them all . . . Captain Raven! (Lady Kai 2001)

Some media characters inspire more AU stories than others. The characters from *The Professionals*, in particular, have been successfully transplanted to almost any universe, future or past, but Starsky and Hutch, for example, seem more a product of their times and are less frequently and with less success placed in extratextual settings. The AUs may be particularly appealing in wrestling fandom because they allow the characters to be removed from the limiting action and activities of the ring and life on the road. However, the characters, as played on television and in the arena, are very much a product of in-ring storylines, which makes it difficult to retain character integrity in a different universe or setting.

Although most evident in AU stories, all wrestling fan fiction plays with the line between real and reel in a way less common in most other kinds of media fan fiction. Only boy-band slash features as much play between character and performers as wrestling stories. Both are universes where the line between "work" (staged) and "shoot" (unplanned) are blurred to a greater extent than in traditional narratives. The public perception of wrestling as completely fake and wrestling fans as dupes has contributed to the importance of being a smart "mark." Fans know the outcomes are predetermined, but the ability of performers to make the matches seem "real" is a key element in their enjoyment of the spectacle. This is a response to both the public stigma of being a wrestling fan and to the industry's tendency to blend real life with in-ring storylines. Much conversation in the Usenet newsgroup rec.sport.pro-wrestling (RSPW), the largest online discussion forum for wrestling, revolves around the issue of real versus fake; fans are obsessed with knowing the difference between a shoot and a work. Characters in wrestling are not fictional creations completely distinct from the actors that portray them; wrestling personae are often based on the men's characters (Austin has said his persona is him at full volume), and real life is often incorporated into storylines to blur the boundary between shoot and work. Frequent heel and face turns make it impossible to treat wrestlers as consistent characters similar to those in traditional drama and comedy. The wrestling universe is also not a separate, self-contained, coherent universe like those in standard television programs. All storylines must take place in the ring and in the present without recourse to flashbacks or flash-forwards. The range of narratives and outcomes is narrow compared to other storytelling forms (angles that feature a tag team have one ending—the end of the team so one or both members can pursue a singles career). Female fans, at least those who write fan fiction, seem to prefer blurring the line rather than maintaining it as male fans tend to.

The issue of real-people slash (RPS) has always been touchy in media fandom. Stories exist which pair the actors (Lewis Collins and Martin Shaw, e.g.) as opposed to the characters (Bodie and Doyle). Most media fans see this as both inappropriate and beside the point. After all, they are interested in the relationship between the characters, not the actors who play them. But in wrestling, the line is far more difficult to draw. A few wrestlers use their own names, and sometimes even they seem to have difficulties separating themselves from their characters (a fault shared by some television actors as well). And while some gimmicks are obviously just that, such as the fraternal relationship between Undertaker and Kane, the distinction between Shane McMahon the character and Shane the person, for example, is less distinct to the extent that, unlike media fans, some wrestling fans feel compelled to explicitly spell out the difference: "The Shane McMahon Angst, Ravishment, and Torture Association for Sadistic Scribblers—for writers of fanfiction about the WWF's Shane McMahon. . . . All Shane fic welcome (humor, angst, het, slash, PWP, etc.)—there is a high slash content on this list, but all stories are rated for content. The only requirement is that you remember, we're writing about the CHARACTER Shane McMahon and not the real person" (shMARTASS 2001).

Some writers keep their wrestlers in character, clearly writing their story about the characters. Such stories often branch off from a particular point in the storyline, such as when Undertaker beats up X-pac during the inferno match of his partner, Kane, with Triple H, or when The Rock defeats Hunter for the WWF heavyweight title. Other stories stay in character (or pretend the storyline is real) but use wrestlers' real names: Mark Calloway instead of Undertaker, Dwayne Johnson instead of The Rock. And yet others portray the men who bring their characters to life as lovers, as is sometimes the case for Kevin Nash and Scott Hall, bringing real-life issues such as Hall's much publicized drinking problems and Nash's divorce into the story. Such blurring of the lines between wrestler and character is only exacerbated by the blurring in pro wrestling itself of whether something is a work (scripted) or a shoot (not scripted). Overall, the proportion of real-people slash is higher in wrestling fandom than in media slash fandom as a whole, probably close to 35 percent, while in media fandom itself, the percentage is closer to 1 or 2.

Constance Penley (1992) has suggested that fantasy identification is an important aspect of slash, focusing in particular on the shifting point of view characteristic of slash stories, whether based on WWF wrestling or *Star Trek*. Because traditionally dominant male characters are made vulnerable in slash, she argues, this creates a space in a relatively closed media text into which the writer or reader may insert herself. And it is certainly true that most of such stories do include both protagonists' perspectives. But the same is often true for Mary Sue stories, and it is certainly true for most romance novels. Women appear to enjoy both characters' points of view, getting to experience the adoption of men as sexual objects, and to experience being the object of their passion (by identifying alternately with both characters). The popularity of fan fiction among wrestling fans as shown in the many discussion lists and Web archives for posting, reading, and commenting on stories, again echoes Dell's (1998) assertion that female fans derive pleasure not only from the expression of their sexuality but from sharing it with other fans. We've also seen that the support and sharing among wrestling fans are similar to how they're practiced by fans of other media. Where wrestling fan fiction differs from media fan fiction is in the absence of gen stories. Just as female fans seem to ignore the analysis of news and angles in their discussion groups, so they ignore the generic fan-fiction equivalent. Similar to discussions that respect textual boundaries, the story-line aspects are picked up by the male fans whose role-playing and fantasy booking equate to gen fan fiction. In this respect, female wrestling fans resemble the fans of boy bands who also write only Mary Sues or slash stories.

"THE WHOLE F'N' SHOW"

American women, young and old, have long treasured the opportunities to ogle scantily clad men offered by professional wrestling. The Internet removes the limits forced on Dell in his study of earlier generations of female wrestling fans and allows us to observe them without a frame created by male reporters or semiofficial newsletters from fan clubs. And yet what we find is a continuation of the two major features Dell identifies: vocal sexual outbursts by women in the audience and pleasure taken in performing and in sharing their performance with other women. While the proffered text excludes or objectifies women, they appear to like it regardless and negotiate its limitations by appropriating the strength and power of the hypermasculine, taming it in the same way that romance novels tame their heroes. Women react to the spectacle of wrestling by focusing on the men's bodies, using the opportunity, as Dell's fans did, to raucously express sexual desire and perform as part of the audience, thereby sharing the experience with other women. Where postwar fans did it in arenas and fan clubs, women now use the Internet to carry on drooling. In spite of the time that has passed, male fans and men in general find outspoken statements of what women want unsettling. Female fans have created their own Internet areas to serve their own interests in sports entertainment.

Female fans of the twenty-first century go beyond earlier generations in two ways, by appropriating images and characters to create their own interpretations of the text, and by bringing wrestling's homoerotic subtext to the forefront. As a spectacle, wrestling's appeal is based on the pleasure of looking, but the gaze represented through the camera is male. Female fans appropriate images for metacommentary on sports entertainment, using isolated seconds out of context to convey unintended and humorous meanings. However, the more common use of images is in filling in what the televised spectacle leaves out: fully developed characters and relationships. Without the narrative tools available to media fans but with the same impulses, female wrestling fans turn to the visual images of wrestling to reconstruct coherent characters and relationships. Picture galleries express not only desire for the body but a desire to know the character and the man. Screens full of close-ups allow fans to capture and study expressions of happiness or intense emotion revealed but not dwelt upon by the camera. Captured shots of hugs and touching allow fans to extend the enjoyment of the relationships beyond the time permitted by angles that separate the performers and camerawork that prevents lingering. Such uses of the visual components of televised wrestling play on the fluid boundary between shoot and work, real and fake at the heart of professional wrestling.

Male wrestling fans use fantasy booking and other versions of fan fiction to play with the narrative of wrestling, but female fans have embraced fan-fiction subgenres from a broader media fandom, such as slash and the Mary Sue story, using them to explore issues of sexuality and attraction. However, there are differences that distinguish female wrestling fans from fans of other texts. Female wrestling fans eschew gen stories, write far more Mary Sue stories, and, probably due to wrestling's blend of shoot versus work, real versus staged, are more likely than media fans to write real-person slash. Relatively impoverished wrestling storylines also influence the form of wrestling fan fiction, distancing it from real-life activities or inspiring writers to turn to AUs in order to fill in perceived gaps. In essence, female wrestling fans have themselves appropriated other media fans' method of appropriation and adapted it, as they have adapted technology, to express themselves. Still working within the discourse of hardcore and smart marks, they take on a more media-fan-type perspective in which the oozing machismo of the hypermasculine is tempered by tenderness for, and by, the characters—a far cry from what Vince McMahon thought he was putting on screen, and from what most male fans perceive as going on. And yet, as Vince so often declares, "anything can happen in the WWF." And that's the bottom line.

NOTE

1. Because the women's online wrestling fan sites analyzed herein utilize low-resolution images, it is impossible to reproduce adequately the photographs discussed in this essay. Readers may find examples of these types of images on fan sites such as those listed in the references to this essay, some of which are still active and some of which are not.

2. Ric Flair was a main-carder for World Championship Wrestling and has continued to be so in the WWE, following Vince McMahon's buyout of WCW.

REFERENCES

Books and Articles

Bacon-Smith, Camille. 1992. *Enterprising Women: Television Fandom and the Creation of Popular Myth*. Philadelphia: University of Pennsylvania Press.

Barthes, Roland. 1972. "The World of Wrestling." In *Mythologies*. Trans. Annette Lavers. New York: Noonday Press.

Clerc, Susan. 1996. "Estrogen Brigades and 'Big Tits' Threads: Media Fandom Online and Off." In *Wired Women: Gender and New Realties in Cyberspace*, ed. Lynn Cherny and Elizabeth Reba Weise. Seattle: Seal Press.

Cole, Judy. 1996. "Wrestling's Heartbreak Kid." *Playgirl*, October, pp. 26–31+.

De Certeau, Michel. 1984. *The Practice of Everyday Life*. Berkeley: University of California Press.

Dell, Chad. 1998. " 'Lookit That Hunk of Man!': Subversive Pleasures, Female Fandom, and Professional Wrestling." In *Theorizing Fandom: Fans, Subculture and Identity*, ed. Cheryl Harris and Alison Alexander. Cresskill, N.J.: Hampton Press.

Fiske, John. 1987. *Television Culture*. New York: Routledge.

Jenkins, Henry. 1992. *Textual Poachers: Television Fans and Participatory Culture*. New York: Routledge.

Mazer, Sharon. 1998. *Professional Wrestling: Sport and Spectacle*. Jackson: University Press of Mississippi.

"Nothing Comes between Me and the Title." 1998. *RAW Magazine*, February 1998, insert.

Penley, Constance. 1992. "Feminism, Psychoanalysis, and the Study of Popular Culture." In *Cultural Studies*, ed. Lawrence Grossberg, Cary Nelson, and Paula A. Treichler. New York: Routledge.

Salmon, Catherine, and Donald Symons. 2001. *Warrior Lovers: Erotic Fiction, Evolution and Female Sexuality*. London: Weidenfeld and Nicolson.

Thorburn, David. 1987. "Television Melodrama." In *Television: The Critical View*, ed. Horace Newcomb. New York: Oxford University Press.

Timberg, Bernard. 1987. "The Rhetoric of the Camera in Television Soap Opera." In *Television: The Critical View*, ed. Horace Newcomb. New York: Oxford University Press, 1987.

Warner, William. 1992. "Spectacular Action: Rambo and the Popular Pleasures of Pain." *Cultural Studies*, ed. Lawrence Grossberg, Cary Nelson, and Paula A. Treichler. New York: Routledge.

van Zoonen, Liesbet. 1994. *Feminist Media Studies*. Thousand Oaks, Calif.: Sage.

Electronic Works

Beach Bum Creations. 2001. "Hunk of the Week: The Top 5 for March 3–9, 2001." 12 April, http://www.tandq.com/Tango/HOTw/hunk135.htm.

Bobby, Dawn L., and JoAnne Mottola. 2001a. MIPB: Men in Pink and Black. 12 April, http://www.webpak.net/~dawnmipb.

———. 2001b. Bakery. 12 April, http://www.webpak.net/~dawnmipb/bake/.

———. 2001c. Posers and Hosers. 12 April, http://www.voicenet.com/~cybermook/p&h.htm.

The Brides. 2001. *The Undertaker's Brides*. 12 April, http://www.geocities.com/Colosseum/Rink/2651/Tales/html.

Catherine. 2001a. "Royal Rumble." Online posting. Wrestlingslashfiction Mailing List. 14 January, http://groups.yahoo.com/group/wrestlingslashfiction.

———. 2001b. "Strong Enough." 12 April, http://www.members.tripod.com/~chica6.6/one/strong.html.

Crow. 2001. Wrestling Babes. 7 November, crow.graphicsnxs.net/archives/wrest.htm.

Flame. 2001. "If I Were You." Wrestlingslashfiction Mailing List. 9 January. http://groups.yahoo.com/group/wrestlingslashfiction.

Glass Tiger. 2001. "The Gift." 12 April, http://www.members.tripod.com/~chica6.6/oneshot/gift.html.

Hart, Bret. 1997. RAW. Television broadcast. 24 March.

Hellfire. 2001a. "Hellfire's Hot Men of Wrestling." 12 April, http://www.hhmow.com/.

———. 2001b. "Best of 2." 12 April, http://www.hhmow.com/bestof/bestof2.htm.

———. 2001c. "Sizzlin' Stud of the Week." 9 April, http://www.hhmow.com/SOTw/index.htm.

———. 2001d. "The Rock Gallery 2." 12 April, http://www.hhmow.com/rock/rockgal2.htm.

JR2sweet. 2001. "Kliq Korner." 13 November, http://www.members.tripod.com/~JR2sweet/.

Ladies Love Wrestling Too Web ring. 2001. Home page. 12 April, http://nav.webring.yahoo.com/hub?ring=llwt&list.

Lady Kai. 2001. "Raven's Prize." 12 April, http://www.geocities.com/ladyjackyl2/RavensPrize.html.

Ortega, Christina. 2001. "The Game Series." 12 April, http://www.geocities.com/rkacat/gameindex.

Pflieger, Pat. 2001. "Too Good To Be True: 150 Years of Mary Sue." 12 April, www.merrycoz.org/papers/marysue.htm.

Powell, Jason. 2001. "Powell's Take." 12 April, http://www.prowrestlingtorch.com/cgi-bin/powellstake.cgi?powellstake/2000/20001107_12812.

Pro-wrestling.com. 2001. Home page. 7 November, http://www.pro-wrestling.com/.

Scaia, Rick. 2001. Part 18 of 18: 00 Fantasy Universe Concluding Thoughts, 6 April. http://www.wrestleline.com/columns/onslaught/apr01/fantasy18.htm.

shMARTASS@yahoogroups.com (Shane McMahon Angst, Ravishment, and Torture Association for Sadistic Scribblers). 2001. Home page. 9 April, http://groups.yahoo.com/group/ShMARTASS.

StevieRichardsandRavenFanfiction@yahoogroups.com. 2001. Home page. 23 April, http://groups.yahoo.com/group/StevieRicahrdsandRavenFanfiction.

Wilson, Melissa. 2001. "The Mary Sue Litmus Test." 12 April, http://missy.reimer.com/library/marysue.html.

Wrestling_hunks@yahoogroups.com. 2001. Home page. 9 April, http://groups.yahoo.com/group/wrestling_hunks.

Wrestlingslashfiction@yahoogroups.com. 2001. Home page. 9 April, http://groups.yahoo.com/group/wrestlingslashfiction.

WWEDivas.com. 2004. 1 November, http://www.wwfdivas.com/lita/index.html.

WWF. 2001. "The Rock." 12 April, http://www.therock.com/photos/index.html.

X-pac Angel. 2001. "Pictures of My Babies Together." 12 April, http://www.angelfire.com/wv/X-pacangel/together.html.

LAURENCE DE GARIS

The "Logic" of Professional Wrestling

The dramatic plot of pro-wrestling matches, as with any sporting contest, is rudimentary: two opponents square off in conflict. There is a crisis in suffering and a climax in victory and defeat. Unlike Roland Barthes's injection of a moral frame into his assertion of pro wrestling as "the great spectacle of Suffering, Defeat, and Justice," there need not be any sense of justice, only victory (1972). The prototype of a wrestling hero was Arrachion of Phigalia, a pankratiast in the ancient Olympic Games in Greece (see Reardon 1999). During the championship match, Arrachion was being choked out as he held an ankle lock submission on his opponent. Just at the time that his opponent raised his hand in defeat, Arrachion died. He was awarded the gold medal posthumously. The plot is so simple, the story so profound. And the medium by which the story is told — a wrestling match — is so immediate, so easily understood. Professional wrestling's structure as a one-on-one athletic contest contributes to its endurance as a performance genre. While gimmicks and storylines come and go according to the vagaries of the times (i.e., the Cold War, the Iranian hostage crisis, etc.), the basic structure of an athletic contest endures.

SUFFERING, DEFEAT, AND VICTORY

Although professional wrestling has recently attracted interest from scholars in theater, performance studies, film, and anthropology — as evidenced by the contributors to this volume — few scholars that frequently write about sport choose to examine professional wrestling. I can only speculate that this noticeable absence is attributable to a bias on the part of sports scholars, in that pro wrestling is not competitive in the sense that most "legitimate" sports are, and that it is part imitation and part parody. I find it curious that those who write about pro wrestling seem to take the stance that there needs to be some kind of explanation for why fans enjoy pro-wrestling matches but seem to feel that competitive sports need no similar explanation, as if "competition" in and of itself is sufficient for pleasure and enjoyment. Among scholars who write about sport, professional wrestling is either ignored or degraded. Most often among sport scholars, professional wrestling is dismissed as "trash" sport (Morgan 1994), not worthy of serious attention.

Wrestling's basic structure is similar to boxing: build up two opponents in a way that the public will pay to see who will win the match. Joyce Carol Oates (1994) calls boxing a "drama without words."[1] There is a common thread between Oates's portrayal of boxing as a "root" metaphor without a point of reference and Barthes's argument that each moment in pro wrestling is intelligible. Oates and Barthes regard hand-to-hand combat between two individuals as an unmediated conflict and, as such, uniquely dramatic. Pro wrestling is unmediated by balls, bats, sticks, or any other kind of sports equipment. Consequently, the dramatic tension is increased and the resolution final. American sports fans seem to be fascinated with one-to-one contests, and team sports are frequently described in terms of individual contests between star players. Historically, professional wrestling promoters have fed this public desire for dramatic one-on-one confrontations.

Increasingly, though, writing about professional wrestling has stripped the performance of any vestige of "sport," whether it be "fake sport," "trash sport," or otherwise. "Drama" has become the dominant metaphor for writing about professional wrestling. Gregory Stone and Ramon Oldenburg (1967) say, "wrestling is drama." Henricks (1974) portrays pro wrestling as "moral order." Eric Zengota (1991) suggests that pro wrestling's appeal lies in the Jungian archetypal images of wrestlers' gimmicks. Other authors (Mondak 1989; and Maguire and Wozniak 1987) refer to the exploitation of racial and ethnic stereotypes as a source of popularity. What is missing from these analyses is "wrestling." At this point in time, one would be hard pressed to find anyone who would seriously defend professional wrestling as a traditional sport. But neither is professional wrestling traditional drama, exhibiting aesthetic choices long considered too "low" for the conventional definition of theater. Professional wrestling's transcendence of boundaries is precisely what makes it so interesting as a cultural phenomenon. The performance genre is not neatly contained by traditional categories. A hybrid of sport, street fight, ballet, spectacle, and soap opera (among other forms), professional wrestling—like jazz—defies easy categorization. Although the dramatic element is crucial to professional wrestling performances, the element of "sport" in professional wrestling has been understated in most analyses. While pro wrestling can be called a dramatic enactment of a sports contest, it certainly is not "drama" proper.

Critics and students of pro wrestling aren't the only ones to contribute to this confusion. During the past few years, officials in the World Wrestling Federation (wwf; now the wwe) have made an effort to distance themselves from professional wrestling, rebranding their product as "sports entertainment." According to the wwf's 1999 prospectus for their initial public stock offering, the company is "an integrated media and entertainment company, principally engaged in the development, production and marketing of television programming, pay-per-view programming and live events, and the licensing and sale of branded consumer products featuring our highly successful World Wrestling Federation brand. We have been involved in the sports entertainment business for over 20 years, and we have developed the World Wrestling Federation into one of the most popular forms of entertainment today" (World Wrestling Federation 1999).

Interestingly, "professional wrestling" is nowhere to be found in the description. The wwf's definition of itself represents a shift in business models away from a sports-based, live-events business and more toward a television show. According to the prospectus, revenue from television advertising and sponsorship accounted for only 12 percent of net revenues ($30.1 million of $251.5 million total). The wwe still receives most of its revenue from promoting professional wrestling, compared to its efforts in "integrated media." In light of failed attempts with the World Bodybuilding Federation (wbf) and the xfl (Extreme Football League) professional football league, the feasibility of wwe brand extensions beyond professional wrestling seems questionable. The hesitation of major corporate advertisers and sponsors to support the wwf speak to not only the questionable content of wwf television programming (i.e., vulgarity and lewdness), but to the structure of pro wrestling itself as "fake" sport. Unlike mainstream professional sports that receive the majority of their revenue from corporate America in the form of television contracts and corporate sponsorships, the majority of revenue for professional wrestling is derived directly from consumers on the foundation of live events. While sports leagues can and have endured for several decades, even the most successful television series rarely make it past their first decade. And, although sports audiences have been in steady decline, they do not experience the wild fluctuations that other entertainment properties often face. In sum, revenues for sports-based properties are more stable. While I can only speculate as to the motivations behind this shift, I believe that the WWF is placing itself in a precarious position.

This focus on television extends to the analysis of wrestling as well. While the premium of analysis among scholars has been television—perhaps because of the convenience it lends to textual readings—televised events only indirectly drive revenue in the form of creating interest for live event attendance and pay-per-view purchasing. Television does play a crucial role in creating interest for live events. But the continued success of the company and the industry as a whole depends on satisfying fans in live events. Television programming can succeed in creating interest in seeing a matchup between two stars, but if fans are not satisfied with the match, they will not continue purchasing pay-per-views or tickets to live events—and analysis that ignores live events misses a vital component of what makes wrestling "wrestling." While promotion and buildup are crucial to short-term success, long-term health of the industry as a whole, and of any individual promotion in particular, requires a cathartic resolution in the form of the match. Good promotion can get fans into an arena, but good matches will bring them back. Matches, then, must be dramatic themselves, a story within a story.

Textual readings of wrestling characters or "gimmicks" overlook the mechanics of the sport as performance, as well as the mechanics of the performance as sport. Despite variations in characters, gimmicks, and storylines, the basic formula of pro-wrestling matches has not changed in the past hundred years. In this essay, I will articulate this basic formula by discussing the traditional craft of pro wrestling, and I will compare it to more recent changes in the form. Drawing on my fourteen years of experience in the ring, I shall examine the core of professional wrestling: the match. In my past six years as a participant-observer in professional wrestling, I have explored its sensuous, performative, and improvisational aspects, wrestling in hundreds of matches and workout sessions (de Garis 1999). Drawing on this work, I shall outline how professional wrestlers put matches together and talk about them (or don't talk about them). Inside the world of professional wrestling, many veterans and old-timers lament that the "art" of wrestling

LARRY BRISCO

A promotional shot, circa 1990. A lot of newcomers try to make a
name with a flamboyant gimmick. I received advice—from Johnny
Valiant in particular—to play it straight. Johnny Rodz gave me the
"Brisco" name when I started. It's a tribute to the Brisco brothers,
whom I apparently resemble and who also wrestled as amateurs.

has disappeared. I plan to detail what that "art" consists of and discuss the
economic and structural changes in the wrestling industry related to its decline. My interest in analyzing the professional wrestling "match" is rooted in
my active professional wrestling career. Although in the past few years there
has been an increasing emphasis on "mic work" and acting ability, as a professional wrestler I am primarily interested in "having matches," hopefully
good ones.

BACKGROUND

I began my professional wrestling training in the autumn of 1987, just at the
demise of the old "territory" system. The United States was divided into, at

its height, more than twenty-five regional circuits. Each territory was known by is regional base and promoter. Eddie Graham ran Florida, the Funks ran Amarillo, Roy Shires ran San Francisco, and so on. Typically, territories ran *cards* several times per week, with the wrestlers traveling by car to the next town. During the time of the territories, and before Vince McMahon's famous appearance on national television in which he conceded that pro wrestling was not a "legitimate sport," the wrestling business was a closely protected, closed society. Its secrets were strongly guarded. "Protecting the business," as it was referred to during the beginning of my career, now seems a quaint notion. But it was taken very seriously at the time. Consequently, gaining acceptance into pro wrestling was no easy task.

Breaking into the wrestling business during the territory days was more of a hazing ritual than training process. As many veterans have described the process, a young initiate would show interest and be invited to the gym for a training session whereupon a veteran "shooter" would rough him up pretty good. Word has it that Hiro Matsuda, the "policeman" for the Florida territory, broke Hulk Hogan's leg when he tried to get into the business in Florida. If you came back after the leg healed, they figured that you had determination and might begin training you.

The training process would only last a few weeks, long enough for you to grasp the basics. Then, you would more than likely be put on the road to wrestle regularly, learning the craft as you went. Preferably, promoters would pair a rookie with a more experienced wrestler who could teach him the ropes. Gene Petit, aka Gene Lewis, or Malakai the Mongol, or Hillbilly Cousin Luke, says he spent only a couple of weeks in the gym before being sent on the road full time. Tom Sullivan, aka Johnny Sullivan, or Johnny Valiant, or Luscious Johnny V, said he learned how to throw a punch by pummeling Dick the Bruiser hundreds of times a night during a program in the old Indiana territory. There was little formal training; wrestlers learned the craft primarily by doing it and talking about it during the long car rides to the next town.

After the demise of the territory system and the rise of the wwf during the 1980s, the old way of training was no longer possible or necessary. First, there were no secrets to be protected, so the screening-out process disappeared. Second, a novice wrestler could no longer learn by doing because there was no place to wrestle on a nightly basis. Consequently, "wrestling schools" began to pop up around the country. While there had always been training facilities in different territories, there was really no such thing as a wrestling school until the mid-1980s. Wrestling schools were new: there was no established curriculum or format, and they were not easy to find.

In 1987, after a search process that took months, I finally stumbled on WWF Hall of Fame member Johnny Rodz's school. At the time, the school consisted pretty much of a ring in a vacant industrial space in Queens, then, by the time I started training, in Brooklyn. Since then, wrestling schools have proliferated. While wrestlers primarily learned by doing during the territory days, wrestlers now learn primarily from workouts in the gym. Although I certainly would have preferred having more work available, I consider myself fortunate in that I came along at a time when many veterans of the territory days were still active. Mostly, I benefited from long, rigorous training sessions working out with Johnny Rodz at Gleason's Gym in Brooklyn. While I was fortunate enough to have matches with acclaimed workers— Jimmy Snuka, Bob Orton Jr., Greg Valentine, Ivan Koloff, and many others— and certainly recognize many other influences, I believe that those regular sessions with Johnny did more to help me learn the craft than anything. Aspiring wrestlers who have begun their training within, say, the past five years have not had those kinds of opportunities. If they do get to work with a veteran of the territory days, it is likely someone who is well past his prime. Mostly, aspiring wrestlers train with each other in the gym and are less likely to perform in front of crowds. Most veteran wrestlers that run schools hire or use a head trainer, most of whom are people like me—someone who has been around the business for a while and maybe has gone through the school but has little or no national television exposure.

There are still a number of locally based promotions throughout the United States, called *independents* or *indies*. There are big differences between the indies and the territories of old. Indies do not run several times per week. Even the most successful indies rarely run more than once a week. Indy promoters are more likely to be fans, or *marks*, than professionals with some kind of background in the industry. Indy wrestlers run the gamut from aging veterans taking a payday, to experienced wrestlers looking for a break, to rank novices trying to get started.

The demise of the territory system and the dominance of the WWF have had a profound effect on the culture and performance of professional wrestling. Perry ("Sports On the Edge" 2000) quotes veteran professional wrestler Bob Orton Jr. describing current professional wrestlers as "Too much concern about style, not enough substance." Perry suggests that "You can now add pro rasslin' to the list of sports where the old-timers say today's athletes lack the fundamentals of their predecessors." But there is more to it than just an old-timer's nostalgia for the way things used to be. As someone whose career spans the time in which territories ended, I argue that the changes in the professional wrestling industry have had a deleterious effect on the performance of professional wrestling and the long-term stability of the industry.

To quote a phrase that I have heard from a number of ring veterans, professional wrestlers today do not know how to "work."

WORKING

Professional wrestlers most commonly refer to what they do as *work*, a loaded term that has several nuanced meanings. The term "wrestling" is seldom used, and usually in special circumstances (e.g., instances where there is more actual wrestling involved). "Sports entertainment," the WWF's official term, has yet to take hold inside or outside the industry aside from official company communications and the spoutings of The Rock. Consequently, inside the industry, professionals are called "workers," not "wrestlers."

"Working" is used to refer to employment and labor, manipulation and deceit, or cooperation or collusion. Probably the most common way that "work" is used is in its everyday meaning of employment and labor. For example, "Are you working this weekend?" I have heard many older wrestlers describe a colleague as "a good hand." The term also emphasizes the focus on labor and money, both as a motivation to get in the ring and as the ultimate by-product. "Work" as a proletarian term also reinforces awareness of labor relations between promoter and employee and reflects professional wrestling's blue-collar roots. Full-time professional wrestlers — though vastly diminished in numbers during the past fifteen years or so — must still focus on basic elements of the *job*. Like all workers, professional wrestlers must show up for work and do what the boss says.

Professional wrestling cannot be considered a full-time career, in that professional careers are limited, and consistent full-time employment without gaps has always been a challenge. Consequently, many professional wrestlers have another trade. For example, many former pro wrestlers work driving trucks or in warehouses for newspaper unions in the New York City area and actually moonlighted in those jobs during their active careers. Professional wrestlers with white-collar trades are much more rare, likely given the tenuous nature of employment in the professional wrestling industry and the financial benefits usually associated with white-collar careers.

The proletarian rhetoric is not limited to "working." I have heard many professional wrestlers, though mostly old-timers, refer to wrestling as a "craft." More common, however, is the term "job," used to refer to losing a match. "Doing the job," means taking a pinfall or submission. Back in the days when televised wrestling consisted mostly of short "squash" matches that pitted a budding star against an overmatched opponent, the loser was called a "jobber" or "job guy." "Working" also refers to the process of manipulation or deceit. "Working the crowd" typically means the process of manipulating the crowd to elicit certain reactions. "Working," which is deceptive, is contrasted to "shooting," which refers to either wrestling for real in the ring or telling the truth in interviews and other forums. "Are you working me?" would mean "Are you lying to me?" In fact, "working" can almost become a worldview. Some professional wrestlers become so used to deception and manipulation that they are skeptical bordering on paranoid. Professional wrestling performances at their core rely on manipulation and, to a lesser degree, deceit. Matches are meant to be "convincing" as are "characters" to use the official wwf (wwe) phrase.

In sum, the goal of most professional wrestlers is to be considered a "good worker" among one's peers. While professional wrestling lacks the objective standards of most sports — it is fitting that parallels were drawn between professional wrestling and figure skating during the judging controversies at the 2002 Olympic Winter Games — professional wrestlers do have a vocabulary for describing their craft. Good workers have good matches. While there are many cultural and technical factors associated with being a good worker — working light, a good record of safety, locker room etiquette, and so on — I shall focus on the performative aspects of having a good match in the remainder of this essay. In sum, a good match is "believable," "logical," and "tells a story."

BELIEVABILITY

When I first started training, I remember legendary wrestling trainer Larry Simon, aka "the Great Malenko," talking about some current wrestlers and whether or not their styles were "believable." These days, I hardly ever hear that description applied to a wrestling style or a wrestler in particular outside of Japan. But I am not alone in thinking that believability is still important to the professional wrestling industry. Now, I am not naive enough to believe that we can turn back the clock over a hundred years and try to establish professional wrestling as a "legitimate" sport. However, I do believe the credibility of professional wrestling as "fake" sport is important to fan enjoyment of the performances. The reason that credibility is important is so that fans can experience a pro-wrestling match as they would a sports event. The best matches in wrestling are those that mimic the oohs and ahs of a sports contest. The best matches have reproduced the formula that makes those "miracle moments" in sports so miraculous: the home run in the bottom of the ninth to win the game, the last-second field goal, the final-round knockout while you are behind on the judges' scorecard.

In order to mimic those moments, a match must be a seamless, impeccable performance of a sports contest. As detailed by Sharon Mazer (1998), professional wrestling fans often look closely for any slip or hole that will give away the secret. A "blown" spot or any mistimed maneuvers will preclude the suspension of disbelief. As Mazer argues, one of the strongest sources of pleasure for fans of spectator sports is the voyeuristic pleasure of seeing something that one is not supposed to see. Professional wrestling fans take pleasure in detecting mistakes or miscues that were not intended for their eyes.

Despite professional wrestling's history of outrageous gimmicks—from cowboys and Indians to spacemen—effective characters must be believable as well. Like Pee Wee Herman, even WWF (WWE) *Superstars* at the top level are never seen out of character. A recent example of how a credible character can be made effective is Bill Goldberg of the now-defunct World Championship Wrestling (WCW) organization. Goldberg is a former professional football player, a very rugged-looking individual. Despite his lack of professional wrestling experience, Goldberg was pushed through the ranks of WCW very quickly, amassing an impressive streak of "victories." Despite the fact that on a cognitive level, almost everyone knows that professional wrestling matches are not legitimate athletic contests, Goldberg became publicly regarded as a legitimate tough guy.

I remember being told by a former student that "if wrestling were real, Goldberg would kill everybody." Apparently, his assertion was based on

Goldberg's string of fake victories. And this was no stranger to sports. This particular student was a former Division I scholarship athlete. It might be easy to poke fun at this student, at his gullibility or naïveté. But there's more to it than that. The are other instances in which wrestling promoters push specific wrestlers to the moon with strings of impressive victories without success. If you ain't selling it, the fans ain't buying it. Goldberg was effective in portraying a believable character, that of a legitimate, serious athlete participating in a rough sport. In public interviews, Goldberg even kept *kayfabe*, maintaining that what he was doing was "real." "Goldberg" the character, and Goldberg the individual were both enormously successful. Likewise, the wwF's "Stone Cold" Steve Austin, the biggest drawing card of the 1990s, maintained a credible, serious character. Despite stints in other promotions as "Stunning" Steve Austin, a member of the "Hollywood Blondes" tag team, Austin was portrayed by the wwF and portrayed himself as a "West Texas Redneck" to great effect.

LOGIC

Pro wrestlers use the term "logic" frequently in evaluating matches. In order to make each moment intelligible, as Barthes says, a wrestler must make each movement logical. This is a challenge I put to my students during their practices. Why did you do that? If you do not have an explanation, you probably shouldn't have done it. Johnny Rodz frequently asks how specific moves or actions fit into the context of a contest. "Would you have done that if you were in a street fight?!" he exhorts. The point is that if you cannot explain in simple terms the purpose and meaning of the action, then it likely will be lost on the audience.

My first match was with territory veteran Charlie Fulton during the spring of 1988 in a high school in Connecticut. After the match, Charlie took the time to talk to me in the locker room about the match. He spent about twenty minutes discussing the different aspects of the match and my performance. Charlie had been working a rear chin-lock for a few minutes during the match. After a few minutes, I reversed the hold and went behind Charlie on the mat. After the match, he commented that while it was good for me to be aggressive in reversing the hold, I neglected to "sell" the cumulative effect of the hold. That is, had I really been in a vice grip rear chin-lock for any period of time my ears would be ringing and, after reversing the hold, I would be feeling the effects and would at the very least have to shake it off. It is a call based on professional judgment because there are no hard and fast rules.

Attention to minute details is essential in creating the overall performance. For example, a headlock is perhaps the most basic of wrestling maneuvers, something a novice might learn during his or her first day of training. While mastering the mechanics of a headlock is important, the "logic" of the headlock is equally important. Grabbing a headlock must be for a purpose besides setting up the next acrobatic high spot, as is the custom in many current matches. That is, when one wrestler takes a headlock, the one giving it pushes his or her opponent into the ropes; shoving the opponent off, the wrestler can then throw a high impact maneuver. Often, the headlock does not even resemble a wrestling hold. A good worker, however, will "work the hold." Instead of simply grabbing a headlock, a good worker will apply it in a way that signifies its purpose: squeezing your opponent's head so as to inflict pain and damage. Of course, you're not really squeezing your opponent's head. But it looks that way.

Both wrestlers must internalize the logic of the headlock in order to be completely effective. Not only does the wrestler applying the hold need to make it look like pressure is being applied; the wrestler in the headlock must "sell" the pain to illustrate the effectiveness of the hold. A "real" headlock exerts enormous pressure on the skull, cuts off circulation to the brain, and can be very uncomfortable for the ears (hence the phenomenon of "cauliflower ear" among so many old-timers, who had a penchant for working "stiff").[2] Following this logic, a headlock is not an easy hold to escape from, or at least it should not be. Now, the degree to which the wrestler who had been in the hold sells the effects depends on the duration and intensity of the hold. Too often, I see novices—and now even professionals on television—who are in a hold for a prolonged or repeated duration, yet do not sell the cumulative effect.

So take a common spot: headlock, go to the ropes, and a shoulder tackle. The logic behind the spot goes something like this. Say I grab a headlock on my opponent. I apply the headlock in order to gain an advantage and inflict pain. Being in a painful hold, my opponent naturally wants to escape. However, I am not too eager to relinquish the hold. My opponent keeps looking for an opening but cannot find one. Finally, almost out of desperation, he shoots me to the ropes, but being disoriented from the pain and damage caused by the headlock—which he indicates by holding his head and stumbling slightly—he finds himself off balance, giving me the chance to hit him with a shoulder tackle and knock him down. Without an internalized logic—both psychic and somatic—even a basic spot like a headlock/shoulder tackle will come off as flat. It may seem simple. If you get hit in the head, hold your head. If you get hit in the stomach, hold your stomach. If you get slammed on your back, hold your back. In fact, the logic *is* simple. Or rather, it is made simple. Each move is not inherently intelligible, as Barthes seems to suggest. Rather, *in a good match*, it is made intelligible by the performers, who include it in a consciously and carefully crafted series of signifiers. In a bad match, each moment is unintelligible.

While there are many creative twists to wrestling logic and endless opportunities for creativity within certain structures, the underlying fundamental is that, at its roots, professional wrestling is a portrayal of some kind of combat between—and now among—different contestants. Whether the logic is a street fight, a no-holds-barred match, or a wrestling match, it still must be a contest. Recently, some novice wrestlers have explained their lack of traditional logic by saying "wrestling is entertainment." I think it's a cop-out, an excuse for a poor performance. For instance, I wrestled a guy in Tacoma, Washington, in 1999 who worked a "baseball" gimmick. He wore a mask that looked like a baseball and a baseball uniform. It was one of his first matches after a very brief training period. Before the match, he said that he wanted to work in his "home run" spot. The way he explained it was that somehow I would end up caught in a corner, with my foot stuck in the rope, upside down. He would then "tag" the other turnbuckles before sliding into "home" and kicking me in the process. My reaction was "I don't understand. How does that fit into the match?" His response was simply: "It's entertaining." I persisted. I just couldn't understand how it made sense in terms of a contest. What am I supposed to be doing while he was tagging the other turnbuckles? If I was so hurt that I couldn't free one leg from the rope, why didn't he just pin me right then and there? I didn't say no categorically; I just wanted an explanation. He couldn't provide it. We didn't do the spot.

Among older veterans, the current lack of logic is somewhat of a joke. I frequently find veterans sitting around locker rooms talking about how wrestlers today will do all kinds of high spots—suplexes, somersaults, throwing opponents through tables, jumping off ladders and balconies, and so on — and then finish the match with a simple roll-up. It just doesn't make sense. But newcomers feel a real pressure to stand out, and high-risk high spots are, unfortunately, a quick way to rise above the clutter.

Other logical transgressions are outright comical. On one overseas tour, a wrestler decided to "get color" in his match (by nicking his forehead with the tip of a razor). The blood was meant to be set up by him being hit with a championship belt, a rather common technique. And that was how it went. Except, he "bladed" in the front of his head but was hit from behind. So, there was no blood on the back of his head where he was hit. I failed to notice, but it was brought to my attention by one of the locker room veterans and we shared a good laugh over it.

The problem is not that the business is given away but that it is a poor performance. Getting hit in the back of the head and bleeding from the front may be perversely entertaining. And while debasing professional wrestling as a sport and wrestlers as individuals may make for entertaining television to some, it will not draw crowds to arenas. What has always drawn crowds to arenas for professional wrestling is a hotly anticipated feud in which fans want to see the score settled. What keeps fans coming back is when the climax pays off.

STORYTELLING

Logic is a prerequisite for a good match, but it is not the end goal. While matches must be logical, they must also "tell a story." Storytelling is a common reference point among wrestlers when they talk about matches. As there exist many types of logic, likewise there are many types of stories. The tradition good guy–bad guy parable, though it still endures, is much less commonplace. One is less likely to see moral tales being played out in the ring than in the past. Still, matches are meant to tell stories. And the good ones do.

In today's wrestling scene, the good guy / bad guy dichotomy has been replaced with a more rudimentary strong/weak dichotomy. Today's pro-wrestling audience, skewing heavily younger and male, cheer the strong and boo the weak. In the absence of a framework of "sportsmanship" that predominated wrestling for so long, it is no longer moral weaknesses or moral turpitude that is vilified; it is simply physical weakness. The sense of justice, in Barthes's terms, is based on a "might makes right" ideology rather than some kind of traditional moral framework. Although possibly simply more "victory" than "justice," there is a sense of order, though not necessarily moral. Simply put, the stronger wrestler should win.

In a match in Calgary in November 1999, I was booked with a relative newcomer. Wrestling as "Professor Oral Payne" in the Stampede promotion, the idea I was given was to portray someone with a wrestling background that is somehow a bit off-key, the referent being Bob Backlund's mid-1990s WWF run.[3] So, I was working heel. At the beginning of the match, I dominated my opponent with technical wrestling, which displeased the six hundred or so fans in attendance. That was the point. My opponent, being somewhat green, became confused after a couple of minutes. Instead of staying aggressive in order to garner fan support, he would do something and then back off, causing an awkward pause. During one of those awkward pauses, I launched across the ring and hit him with a pretty solid clothesline. Immediately, I could hear the fans start to turn in my favor. If I wanted to stay out of favor, I had to back off, which I did. In that respect, I "stole" the match when I won because I was weaker. The basic story of the match is that I had better skills; my opponent was stronger and more rugged, but I managed to "steal" the victory by a combination of guile and luck.

The basic structure of the story in the match I just recounted is similar to most good matches: build a dramatic tension and reach a climax. In fact, when wrestlers themselves describe the basic elements of a match or a storyline, they frequently use sexual metaphors. The audience should "pop" at the finish and not "shoot its wad" before. In my role as informant in Mazer's *Professional Wrestling: Sport and Spectacle* (1998), I said, "wrestling is like making love to a woman," a phrase that has repeatedly come back to me since. What I meant is that wrestlers can gently or rigorously tease a crowd to build to a climax the same way lovers can sexually tease their partners to build the intensity of an orgasm. I recall one veteran in particular frequently gyrating his hips to simulate sexual activity while describing a good match, intimating that it was like making love to the crowd.

The underlying structure illustrated here is that matches must be constructed in a dialogue (or maybe colloquy) between or among the wrestlers and the crowd. Thus, the crowd has a say in constructing the story. The wrestlers are never in total control of the crowd — though they are frequently the manipulators or at least the facilitators. In effect, the crowd tells the wrestlers the story it wants to hear. It is up to the wrestlers to listen and react.

Sadly, the growing (and misplaced, I argue) emphasis on televised performance has led to an overall decline in wrestlers' ability to react to a crowd and construct an ad hoc story. As one veteran wrestler and booker told me, "All the great workers will tell you that the best work is the result of spontaneous improvisation."

I would like to be clear about the relationship between the wrestlers and crowds. While crowds do have input into how matches are performed, they do not — or at least should not — dictate the pace and outcome of a match. During "independent" matches at Gleason's Arena, Mazer observed that wrestlers responded to the all-too-common "boring" chants by immediately picking up the pace of the match. I attribute that to a lack of experience. Nickolai Volkoff told me that when someone chants "boring," he says, "Go home. I didn't ask you to come." Other veterans say they refuse to allow fans to dictate the pace of the match. When members of the crowd start a "bor-ing" chant, they just grab a hold and demand attention.

Despite the amount of play and flexibility, professional wrestling matches are guided by some fairly predictable, if not rigid, structures. The persistence of the hero/villain dichotomy, even in the absence of a moral framework, is perhaps attributable to the persistence of the dramatic form. While not all matches are "pyramidic" as Mazer suggests, there are certain formats that are typically followed. Jimmy Snuka summarized the process of putting a match together very succinctly: "Go out, get your heel heat, one big babyface comeback, and go home." Although the stories that many matches tell are more complicated, the basic structure is remarkably consistent. Typically, no matter how a match begins, the heel will take over at some point. The babyface then comes back with some "hope spots" or false finishes before the big comeback and the finish, regardless of who wins the match. The structure is consistent with traditional dramatic form: conflict, crisis, and resolution. The conflict is performed in the beginning of the match, the crisis with the heel heat, and the resolution with the finish.

Of course, there are an infinite number of possibilities within the basic story of a professional wrestling match. There are also a number of ways in which the story that is created can be more complex, especially in light of inserting elements of the wrestler's gimmick into the match. It takes more than putting on a costume and giving charismatic or entertaining interviews to make a gimmick effective. Any effective gimmick must be "worked" in the match. That is, elements of the "character" must be performed consis-

A promo shot from a 1997 tour in Malaysia. I didn't know
if I was going to work babyface or heel on the tour, so I
went for a bit of a "'tweener" look: enthusiastic, energetic
babyface, and/or psychotic heel.

tently and seamlessly. For example, for a wrestler to do a "dancer" gimmick,
it takes more than just doing a couple of dance moves in between spots; the
dancer must move gracefully throughout.

In another Calgary match — this time in the March, 2000 — I was pitted,
again as Professor Oral Payne, against one of the promotion's top babyfaces,
a young, athletic, acrobatic light heavyweight who had an amateur background. A group of heel wrestlers called "the Honor Roll" accompanied me
to the ring. The match started with a display of technical wrestling — "chain"
wrestling as it's referred to in the business. After a little bit of back and forth
to establish the nature of the contest, I decided to take my heel heat by raking
my opponent's eyes. I then threw my opponent out of the ring and grabbed

the referee. While the referee was occupied with me, the Honor Roll had the opportunity to jump my opponent.

The story behind the match is one of the more persistent in sports: the crafty veteran versus the enthusiastic upstart. As the crafty veteran, Professor Payne needed to exhibit guile, cunning, and, because he is a heel, deceit. As the young upstart, my opponent needed to display enthusiasm and vigor. After I cut off my opponent and he started to sell for me, I maintained control despite his efforts to the contrary. He would make a comeback by throwing some punches to my midsection; I would cut him off with a knee to the stomach or a rake of the eyes.

After a series of fake comebacks and false finishes to build tension, the stage was set for the big babyface comeback. During the big comeback, I was "unable" to cut him off. He gave me a big back body drop, shot me into the corner a couple of times, and set me up for his big finish: a *huracanrana* off the top rope. While he wanted to do a huracanrana, any move here would have sufficed because it is the part of the story where fans know that a resolution is near—kind of like reaching the last chapter in a suspense novel. Unfortunately, my opponent slipped off the rope and injured his shoulder. While I managed to hit a forward roll safely, my opponent's awkward fall caused him to kick me in the face. I wasn't too happy about that.

I was even less happy that because of his injury, he could not move in for the cover as would make sense for the match and the story. According to the characters, the story of the match would dictate outside interference (successful or not) by the Honor Roll at a point in the match where Professor Payne's victory was in jeopardy. Despite the missed spot, we recovered well and moved into the finish in which I applied a submission ankle lock after the outside interference. Afterward, we received compliments about having a "good match."

The favorable comments about the match centered on believability in applying holds and delivering blows without missed spots; on logic in not over- or underselling moves and building the match in a way that made sense; and on telling a story in that we produced a match that made sense given the context of our characters. Typically, professional wrestling angles are evaluated in the context of storylines and, more recently, writing. While it is important to get a solid storyline from bookers and writers—and we certainly did in Calgary—the execution of the angle still must take place in the ring. In that sense, the matches become stories within a story.

In this essay, I have attempted to provide an outline of what pro-wrestling veterans have taught me about pro wrestling during the past fourteen years. More to the point, I have discussed what, in my view, pro wrestling *should* be rather than what it *is*. As the business progresses away from pro wrestling and more toward "sports entertainment," you are less likely to find what I would call a good match on television or at an event. This is a fairly common view that can be found easily on a variety of pro-wrestling-related Web sites.

Within the past few years, droves of pro-wrestling fans have left the sport, especially older fans. As pro-wrestling television programming has evolved from a complex performance form referring to broadcast sport, to low-quality sketch comedy, traditional fans have turned the channel. As matches have evolved from a stylized sports contest to an almost randomly assembled series of acrobatic displays, some fans have stopped going to live events. For the pro-wrestling industry as a whole, these are disturbing signs. While exact figures are difficult to obtain, many who follow the industry believe that overall attendance at live pro-wrestling events is at its lowest in many years. The WWE receives a lot of press for its success because it is now the only game in town. But while the WWE may dominate market share, the overall pro-wrestling market has shrunk and continues to shrink.

Frequently, I find that I don't speak the same language as many of the younger guys in the locker room. I suppose that many of the younger guys look at me as somewhat of a dinosaur. I know that at least some of them do. From what I understand, their position is that I am stuck in the past; that the business evolved and I didn't. I feel differently. I believe that vague asser-tions of "necessary change" are an easy way to defend an inferior product; that the business didn't just change, but the in-ring product deteriorated.

Still, the decline in the product cannot be totally ascribed to booking or promotion. Talent on the part of pro wrestlers has deteriorated as well. When I broke into the business, there was very little choreography to matches. You would get your finish from the booker, maybe work out a few spots, and that's it. Everything else you would "play by ear." I have noticed a defi-nite trend in locker rooms toward a much more detailed choreography of matches. When I started, scripting matches was a joke. Within the past few years, I have seen detailed written scripts of matches. I have even witnessed "dress rehearsals" for matches. It's a downward spiral. Well-meaning promoters and bookers may provide detailed match scripts because their in-ring talent lacks the ability to improvise in the ring and create ad hoc responses to the crowd. But developing performers become reliant on the script and never learn to work. The end result is that matches come across as choreographed and robotic, even to the untrained eye. So while there may be polite applause or some oohs and ahs for a particularly acrobatic maneuver, there is no genuine heat generated.

Without a compelling story, pro wrestlers today must resort to the spectacular to get noticed. The bar continues to be raised with respect to acrobatics. The end result is a rate of injury that I believe is unprecedented in the history of the business. These days, top-level performers are retiring in their mid-thirties, just when pro wrestlers hit their prime not too long ago. The sad part is that so many of these injuries are unnecessary. The top pro-wrestling draws of the last decade — Stone Cold Steve Austin, The Rock, Goldberg — generally conformed to a traditional pro-wrestling repertoire.

The pro-wrestling business has always gone through up and down cycles. This time, I think it's different. I think there's a strong possibility for a prolonged down period for the industry as a whole. Long-term, however, I am bullish on pro wrestling. A veteran of the 1950s and 1960s once told me that the wrestling business always finds a way to reinvent itself. If the current style of sports entertainment eventually disappears, I still believe that pro wrestling's underlying appeal will endure. In the various mixed martial arts promotions around the country, I see a modern version of what pro wrestling was a hundred years ago. As talent and technique have declined in the United States, they have advanced in Japan. I am not sure what pro wrestling's next incarnation will look like. But I look forward to finding out.

NOTES

1. The histories of boxing and professional wrestling are intertwined. The *Ring* magazine continued to cover both boxing and professional wrestling up until the late 1960s. Primo Carnera started his career as a wrestler, switched to boxing, and finished his career as a professional wrestler. Professional wrestling influenced Muhammad Ali's public persona, leading to a close relationship between the boxer and professional wrestling during his professional career. The relationship continues to recent years, where Mike Tyson made an appearance on the World Wrestling Federation's *Wrestlemania*, and boxing and professional wrestling share fan bases.

2. There is a specific vocabulary used in describing the tactile sensations in a match. Working "stiff" means delivering blows and applying holds with excessive force. Although it doesn't always make the performance more believable, it always hurts more. Working "light" is the generally preferred feeling, though there are varying degrees of stiffness. Some wrestlers like to work "snug," a little stiff but not enough to be painful. Others use the term "solid" to describe a feeling somewhere between light and stiff.

3. Bob Backlund started his career as a clean-cut All-American, scientific wrestler. During the late 1970s and early 1980s, he was the wwf champion (which was the wwwf at the time). Word has it that Vince McMahon Jr. wanted him to dye his red hair black and turn heel after Hulk Hogan became champion in 1983. Backlund allegedly refused the request. Years later, he reappeared in the wwf and underwent his heel transformation, playing off his straightlaced persona in an offbeat manner. He started to wear a bow tie, launch into Elmer Gantry–type tirades, and lecture fans on proper conduct.

REFERENCES

Barthes, Roland. 1972 [1957]. "The World of Wrestling." In *Mythologies*. Trans. Annette Lavers. New York: Hill and Wang.

De Garis, Laurence. 1999. "Experiments in Pro Wrestling: Toward a Performative and Sensuous Sport Ethnography." *Sociology of Sport Journal* 16:65–74.

Henricks, Thomas. 1974. "Professional Wrestling as Moral Order." *Sociological Inquiry* 44, no. 3:177–88.

Levi, Heather. 1999. "On Mexican Pro Wrestling: Sport as Melodrama." In *Sportcult*, ed. Randy Martin and Toby Miller. Minneapolis: University of Minnesota Press.

Maguire, Brendan, and John Wozniak. 1987. "Racial and Ethnic Stereotypes in Professional Wrestling." *Social Science Journal* 24, no. 3:261–73.

Mazer, Sharon. 1998. *Professional Wrestling: Sport and Spectacle.* Jackson: University Press of Mississippi.

Mondak, Jeffrey. 1989. The Politics of Professional Wrestling. *Journal of Popular Culture* 23, no. 2:139–49.

Morgan, William. 1994. *Leftist Theories of Sport: A Critique and Reconstruction.* Chicago: University of Illinois Press.

Oates, Joyce Carol. 1994. *On Boxing.* Hopewell, N.J.: Ecco Press.

"Sports On the Edge." 2000. *San Angelo Standard Times*, 30 December.

Stone, Gregory, and Ramon Oldenburg. 1967. "Wrestling." In *Motivations in Play, Games and Sports*, ed. Ralph Slovenko and James A. Knight. Springfield, Ill.: Charles C. Thomas.

World Wrestling Federation Enterprises, Inc. 1999. Class A Common Stock. Bear, Stearns and Co., Inc.; Credit Suisse First Boston; Merrill Lynch and Co.; Wit Capital Production. 18 October.

Zengota, Eric G. 1991. "Versus: Archetypal Images in Professional Wrestling." *Quadrant* 24, no. 2:27–39.

LUCIA RAHILLY

Is *RAW* War?: Professional Wrestling

as Popular S/M Narrative

On 1 April 2001, the World Wrestling Federation (WWF, now WWE) stages its seventeenth annual championship contest, *Wrestlemania X-Seven,* a ratings juggernaut and the highest-grossing live event in WWF history. At the crux of the marathon series of matches—each consummating months of animosity and grudge-fueled foreplay between the competitors—the legendary McMahon family engages in an epic and intergenerational power struggle for control of the wrestling empire. With McMahon matriarch Linda apparently sedated and relegated to a wheelchair, Vince and his only son, Shane, pummel each other with a variety of improvised weaponry, including folding chairs, trash cans, and even, ironically, the agent of their much-publicized success—a television monitor. Daughter Stephanie, sporting a crystal-studded jersey reading "Daddy's Girl," jumps into the fray to land a petulant slap on her brother's cheek, only to flee offstage after a catfight with her principal rival for her father's affections, WWF diva and former McMahon sex toy Trish Stratus. Ultimately, Linda precipitates Shane's triumph, retaining her catatonic affect but delivering a crippling kick to her husband's groin. Capitalizing on his father's vulnerability, Shane knocks Vince unconscious, earning his mother's embrace and the respect necessary to assert his leadership status in the formidable McMahon machine.

The McMahon match at *Wrestlemania* represents the inevitable culmination of a Byzantine series of confrontations, including innumerable instances of jealousy, allegiance shifting, and betrayal—all enacted via typically outrageous threats and "unforgivable" insults. Located within an emotionally charged, open-ended narrative trajectory, the battle fits easily under the rubric of soap opera or, as Henry Jenkins describes professional wrestling, "serial fiction for men" (Jenkins 1997: 50, and in this volume). Unlike traditional melodrama, however—which maps the landscape of cultural norms, limning the boundaries between good and evil—the McMahon blowout actually foregrounds a host of physical pleasures typically suppressed or pathologized among "normal" citizens in the culture at large.[1] Specifically, the intrafamilial clash recycles a conventional melodramatic pretext for conflict—the struggle against a corrupt agent of power and its excesses—to contain and legitimize an otherwise brash celebration of bodily torment. Pointing toward a broader trend in wrestling performance, the episode conflates pleasure with violence and the apperception of pain, attempting to veil a queer-inflected, sadomasochistic extravaganza behind little more than a flimsy, melodramatic scrim.

Like professional wrestling generally, the McMahon match appeals to the popular yearning to "act out"—to react against cultural strictures enforcing normative behavior. Civilized deportment—the ability to govern oneself in an orderly and socially productive fashion—serves as a baseline marker for citizenship and cultural coherence; class mobility depends, at least in part, on adherence to the disciplined behavioral code of the bourgeois. Indeed, the historical emergence of a cultural infrastructure of "norms"—standards that both evaluate and regulate bodily conduct—coincided, Michel Foucault argues, with the burgeoning of the bourgeois class. To prosper in an industrializing economy based increasingly on the production and sales of goods and property, the bourgeoisie required an efficient means of ensuring a docile, law-abiding populace, and thus of safeguarding its investments and perpetuating its financial success (see "The Carceral," in Foucault 1995). Rights-based post-Enlightenment discourses, mirroring bourgeois economic aspirations, linked "acting out" and public instances of bodily harm—most visibly the spectacles of torture previously enacted to redress crimes—to vice and the excesses of the libertine-leaning aristocracy. The evolution of norms, in this formulation, functioned to eliminate and replace the public performance of pain, producing a society of docile citizens and ideal laborers in "an art of the human body directed . . . at the formation of a relation that makes [the body] more obedient as it becomes more useful, and [vice versa]" (Foucault 1995: 138).

At least on the surface, then, the McMahon episode inverts the cultural

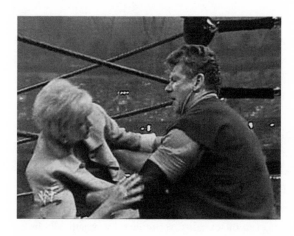

Vince McMahon and wife Linda embroiled in their internecine clash at *Wrestlemania X-Seven.*

value of "discipline" by lampooning the docile body. Ostensibly drugged, Linda McMahon—forced, apparently helpless, to watch her loved ones batter one another—literalizes the concept of docility, playing the foil to her family's flagrantly "uncivilized" behavior. Her passivity highlights her husband's most truculent transgression—not, in fact, his assault against his son, but his obstreperous insistence that Linda watch the bloody exchange of blows; as the match intensifies, he actually moves Linda into the ring to observe at closer proximity. Vince intends that watching this performance of violence and pain—for Linda, an ironic exemplar of a normal citizen—will constitute the ultimate punishment. For the thousands of cheering fans, however, watching is sheer pleasure, a much-anticipated privilege for which they've paid plenty. And while, in her status as an observer of an ongoing spectacle, Linda should represent a point of identification for the audience of fellow onlookers, she actually marks the gap between the contained conduct characterizing conventional spectatorship and the actively participatory, rowdy, and "undisciplined" behavior of wrestling fans. Her crowning moment, and the climax of the match, entails momentarily joining the fray. By rising to kick her husband, she comes alive, facilitating the predictably melodramatic outcome—the vanquishing of Vince, the embodiment of evil and corruption—and provoking a frenzy of support from the *Wrestlemania* fans.

Laden with libidinal dynamics, moreover—and narratively fueled, at least in part, by Vince's shameless extramarital betrayal with Trish Stratus—the McMahon match intensifies its challenge to cultural norms by skewering a chief measure of behavioral discipline: the well-ordered family. A critical example of one's capacity to govern, the family serves as a kind of test of citizenship; the "normal" family, as the principal locus for the transmission of cultural values, plays an instrumental role in preserving the dominant social order. To perpetuate its own stability — and thus fulfill this role effectively over the long term — the family is expected to strictly regulate sexual attitudes, containing sexuality while simultaneously denying its intrahousehold existence to the culture at large. In his boisterous flaunting of his mistress before his family and kids — and in his Oedipally resonant allegiance with his jealous, possessive daughter against his wife — Vince flaunts the family's status as "a hotbed of constant sexual incitement" (Foucault 1978: 109). He further complicates this notion of sexuality, moreover, by specifically linking pleasure to the performance of pain; at the nadir of Shane's suffering, he taunts his wife, "You like this, don't you — well watch this!" His words — intended, apparently, to insult her — prove solicitous to his fans, titillating them with the promise of an imminent wallop. Ironically, therefore, despite its rigorously heterosexual narrative format, the McMahon match points toward a facet of desire that falls definitively outside the rubric of straight sexual norms, highlighting the paradoxical pain/pleasure relationship at the core of the sadomasochistic dynamic.

Does the McMahon family's send-up of docile conduct implicitly destabilize dominant cultural norms? Arguably not. From one perspective, in fact, the kind of "acting out" mobilized in professional wrestling actually perpetuates the pervasive exercise of discipline by providing a safe, acceptable arena for the production and expression of powerfully charged emotions. As Jenkins argues, emotional restraint — particularly for men — proves critical to social integration (Jenkins 1997: 52, and in this volume); emotional display baldly violates cultural norms, coding vulnerability and a dangerous incapacity for self-control. Cathartic and libratory for both participants and fans, therefore, wrestling catalyzes a necessary emotional release that allows them to comport themselves, otherwise, in a definitively docile fashion. Providing a periodic emotional steam valve, moreover, professional wrestling provides no lasting solution to the larger cultural problem of affective distance, to which Celeste Olalquiaga attributes the increasing popularity and visibility of pain practices in contemporary culture. In an era where high-powered technological development has threatened to alter traditional corporeal functions and boundaries — fueling, in Olalquiaga's words, a "collective fear of organic disappearance and human alienation" (1999: 257) — sadomasochism provides a means of affirming the body, identifying its surface as the privileged site for the expression and experience of feeling. Enacting the performance of pain as a fetishistic substitute for more conventionally "authentic" emotional interaction, however — contriving a scenario to both prompt and police the fugacious expression of feeling — simply staves off eruptions of postmodern anxiety, exacerbating the wane of affect over the long term.

But professional wrestling certainly does more than supply a safe forum for acting out; in its appropriation and fundamental parody of athletic culture, wrestling actively illuminates the role of sport in preserving the power status quo. Serving a directly "civilizing" role, sport trains bodies to become both strong — and thus potentially useful in an industrial, manufacturing economy — and obedient to a coach or other authority figure. By promoting "sportsmanlike values," furthermore, which clearly correlate to the norms of citizenship, sport helps stabilize illusions of a cultural meritocracy — the myth of structurally unimpeded upward mobility that undergirds capitalist society. While professional wrestling apes the grammar of the conventional sporting event, its performance derives much of its dramatic punch from the jarring juxtaposition of the "vulgar" or "inappropriate" with the "normal" codes of athletic competition. Mocking "fair play" with its blatant violation of rules and cheerful celebration of trickery, professional wrestling fractures the athlete-citizen paradigm of impartially judged, equitable competition, highlighting instead the kinds of behind-the-scenes politics and prejudices that obstruct mobility for the majority of nonbourgeois subjects. In this context, the exaggerated, broadly drawn characterization typical of professional wrestling — often criticized for mobilizing racial, ethnic, class, and regional stereotyping — can be seen to foreground the biases operative in contemporary culture. For the nonelite, mobility on the broader cultural playing fields is clearly linked to the unfairly refereed politics of appearance characteristic of wrestling drama.

As a kind of athletic drag performance, therefore, professional wrestling resonates ambivalently as cultural critique: On the one hand, its incompatibility with dominant norms conflicts clearly with necessary preconditions for class mobility, assuring the compulsive repetition of its narrative as an ever-failing melodrama. On the other, its elucidation of the self-serving bourgeois logic structuring these norms opens up the possibility —

through its very reiterative tendency—for increased awareness and productive change. In its depiction of Vince McMahon's notorious double-cross of WWF veteran Bret Hart, Paul Jay's 1998 documentary *Hitman Hart: Wrestling with Shadows* problematizes the relationship between acting out and ascension in the class system, simultaneously blurring the boundaries between the performed self and the private citizen, and between wrestling artifice and "reality." After fourteen years of loyal service, Hart finds himself no longer popular enough to compete with his younger, bawdier competitors. The epitome of the "company man," Hart agrees, at Vince's behest, to commit the ultimate corporate sacrifice: to help Vince alleviate his organization's imminent "financial peril" by resigning from the WWF and moving to the WCW (World Championship Wrestling). But while Vince promises Hart the flexibility to leave on his own terms—to relinquish the belt "voluntarily" upon his departure—McMahon reneges on his word. Requesting that the referee ring the match-end bell while Hart is trapped in a submission hold, Vince effectively humiliates the Hitman, stripping him of his title during a championship bout on his own turf. Hart, bilious, stalks around the ring, swearing and spitting in what appears, ironically, a fairly typical performance of postmatch venom. The confrontation culminates off camera, when Hart decks Vince in the locker room—a "real" showdown that, as described by Hart in a voiceover, precisely mimes innumerable prior conflicts staged between the two.

Unable to accept the terms of his "failure," Hart points indignantly to a stylistic shift in wrestling performance, marking his ideological distance from what he perceives as a "raunchier, sleazier WWF not fit for kids." Waxing nostalgic for a morally binary landscape populated by faces and heels—wrestling jargon for "good guys" and "bad guys"—Hart denigrates the current trend toward openly lewd gestures and gratuitous, narratively unjustified violence. In doing so, he aligns himself with the tradition of melodrama; historically, the melodramatic "good/evil" character structure —and the genre's formal preoccupation with conflict between the moral, innocent poor and the malignant agents of power—has functioned to help embed values within a secular society, serving as "the principal mode for uncovering, demonstrating, and making operative the essential moral universe for the post-sacred era" (Olalquiaga 1999: 15). Ultimately transparent to bourgeois aims, the melodramatic narrative format reiterates the virtues of discipline and docility, celebrating a kind of ethical powerlessness much as Hart, in the aftermath of his rift from Vince, clings to the value of his own honor in *Hitman Hart*, claiming "It was almost a fitting end to the Hitman character, because he never sold out, he never lost his integrity."

Hearkening back to wrestling's formerly explicit moral framework, Hart underlines his desire to be "normal." At several points in the documentary, both he and his wife describe their yearning "to live a normal existence." What he perhaps fails to realize, however, is that historically, the adoption of the melodramatic good/evil format served simply to justify an otherwise blatantly sadomasochistic performance; as one critic articulates, wrestling "turned to the . . . tradition of melodrama . . . to provide a legitimizing morality for a spectacle of pain and suffering" (Rickard 1999: 136). Significantly, wrestling acquired its moral justification as part of its then-tacit transition to choreographed, scripted performance in the second and third decades of the twentieth century, a period often noted for the sensationalism of its popular entertainment. Reflecting and reiterating cultural anxieties regarding accelerating lifestyle tempos and intensifying sensory stimuli within the industrial metropolis, turn-of-the-century commercial amusement became obsessively concerned with the incitement of visceral shock.[2] Even the melodrama of this period, while preserving its characteristically definitive moral message, enacted the kind of visually superabundant, violent actions and stunts feeding the burgeoning modern appetite for spectacle. Instantiating a broader, thrill-seeking cultural aesthetic that celebrated the appearance of physical imperilment, therefore, professional wrestling deliberately recycled bourgeois moral mechanisms to contain its increasing violence quotient, thus ensuring its continued popularity within the growing commercial entertainment market.

Even justified by the moral pretext, therefore, wrestling celebrates the performance of pain—a pleasure falling distinctly outside the realm of cultural approbation. Try as he might to comport himself "normally," Hart pursues a lifestyle at odds with the values of citizenship; even as a face or hero, Hart—not unlike Vince—incorporates the sexualized experience of sadomasochism into the family space. Hart himself concedes that wrestling has impeded his family life; reflecting on his career, he remarks ruefully, "I've been gone a lot, which hasn't been fair to my wife. I can't say I've been the best husband in the world." But Hart—in large part a gentle father and loving son—spent his childhood listening to the whimpering cries of men being tortured in the dungeon of his home, his father allegedly "salivating

with pleasure" upon the discovery of willing participants in his own basement wrestling tourneys. As an adult, Hart maintains his own dungeon; he
poses—smiling for the filmmaker—beside a life-size mannequin, strapped
into an electric chair, that he activates remotely to visualize the experience
of pain. Hart's temporary work-related departures, therefore, fail to define
the scope of his cultural offense; without a moral structure to mask his sadomasochistic pleasures, Hart exhibits a nakedly nonnormative relationship
to violence, a cultural position uncomfortably at odds with his insistently
"pro-family" platform.

The incompatibility of wrestling with the norms of family and citizenship are taken up again in Barry W. Blaustein's *Beyond the Mat* (1999), a
documentary aiming—as its title indicates—to depict wrestlers in the "real"
world, beyond and in contradistinction to the spectacular artifice of their
live and televised quasi-competitions. Predictably determining "reality" via
attention to conventional family values, the film depicts the effects of wrestling performance—and particularly of the pain thus incurred—on various athletes' parents, spouses, and children. In one segment, for example,
the furious competitive antics of enormously popular wwf wrestler Mick
Foley[3]—one of the organization's most successful athletes—are juxtaposed
with images of Foley wallowing in domestic bliss: cuddling on an outdoor
hammock with his wife, praising his son for his achievement on his report
card, and patiently allowing his toddler-aged daughter to style his shoulder-
length hair into a ponytail. Underscoring its visualization of Foley's harmo-
nious "real-life" existence, the film approximates emotional intimacy with
Foley via a number of extreme close-ups, during which he articulates that his
"true" priorities are to retire from the dysfunctional world of wrestling and
dedicate himself completely to his responsibilities within the household.

After establishing his character as a committed "family man," however,
the film proceeds to undercut Foley's current capacity to father by linking
the disorder of his wrestling performance to familial emotional chaos. Opt-
ing to bring his children to a major "championship" match, Foley carefully
describes his impending performance to the children as "pretend," introducing them to his opponent and attempting to demonstrate their mutual
friendship; the violence of the extremely bloody match, however, spurs both
his daughter and wife to tears. On a later visit to Foley, moreover, the filmmaker confronts him with the footage in question—several minutes of reaction shots featuring his anxiety-ridden family, who eventually leave their

seats, continuing to watch the match via backstage monitors—thus forcing him to concede the incompatibility of wrestling indiscipline with familial governance. Chagrined, Foley confesses his failure to the camera, admitting: "Wow . . . I feel like a bad dad . . . I've never felt this way before."

Hinging on the question of identity, the episode reproduces a central narrative mechanism of traditional melodrama, that is, the visible clarification of "good" and "evil": the moment of ethical evidence and recognition, in Peter Brooks's terms, at which "characters will name the wellsprings of their being . . . proffer to one another, and to us, a clear figuration of their souls. . . . [S]uch moments provide us with the joy of a full emotional indulgence, the pleasures of an unadulterated exploitation of what we recognize from our psychic lives as one possible way to be, the victory of one integral inner force" (1985: 41). Affirming the bourgeois construct of the unified self, the film produces the "truth" of Mick Foley: within the conventional melodramatic space of the family, Foley—ironically, a professional face, or in wrestling terms, "good guy"—is proven to be "bad," a corrupted patriarch inflicting injury on his innocent, powerless family. What is particularly interesting about this segment, moreover, is the way that the truth of Foley—his moment of self-realization and confession—is entirely produced and mediated via the machinations of technology. For the Foley family observing the bloody spectacle, the proximity of liveness proves excessive; Foley's wife and children retire from their ringside seats, preferring to watch the event via the safely removed frame of a television screen. Their articulations of anguish—the evidence of Foley's "badness" revealed by the documentary, which, as a genre, takes "truth" as its central concern—stand in apparent contrast to the "inauthentic," performed version of affect occurring in the capital-driven spectacle onstage.

As in Olalquiaga's formulation, the enactment of pain—necessitated by a technologically induced sense of alienation and yet itself a technologically driven spectacle—serves as an invocation of affect. Foley's ultimate revelation is provoked not by intrafamilial, interpersonal communication, but by the electronically mediated visualization of emotional pain presented by the filmmaker. Usurping the fundamental visual technique of wrestling—that is, the imaging of both pain and uninhibited emotional expression—and reinserting it within a more functionally melodramatic format, *Beyond the Mat* illuminates the mutually inflecting processes of technology, "truth" production, and a particular, "normally" contoured value system; in the real-world representational economy of the documentary film, violence not legitimated by its cultural productivity becomes aligned with the "immoral."

Like both Vince and Hart, moreover, Foley further violates citizenship norms by publicly welding together constructs that are culturally defined as contradictory and yet mutually constituting and coexistent: sexuality and the family. Celebrated among wrestlers as a kind of limit case in the ability to endure bodily suffering—as one WWF executive queried in the film remarks, "I don't know if he's a masochist, but I don't think he minds feeling pain"—Foley openly combines the (arguably) pleasurable, sexualized experience of inflicting and enduring injury with what he and others have construed as a "family event."[4] The filmmaker's intervention into Foley's apparently shameless actions—his attempt to discipline Foley's seemingly untamable body via the infliction of guilt on his "soul"—reframes Foley's confession within the larger phenomenon of the pathologization and psychiatrization of the family.[5]

A consistent narrative strategy throughout *Beyond the Mat*, the eliciting of a confessional articulation—a disclosure of "truth"—functions to stabilize conventional cultural structuring of "truth" claims, whereby statements become intelligible as truths only via the affirmation of authority figures external to the wrestling scenario (such as, in the latter instance, the filmmaker). In another of the film's segments, fifty-five-year-old wrestler Terry Funk is featured examining x-rays of both of his knees with an orthopedic doctor. Advising him to retire from the ring, the doctor informs Funk that due to the deteriorated condition of his joints, he should not so much as walk without assistance—and optimally, without undergoing surgery. Linking Funk's desire to continue performing with medically diagnosed pathology, the film again mobilizes familial norms to situate wrestling as incompatible with citizenship; in light of the "truth about Funk's physical condition, the filmmaker solicits verbal confessions from Funk's wife and grown daughters regarding their father's dangerous profession and, failing to extract suitably affective responses, reveals their "true" emotional distress visually via reaction-shot footage taken during a match. Funk's subsequent decision to retire, appropriately announced on camera at his daughter's wedding, represents his accession to both familial duty and professionally authorized "truth"; his ensuing return to wrestling performance—occurring after the completion of the film—marks his culturally defined "madness," as Funk himself articulates it: "I guess I'm crazy, but it's hard for me to say no when I'm asked to get in that ring . . . it's just my way of life" ("Dropkicks" 2000: 7).

From one standpoint, preoccupation with the "real" or "true" injurious effects of professional wrestling on the physical health of its performers in *Beyond the Mat* is clearly contingent on the openness of wrestling artifice. The utter outrageousness of the wrestling spectacle—regularly synthesizing pyrotechnics, laser-light displays, heavy-metal music, and a panoply of high-flying body slams and potentially dangerous stunts, in addition to the conventional hand-to-hand combat—contextualizes blood and pain within a broader landscape of technologically facilitated illusion. Indeed, the reclassification of wrestling from sport to the hybrid genre "sports entertainment" in the mid-1980s facilitates the consideration of its corporeal effects as merely acted, linking wrestling to other forms of "action-adventure" entertainment such as the martial arts film. Constantly upping its violence and danger ante to vie with the quasi-chimerical visual effects of editing and digital manipulation possible in other formats, however, wrestling differs critically from its commercial competitors in the fact of its "liveness."

As a live event, wrestling is grounded in a kind of productive instability, a tension that wrestlers endeavor to contain via careful rehearsal of the scripted choreography, but that simultaneously functions to fuel wrestling narrative and generate increased interest in its performance. Operating similarly to the talk show—the "cousin genre of professional wrestling"[6] for which the moment of raw, uncontrived emotional orgasm comprises the "money shot"—wrestling offers the potential to view a breakthrough of spontaneously experienced, "true" affect, in the form of physical pain.[7] By illuminating the consistently "real," detrimental somatic effects of wrestling, therefore, even when such effects are spectacularly contained and endured without immediate medical attention, *Beyond the Mat* ambivalently reinforces and undermines the "truth" of wrestlers' enactment of pain, affirming the "reality" of their performed, corporeal experience while simultaneously pathologizing their willingness to engage in injury for the purposes of entertainment.

From another standpoint, however, situating wrestling within the dynamic of confession belies its preoccupation with surfaces, in which the reformulation of pain as pleasurable is inevitably bound up. Wrestlers' critical offensive tactic, the *hold*—a physical configuration allowing the indefinite immobilization of one's adversary—not only functions to visualize the dramatization of powerlessness (as per Barthes 1972: 20), but to freeze the body into a range of poses effecting an unusual degree of bodily display. Constant innovation into the types and arrangements of holds, which early on became contrived enough to require the cooperative participation of the "victim," pushes to frame and reframe every segment of the wrestler's anatomy in an expanding variety of combinations. The recent incorporation of quasi-weaponry into ring combat—in combination with prematch infliction of superficial cuts, loosely stitched to burst open under forceful impact—further enlarges the field of visibility, extending the network of viewable surfaces via the depiction of blood and flayed skin.[8] Excessive in its attempts to transgress the boundaries of televisual representation, wrestling is simultaneously contained by the limits of bodily endurance, functionally replicating a sadist dynamic that oscillates between excess and deficiency.

The appearance of extreme somatic violence, moreover, highlights the reduction of the body to a prediscursive state of "flesh." The wrestlers' groans and expressions of affect, in this formulation, signify their accession to embodiment in "its barest materiality: a mass of flesh, a network of nerves, and an expanse of skin" (Henaff 1999: 80). The disarticulation of the body as discursive construct—noted to be a critical effect of s/m practice generally (see Hart 1998: esp. chap. 2)—has a particular resonance within the wrestling context, where corporeal contours seem so heavily inflected by developments in capital and technology. Obviously "built," the wrestling body emerged as part of a broader "muscle body" trend amid the late-nineteenth-century climate of industrialism, reflecting and reiterating manufacturing ethos in its reconceptualization of the body as mechanistic "product."[9] Within the large-scale celebration of capitalism via the display of commodities—the opening of the Crystal Palace, for example, and the beginning of the World's Fairs—"muscle bodies" became subject to the same spectacularizing processes as industrial products more generally.

Although affiliation with the traveling-show circuit led rapidly to exhibition contexts more conventionally considered carnivalesque—and, concomitantly, to a refiguring of the wrestler's body as grotesque, rather than athleticized and muscular—wrestlers' recent return to the aesthetic of the muscle body points again toward the question of the body's position within the discourses of the contemporary economy. If public spectacles of corporeal torture are indeed preindustrial—the "effect of a system of production in which labour power, and therefore the human body, has neither the utility nor the commercial value conferred on them in an economy of industrial type" (Foucault 1995: 54) — then the present popularity and increased violence quotient of professional wrestling can be seen to articulate the inutility of the body within the postindustrial, information services economy. The mutual interchange of violence between evenly "built" bodies, moreover — and the perpetual reversibility of "top"/"bottom" status — provides a local example of a formulation of power not as an effect of laws, but rather as constantly shifting, relational, and unstable.[10]

Within a Foucauldian formulation, significantly, the practice of deconstructing the discursive body represents a method of askesis, a process of cultivating, fashioning, and styling the self in order to effect a specific kind of self-transformation.[11] Less the inner exploration of a unique, private space — the true self constructed and confessed in the tradition of bourgeois humanism — than a rigorous strategy of self-scrutiny deployed to achieve a new relationship of self-reflexivity, askesis provokes an encounter with the self as other, ultimately leading beyond the limits of the self to a place of transcendence. The performance of sadomasochism is significant, among a range of practices constituting askesis, as a means of achieving a new experience of bodily pleasure, and thus of effecting a fundamental change in the relationship between self and body; deprivileging the erotic monopoly held by the genitals, s/m remaps and redistributes erogenous zones to include the entire corporeal surface. Detaching power from the site of the penis, sadomasochistic practice reconstructs the body as a sort of diffuse, sensorial continuum, decentering the subject and disarticulating the psychic and bodily integrity of the self to which sexual identity has become attached.[12]

Retraining focus from the bourgeois system of norms and their pathologizing effects, Foucault illuminates the political implications of sadomasochism, refiguring pain and sex as interconnected mechanisms critical to the productive work of pleasure and the care of the self. Interestingly, while acknowledgment of the intermingling of pain and pleasure seems increasingly unavoidable in professional wrestling — particularly given the flimsy tenability of its moral framework — the linkage between pain and sexuality as a particular strand of pleasure is consistently elided. Even in its more conventionally intelligible heterosexual format — the gendered "female/top, male/bottom" masochistic paradigm established by Sacher-Masoch — the issue of wrestling as sexually provocative sadomasochism is publicly confounded. Whip-bearing female wrestlers in dominatrix-style leather corsets humiliate their male opponents, yet the quasi-pornographic body aesthetic of many female wrestlers and valets — often accentuated by scanty costuming and occasional mid-match breast baring — seems to constitute legible sexuality in professional wrestling to the exclusion of either straight or queer s/M.

Indeed, in its brief portrayal of WWF wrestler Chyna — the only female athlete depicted in the film, and one of the most popular of the dominatrix-style characters — *Beyond the Mat* focuses solely on the apparently problematic status of her "femininity" and by extension, presumably, her (hetero)-sexual allure. Attempting to contain the destabilizing threat of her muscular physique, the film depicts Chyna in the exaggeratedly gender-coded act of having her toenails painted; simultaneously, she reassures the audience that despite the suspicions of her family, she is "not a lesbian . . . just a girl who loves lifting weights." Again citing the family as the proper locus for the confession of sexual "truths," the scenario transitions visually to the gym, where Chyna performs bicep curls under the now-approving gaze of her parents. The segment concludes by apprising the audience of Chyna's recent cosmetic jaw surgery, performed — from the filmmaker's perspective — to enhance the femininity of her appearance. Ultimately preserving the integrity of gender boundaries, the film's treatment of Chyna functions to reinforce the distinction between male and female, problematizing the discrete aberrance of her body rather than the broader dimorphic conceptualization of gender categories. Legitimizing Chyna's popularity by extracting the "truth" of her femininity (and overlapping heterosexuality), moreover, the film dissociates the construct of "self" from "surface," effectively denying the potential attractiveness of her musculature, costume, and in-ring behavior as they resonate within the semiotics of sexual s/M.

In this context, the incorporation of female characters embodying a more stereotypically feminine, exaggeratedly legible sexual aesthetic into the wrestling spectacle provides a correlatively moral, gendered substitute for the melodramatic "good/evil" structure, functioning to contain and — at least superficially — to discipline the excesses of "perverse" or "pathological" sexuality. More specifically, the incitement to sexual provocation via the performance of pain — and further, via the visualization of excessive, undisciplined bodies potentially complecting the categories of gender — is both masked and "properly" reoriented by the obvious and regular display

The WWE's Chyna posing in quasi-dominatrix garb.

of, for both male and female spectators, the culturally sanctioned hetero-sexual object-choice. Putatively desirable for the straight female viewer,[13] the male wrestling body — sensationally muscle-bound, bronzed, and cleanly waxed — blurs codes in its aesthetic overlap with gay male "butch drag,"[14] underlining the necessity for the female tits-and-ass burlesque.

Unlike other athletes, who build and deploy their muscles to effect en-hanced performance, developing specialized physiques according to the de-mands of their respective sports, wrestlers — and, similarly, gay musclemen — construct and display their musculature to visually cue strength, power, and, at least in gay culture, erotic desire; in the words of queer theorist David Halperin, "the exaggerated, arcane, highly defined, elaborately sculpted muscles of the gay male gym body derive from no useful pursuit and serve no practical function: they are the sort of muscles that could only have been developed in the gym. They are explicitly designed to be an erotic turn-on, and . . . they deliberately flaunt the visual norms of straight masculinity, which impose discretion on masculine self-display and require that straight male beauty exhibit itself only casually or inadvertently, that it refuse to acknowledge its own strategies" (Halperin 1995: 117).

Mirroring "butch" performance of a kind of hypermasculinized effeminacy, male wrestlers similarly transgress culturally constructed gender codes via practices of self-flaunting and quasi-solicitous, vain display, as rhetorically manifest in the naming of wrestling characters such as "Gorgeous George," "Scotty Too Hotty," and "Sexual Chocolate." Without the rigorously policed disavowal of the link between pain and sexual pleasure, therefore—facilitated and, paradoxically, necessitated by the hypereroticization of both male and female wrestling competitors—the spectacle of overtly sexualized, barely clad, intimately grappling same-sex bodies would threaten the stability of the boundaries of heterosexual identity. In its very amplification of erotics within an ostensibly heterosexual matrix, therefore, wrestling serves to illuminate the normalizing role of sport more generally as it preserves the integrity of the categories of gender and sexual orientation, serving as a forum for "men to watch and dissect other men's bodies . . . a legitimate space for gazing at the male form without homosexuality alleged or feared" (Miller 1998: 103).

In the context of increasing cultural attention to pain practices and the construction of subjectivity—exemplified by the recent Hollywood films *Fight Club* (1999) and *American Psycho* (2000), as well as by the broadening visibility of s/m and pain practices such as tattooing and piercing—professional wrestling points toward what appears to be widespread ambivalence regarding the postindustrial body in pain. Marked advances in technology strive constantly toward the elimination of corporeal suffering. As the narrowing field of the "normal" paradoxically assures the proliferation of delinquencies (see Foucault 1995: esp. 296–308), however, so advancements in the diagnosis and treatment of pathology function to organize and produce bodily pain, engendering forms of knowledge by which individuals understand and map corporeal sensations: "If the medical industry has succeeded in one thing over the past two centuries, it is in democratizing hypochondria. . . . We are involved in a process of self-evaluation, or self-incrimination, within the broad apparatus of the health and medical industries" (Acland 1999: 209).

The practice of pain in professional wrestling—although framed in the terms of "acting out," of defying the codes of disciplined comportment — derives its impetus and structure from developments in technology. The sheer accumulation of capital constituting its spectacle means that wrestling must deliver according to audiences' technologically framed expectations for the exhibition of violence and gore. Repeatedly testing the limits of bodily endurance, moreover, wrestling manipulates sexuality to mask the linkage between pain and sadomasochistic pleasure, occluding potentially productive implications for the reformulation of the "perverse." The involvement of minoritarian subjects on the production side of professional wrestling — the outrageously popular "Goldberg," for example, whose enormous physique counters stereotypes regarding "weak" Jewish bodies,[15] or queer pop star Bob Mould, who recently finished a stint as creative director for the WCW — points toward the possibility for positive intervention into corporeal dynamics in wrestling. Ultimately, however, the burden for the refiguration of pain, sexuality, and subjectivity is inextricably bound up in the culturally determined conditions of visibility, and in destabilizing the insistently heterosexual matrix through which wrestling is perceived.

NOTES

1. For a discussion of the characteristics of melodrama, see Peter Brooks (1985: chaps. 1–3).

2. For a discussion drawing on the writings of Walter Benjamin and Siegfried Kracauer in this vein, see Ben Singer (1995: 72–99).

3. Consistently ranked in the WWF top five as one of his multiple wrestling personae, Mick Foley authored a biography that immediately rocketed to number one on the *New York Times* Nonfiction Bestseller List.

4. As described in Neil Strauss (1999: 33). See also Barbara Kantrowitz (2000: 52).

5. As Foucault describes in *History of Sexuality* (1978: 111), "a pressing demand emanated from the family: a plea for help in reconciling these unfortunate conflicts between sexuality and alliance . . . the family broadcast the long complaint of its sexual suffering to doctors, educators, psychiatrists, priests . . . to all the 'experts' who would listen."

6. Joshua Gamson (1998: 92). For a discussion of the talk show "money shot," see pp. 90–95.

7. As wrestlers incur greater risks in performance, injuries requiring immediate, in-ring medical attention have become increasingly regular. In addition to the much-publicized on-air death of wrestler Owen Hart after a fatal fall in 1999 and several recent paralyses, wrestlers frequently require assistance for broken bones, torn muscles, and severe lacerations. Although several states have effectively prevented wrestling performance within their borders due to its potentially hazardous effects, the designation *sports entertainment* limits the kind of governmental regulation of wrestling that occurs in conventional sport.

8. *Beyond the Mat* features Vince McMahon engaging in the pre-match cutting and stitching of the crown of his head, apparently under the supervision of specialists, although the film does not explain or comment on this occurrence. Lacerations to the skin of the head generally produce a relative abundance of blood, facilitating the appearance of a blood-covered face commonly described in wrestling terms as a "crimson mask."

9. For a discussion of the emergence of the "muscle body" within a capitalized framework, see Jon Stratton (1999: 151–72).

10. In Foucault's words, power is "a conception . . . which replaces the privilege of sovereignty with the analysis of a multiple and mobile field of force relations, wherein far-reaching, but never completely stable, effects of domination are produced. The strategical model, rather than the model based on law." See Foucault (1978: 102).

11. "*Askesis* means . . . the progressive consideration of the self, or mastery over oneself, obtained not through the renunciation of reality but through the acquisition and assimilation of truth. It has as its final aim not preparation for another reality, but access to the reality of this world. . . . It is a process of becoming more subjective." See Foucault (1988: 35).

12. "It is sexuality that amalgamates desire and identity into a unitary and stable feature of the individual person and thereby imparts to the subject a 'true self' — a 'self' that constitutes the 'truth' of the person and functions as an object both of social regulation and personal administration." See David Halperin (1995: 95).

13. For a discussion of the public exhibition of sexual desire for male wrestlers by female wrestling fans in the 1940s and 1950s, see Chad Dell (1998).

14. See Brian Pronger's discussion of the muscle body as gay "butch drag" in Pronger (1990: 116–19).

15. For a discussion of the perceptions of the Jew as weak and sickly, and further, for implications of this stereotype in the racist scientific practice of eugenics, see Sander Gilman (1991). José Muñoz also takes up this trope in Muñoz (1999) in demonstrating the disidentificatory potential of the Superman comic, originally authored by Jews, which seems relevant here given the oft-noted influence of comics on the wrestling genre.

REFERENCES

Acland, Charles R. 1999. "Take Two: Post-Fordist Discourses of the Corporate and the Corporeal." In *When Pain Strikes*, ed. Bill Burns, Cathy Busby, and Kim Sawchuk. Minneapolis: University of Minnesota Press.

Barthes, Roland. 1972 [1957]. "The World of Wrestling." In *Mythologies*. Trans. Annette Lavers. New York: Hill and Wang.

Blaustein, Barry W., director. 1999. *Beyond the Mat*. Film. Imagine Entertainment.

Brooks, Peter. 1985. *The Melodramatic Imagination: Balzac, Henry James, Melodrama, and the Mode of Excess*. New York: Columbia University Press.

Dell, Chad. 1998. "Lookit That Hunk of a Man! Subversive Pleasures, Female Fandom, and Professional Wrestling." In *Theorizing Fandom: Fans, Subculture, and Identity*, ed. Cheryl Harris and Alison Alexander. Cresskill, N.J.: Hampton Press.

"Dropkicks." 2000. *World of Wrestling Magazine* 1, no. 12 (April): 7.

Foucault, Michel. 1978. *History of Sexuality*. New York: Vintage Books.

———. 1988. "Technologies of the Self." In *Technologies of the Self*, ed. Luther H. Martin, Huck Gutman, and Patrick Hutton. Amherst: University of Massachusetts Press.

———. 1994. "Language to Infinity." In *Essential Works of Michel Foucault*. Vol. 2: *Aesthetics, Method, and Epistemology*. New York: New Press.

Gamson, Joshua. 1998. *Freaks Talk Back: Tabloid Talk Shows and Sexual Nonconformity*. Chicago: University of Chicago Press.

Gilman, Sander. 1991. *The Jew's Body*. New York: Routledge.

Halperin, David. 1995. *Saint Foucault*. New York: Oxford University Press.

Hart, Lynda. 1998. *Between the Body and the Flesh: Performing Sadomasochism*. New York: Columbia University Press.

Henaff, Marcel. 1999. *Sade: The Invention of the Libertine Body*. Minneapolis: University of Minnesota Press.

Jay, Paul. 1998. *Hitman Hart: Wrestling with Shadows*. Documentary. A&E Cable.

Jenkins, Henry. 1997. " 'Never Trust a Snake': WWF Wrestling as Masculine Melodrama." In *Out of Bounds: Sports, Media, and the Politics of Identity*, ed. Aaron Baker and Todd Boyd. Bloomington: Indiana University Press.

Kantrowitz, Barbara. 2000. "Is This Too Raw for Kids? What Parents Should Know About Wrestlemania," *Newsweek*, 7 February, p. 52.

Miller, Toby. 1998. *Technologies of Truth*. Minneapolis: University of Minnesota Press.

Muñoz, José. 1999. *Disidentifications: Queers of Color and the Performance of Politics*. Minneapolis: University of Minnesota Press.

Olalquiaga, Celeste. 1999. "Pain Practices and the Reconfiguration of Physical Experience." In *When Pain Strikes*, ed. Bill Burns, Cathy Busby, and Kim Sawchuk. Minneapolis: University of Minnesota Press.

Pronger, Brian. 1990. *The Arena of Masculinity: Sports, Homosexuality, and the Meaning of Sex*. New York: GMP (Gay Men's Press).

Rickard, John. 1999. "The Spectacle of Excess: The Emergence of Modern Professional Wrestling in the United States and Australia." *Journal of Popular Culture* 33, no. 1 (summer): 129–38.

Singer, Ben. 1995. "Modernity, Hyperstimulus, and the Rise of Popular Sensationalism." In *Cinema and the Invention of Modern Life*, ed. Leo Charney and Vanessa R. Schwartz. Berkeley: University of California Press.

Stratton, Jon. 1999. "Building a Better Body." In *Sportcult*, ed. Randy Martin and Toby Miller. Minneapolis: University of Minnesota Press.

Strauss, Neil. 1999. "What Rock Could Learn from the WWF." *New York Times*, 28 March, sec. 2, p. 33.

PHILLIP SERRATO

Not Quite Heroes: Race, Masculinity,

and Latino Professional Wrestlers

It's about spectacle, not who wins or loses.
—*Beyond the Mat*

The spectacle is not a collection of images;
rather, it is a social relationship between people
that is mediated by images.—Guy Debord,
The Society of the Spectacle

In 1999, toy manufacturer Toy Biz released a line of nine "Smash 'N Slam Wrestlers" action figures. The series immortalized the biggest and "baddest" white stars of World Championship Wrestling, such as Kevin Nash, Lex Luger, Hollywood Hogan, and Sting. Along with a mean snarl and an unrealistically hypermuscularized body, each eight-inch figure came with an accessory such as a breakaway table, a breakaway crowd-control gate, or a folding chair. In every case, the toy wrestler had the capacity to act out supermasculine rage by throwing or breaking the accessory or by using it to brutalize an opponent.[1]

Interestingly, a 4.5-inch Rey Mysterio Jr. figure serves as Smash 'N Slam Giant's accessory. This pairing is notable because in real life, Giant, who is white, stands nearly two feet taller and weighs 350 pounds more than Mysterio, a muscular yet diminutive *luchador* from Mexico. Clearly, Toy Biz designers did not intend the much smaller Mysterio to function as a competitor for Giant. They included the Mysterio figure to make Giant look unusually large and domineering. The two figures are grossly disproportionate to

Smash 'N Slam Giant clutches a pathetically tiny and helpless Smash 'N Slam Rey Mysterio Jr. Photo By Laura E. Ramirez-Diaz.

emphasize Giant's physical superiority and, presumably, to offer consumers greater amusement.[2] Besides making Giant look intriguingly enormous, the disproportionately smaller Mysterio figure serves as the victim of his signature choke slam, and, thus, he additionally enables the performance of Giant's superior power. As the instructions on the packaging explain, for fun one can slip Mysterio's tiny neck into the grip of Giant's enormous right hand and then squeeze the larger figure's legs together to see him sadistically lift, lower, and strangle the hapless Mexican.

This unequal relationship between the Mysterio and Giant toys reflects the unequal relationship that wrestling promotions have maintained between Latino and white wrestlers over the past twenty years. In the 1980s and 1990s, profit-minded promoters sacrificed the prominence and respectability of Latino performers such as Tito Santana, Rey Mysterio Jr., and Eddie Guerrero, while they made large and powerful white wrestlers their star attractions. As part of an effort to bolster the primacy of their white stars, promoters oversaw the development of storylines and characteriza-

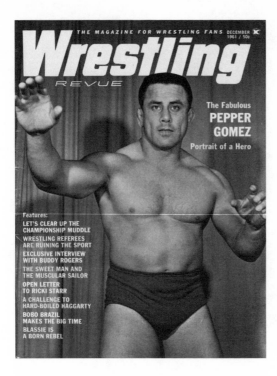

The Fabulous
PEPPER
GOMEZ
Portrait of a Hero

Pepper Gomez enjoyed wide-spread popularity and was seen as a "fabulous hero." Courtesy of Arena Publishing (www.wrestleprints.com).

tions that positioned Latino wrestlers as weaker and smaller, embodying a masculinity that was inferior to the monolithic masculinity that larger white wrestlers embodied. Importantly, this debasement of Latino wrestlers and Latino masculinity represented a dramatic shift from the more positive portrayals in the 1950s–1970s of Latinos such as Pepper Gomez, Pedro Morales, and Mil Mascaras. Prior to the 1980s, promoters tended to cast their Latino wrestlers as fan-friendly characters who were often champions and who embodied admirable personal qualities. Moreover, representations of Latinos in the earlier decades encouraged audiences to identify with those wrestlers, even across racial differences between the wrestlers and wrestling fans. In contrast, promoters' increased reliance in the 1980s on large white wrestlers to entertain audiences, combined with more contentious racial politics within wrestling leagues themselves, precipitated more derogatory portrayals of Latino performers that invited fans to limit their esteem for Latinos and for Latino masculinity.

What does it mean to describe the masculinity of heavyweight white wrestlers as "monolithic" in comparison to representations of Latino masculinity? To be sure, the history of professional wrestling has seen its share of oversized wrestlers, Andre the Giant being perhaps the most famous. And more recently, the two main venues — the WWF (now WWE) and the WCW — have given pushes to wrestlers of color, particularly The Rock and Booker T. But in terms of ring time and title shots, Latino wrestlers have been increasingly pushed to the margins. More than that, the meaning of an idealized masculinity in professional wrestling has come to be equated with the brute force and excessive violence of huge, white superstars. Not only has. this choice limited the career opportunities of the best Latino wrestlers, who tend to be smaller than their white counterparts, but it has limited the range of acceptable meanings for masculinity available for public consideration and consumption. Generally speaking, smaller and faster Latino male wrestlers have drawn upon the Mexican *lucha libre* tradition — which favors speed, finesse, and acrobatic agility over brute force — and have incorporated positive references to *la raza* into their performative personas. Yet while Latino wrestlers of the 1950s, 1960s, and 1970s could build positive and winning characters out of these performative choices, in the last two decades, storylines and character choices have increasingly limited the meanings assigned to Latino culture and masculinity, positioning these qualities as signs of cowardice, weakness, and a ghetto-style animality in the face of fearsome white power. In this sense, *monolithic* whiteness refers both to an increased emphasis in size and power, and to the positioning of Latino masculinity as inherently inferior. A glance at the history of Latino male wrestlers in U.S. professional wrestling suggests that this trend is not only disempowering to individual wrestlers, but a source of regressive racial formations in general.

PEPPER GOMEZ, PEDRO MORALES, MIL MASCARAS, TITO SANTANA, AND JOSE LUIS RIVERA

One might intuitively want to approach the subject of Latinos in professional wrestling by identifying the ways that racism has haunted the representation and reception of these wrestlers. It might therefore surprise some (if not many) to realize that several Latino wrestlers have managed to become quite popular. In the 1950s, 1960s, and 1970s, U.S. fans cheered without restraint for Pepper Gomez, an amiable "Latin" wrestler renowned for his toughness in the ring (as well as his ability to withstand the weight of a Volkswagen

Bug on his abdomen). Throughout the 1960s, 1970s, and early 1980s, Pedro Morales and Mexican lucha libre legend Mil Mascaras also reigned as renowned stars and huge fan favorites. The Puerto Rican Morales even enjoyed lengthy stints as the WWF heavyweight and Intercontinental champion. By the early 1980s, as Morales's career began to wane, Tito Santana emerged as an extremely popular Mexican who won the WWF Intercontinental belt twice and became so well liked that in December 1984 the magazine *Wrestling's Main Event* declared him "The New People's Champion."

These four Latinos — Gomez, Morales, Mascaras, and Santana — garnered the support of fans and the high esteem of wrestling commentators and journalists because of their moral integrity and solid wrestling talent. Indeed, the four Latinos fit perfectly folklorist John Gutowski's definition of the wrestling hero as distinguished by "his skill and sportsmanlike supremacy" (1972: 45). In contrast to heels such as Bobby Heenan, Don Muraco, Freddie Blassie, and "Mr. Wonderful" Paul Orndorff, the four Latinos were venerated for their discipline, hard work, cordial demeanor during interviews, and appreciation of fans' support. Commentators also consistently praised the four men as gifted technical wrestlers who could stand up to the power and shenanigans of their dastardly rivals without compromising their own superior sportsmanship. Whenever one of the four Latinos had to contend with a heel's cheating, racial slurs, or other unethical behavior, he would become justly angered but never lose control of himself. Rather, he would promise — like a true sportsman — to settle matters in the ring under the auspices of fair athletic competition.

The popularity of these four wrestlers serves as an example of the idea that "most forms of popular culture ask the public . . . to play ambiguously with class, gender, or ethnic identification" and that wrestling audiences were more than happy to do so (Rowe, McKay, and Miller 1998: 128). Interestingly, at the same time that Gomez, Morales, Mascaras, and Santana enjoyed the boisterous support of many white wrestling fans, racism against Latinos was actually rampant in American society and manifested itself in racist parodies of Latinos in other popular media, and in discrimination in housing, education, and the workplace. For example, surveys conducted across the United States during these decades revealed widespread resentment of Latinos, namely, persons of Mexican and Puerto Rican descent, as morally deficient people responsible for numerous social ills (see Moore and Pachon 1985: 8–11). For a sense of the racist contempt with which white

America held Latinos, one need only to scan print ads and television commercials of the 1950s, '60s, and '70s, which reduced Latino identity to vulgar caricatures such as bandits and lazy sleepyheads (see Martínez 1971). During the 1960s and 1970s, the increasingly militant Chicano and Puerto Rican civil rights movements exacerbated tensions between Latino and Anglo America, forcing into public visibility and debate the antagonistic attitude of most Anglos toward Latinos.

With so much animosity existing between Latinos and Anglo America in the "real world," how did four Latino wrestlers manage to become so well liked? What exactly occurred in wrestling venues across the country with the result that fans enthusiastically sided with the likes of Gomez, Morales, Mascaras, and Santana? Were these fans simply not racist, or were they, for some reason, willing to cheer for the Latinos even in spite of any racist feelings they might have harbored? Henry Jenkins's essay, " 'Never Trust a Snake': WWF Wrestling as Masculine Melodrama" (1997 and in this volume), provides an avenue for understanding their popularity. Jenkins describes class conflict as the primary structuring principle of wrestling plots and as most responsible for drawing working-class male audiences. According to Jenkins, "Melodramatic wrestling allows working-class men to confront their own feelings of vulnerability, their own frustrations at a world which promises them patriarchal authority but which is experienced through relations of economic subordination" (56). He then goes on to explain, "The patriotic laborer (Hacksaw Jim Duggan), the virtuous farm boy (Hillbilly Jim), the small-town boy made good (Big Boss Man), the Horatio Alger character (Virgil, Rowdy Roddy Piper, Tito Santana) are stock figures within this morality play, much as they have been basic tropes in populist discourse for more than a century. WWF heroes hail from humble origins and can therefore act as appropriate champions within fantasies of economic empowerment and social justice" (1997: 71). With Jenkins's argument in mind, it becomes possible to imagine that wrestling fans' allegiance to the underdog (because of their own experiences as underdogs in their own lives) were powerful enough to result in the transcendence of the prevailing racist attitudes and hostilities that may otherwise inflect interracial relations at a given social moment.

The status of Gomez, Morales, Mascaras, and Santana as working-class men worked in their favor. Throughout their careers, the four Latino wrestlers played the roles of victims, underdogs, and hard workers, and this rendered them similar to the disempowered, disenchanted working-class wrestling fans that Jenkins imagines. The Latinos portrayed characters who were common, humble men trying to make an honest living; support their families; and accomplish their goals and dreams. Also like their working-class fans, the Latinos always appeared to be struggling to overcome adversity. As they pursued their honest goals of championship belts and masculine integrity, these wrestlers supposedly fought to surmount injuries and injustices. In one of the more popular angles concocted by the WWF in 1984, for instance, Intercontinental champion Santana had to fend off Paul Orndorff's pursuit of the title—which represented the fruit of Santana's hard work and discipline—as well as Orndorff's efforts to incapacitate Santana. During a scripted interview with Gene Okerlund during *World Championship Wrestling* (14 April 1984), Santana accused Orndorff of threatening his career and, in turn, his ability to feed his family. In this and other angles that involved the four Latinos, fans saw performed the kind of working-class drama of "honest men meeting misfortune in the land of equality" which Jim Freedman suggests makes wrestling especially appealing to working-class men (Freedman 1983: 73). It is thus possible that the parallels between Gomez, Morales, Mascaras, and Santana and working-class fans were strong enough to render the Latinos convenient objects of fans' interest, support, and, perhaps, projections of identification.

An angle that Pedro Morales had with Sgt. Slaughter in 1981 serves as one of the best examples in which a Latino wrestler managed to become a champion for disenchanted working-class fans. In this angle, Morales committed himself to punishing Slaughter for abusing an unnamed young fan who, the story goes, went to Morales to complain about the drill instructor's sadistic treatment of him and other new recruits in boot camp. According to an article in *Pro Wrestling Illustrated*, Morales reportedly responded to the young man's story, in endearingly broken English: "I am going to pay back that Slaughter. I will make him regret what he done to that poor boy. I not afraid of him. I want that young boy to know he has a friend, and I will make Slaughter have great pain for doing such a terrible, terrible thing to him" ("Sgt. Slaughter Learns" 1981: 64–65). On one level, the subsequent spectacle of Morales's punishment of Slaughter represented the realization of disenfranchised fans' fantasies of violently avenging their own humiliating oppression. On another level, Morales assumed the symbolic role of savior for disenchanted young men everywhere. By challenging Slaughter, Morales offered to restore a liberal democratic social and moral order founded not on the unequal distribution of power, but on equal opportunity and the rewarding of honest, hard work.

Gomez, Morales, Mascaras, and Santana also garnered broad appeal because their racial identities did not alienate or incite white audiences to hostility. The four Latinos remained "ethnically neutral," a quality, according to Gutowski, necessary for the evolution of a nonwhite American wrestler into a mainstream wrestling hero (1972: 43). Gutowski suggests that ethnic or national differences carry the potential to drive a wedge of alienation between fans and wrestlers who belong to different ethnic and national groups. Consequently, he argues, in order for nonwhite American wrestlers to become mainstream heroes, their characters must be crafted and performed in ways that downplay their alienating differences and, instead, foreground their compatibility with (white) American values. Such downplaying clearly occurred with Gomez, Morales, Mascaras, and Santana. They came across as "good" Latinos, and fans therefore liked them because of their commitment to "American" values of hard work and honesty. If fans had any questions about the wrestlers' moral character, they had commentators to vouch for them as fine men and fine athletes. By this process, these Latinos emerged as distinctly unlike the lazy, indolent, or politically radical Latinos that filled the popular American imagination throughout their careers.

Gutowski's point anticipates Guillermo Gómez-Peña's more recent contention that American popular culture only welcomes " 'domesticated Latino[s]' who can provide enlightenment without irritation, entertainment without confrontation" (1993: 51). In fact, Gómez-Peña's argument seems especially appropriate for accounting for the popularity of Gomez, Morales, Mascaras, and Santana amidst the volatile relations that existed more generally between Latinos and Anglo America at that time. Although always racially marked—Santana, for instance, wore a cartoonish sombrero emblazoned on his wrestling trunks—the Latinos always came across as benign characters. Any uncomfortable, political meanings that the wrestlers might have embodied were carefully disarmed by plotlines that maintained the wrestlers' benign, and therefore likable, characterizations.

Without a doubt, real-world racial conflicts could have played out violently—and perhaps to the pleasure of white fans—through rivalries between the Latinos and white competitors. With so much real resentment of Latinos prevalent in the United States, wrestling writers and promoters could have chosen to tap into a volatile reservoir of fan emotions. On several occasions, the full development of an Anglo-Latino race war in wrestling even seemed imminent. When "Handsome" Jimmy Valiant called Morales a "Mexican jumping bean"; when Freddie Blassie called Mascaras a "wetback" and Santana a "taco-eater"; and when Bobby Heenan and recent Minnesota governor Jesse Ventura took turns calling Santana "Chico Santana," while claiming that he sold tacos in Tijuana and lived with his family in a '57 Chevy, stages were set for outright racialized conflict. These antagonisms, however, never went beyond the heels' racial slurs. The Latinos never directed any slurs back toward their racist antagonists. Instead, they promised to respond to the heels' disrespectful remarks man-to-man in the ring. With the Latinos thus not escalating the race-baiting or conflict, the rivalries remained grounded as class-based, moral oppositions between good guys and bad guys with which working-class fans could more easily identify.

Of course, one cannot take promoters' refusal to develop full-blown racial conflicts involving the Latinos as indicative of their unwillingness to script potentially racist storylines. Promoters had already revealed their insensitivity to political correctness through their recurring willingness to cast Germans, Russians, and Arabs as despicable heels to intrigue fans and secure their emotional involvement. Angles involving Gomez, Morales, Mascaras, and Santana simply reflected promoters' desires to maximize their revenue by drawing simultaneously both Latino and non-Latino audiences. Such a goal, though, required a careful balancing act between creating appeal for Latino fans and not upsetting non-Latinos, especially whites, who represented the primary consumers of wrestling.

Tito Santana's character most successfully managed to appeal to both Latino and non-Latino fans. Although Santana's persona carried a racialized agenda of Mexican pride that attracted the interest of Latino audiences, its potency was brilliantly controlled to guard against the alienation of white fans. In scripted interviews, Santana always spoke of his Mexican ethnicity and figured himself as a representative of the Mexican people. When he reigned as Intercontinental champion, he promised to continue his winning ways in the name of oppressed Mexican people everywhere. More important, though, he delivered all of these articulations of his ethnic pride in Spanish. Moreover, the Spanish monologues always came at the end of interviews that had begun in English and in which he would express a general, working-class pride in realizing his dream of winning the Intercontinental championship. From a marketing perspective, this English/Spanish split was a brilliant move. In English, he was "ethnically neutral," and he activated class identification rather than racial disidentification. He thus remained able to draw non-Latino fans to his character and, by extension, to the WWF. With his more racially pointed messages delivered in Spanish, most non-Latinos, presumably, would not realize what he was saying and would perceive him as a cutely unintelligible, benign Latin caricature rather than as an uncomfortably confrontational Mexican nationalist. In addition, speaking in English first and then in Spanish (rather than the other way around) reduced the chance that Santana would fail to secure the attention and interest of non-Latinos. Then, when he did finally speak Spanish, he could address disenchanted Latinos, which helped him mobilize their interest and support as well. This meant that Spanish-speaking Latinos could become WWF consumers, too.

A potentially dangerous situation arose (accidentally?) when Santana appeared on the interview spot "Piper's Pit" on *World Championship Wrestling* on 24 March 1984. As part of his usual effort to insult his guest and as many people in the audience as possible, the irascible Rowdy Roddy Piper began his interview of Santana by asserting "As the history of wrestling goes on . . . there is [*sic*] not too many Latins that go on to be champion, mostly because Latins are a little on the slow side, some of them are flat-footed . . ." Before Piper could finish his sentence, a visibly seething Santana stood up and interjected, "Roddy Piper, let me straighten you out before you go on too far, brother. Latins are not around because they haven't had the opportunity to prove ourselves [*sic*], and get that through your head." Although Santana's response was consistent with his working-class, underdog identification, his racially specific — and legitimate — statement threatened to bring into wrestling the real-world problem of racial discrimination and oppression. In addition, Santana suddenly resembled a disgruntled Chicano activist committed to indicting white racism in wrestling and in American society. Such a development certainly could have alienated white fans, especially those who might have held unsettling memories of the Chicano Movement (with its demonstrations, protests, and blowouts) of the 1970s. Unsurprisingly, this potential Santana-as-disgruntled-Chicano angle quietly disappeared; by the next episode of *Championship Wrestling*, he went back to being the ethnically neutral, hard-working, working-class Mexican that everyone could like because he did not say anything controversial about racial discrimination or oppression.

Unfortunately for Santana, his prominent position in the wwf did not last much longer anyway. By the early 1980s, changes began evolving in wrestling that eventually left Santana and Morales—along with other Latino hopefuls—without a place in professional wrestling. When Vince McMahon assumed control of the wwf in 1982, he began pushing the careers of hard-bodied white wrestlers such as Paul Orndorff, Hulk Hogan, "Macho Man" Randy Savage, and Greg "The Hammer" Valentine. His strategy was to draw audiences with white wrestlers who had admirably sculpted bodies and who could perform awesome demonstrations of power. Especially indicative of the new primacy he accorded to the hard, white male body was that after orchestrating Hulk Hogan's defeat of the Iron Sheik in a heavyweight title match in 1984, McMahon allowed Hogan to hold the title for four years. As large, white wrestlers like Hogan became the primary stars of the wwf, the careers of Santana, Morales, and other Latinos went nowhere.

Jobbers in the 1980s had an important role in enabling the staging of the new preeminence of the hard white male body. On *Championship Wrestling*, for instance, Orndorff, Valentine, and other white strongmen such as Iron Mike Sharpe and "Dr. D." David Schultz were weekly fed wrestlers such as Rudy Diamond and Frank Williams, whom they could pulverize. In these matches, the jobbers served as nothing more than vehicles for the establishment of the white strongmen's awesome invincibility. In an especially disturbing trend on *Championship Wrestling*, the white strongmen regularly faced Mexican and Puerto Rican jobbers such as Angelo Gomez, Frank Ruiz, Victor Mercado, Francisco Vasquez, and Santiago Rios. During these matches, commentator Vince McMahon repeatedly mentioned that the Latino jobbers could provide absolutely no competition for the strongmen ruthlessly overpowering them. Ultimately, with each brutal pile driver, merciless figure-four leglock, and tremendous body slam that McMahon extolled, the new place of Latinos in wrestling became more apparent.

A match José Luis Rivera had with Greg Valentine shortly after Rivera's debut in 1984 illustrated the new place of Latinos in the wwf in the 1980s. When the Puerto Rican Rivera made his first wwf appearance during an episode of *Championship Wrestling*, commentators advertised him as a promising new wrestler. After his debut, however, Rivera worked as an undefeated main-event wrestler for only a month. When he wrestled Valentine on 17 March 1984, he assumed his new, permanent role as a jobber for the wwf's white strongmen. From the opening bell of a match in which Valentine absolutely decimated Rivera, Valentine tossed Rivera around helplessly. At one point, in a demonstration of Rivera's inadequacy to even be in the ring with the strong white man, Valentine lobbed the Puerto Rican out of the ring. Eventually, in a show of Valentine's unequivocal superiority, he wrapped Rivera up in his patented submission hold, the torturous figure-four leglock. Unfortunately for Rivera, however, his humiliation did not end with his submission to the leglock. The performance of the white wrestler's dominance continued as Valentine pummeled Rivera after the bell and proceeded to lock him up in a second leglock. In the course of this after-the-bell mauling, Valentine further signaled the inferiority of the Puerto Rican by looking with disdain at his victim flailing and wailing on the mat. After several minutes of this, medical technicians finally arrived with a stretcher to take away a supposedly devastated Rivera, whose exaggerated groans of "¡Ay, coño!" suggested his excruciating pain and were supposed to index the power of Valentine. Two weeks later, Rivera returned to *Championship Wrestling*, but as nothing more than a nondescript jobber who enabled the performance of white stars' physical superiority.

Comparable fates befell Morales and Santana. In the course of the 1980s, these wrestlers gradually disappeared from their perches in wrestling. After Morales lost his Intercontinental belt to Don Muraco in 1983, he inconspicuously faded from the wrestling scene. As for Santana, after he lost his Intercontinental title for the second and final time in 1985, he briefly worked as a member of the cheesy championship tag-team Strike Force, but for the most part he found himself without a decent push. He relates in the video *Shoot Interview: Tito Santana* (Santana 2000), that by the late 1980s he was "fighting" with Vince McMahon to do something with him, but only a stint as "El Matador" in 1991 came out of these talks. As Santana points out in the interview, the caricatural El Matador character garnered little interest from fans and led to his retirement. Audiences and promoters had lost interest in benevolent, hardworking Latino underdogs.

SPECTACLES OF CONTAINMENT AND INEFFECTUALITY IN THE 1990S

In the 1990s, large white wrestlers intrigued audiences with their super-human demonstrations of power and their uncanny size. Because of these wrestlers' ability to fascinate spectators, promoters positioned them as their feature attractions and organized their most important storylines around them. As wrestling journalist Steve Anderson observed in a 2001 article in *wow Magazine* about the importance of bulk in wrestling in the 1990s: "While light-heavyweight professional wrestlers struggle to establish their identities in both World Championship Wrestling and the World Wrestling Federation, their more weighty counterparts dominate. In the mid-1980s, the emphasis was on size and mass. Promoters preferred the taller and more muscular performers. Today, wrestlers of a smaller stature receive significant pushes, sometimes to the top of a promotion, but super-heavyweights remain a force" (Anderson 2001: 66). Unlike the smaller wrestlers, Anderson concluded, "Super-heavyweights are champions, top challengers, and living legends" (67). The preeminence of super-heavyweights in the 1990s in both the wwf and its competitor, the wcw, did not favor Latino wrestlers and their typically smaller builds. The most prominent Latinos of the 1990s included relatively unimposing men such as Eddie Guerrero (5′ 9″, 205 pounds), Chavo Guerrero Jr. (5′ 10″, 190 pounds), Juventud Guerrera (5′ 5″, 165 pounds), Essa Rios (5′ 10″, 190 pounds), and Rey Mysterio Jr. (a mere 5′ 3″, 140 pounds). As these men shared performance spaces with white giants such as 6′ 8″, 318-pound Sid Vicious, 6′ 3″, 368-pound Bam Bam Bigelow, and 6′ 11″, 329-pound Kevin Nash, their smaller statures came across sharply. Such physical disparities visually positioned Latino masculinity as inferior to the monolithic masculinity that the Latinos' larger white colleagues embodied.

This visual regime was reinforced by ringside commentary, and by discussions in the wrestling press, that adulated the new white behemoths while portraying Latino wrestlers as easily overpowered and intimidated by them. Although commentators and journalists regularly praised Mysterio, Guerrera, and the Guerreros as admirably acrobatic and technical wrestlers, they just as often described the Latinos as handicapped by their smaller statures and lack of power. More often than not, boasts about the talents and potential of the Latinos quickly ended up undercut by qualifying references to these men's small bodies and limited strength. For instance, in a 1999 article on Mysterio in *Pro Wrestling Illustrated*, wrestling journalist Dan Murphy frankly remarked, "The road to respect for Mysterio has been a long and bumpy one. . . . At 5′ 3″ and 140 pounds after a big dinner, Mysterio learned early that he had to give his all in each and every match to not only win, but survive. That meant sticking with his fast-paced, high-risk aerial attack . . . and remaining alert at all times, knowing full well that virtually any opponent could overpower him if he was lured into following that man's game plan" (1999: 57). Within this passage, a nervous obsession with Mysterio's small size hastily overwhelms the admiration the writer initially sought to convey, and it exemplifies what usually occurred with all of the other prominent, smaller-bodied Latino wrestlers of the 1990s.

These same commentators and journalists, meanwhile, gushed uninhibitedly over the strength and size of large white wrestlers such as Nash, Bigelow, and the Undertaker. They regularly deployed adjectives such as *awesome* and *incredible* to describe the big men and their ability to dramatically smash another wrestler onto the mat or into a ring post. Camera work simultaneously invited television audiences to share their admiration. Slow-motion replays allowed viewers to dwell upon the power of the giants' huge bodies, while longer shots encouraged admiration of their comparative bulk. The use of low-angle shots further enabled the fetishization of these wrestlers' size and power, for as viewers literally looked up at them, they were encouraged to see them as awe-inspiring, supermen.

The unequal relationship in wrestling between Latino and white masculinity came across most painfully whenever a Latino and a larger white wrestler encountered each other. In earlier years, Gomez, Morales, Mascaras, and Santana backed down from no one; in fact, the venerability of their underdog personas hinged significantly on their willingness and ability to confront large men such as "Handsome" Jimmy Valiant, Sgt. Slaughter, and Paul Orndorff. In the 1990s, though, with astonishingly greater size differentials visible between Latino wrestlers and their white colleagues, even if a Latino didn't first cower in the presence of someone such as Nash or Bigelow, he usually ended up thrown around (just as José Luis Rivera was when he first encountered Greg Valentine). If, in an act of self-preservation or in an attempt to generate some offense, a Latino tried some creative aerial move, he invariably found himself caught midair, carried around helplessly, and then slammed with authority into a corner or onto the mat. The manhandling of Latinos effectively relegated them to the bottom of wrestling's racial and gender hierarchies by trivializing their abilities as wrestlers and suggesting graphically the inability of Latino men to compete with exceptionally powerful forms of white masculinity.

Of course, the wcw—which by the late 1990s employed far more Latinos than did the wwf—did not start importing renowned Mexican *lucha-*

dores in 1996 simply so that they could serve as vehicles for the establishment of the primacy of the league's white stars. The wcw contracted Mysterio, Guerrera, Psichosis, La Parka, and others to thrill audiences with their high-flying acrobatics and, in the process, help the promotion in its ratings wars with the wwf. When the luchadores began to appear in the wcw, commentators, journalists, and fans celebrated their unique abilities. With so much excitement generated, Konnan, another product of Mexico's lucha libre leagues who had already established himself in the wcw by the time the luchadores had arrived, declared, "I'm sure every kid watching wrestling right now wants to do what they do. [This] is the future of wrestling" (quoted in Esparza online 1998).

Widespread enthusiasm for the luchadores suggested a potential shift in the emphasis of wcw programming. The luchadores reinvigorated the cruiserweight division and suddenly made it the site of particularly exciting matches. Previously, this division had been an afterthought; powerful white wrestlers such as Hulk Hogan, Sting, Lex Luger, Randy Savage, and Giant reigned as the primary stars of the wcw, and their competition for the World Heavyweight title dominated wcw coverage. New and growing interest in the luchadores, however, suddenly threatened the organization of the wcw around its large white stars.

Wrestling fans' excitement over the luchadores in the late 1990s also represented a noteworthy turn away from their fascination with monolithic forms of white masculinity that emerged in the 1980s. Unlike Hogan, Luger, and the other large white stars of the 1980s and 1990s, the luchadores had amazingly flexible bodies, not unflinchingly erect ones, and they based their performances more on acrobatics and style than on power and violence. Sharon Mazer relates that these attributes prompted some of the students she interviewed at a wrestling school to dismiss what luchadores do as somehow less masculine: "Other wrestlers tend to be dismissive of . . . *luchadores*, in large part because of the way in which [their stunts are] obviously choreographed, appearing almost balletic in performance" (1998: 67). One student wrestler even remarked to her, "It's too fake. . . . American wrestling is more violent and aggressive. It's more real" (171). Such a comment suggests that the wcw's luchadores embodied a unique type of masculinity that, because of its difference from the monolithic masculinity that the wcw's large white stars embodied, fans could have regarded as inferior. The fact that the luchadores often attired themselves in spectacular tights and masks only compounded their apparent "deviance"; in this attire, the luchadores betrayed excessive and, some might say "nonmasculine" attention to ostentation which threatened to undermine others' ability to take them seriously as men and as athletes. As with other "showy" wrestlers such as Gorgeous George or Golddust, it suggested the possibility of the always-threatening appearance of overt homoeroticism.

Interestingly, rather than deride the luchadores as less-than-masculine or as too ridiculous, American fans became enthralled with them. On one level, fans simply found the aerial abilities of the luchadores exciting and admirable. In addition, the luchadores entertained audiences with their colorful personae and costumes. By the time luchadores began to enter the ranks of the wcw, many fans already had an appreciation for their acrobatic style of wrestling, and others grew to respect it. Importantly, such receptiveness to the luchadores represented a new willingness on the part of fans to celebrate an alternative masculine tradition and suggested an emerging interest in the late 1990s in forms of masculinity other than the monolithic version that distinguished the primary white stars of the wcw.

Rapidly, not-so-subtle efforts to contain the importance of the luchadores in the wcw and reestablish the preeminence of veteran white stars' monolithic masculinity over Latino masculinity accompanied the emergence of the luchadores. In the videos *Shoot Interview with Rey Mysterio Jr.* (Mysterio 2000) and *Shoot Interview with Juventud Guerrera* (Guerrera 2000), Mysterio and Guerrera reveal that their popularity made established white performers such as Hogan uncomfortable and prompted several white stars to seek the curtailment of pushes being given to the Latino newcomers. According to Mysterio and Guerrera, the complaints of the white stars quickly led to a number of developments in wcw programming that undermined the visibility and popularity of the Latinos. One of the most important angles hatched to restore the primacy of Hogan, et al. was the creation of the nwo (New World Order). Nash, Hogan, and Scott Hall formed the nwo at *Bash at the Beach* on 7 July 1996—incidentally, just one day before Mysterio's push climaxed in his first cruiserweight championship. As part of the nwo angle, Hall, Nash, and Hogan declared a coup in the wcw. Professing themselves unhappy with their treatment and with the direction of the company, they supposedly seized control of the promotion so that they could correct what they deemed wrong with it.

Although wrestling rhetoric is always hyperbolic and theatrical, one can read the NWO angle and its "agenda" as reflecting a real crisis that the WCW's white stars faced in the late 1990s. In a series of scripted television spots, members of the NWO performed their commitment to being the most important names in the world of wrestling. At the inception of the NWO, for instance, Hogan gestured to himself, Nash, and Hall and announced to ring announcer Gene Okerlund, "This right here is the future of wrestling. You can call this the New World Order of wrestling, brother." In later television spots (*Superstar: NWO 4 Life!* 1999), Hogan declared, "We're gonna take over the whole planet," while Marcus "Buff" Bagwell, a later NWO recruit, revealed the NWO's desire "to control all power, to control the world of wrestling." Ambitious promises such as these were especially meaningful because as workers, those who constituted the NWO saw their standing in the world of wrestling weakening. As fans became increasingly interested in the cruiserweights and grew tired of stale plots in the heavyweight division, the preeminence of the league's white stars began to slip. Consequently, the concoction of the NWO and its commitment to (re)dominate the world of wrestling seemed grounded in more than just marketable melodrama.

The terror campaign that the NWO carried out ended up allowing for the reperformance of the primacy of monolithic white masculinity. As one wrestling journalist commented, in the embryonic stages of the NWO angle, "Hall began terrorizing the announcers out of nowhere, making veiled threats [of] a 'takeover' and generally being a huge bully" (Keith 2001: 160). In the angle's next stages, Hall and Nash both began randomly assaulting other WCW stars. Even Eric Bischoff, president of WCW, suffered a powerbomb through a table at the hands of Nash. As soon as Hogan joined Hall and Nash and officially christened the group the New World Order, the three wrestlers stepped up the terror by attacking everyone. This endless string of attacks made the group's invincibility violently visible and resulted in its emergence as the most dangerous force in wrestling. In one of the most notorious of the NWO's attacks, Kevin Nash tossed a helpless Rey Mysterio Jr. into the side of a trailer. This incident rendered the diminutive Mysterio a pathetically ineffectual figure, and succinctly and graphically suggested the (re)subordination of Latino masculinity to its more powerful white cousin.

By 1998, Mysterio, Guerrera, Psichosis, and Eddie Guerrero took turns reigning as cruiserweight champion, but NWO dramas consistently eclipsed the Latinos' profiles. In late 1998, however, the Latinos had a chance to become an important WCW force. On 5 October, during an episode of *Nitro*,

Eddie Guerrero interrupted a match between Hector Garza and Damian Garza and pointed out to both of them their mistreatment by Bischoff. He indicated (rightly) that the Latinos always had to wrestle each other and received limited television time. Guerrero declared that the Latinos had to unite to demand more television time and more championship opportunities. With Garza and Damian assenting to join Guerrero's campaign against the continued suppression of Latino wrestlers, the Latino World Order (LWO) came into existence. In subsequent WCW telecasts, Guerrero regularly emerged to rearticulate the agenda of the LWO and recruit other Latino wrestlers into the LWO fold.

The appearance of the LWO represents one of the most notable moments in the history of Latinos in professional wrestling. For the first time, a promotion allowed an angle that saw its Latino wrestlers organized around a valid and radical political agenda. Moreover, it appeared — at least initially — that the LWO angle was really going to lead to the destabilization of the unfair racial organization of the "sport." In another first, the legitimacy of the LWO's complaints forced audiences to acknowledge the real racist treatment and containment of Latinos in American popular culture. Particularly interesting about the LWO was how audiences did not know whether the Latinos were heroes or heels. The LWO was not immediately framed with any obvious cues for audiences to cheer or jeer. Compared to the 1960s and 1970s, there was less anti-Latino rhetoric and sentiment circulating in the United States, upon which fans could draw to imagine the LWO as loathsome. If anything, the validity of the LWO's agenda precluded any interpretation of the LWO as heels and compelled fans to try to come to terms with an angle that figured white America as the actual villain.

The flatness of audiences' responses to initial LWO appearances reflected their uncertainty about the Latino clique, as well as the amount of discomfort that the implications of the angle generated. Were fans supposed to boo the group as un-American heels, or were they supposed to cheer on the group's apparently just indictment of white racism against Latinos? When Guerrero came out and boldly leveled his legitimate complaints, even his status lacked obviousness. Was he still the dastardly Eddie, notorious for his selfishness and affinity for cheating? Or, was he playing a new part as a respectable crusader for the rights of his mistreated brothers? It was not even clear whether the LWO was a shoot or a work because agenda appeared valid and commentators seemed honestly befuddled. At an apparent loss for how to understand the LWO, WCW television commentators wondered aloud about the genuineness of Guerrero's intentions. Although the whole setup was a work, in the process, they stoked audiences' uncertainty about the status of the LWO.

Soon enough, though, the unequivocal reprehensibility of the LWO and Guerrero emerged. Plotlines eventually led to the depiction of Guerrero as a corrupt leader driven by self-interest. Within a few weeks of the inception of the LWO, audiences learned that he had been angling from the outset to secure for himself wealth, power, beautiful women, and championship opportunities. As a result of such revelations, audiences' silence and uncertainty gave way to vehement jeers and chants of "Eddie sucks!" The energy with which fans began to heap scorn upon Guerrero and his LWO derived from their relief in finally knowing how to respond to the group. In addition, some white audiences appeared relieved to know that the LWO's indictment of white racism would cease because the Latinos, not white America, were the bad guys all along: in a good example of how the logic of racism works, one conclusion that audiences could draw was that the Latinos actually deserved whatever unjust treatment they had previously received (and would now continue to receive) because they were morally corrupt to begin with.[3]

The degeneration of the LWO angle ultimately represented a corrective maneuver on the part of the WCW to contain the political validity of the group and neutralize whatever alienating or discomfiting effects the angle might have had on WCW fans. From the start, the LWO seemed a dangerous angle to implement. Realization of the full potential of the angle would have required continued escalation of the group's critical agenda, and in all likelihood this would have resulted in increasing discomfort for wrestling fans. To confront white audiences in particular with "entertainment" that actually foregrounded their own racism risked the alienation of the WCW's primary consumer sector. In an apparent effort to undo this marketing mistake, the WCW first arranged for a reunified NWO to make its return during an episode of *Thunder* (11 January 1999) by interrupting a match between Psichosis and Mysterio. Then, in an offensively ludicrous routine during the following week's *Nitro*, WCW President — and legendary white wrestler — Ric Flair completed the dissolution of the LWO by bribing its members with promises of money, liquor, and women to remove their LWO shirts and renounce their membership in the clique. Besides bringing to a close the LWO debacle, the spectacle of the Latinos hurriedly removing their shirts in response to

Flair's offer effectively stabilized the WCW's white-dominated racial order by reinscribing the "actual" indolence and depravity of the Latino wrestlers.

Through the dismantling of the LWO, audiences saw not just the disarming of a Latino man who articulated legitimate political concerns, but also the reinscription of Latino men as cunning, untrustworthy, and morally and intellectually inferior. The dissolution of the LWO also served as an emasculating spectacle of Latinos' inability to secure more power within an organization dominated by big white men. In the end, the debasement of Latinos enabled the primacy of the NWO and the monolithic version of white masculinity that they embodied to reemerge more incontrovertibly.

"LATINO HEAT," "FILTHY ANIMALS," AND LATINOS' FUTURE IN PROFESSIONAL WRESTLING

In the period after the LWO fiasco, both the WCW and the WWF marked and marketed their Latino wrestlers in especially demeaning ways. When Eddie Guerrero first left the WCW for the WWF in January 2000, WWF commentators hyped him as a respected member of the Radicalz and as an important new contender for the Intercontinental title. Soon after his arrival, though, he assumed the persona of "Latino Heat," a sleazy Latin lover who embodied the worst of the greaser Mexican stereotype. Meanwhile, in the WCW (before Vince McMahon purchased the organization), Konnan, Guerrera, and Mysterio played the parts of "Filthy Animals," characters who, according to one wrestling journalist, "party as hard as they work in the ring" and "live by their own code of ethics, which is probably something along the lines of 'the nastier, the better'" (Adeline 2000: 36, 38). Although the Latino Heat and Filthy Animals angles emerged separately in different wrestling organizations, they simultaneously portrayed Latino masculinity and identity in deliberately disgraceful ways.

As Latino Heat, Guerrero became an arrogant, macho, womanizing Latin lover who spoke with a ridiculously harsh accent and enjoyed driving lowriders. In shoot interviews conducted shortly after the birth of Latino Heat, Guerrero claimed that he proposed this character, that WWF officials did not impose it upon him, and that he regarded it an "entertaining" character.[4] He never acknowledged (or recognized), however, the complicity of this characterization with the continued degradation of Latino masculinity. When one interviewer asked him, "While a lot of people enjoy Latino Heat, some critics believe it's the kind of racial stereotyping that wrestling needs to move away from. How do you respond to that?" Guerrero insisted,

> That's very stupid if people are thinking that way because they see my character. Latino Heat is what I am. I am Latino. That's the character I play, and it's an extension of myself. I grew up in El Paso, Texas, and there are a lot of people like Latino Heat. I grew up with guys who were, and still are, exactly like the character. How can I not have fun with that? I'm proud of my ethnic background. But I'm also a person who knows how to have fun. This character is a reflection of that. Anyone who can't see that, can't have fun. I think that's really a stupid way of looking at it. (Chamberlin 2001: 23)

While Guerrero assumed agency in the crafting and performance of his Latino Heat persona, he overlooked the role of the WWF in permitting the development of this character. In the cases of Tito Santana and the LWO, for example, wrestling promotions have demonstrated their willingness to act promptly to clip or redirect an angle whenever it starts to become too subversive or too discomfiting, especially for white audiences. WWF officials perhaps deemed Latino Heat "safe" because the character threatened neither white audiences nor the central importance of established white stars. The primary effect of the Latino Heat character was the bolstering of the superiority of white identity and masculinity via his contemptibility and cowardliness. If anything, he contributed to the generation of revenue for the WWF through the safe "entertainment" that he provided. As for Latino audiences, it would be a valuable audience research question to ask if they enjoyed the *vato* character or if they took offense at seeing Latino identity and masculinity reduced to such a loathsome caricature. In any case, in its inclination to let Latino Heat become more and more despicable, the WWF never appeared too worried about the potential alienation of the Latino consumer sector.

The degradation of Latino Heat occurred mostly through the staging of his romantic affair with white femme behemoth Chyna. Initially, fans and commentators found amusing the spectacle of the smaller Latino Heat deferring courteously to Chyna and presenting her roses at every turn. Latino Heat's successful courtship had actually rendered him somewhat admirable, for he accomplished with the intimidating and imposing woman what no other man had previously managed. Gradually, though, the distinct physical and racial contrasts between Chyna and Latino Heat played out to his disadvantage. Latino Heat's courteous deferrals increasingly threw his smaller size into relief and rendered him more silly than romantic. The fact that Chyna regularly intervened in Latino Heat's matches to protect him undermined his credibility both as a wrestler and as a man. On a few occasions, Chyna herself effortlessly tossed around and slammed Latino Heat, and such manhandling furthered his denigration.

As the angle progressed, Latino Heat went from playing a ridiculously subservient role to playing an abusive and misogynistic macho. When Chyna announced her intent to do a photo shoot for *Playboy*, Latino Heat became excessively jealous and abusive, and subsequent spectacles of him acting irrationally and reducing Chyna to tears rendered him an unusually repugnant character. Of course, this development — which occurred under the direction of McMahon — only reinscribed stereotypes of the Latino man as inappropriately volatile and domineering in relationships with women.[5] Eventually, the character of Latino Heat reached its low point with the "discovery" of a videotape of him showering with Mandy and Victoria, two of the wwf's notorious "hos." With this development, Latino Heat emerged in his full decadence as unfaithful and sexually depraved. Once again, as had occurred when he led the lwo, Guerrero ended up being exposed as immoral and worthy of all the scorn that fans might heap on him. More generally, the exposure of Latino Heat's moral bankruptcy implied that suspicions fans might have had about the moral character of Latino men were, more often than not, justified.[6]

Racist dynamics also operated in the wcw, where the Filthy Animals angle rendered Konnan, Guerrera, and Mysterio an uncivilized and uncouth sideshow that excited and engaged audiences without threatening the primary status of the wcw's white wrestlers. Positioning the Animals as a fusion of hip-hop style, professional wrestling, and Latino exoticism, the wcw attempted to capitalize on three of the strongest cultural forces of the past few years.[7] A letter to the editor that appeared in *wcw Magazine* demonstrates the promotion's success in drawing diverse fans through the Animals: "I love the Filthy Animals. I'm not Hispanic and I don't come from the streets, but I look up to them. . . . Rey and Konnan, keep up the good work, and Rey, you are hot! Filthy Animals forever! [signed, Ashley Bird, Kalamazoo, mi]" (Bird 2001).

This letter suggests that the convergence of popular cultural forces in the characterizations of the Filthy Animals facilitated the transcendence of racial difference and helped the WCW arouse the interest of non-Latino as well as Latino fans, male and female. The thunderous applause that greeted the Animals every time they appeared in an arena also indicated their ability to animate spectators. Whenever the Animals' soundtrack began thumping over the sound system, fans of all colors immediately, and with obvious enjoyment, cheered and imitated the poses that the Animals liked to strike. Moreover, when prompted by Konnan, the heavily white audiences that filled arenas across the United States always responded with striking enthusiasm, "¡Órale!" and "¡Viva la raza!"

As was the case with Latino Heat, however, a degradation of Latino masculinity was built into the Filthy Animals angle. At first, the angle involved Konnan, Guerrera, and Mysterio embracing a bacchanalian, party-hardy ethos. But while the Animals donned hip attire to suggest their new, more urban orientation, their fashion began to look more and more absurd. For instance, as Mysterio began appearing in yellow vinyl overalls with leopard-print accessories, the stylistic sensibilities of the Filthy Animals increasingly put them at odds with dominant figurations of masculinity. Mysterio's eventual, and ridiculous, appearance with devil horns glued to his temples served not just as the culminating signifier of the Animals' supposed moral depravity, but also as the WCW's culminating effort to challenge fans' willingness to identify with the Latinos and applaud them.

In spite of the increasing depravity and ridiculousness that suffused the Animals' portrayals, not to mention a simultaneous drop in the amount of attention (or push) accorded to them by the WCW, Konnan, Guerrera, and Mysterio remained popular. The enthusiastic reception that they continued to receive when they appeared in arenas suggested fans' interest in the hipness, narcissism, and sensuality or sexuality that the Animals embodied. Male fans in particular appeared to envy the Animals, who enjoyed an uncommonly raucous lifestyle and surrounded themselves with the types of beautiful women that heterosexual young males are supposed to fantasize about. For a time, Mysterio even appeared in arenas frolicking and bumping and grinding with Tygress, a popular "Nitro Girl" whom many male fans lusted after, and this resulted in an increase in many male fans' audible appreciation for him, and for the other Animals.

Unfortunately, the persistent popularity of the Filthy Animals carried undesirable implications. Obviously, their popularity could have destabilized the racist racial order of the WCW and represented fans' color-blind respect for Latino wrestlers. In addition, fans' applause for the Animals could have signaled another noteworthy shift in their interest away from monolithic forms of masculinity and toward something less violent and more nuanced. After all, the Animals were renowned for their hip-hop and urban style, not for an ability to brutalize others. Depictions of the Animals' aggressive pursuit of women, though, ultimately ended up rendering their masculinity animalistic in comparison to the monolithic power of Hall, Nash, Hogan, and the other white strongmen of the WCW. The Animals' apparent commitment to having beautiful women at their disposal only rearticulated the problematic heterosexual male fantasy of possessing women solely to serve as sexual objects. Even more disturbing was that fans' celebration of the Animals basically constituted a mass celebration of misogynistic heterosexual masculinity. The Animals' hard partying reproduced the rather stale cliché of persons of color as embodying unbridled libidinal energy, a sexuality which ruled their bodies and minds; it provided fans permission to revel in regressive sexual excess while reducing Latino men to a less-than-human status in which their appetites won out over any higher aspirations they might have had.

The Animals thus ultimately did not offer audiences an example of a decent alternative to the excessively violent forms of masculinity that one most often encounters in professional wrestling. Their portrayals only supported the heteronormative and sexist values that continue to circulate freely within professional wrestling. Interestingly, the ironic recuperation of the Animals' difference or "deviance" invites a more detailed consideration of Mazer's idea that in wrestling, fans encounter a range of possible forms of masculinity. In *Professional Wrestling*, she suggests,

> Instead of offering fans a presentation of masculinity that is singular and conservative, the professional wrestling performance presents two or more contradictory possibilities poised against and coexisting with each other. Masculinity is both a choice and an essence, simultaneously an option and an imperative. While the professional wrestling performance always presents a version of masculinity that is sanctioned by the dominant culture, its presentation of alternative masculinities as concurrent proposes a community of men that is inclusive of a wide range of

identities and behaviors, as such heterogeneous rather than homogenous. Rather than prescribing limitations to masculine behavior, professional wrestling recognizes the official version at the same time that it acknowledges and, it might be argued, even encourages the unleashing of masculine expressivity in all forms. (1998: 107)

The problem posed by the Filthy Animals, which complicates Mazer's argument that wrestling offers its fans a wide spectrum of possible masculine identities, is that the version that the Animals offer is merely a degenerate form that simultaneously affirms heteronormative misogyny while debasing Latinos. This fundamental "normalization" of the Animals then forces one to question the extent to which one can say that wrestling promoters parade out, without bias, a diverse range of masculine identities. The Animals' normalization suggests that in "different," apparently subversive masculine images, dominant ideas and attitudes can be reinscribed anyway.

Whether Latino masculinity can assume more dignified, more productive, or even more subversive forms in the future is debatable. Over the past twenty years, promoters have proven themselves predisposed to contain and debase their Latino performers. Vince McMahon's ownership of the new WWF/WCW conglomerate, the WWE (World Wrestling Entertainment, Inc.), makes it even less likely that Latinos will be portrayed in either decent or productively subversive ways in the near future. McMahon, who has already demonstrated his predilection for brutal violence by large white wrestlers, has a history of handling his Latino performers in problematic ways. One need only consider the fates of Tito Santana and Latino Heat to realize McMahon's lack of interest in creating opportunities for Latino wrestlers to become successful and respected. Over the past year, he has given only Chavo Guerrero a limited push while leaving the other former WCW Latino cruiserweights unemployed. Apparently, luchadores do not fit into his present marketing strategies. If at some point he does decide to bring some of the luchadores into his new conglomerate, will he just ask them to become new Latino Heats? Or will he feed them to the likes of The Undertaker and Triple H to be pulverized in a demonstration of his strongmen's awesome reserves of power and violence? In any case, in order for less destructive images of masculinity in general, and less degraded images of Latino masculinity in particular, to appear, McMahon has to see some profitability in the promotion of these alternative images. His business is to offer audiences spectacles that will entertain and intrigue them. The political meanings of these spectacles that he stages apparently do not concern him.

NOTES

1. The incredibly ripped physiques of the Smash 'N Slam action figures participate in a larger trend identified by Harrison G. Pope Jr., Katharine A. Phillips, and Roberto Olivardia, in which male action figures from GI Joe to Batman to Luke Skywalker have undergone massive muscularization. According to Pope and colleagues, rather than displaying "reasonably attainable figure[s]," male action figures in recent years have sported "hugely muscular figure[s] that . . . no man could attain without massive doses of steroids" (2000: 44). Pope and colleagues then go on to question the potentially destructive effects that hypermuscularized action figures as well as hypermuscularized real-life professional wrestlers' bodies might have on young boys' understandings of what their own bodies should look like when they grow up.

2. According to the relative heights of the two action figures, Giant would stand four feet taller than the 5′ 3″ Mysterio.

3. Many Latino fans were perhaps left disappointed by the deterioration of the LWO. As evidenced by the LWO signs and T-shirts that Latinos and Latinas at wrestling events displayed, the LWO became a focal point for Latino pride. It facilitated what sociologist Félix Padilla (1985) has termed *Latinismo*, an ethnic consciousness that involves the crystallization of Latino unity in response to diverse Latino groups' collective experience with injustice. The LWO managed to inspire Latinismo because Latino audiences saw raza actively resisting its continued oppression and articulating an agenda of raza dignity. Fan Web sites devoted to the LWO further suggested the imbrication of the LWO and Latino pride, for these Web sites framed LWO news and information with various icons of Latino pride, such as Mexican flags, lowrider cars, and Chicano slang. When the LWO fell apart, Latinos lost a surprisingly powerful source of Latinismo — and the WCW failed to take advantage of an opportunity to secure for itself a Latino market.

4. Interviews with Dave Meltzer on *Wrestling Observer Live* and in Thomas Chamberlin (2001).

5. In the Thomas Chamberlin shoot interview "5 Minutes with Eddie Guerrero," Guerrero explains that he went to the Playboy mansion to perform a scene that had him erupt in a jealous rage and demand that Chyna's photographs be suppressed because "Vince McMahon wanted me to do [it], so it was just part of my job" (2001: 23). Interestingly, Guerrero suggests through this statement his own passivity in the problematic development of the Latino Heat angle and thus contradicts his own belief in his agency in the performance of his character.

6. While the degradation of Latino Heat reduced Latino masculinity to a loathsome status and left white identity in a privileged position, it also facilitated another WWF marketing move, the humanization and feminization of Chyna. Images of her weeping and suffering emotionally in response to the rage that Latino Heat directed at her served to soften her persona and increase her appeal to fans.

7. In a May 2000 article in the magazine *Brandweek*, Terry Lefton reported that a group of TV production executives sensitive to the profit potential of commodifying hip-hop style, professional wrestling, and Latino exoticism planned on launching the Urban Wrestling Federation, or UWF.

REFERENCES

Adeline, Ben. 2000. "Party Animals: WCW's Filthy Animals Party as Hard as They Work in the Ring." *WOW Magazine*, December 2000, pp. 36–39.

Anderson, Steve. 2001. "Giants of the Ring." *WOW Magazine*, the Best of *WOW Magazine*, pp. 66–70.

Blaustein, Barry W., director. 1999. *Beyond the Mat*. 1999. Film, Universal Studios.

Bird, Ashley. 2001. Letter to the Editor. *WCW Magazine*, May, p. 8.

Chamberlin, Thomas. 2001. "5 Minutes with Eddie Guerrero." *WOW Magazine*, April, pp. 20–23.

Debord, Guy. 1994. *The Society of the Spectacle*. New York: Zone Books.

Esparza, Santiago. 1998. "WCW Goes South for New Talent." *Detroit News*, 23 November. Accessed 14 March 2001 at http://www.detnews.com/1998/sports/9811/23/11230185 .htm.

Freedman, Jim. 1983. "Will the Sheik Use His Blinding Fireball? The Ideology of Professional Wrestling." In *The Celebration of Society: Perspectives on Contemporary Cultural Performance*, ed. Frank E. Manning. Bowling Green: Bowling Green University Popular Press.

Gómez-Peña, Guillermo. 1993. "The Multicultural Paradigm: An Open Letter to the National Arts Community." In *Warrior for Gringostroika*. Saint Paul: Graywolf Press.

Guerrera, Juventud. 2000. *Shoot Interview with Juventud Guerrera*. Videocassette. RF Video, Langhorne, Pa.

Gutowski, John A. 1972. "The Art of Professional Wrestling." *Keystone Folklore Quarterly* 17, no. 2:41–50.

Jenkins, Henry. 1997. " 'Never Trust a Snake': WWF Wrestling as Masculine Melodrama." In *Out of Bounds: Sports, Media, and the Politics of American Identity*, ed. Aaron Baker and Todd Boyd. Bloomington: Indiana University Press.

Keith, Scott. 2001. *The Buzz on Professional Wrestling*. New York: Lebhar-Friedman Books.

Lefton, Terry. 2000. "Into the Cage with WWF." *Brandweek* (29 May): 1.

Martínez, Tomás M. 1971. "Advertising and Racism: The Case of the Mexican American." In *Voices*, ed. Octavio L. Romano. Berkeley: Quinto Sol.

Mazer, Sharon. 1998. *Professional Wrestling: Sport and Spectacle*. Jackson: University Press of Mississippi.

Meltzer, Dave. 2000. Interview with Guerrero, Eddie. *Wrestling Observer Live*. 14 June. www.eyada.com.

Moore, Joan, and Harry Pachon. 1985. *Hispanics in the United States*. Englewood Cliffs, N.J.: Prentice-Hall.

Murphy, Dan. 1999. "Out of Alignment: Rey Mysterio Jr. Must Fly Solo." *Wrestler Digest*, winter, pp. 57–59.

Mysterio, Rey, Jr. 2000. *Shoot Interview with Rey Mysterio Jr.* Videocassette. RF Video, Langhorne, Pa.

Oherlund, Gene. 1984. Interview. *World Championship Wrestling*, 14 April.

Padilla, Félix. 1985. *Latino Ethnic Consciousness: The Case of Mexican Americans and Puerto Ricans in Chicago*. Notre Dame, Ind.: University of Notre Dame Press.

Pope, Harrison G., Jr., Katharine A. Phillips, and Roberto Olivardia. 2000. *The Adonis Complex: The Secret Crisis of Male Body Obsession*. New York: Free Press.

Rowe, David, Jim McKay, and Toby Miller. 1998. "Come Together: Sport, Nationalism, and the Media Image." *Mediasport*, ed. Lawrence A. Wenner. New York: Routledge.

Santana, Tito. 1984. Interview, "Piper's Pit." *World Championship Wrestling*, 24 March.

———. 2000. *Shoot Interview: Tito Santana*. Videocassette. Harrington Talents, New York.

"Sgt. Slaughter Learns: The Painful Vengeance of Pedro Morales." 1981. *Pro Wrestling Illustrated*, July, pp. 32+.

Superstar: NWO 4 Life! 1999. Turner Home Video.

World Championship Wrestling. 1984. KCOP, Los Angeles.

DOUGLAS BATTEMA AND PHILIP SEWELL

Trading in Masculinity: Muscles, Money,

and Market Discourse in the WWF

I n the late 1990s, partly in reaction to the perception that television was more devoted to the female consumer than the male viewer, a distinctive strain of strongly masculinist programming took to the airwaves and cable wires. Though falling short of critical approval, programs such as FOX's *Titus*, NBC's *Men Behaving Badly*, Comedy Central's *The Man Show*, and anything involving Howard Stern won Nielsen ratings points, grabbed advertisers' dollars, and invited scores of emulators. The *New York Daily News* suggested in early 2000 that "After all but giving up on men, TV is pumping with testosterone again. Marking a big shift in a medium where girls rule, everyone from Comedy Central, to massive cable TV channel TBS, to up and coming Viacom network, UPN, is plunging into the Y-chromosome world with edgy, guy fare" (Furman 2000: 28). With formerly dependable programming such as *Monday Night Football* and professional basketball losing male viewers at an alarming rate, networks sought new fare that appealed to the elusive eighteen-to-thirty-four "guy" demographic—with an emphasis on white guys. The success enjoyed by the World Wrestling Federation (WWF) was symptomatic of this programming trend, which articulated a certain brand of masculine presence within the feminine sphere of television.

Despite their overt embrace of vulgarity and simplicity—the reliance on "babes in bikinis," fisticuffs, farting, belching, and drinking as plot devices—the programs targeting men during this neoconservative era are intriguingly complex. These shows appear to be of a piece with the backlash against classic liberalism, second-wave feminism, civil rights movements for racial minorities and gays/lesbians, and environmental movements. The programs indulged in masculine excesses and lewdness while expressing skepticism of or hostility against anything perceived as politically correct, overlapping at times with free-market liberalism and a radical individualism that underpinned movements such as anti-affirmative action campaigns. Importantly, the kind of male-oriented programs described above inoculated themselves against criticism by using irony and play to justify their excesses. When detractors pointed out the racism, sexism, classism, homophobia, and xenophobia of such programming, they were charged with lacking a sense of humor. By mocking themselves and adopting a reflexive, wink-and-a-smile approach, these shows attempted to disarm critics by willfully reveling in misogynist vulgarity and uncompromisingly offensive content.

The deliberate absence of intellectual content, equated with elitism, facilitated a culturally conservative neopopulism reminiscent of Reagan-era politics which broadly aligned white males of all classes against women and minorities. These shows also abandoned the pretenses of seriousness and taste, an ironic move which preempted or resisted attempts to challenge cultural hierarchies. For example, when asked by a *New York Times* reporter about "the suitability of an octogenarian 'pregnant' female wrestler being body-slammed by [former Olympic wrestler] Kurt Angle, [WWF owner Vince] McMahon asked, 'Where's your sense of humor?'" (Sandomir 2000: D4). In the words of *Newsweek*, the WWF offered "a second layer of unreality, creating ironic distance from the first. You could take it straight, or with a twist. Here was something to believe in: the candidly, honestly fake" (Leland 2000: 46). Such recourse to ironic humor allowed regressive, recidivist masculinity to emerge relatively unscathed from ongoing cultural struggles.

We argue that the WWF's resurgence represented the apotheosis of this ironic masculinist trend, offering a case study of cultural industries' willingness to attract male viewers by adapting an economy of stereotypes—a shorthand system that provides a streamlined set of narrative tropes and characters that allow for easy legibility—to a contemporary context. Merging the logic of market discourses that privilege flexibility and individual accomplishment with those that favor the increasing fluidity of identities made it possible for the WWF to overwrite histories of economic inequalities and historical injustices. Resulting from this convergence was a slippery set of texts with characters and narrative trajectories that resisted definitive articulation and provided a rhetorical shield against critics, while offering viewers a privileged position as idealized consumers from which they could choose either to take the text as is or to unveil its various conceits. We also contend that the World Wrestling Federation Entertainment, Inc.'s (WWFE)[1] initial public stock offering (IPO) in 1999 and the short-lived XFL (Xtreme Football League) helped to connect this increasingly visible masculine ethos to more respectable economic and cultural realms. In effect, WWF wrestling texts exploited narratives of economic and symbolic abundance to redraw the boundaries among production, consumption, and investment, effectively recasting them within a particular masculine mold.

STONE COLD TEXTUAL DECONSTRUCTION

The most obvious place to see this reactionary new masculinity is within the WWF's television programming, which Henry Jenkins identified in the late 1990s as "a form of masculine melodrama" which "embodies the fundamental contradictions of the American populist tradition," championing the powerless and positing a space for homosocial bonding and class solidarity while simultaneously exploiting stereotypes and nationalism and "depicting a world where might makes right and moral authority is exercised by brute force" (1997: 76, and in this volume). Yet the existence of "masculine melodrama" accentuates the contradictions inherent in the gendering of American television and its generic forms. That is, melodramas and soap operas are considered feminine programming, whereas sports and action-adventure are typically considered masculine programming. But the connections between gender and genre are not essential or intrinsic to gender or genre, as Lynne Joyrich has pointed out. Joyrich has argued that the melodramatic mode began to increase in prominence as conditions of postmodernity took hold, theorizing that the uncertainties of postmodernity provoked a demand for the clear legibility of melodrama, while evacuating a "stable site of mastery, the ideal of masculinity" (1988: 131, 141–42). In other words, melodrama as a form of televisual representation can provide a sort of moral anchor or stabilizing force without necessarily resorting to traditional masculine social and cultural authority.

Joyrich has further argued that both melodrama and postmodernity give "free reign to consumer fantasies," linking consumerism to constructions of femininity. For Joyrich, the conflation of femininity with consumerism, of femininity with passivity and overidentification or closeness, and of consumerism with television creates tensions within U.S. culture which melodrama is ideally poised to negotiate, offering "legible meaning even as it plays on the closeness associated with a spectator-consumer" (1988: 146–47). Melodrama, she concludes, lacks a fixed political vector — neither always progressive nor always regressive — but serves as a productive site for analysis aimed at interrogating and interrupting the linkages among gender, consumption, and passivity or powerlessness. Similarly, Jenkins has suggested that the populist narratives depicted within wwf programming of the late 1980s and early 1990s became a productive site for interrogating and interrupting a similar web of linkages among class, gender, consumption, and cultural authority: "Although rarely described in these terms, populism offers a melodramatic vision of political and economic relationships. . . . American populism sees virtue as originating through physical labor, as a trait possessed by those who are closest to the moment of production (and therefore embodied through manual strength), while moral transgression, particularly greed and ruthlessness, reflects alienation from the production process (often embodied as physical frailty and sniveling cowardice)" (1997: 70, and in this volume).

We contend that with the rise of a libertarian economic and social paradigm during the latter half of the 1990s, wwf texts adjusted by resolving some of these contradictions while exploiting others — albeit in ways that created additional contradictions. Melodrama has been at least partially supplanted by irony, while populism has been disarticulated from a politics of solidarity or commonality and rearticulated to a market-based politics of individual opportunism. In place of moral legibility and a sense of righteousness, wwf texts celebrate the opportunity to purchase and exchange physical and symbolic goods ranging from plastic action figures to stock certificates, from a masculine physical ideal to a capitalist fiscal ideal. Whereas Jenkins claimed that in the late 1980s and early 1990s wwf "villains offer[ed] vivid images of capitalist greed and conspicuous consumption," by the late 1990s, the same could be said of its most celebrated heroes. The wwf has blurred and manipulated the boundaries between good and evil, real and fake, and text and context. In short, the underlying inconsistencies and political and cultural tensions identified by Jenkins within wwf texts of the late 1980s and early 1990s have become the fuel for the textual machinery that produces an ironic play within more recent texts.

In the ironic performances of wwf texts during the late 1990s and early twenty-first century, certainty comes not from the moral but from the physical and fiscal. The dangerous, feminized "consumer passions" and "the dissolution of a stable site of mastery," identified by Joyrich as threatening and anxiety-producing elements of the postmodern, are replaced within WWF texts by the possibility of an ironic mastery, readily available to men as well as to women, that embraces unstable meanings and blurred boundaries as the programs' principal joys. As we will explore below, however, the apparently unstable meanings such texts provide are consistently undergirded by appeals to the imperatives of biological and economic laws. As a result, irony—which Joyrich sees as a tool for feminist critique—becomes an excuse for smutty double entendre; and the blurring of boundaries, a process often linked to the destabilizing of cultural hierarchies, blunts the development of critical positions from which such hierarchies might be challenged. This is particularly the case with respect to distinguishing between good and evil and the real and the fake in WWF texts.

Within the arena and the television programs, WWF texts primarily center on contests or arguments between a *babyface* (good guy) and *heel* (bad guy) or announcers who are either fool or sage. Although this quasi-Manichaean scheme provided the moral and political legibility identified by Jenkins, the late 1990s fandom for heels and the framing of the program as a set of rhetorical and physical contests, in which babyfaces do not always emerge clearly physically and morally victorious and perhaps more important aren't always cheered, co-opts or contains oppositional readings. Complicating the distinction between "good" and "bad" reverses the rationale behind success: being right does not result in success, but being successful results in being right. (This maneuver has numerous analogs in late 1990s culture, the most prominent of which may be the continued popularity of Bill Clinton, who was considered a successful president in opinion polls in part for overseeing a booming economy, despite his purported sexual malfeasance, questionable ethics, and scandalous behavior.) In WWF texts, this logic is more than simply the notion that everybody loves a winner: the blurring of boundaries between proper conduct and success—as well as the exaggerated and ironic tone—provides a justification for audiences to cheer on morally questionable characters constructed as heels because of the quality of their performance, where in previous years the heel role was written and performed in such a way as to lose the climactic match (or "blow-off") and to encourage the audience's disrespect for the character.[2] This enables the grafting of stereotypical traits generally construed as negative, such as improper dialect or behavior associated with a particular racial or class group, onto highly productive and accomplished characters.

While linking stereotypical attributes to successful, celebrated figures might be politically progressive and provide an opportunity to overturn stereotypes, the ironic and hyperbolic environment in which these characters appear may reinforce rather than destroy such stereotypes. As Peter Stallybrass and Allon White (1986) have suggested regarding the carnivalesque, situating the struggles within a somewhat clearly delineated arena (both the ropes of the ring and the frame of the television screen) contains them and effectively constrains any critical or subversive potential within the programming. What appear to be transgressive and potentially empowering moments are simulated, scripted, and planned—hence not genuinely transgressive or empowering, because the audience does not have to take a critical stance but merely adopt a proffered faux-critical stance. We are not arguing that the meanings and political utility of wwf texts are fixed, but simply that the opportunity for struggle is more severely circumscribed than it might initially appear.

These limitations are exacerbated by the textual potential for making claims to reality and producing an I-call-'em-as-I-see-'em discursive truth: we are encouraged to believe what we see and not to question its validity, particularly because the texts are structured in such a way as to enable the audience to recognize a distinction between real and fake. The admission that wwf events are scripted is a form of honesty of which regular viewers are aware. *Smart* viewers, unlike *marks*, recognize that the events are planned and that wrestlers are engaging in choreographed acts of violence—and at the same time they recognize that these acts have real consequences upon real bodies, require skill to perform, and carry great physical risk. Thus the viewers, interpellated as smart and knowing, are offered a privileged place from which they can supposedly distinguish between the real and the fake, even though the distinction between the two has been compromised. Although prime-time television programs such as *Smackdown!* generally do not foreground their own constructedness, other wwf products that circulate among fans, such as *raw Magazine* and the webcast radio report *Byte This*, occasionally discuss the alter egos of the in-ring personae and the scripting of wwf sports entertainment. Behind-the-scenes accounts mark some elements within the texts as fictional and, by implication, other elements as real. The core of these reality claims are rooted in the body: even if everything else is fake, the bodies are real — or, more specifically, the male body is real. While announcers and performers may allude to female breast enhancement, any discussion of steroid use and cosmetic surgery for men is silenced. Thus, the indisputably genuine pain and suffering of male bodies becomes one of the primary claims to reality and truth within WWF texts. Yet there is a twist to the positing of the muscled male body as the site for the production of truth: this body can be bought, principally through the nutritional supplements hawked by the wrestlers via commercials. Consumption is thus at least partially recuperated as a masculine activity through an ironic wink and a cynical rebellious posture.

Drawing on long-standing masculine traditions of excess, typified by eating and drinking contests, the shows and their commercials link consumption with both masculinity and marginality. While maintaining a clear social sanction for consumption, these segments of televisual flow divest consumption of its associations with the feminine and instead mark it as masculine and edgy. For example, Stone Cold Steve Austin, the WWF's rebellious redneck, is associated with excess on the program through such acts as chugging multiple beers simultaneously, driving monster trucks, and generally "deconstructing" things. The most obvious form of excess and waste occurs in the wanton destruction wreaked in the course of the matches, particularly the "hardcore" matches in which there are no disqualifications, and in prop-driven stunts such as a table match (in which the objective is to throw an opponent through a folding table). Advertisements typically replicate this outlaw masculine attitude as well; for instance, both Mankind and Big Show appeared in advertisements for Chef Boyardee in which they indulged in ravenous ravioli repasts. Of course, ads are supposed to promote consumption, but there is little difference between the programs and the advertisements. Indeed, the prime-time shows are themselves largely commercials for upcoming pay-per-view events. Even when ads do not involve WWF stars, they often promote toughness and excess. For example, one frequently aired commercial has had Tom Berenger (of *Platoon* fame) pitching a type of Quaker State motor oil that allows drivers to push their car past the recommended mileage. Another set of oil advertisements by Castrol linked the abuse endured by police cars to the toughness of the product and of wrestlers via the "WWF/Castrol Slam of the Week." In place of the consumer passions articulated toward femininity, the shows and commercials deploy irony and excess to reframe consumption as a highly masculine endeavor.

When irony, appeals to a particular sort of truth, and celebration of consumption and purchasing power are combined with stereotyped representations, they provide the raw materials for a recentering of a white, middle- or lower-middle class masculinity which calls-'em-as-it-sees-'em and appears justified in its relative material success or cultural valorization. As we discuss in the following section, the appeals to irony and to biological and economic truths have enabled a novel reconfiguration and deployment of stereotypes.

THE NEW ECONOMY OF STEREOTYPE

Professional wrestling has trafficked in stereotypes for decades. Roland Barthes (1972 [1957] and in this volume) recognized this in discussing how professional wrestlers embodied cultural myths. In addition to fulfilling ideological functions, stereotypes have offered a partial remedy to the narrative constraints placed on wrestling by its emphasis on spectacle and its road-show format. Since wrestling does not spend a great deal of time on character development, yet needs motivations and explanations for wrestlers' actions, drawing upon cultural stereotypes provides an efficient shorthand method for developing viable characters. For example, in the 1980s, you did not need to know the Iron Sheik's backstory to understand why he attacked Sgt. Slaughter: racist, jingoistic stereotypes provided a quasi-melodramatic moral legibility that largely displaced concerns about motivation and character development. However, the use of stereotypes within professional wrestling has shifted considerably within the last decade. No longer do fixed stereotypes merely serve as the foundation for an easy legibility; in recent years, the fluidity and mutability of character traits have allowed for the articulation of modified stereotypes that provide raw materials for the WWF's current marketing scheme predicated on an in-your-face attitude. The interplay and hybridization of stereotypes offer the appearance of diversity (articulated to rebellion and nonconformism) and the ingredients of product innovation and differentiation, with easily acquired and discarded stereotypes providing the impetus for different action figures for the same wrestler. While this section will describe some stereotypes and other troublesome content, our primary interest is in how these negative traits are discursively explained away by appeals to irony, masculinity, and economic performance.

In addition to their mythical/ideological and narrative functions, the deployment of stereotypes within recent w w f programming seems predicated on the notion that the operations of power along axes of race, gender and sexuality, and class are rendered irrelevant by the promise of ever-expanding market choice and opportunities for masculine empowerment. For example, some recent fan favorites such as The Godfather (a Black pimp) and Eddie Guerrero (aka Latino Heat, a lowrider-driving Latin lover) have tapped into long-standing racial stereotypes. Certainly, some fans have derived pleasure from sharing these characters' racial identity and viewing their physical prowess, but, judging from the fans cheering their entrance, such characteristics were not the sole sources of their popularity: their excessive masculine behavior contributed greatly to their popularity. When white fans chanted along with The Godfather's boast to "be pimpin' hos nationwide" and his exhortation to "step aboard the Ho Train," for instance, they were readily able to embrace a particular brand of misogyny, in which women are mere commodities—yet they could also distance themselves from this misogynous belief because of the "cover" that Blackness offered. In other words, the combination of racial stereotyping with misogyny allowed a vicarious performance of extreme, hypermasculine behavior associated with Blackness—from which fans could later retreat into a more moderate whitened masculinity (while perhaps retaining uncritically the perception that women may be mere commodities). Of course, it is possible to read characters such as D'Lo Brown, The Godfather, or Mark "Sexual Chocolate" Henry as ironic critiques of racist stereotypes—but while the open-endedness of w w f programming makes such opportunities available, it does not encourage viewers to engage seriously in a critique of this form of racism. Vince McMahon has even mocked those who would do so, justifying the reiteration of stereotypes by stating, "We're not concerned about being politically incorrect" (Rosellini 1999: 52).

Independent of egregiously and overtly racist readings, more insidiously racist and politically problematic readings are possible. For instance, one possible reading of a character like the Godfather is that because Black men can make fun of these stereotypes and be well paid while doing so, we can relax and recognize how this market-based employment opportunity has apparently leveled the playing field. In fact, the individual wrestlers may have much to gain from adopting a gimmick that relies on stereotype: The Godfather character, for instance, became popular enough through TV appearances to sell many action-figure toys, but the same wrestler's next character, The *Good*father, has failed to capture the imagination of fans. (It's worth noting that The Goodfather is a member of the Right to Censor [RTC], a group of WWF wrestlers whose sanctimonious task is to crack down on sexual display in and around the ring, representing a jab at the Parents Television Council [PTC]—emblematic of how the WWF takes on its critics by reducing them to stereotypes and mocking them in performances.) Yet the relative freedom of choice in consuming broadcast or expanded basic cable programming does not necessarily signify a free labor market in which skill unproblematically translates into employment and economic success, regardless of what the inter-Bush boom may have led one to believe. Furthermore, the fans' ability to play with stereotypes, whether in televisual or plastic form, does not evacuate them of their dominant cultural meanings. In other words, to return to the example of The Godfather, a Black pimp is still a racist stereotype, even if articulated as a face within the ring. The audience's ability to fracture the stereotype and reassemble some its constituent parts into a pleasurable character does not make the stereotype any less potent or potentially damaging in the wider social context. If anything, this may make it more potent or resistant to challenge, especially because a Black man is profiting economically from the exploitation of this stereotype.

Similar problems arise from the WWF's representations of women, which serve a consistent set of narrative functions. The use of female figures to incite voyeuristic activity is obvious, and even explicitly acknowledged by wrestlers proclaiming the need for what they term "eye candy" during matches, but should not distract from their crucial narrative and character-defining roles—since their presence underpins a misogynist version of heterosexual masculinity concerned with defending its entitlements from competing visions of masculinity and sexuality. Furthermore, sex, attraction, and heterosexual romance are key narrative elements within specific matches as well as in longer narrative arcs, such as a character's heel turn or the formation of an alliance. Whether female characters assume the role of manager for or manipulator of male wrestlers, they are always on display, distracting referees or opposing wrestlers with skimpy attire. On rare occasions female characters wrestle for their own titles, but the stakes are typically diminished to a voyeuristic display (as in an evening gown or bra-

and-panties matches where the first woman to disrobe her opponent wins) or framed as part of a larger power struggle (as when Stephanie McMahon won the title in a match that secured the men's and women's titles for the McMahon-Helmsley Regime).

Perhaps the most remarkable aspect of WWF programs' representations of women is how often they appear to be hurt—an element that suggests a severe constraint on the articulation of both femininity and masculinity. We categorize the narrative portrayal of physical abuse women receive from male wrestlers as either "uncalled-for" or "justified" violence. The uncalled-for trope relies on conventional "women in jeopardy" storylines to assert the goodness of the babyface or the badness of the heel. The justified assault opens up a potentially uncomfortable debate over what constitutes the acceptable consequences of female agency and masculine action. For example, when a female manager interferes with a match by dealing her wrestler's opponent a blow to the crotch, what is the precise narrative and moral calculus by which retaliation is either condemned or sanctioned?

WWF programming answers the question by assessing the status of the male wrestler: judgment about the propriety of a response is predicated upon the retaliator's heel or babyface status rather than the female object of violence. Even Chyna, who wrestled men rather than other women, often played a role principally designed to demonstrate the heel credentials of male wrestlers. Thus a babyface may retaliate by hitting a woman without being criticized by the wise announcer or the fans as long as she has apparently done something to warrant retaliation, while a heel will hit women indiscriminately. Or, rather, she deserves it because he's a babyface, or he's abusive simply because he's a heel: the violence comments on and develops the male character more than encouraging an understanding of or sympathy toward the woman in question, thus leaving the female character less developed, less valued, and less important except insofar as she provokes or justifies masculine activity. Thus while the violence perpetrated by heels is judged an affront to moral sensibilities, the violence perpetrated by babyfaces is construed as justified retaliation. Given widespread domestic abuse falling inexcusably and disproportionately on women, such a story is far from a testament to progress, particularly within a set of texts that makes no pretense toward equality beyond the simplistic notion that might makes right.[3] In other words, the struggle for gender equity that drove second-wave feminism and challenged traditional patriarchal gender roles receives a discursive backhand: heels have abandoned any pretense of civilized masculine behavior by refusing to abide by the principle that women should be protected, while faces will be chivalrous as a rule and will protect women who behave properly—but may legitimately use violence against women who don't.

The WWF articulates a tremendously limited masculinity which paradoxically claims to transgress unnatural limits imposed on men by civilized society. In other words, in the WWF, masculinity is defined by body, action, and attitude, and the preferred mode is big brutal guys who play by their own rules. Triple H may sometimes be a heel, but he will always be more of a man than skinny announcer Michael Cole, an infamously easy pushover. Even Vince and Shane McMahon, the owners who exercise both physical and economic power willfully and vengefully, demonstrate how this vision of masculinity is not only racist and sexist but also restricts the range of acceptable masculine behavior or, more precisely, how racism and sexism work along with other techniques to construct a very narrow white, masculine, heterosexual position. The WWF's version of masculinity combines discourses of racism, misogyny, and excess with a glorification of physical and economic power and a derision of fair play, offering a construct called masculinity through its explicit articulation to male anatomy.

The combination of biological features with cultural gender roles can play out in a variety of ways, often presenting competing versions of ideal masculinity without firmly articulating which is best. On an 8 May 2000 episode of *Raw Is War*, for example, Chris Jericho complimented Vince McMahon on his ability to acquire billions, but then asserted that he was driven to do so because he had a small penis. McMahon retorted by extolling the size of his genitals—referring to them as "grapefruits" on a big "trunk"—and then promised punishment for Jericho. And punishment Jericho received: he was forced to fight three title defenses in one evening and lost his Intercontinental title in a match officiated by Triple H, McMahon's son-in-law (within the storyline). This conflict offered two competing models of authentic masculinity, with the audience free to choose either McMahon, Jericho, or both as their champions. McMahon pitted his organizational stature, his intellect, and his purportedly massive male member against Jericho's muscular body, wrestling prowess, and gutsy willingness to challenge the boss in a battle of will and skill. And it's not clear which character is preferred, since both are big, brutal guys who play by their own rules: McMahon won this conflict by using the brutal power of his corporation and the hypermasculine attitude apparently derived from huge genitalia to revise the wwf's rules and strip Jericho of his title, but Jericho retained the sympathies of the principally working- and middle-class wrestling audience by audaciously inciting the fight and using his powerful body to defend himself in the ensuing brutal struggle. Thus while power, wealth, and biology coalesce to define at least one model of authentic masculinity (McMahon's), whether or not this model is preferable is ambiguous.

This ambiguity is the product of conflicted and contradictory processes which attempt to resituate masculinity within a changing economy. Within and around the wwf texts of the late 1990s and early 2000s, there are at least three distinct processes which locate masculinity in economic discourses: the aforementioned recuperation of both textual and commodity consumption as an appropriate masculine activity; the commodification of the male form through both the specular processes of the text and the reproduction of male bodies in the form of action figures; and the discourses of work and ownership that link masculinity to production. Any one of these processes can conflict with either or both of the others. For example, the positioning of masculinity as a new terrain of consumption and as an object to be consumed provokes contradictions and tensions that require careful textual negotiation. In addition, there can be conflict within these processes, with the conflict between Vince as owner and Jericho as employee serving as a prime example.

All of these contradictions play out most often and openly in the discourses circulating around the McMahon family, particularly Vince. The nefarious character of Vince is generally considered a product of the infamous 1997 Survivor Series pay-per-view in which Vince "screwed" Bret "the Hitman" Hart out of his wwf title in Montreal.[4] The event remains a subject of intense debate, both as to whether or not Vince's actions were just and whether the whole affair was a *work* (a performance) or a *shoot* (real). Certainly the event broke down many of the walls separating the wrestling business from the wrestling narrative. The real-world circumstances in which Hart was hired away by rival company wcw necessitated giving the wwf world title to a wrestler who would remain with the wwf. Secondary texts — most notably underground newsletters and the documentary *Wrestling with Shadows* (Jay 1998) — allowed the dissemination of the economic rationale for Vince's textual treachery. Whether work or shoot, the contradictions

Executive Action Figures: Vince takes it on the chin from storyline co-owner Ric Flair. McMahon's evil genius entrepreneur persona allows him multiple poses. This and other WWE merchandise provide opportunities to play with models of masculinity, with Vince's as a premium brand.

embodied in Vince—simultaneously the duplicitous, overbearing boss portrayed on WWF programming and the protector and proprietor of WWF business interests—were worked and reworked during subsequent years. These contradictions are most visible in Vince's ongoing and convoluted feud with Stone Cold Steve Austin, which began in 1997, the general parameters of which posed Austin's working-class antiauthoritarian persona in sustained conflict with Vince's embodiment of dictatorial economic power.

Vince McMahon is the site of profound ambivalence. When he lambastes fans for being low class or stupid and supporting the targets of his machinations, the owner is both vilified as the evil rich and celebrated for his wealth, which finances the entertainment. Vince is also typically praised for his financial acumen before being insulted, generally by having his masculinity called into question as in the Jericho example just cited. Ultimately, Vince has a split textual persona that is simultaneously celebrated as entrepreneur and entertainer and maligned as coward and corporate bigwig. Even his position as capitalist par excellence is complicated by his positioning as a commodity—both as object to be viewed and to be owned (in action-figure form). Furthermore, his and his children's willingness to take a punch or a folding metal chair for the good of the family enterprise blur the distinctions between owner and worker. While Shane, currently the most active in-ring performer among the McMahons, may never be a worker in the sense that term has among professional wrestlers, Vince and Shane have complicated a class-based interpretation of the relationship between owners and workers, thus successfully exploiting and negotiating the processes that situate masculinity within economic discourses.

Their in-ring performance, though, constitutes only part of this negotiation. The performance of ownership within the skit portions of the programs is equally important, as the narrativized power struggles among members of the McMahon family have been as prominent as the struggles of the workers against the owners. In the most overt textual positioning of the wrestlers as Labor, the spring 1999 formation of the Union of People You OUght to ReSpect (aka UP YOURS), the wrestlers supported Vince in the face of a hostile takeover by son, Shane. The McMahon family's narrative quarrels draw heavily on the conventions of prime-time family melodramas such as *Dallas* and *Dynasty*, albeit with male characters rather than male and female characters dominating the action. Of course, the women of the McMahon family also wield considerable power over the family business. Textually, Stephanie—who has filled multiple roles in front of and behind the camera, including a stint as head writer—is perhaps a more competent adversary for her father than Shane, while Linda (the real-life CEO of the WWFE) serves as the mostly absent authority figure. Thus, as the positions of Stephanie and Linda suggest, ownership, economic power, and masculinity are not completely congruent.

However, a gendered hierarchy of sorts remains in place. The key distinction between Stephanie and Linda and Vince and Shane is that the latter pair performs regularly in pay-per-view matches and regular television contests, staking a claim to both of the WWF's sources of power and reality. Everything else may be fake, a gimmick planned for entertainment purposes, but muscles and money become the twin measures of masculinity and the common currency in the text's negotiations with itself and its audience. Vince and Shane provide much more physical performances, often getting bloodied or engaging in high-risk stunts, than does Stephanie, who wrestles on occasion but principally serves as a manager for male wrestlers—particularly her husband in wwf storylines, Triple H. Given this dynamic, we suggest that the texts articulate a sort of three-tiered cultural hierarchy that locates Vince and Shane at the top (as paragons of hypermasculine behavior, able to exercise both tremendous economic and physical power), Stephanie and Linda along with the stable of wrestlers in the middle (as capable of either exercising economic influence or demonstrating physical prowess, but almost never both), and wrestling fans at the base (in the feminized position of consumers merely watching the spectacle, captivated by the excitingly ambiguous and multifaceted texts offered in a variety of venues). In short, the narrative economy of the wwf has undergone a shift during the late 1990s and the early twenty-first century in which difference is created and exploited to sell a spectacle increasingly less focused on producing a clear moral tale of good versus evil. Instead, texts have been built on celebrating the accumulation of monetary wealth and the unfettered exercise of masculine power—a theme resonating with other discourses circulating within U.S. culture during this period.

WHATEVER BULLISH BRAVADO THE MARKET CAN BEAR

The metaphor of an economy of stereotypes described in the previous section is apropos, suggesting the extent to which financially oriented discourses have suffused U.S. culture around the turn of the millennium. According to such discourses, the invisible hand of the market offers the optimal regulating mechanism for social and cultural interaction, with claims about the desirability and necessity of opportunities for consumer choice and unregulated competition for resources—for example, the appearance of absolute choice provided by cable or the illusion of equal access to an evidently democratic stock market—deployed to blunt any criticism of or objection to this economic model. Although class has been opened up as a site for struggle within wwf texts, this potential conflict is complicated by the dual discourses of investment and consumption provoked most overtly by the initial public offering of wwfe shares, which offered fans the symbolic opportunity to transgress class boundaries by investing in the stock market (traditionally considered a long-term activity), against the more immediate pleasure of indulging in the consumption of pay-per-view events. The wwfe's initial public offering provides an intriguing example

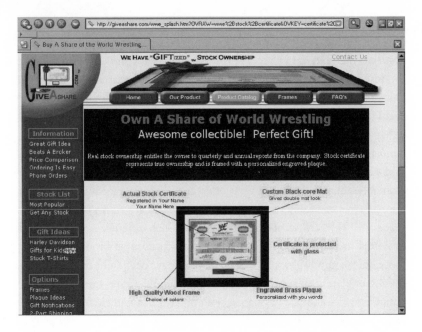

You Can Own These Guys: The WWE's initial public offering was hailed as evidence of the continued democratization of the stock market, a milestone in the ascendance of the common investor into the rarified halls of stock trading. Sites such as giveashare.com suggest that it also blurred the distinctions among capital, commodity, and keepsake.

of the paradoxes emerging as U.S. culture increasingly interprets economic models and measures as indexes of democratic and rational behavior: fans were exhorted to expend economic assets to attain the status of investor or shareholder, a position of privilege that has come to be associated with a kind of masculine activity.

We argue that in an age dominated by what Thomas Frank refers to as "market populism," economic laws and market logic have been inextricably fused with a variety of cultural discourses. Frank's work helps to account not only for part of the WWF's surge in prominence and popularity, but also for why the McMahons believed WWFE stock would be an attractive option for fans. Frank argues that 1990s U.S. culture was defined by "our diversity, our nonconformity, our radicalism, our differentness. It was an era of many and spectacular avant-gardes, of loud and highly visible youth cultures, of emphatic multiculturalism, of extreme sports, extreme diets and extreme investing" (2000: 13). Yet this era was also marked by a widespread agreement that market forces and business needs were the proper avenues for ensuring the proper distribution and allocation of resources and for democratic choice. "In addition to being mediums of exchange," Frank suggests, "markets are [conceived of as] mediums of consent . . . [and] an anti-elitist machine" (2000: 14).

Market populism resembles the neoconservative backlash against liberal elites that brought Ronald Reagan and Newt Gingrich to power, particularly for its sotto voce appeals to (white) working-class male voters. Yet the crucial difference is that market populism is hip, cool, edgy: not rooted in a religious fundamentalism, nor in the notion that violence, sexuality, and coarse language must be suppressed, but in the belief that self-expression is safeguarded by market forces. Moreover, market populism often asserts the desirability of difference, nonconformity, and radical change while providing an ostensibly nonideological basis for choosing to reject anything too different or disturbing, thus defending neoconservative political retrenchment against charges of explicit or systematic bias by referring to the exercise of individual rights and free will. In essence, the appearance of absolute autonomy for individuals (and corporations, which have the same legal status as individuals), self-regulation, and difference enabled by a market-based society seem to emerge naturally rather than out of intentionally constructed cultural systems.

Thus the apparent democratization of the stock market and the evidently universal benefits of the ever-expanding economy became a paramount yet seemingly value-neutral ideological component of this neoconservative era. Differences in economic and cultural capital have been washed away by the seeming abundance and fluidity of cultural and economic currency. David Harvey suggests that one characteristic of postmodern societies such as the contemporary United States is that "money unifies precisely *through* its capacity to accommodate individualism, otherness, and extraordinary social fragmentation" (1995 [1990]: 103). Despite the vast class-based disparities and economic distortions manifest in the United States by most economic measures, the average American can thus envision him- or herself as empowered and valued by choosing to purchase particular symbols of the seeming abundance offered by the marketplace. Frank contends that anyone can use the rhetoric of market populism to articulate almost anything — no matter how illogical — even to the relatively economically disadvantaged. For instance, he observed, analysts claimed that "the NASDAQ was soaring because the buy-and-hold common man had finally been allowed to participate" (2000: 18). This discursive truth became so profound that James Taranto of the *Wall Street Journal*'s online edition could fantasize that " 'the U.S. is now closer to [the] Marxian ideal than any society in history' " as a result of " 'the democracy of the market' and the widespread ownership of stock" (quoted in Frank 2000: 19).

It was in this ostensibly liberated economic and cultural environment that the WWFE offered fans and investors the opportunity to cheer on the company's performance in the stock market as they would root on the performance of their favorite wrestlers in the ring. News stories and opinion columns about the WWFE's initial public offering suggested the extent to which market populism had become both naturalized and linked to distinctly masculine traits. The WWFE announced that it would begin selling stock publicly in October 1999, a maneuver that one critic said combined "two of the biggest pop cultural phenomena of the '90s, stock market mania and wrestlemania" (cited in Schwartz and Liebowitz 1999: E01). Although this critic questioned whether or not pro-wrestling fans "are investor types who can affect the price of a stock," others argued that the IPO marked "at least a symbolic milestone in the ongoing democratization of the stock market, further choke-holding the notion that investing is the sole province of the buttoned-down" (E01). Some speculated that fans might buy stock as souvenirs; said one investor, fans could look at a poster of wrestlers "and say, 'I own you guys' " (E01). Dave Meltzer, publisher of the *Wrestling Observer Newsletter*, suggested that if the price was right, fans would feel invited to participate in the stock market boom and snap up shares (Roberts 1999: 42). As such quotations suggest, the investment opportunity was construed as giving fans the chance to supplement their consumption of melodramatic wrestling texts and wrestling-related products with activities that would make them owners: to change their actions from being ones that would profit only others, to actions that would profit themselves as well as others. In essence, they promoted the material and economically reproductive cycle afforded by the investment opportunity, such that the roles of feminized fan and of masculinized breadwinner could overlap.[5] Yet such a strategy was also criticized on the grounds that the WWF's core demographic of young men and teens resided largely in lower income brackets. Though inviting all economic classes to participate directly in the market conformed with the intellectual tenets of market populism, the stories rec-

ognized that the majority of fans purchasing WWF broadcasts and paraphernalia may have lacked adequate investment capital to purchase stock.

On the other hand, wealthier and institutional investors might have been
expected to avoid the firm because of its programs' controversial content,
because the vast majority of WWFE stock remained in McMahon's hands,
and because of the inability to influence corporate practices, since the public
stock had no voting rights. Thus the typically empowering exercise of economic strength and self-determination through stock purchase was structurally emasculated by the limited amount of input WWFE stockholders
could possibly have. Given the limited number of shares available plus the
absence of voting rights, the stock offering may have been perceived as one
in which McMahon invited investors along for a ride but asked them to pay
for the gas. (In fact, it is possible that audiences have far more influence over
the company's practices than shareholders, since the company will respond
to fans' rejection of a particular textual turn or wrestler but is unlikely to
respond to the desires of a relatively small number of stockholders lacking
voting rights.) Such concerns, combined with well-justified historical skepticism about the duration of the bull market, caused the London *Financial
Times* to express wariness about purchasing WWFE stock ("Fighting a Delusion" 1999: 14). Yet McMahon's skill in attracting audiences to the arena and
television screen combined with the company's strong financial reserves and
cash flow to intrigue some commentators: "When World Wrestling Federation Entertainment Inc. announced its plan to go public last August, wrestling was suddenly taken seriously by the "serious" media. . . . With annual
revenues of more than $250 million, and the rising profile of its matches on
both cable and network television — not to mention successful tie-in ven-
tures in the home video and toy markets — WWFE has the potential to become the hulking 800-pound gorilla of the entertainment world" (Clancy
1999: 8).

Moreover, the potentially problematic content of WWF telecasts was described by McMahon as filling a market niche and serving WWF audiences or
consumers (and thus investors) well: "It behooves us, business-wise, to listen
to our audience and give them what they want. . . . They are far more sophisticated now than they've ever been. This is a complex world. To have the whole
black-and-white issue jammed down their throat — they'd find that boring"
(Ahrens 1998: D01). Finally, as will be discussed in this section, McMahon
the CEO and McMahon the WWF character both match up nicely with the

image of the "New Economy" investor: innovative, risk taking, cocky—in other words, thoroughly masculine.

Both the mainstream and financial presses noted the apparently inappropriate or incongruous match of the low-class company and its maverick owner McMahon with the upper-class financial sector. The *Independent* of London, for example, characterized the bout as one between "the redneck corner" of the WWF and "the blue-blooded corner" of "Wall Street financiers who scorn the vulgarity of Mr. McMahon's over-hyped set-pieces" (Gledhill 1999: 5). Yet as signaled by the subtitle of an article in the London *Financial Times*, "Wrestling's Bravado Appeals to Bullish Traders," parallels existed between the hypermasculine realms of professional wrestling and investing. The *Financial Times* asserted that the WWF's economic clout rendered it "a parable of pre-millennial American finance," and indicated that "the rough-cut bravado of professional wrestling appeals not only to the American teenager, but also to the American equity day trader, who has become accustomed to a never-changing storyline, the bullish one" ("Fighting a Delusion" 1999: 14). The article labeled this bravado as a clearly masculine discourse, though citing an example that featured a female figure:

> "I don't want to just beat the market," is the testimony of a tough and savvy-looking young woman, pictured in a newspaper advertisement for Ameritrade, an online brokerage firm. "I want to wrestle its scrawny little body to the ground and make it beg for mercy. . . ." This kind of talk has made *Raw is War*, *SmackDown*, and other WWF video delights mustviewing in college fraternity houses. But it is not the language of finance, or was not, at least, until the Wall Street scriptwriters allegedly wrote risk out of the plot. . . . Looking into the eyes of the tough-as-nails Ameritrade lady, one can intuit a comprehensive financial theory. Evidently fearless, she seems to believe that she, or a power she understands, is in control of events. (1999: 14)

The power to subjugate, the thrill of risk without the fear of negative consequences, the take-no-prisoners attitude, and perhaps above all the ascendance of corporate monarchs over the teeming masses—all are key discursive goals manifest in WWF texts and their economic counterpart, the stock offering. In its analysis of the ad, the *Financial Times* nicely critiques the hypermasculine traits that accompanied the dominant narrative of market populism in the 1990s, especially the self-interested, shortsighted goals it ascribes to the rhetorical figures of the U.S. equity day trader and the college frat boy.

Moreover, the portable character of masculine traits such as the financial acumen and ruthlessness displayed in the Ameritrade advertisement is congruent with the logic underpinning the economy of stereotypes outlined above: certain forms of masculine power and authority can in theory be taken up and deployed by anyone willing to develop the skills and knowledge necessary to engage in a performance that is discursively marked as masculine regardless of biological gender. If power and authority are so freely and naturally available, it becomes easier to criticize those who are unwilling or unable to exercise it as somehow deficient, deviant, or weak—and to celebrate those who are willing or able to exercise such power, regardless of the ends to which it is put or the consequences incurred. In effect, market populism enables and excuses the rampant racism, sexism, and other regressive features of wwf programming. The way in which wwf characters such as The Rock and Chyna have been celebrated for their performance in the ring (and their status as profitable and highly marketable stars) implies that race, gender, class, and other characteristics do not have an intrinsic and immutable meaning, and thus appear to be arbitrary and irrelevant signs that can be obviated by repeatedly successful performances. This stance, while echoing laudable ideas long espoused by progressives, effectively masks the ways in which free-market ideologies and wwf texts are invested in and underwritten by gendered, classed, and racialized discourses that work to constrain the potential for social change.

In February 2000, *Newsweek* featured The Rock and Chyna on its cover to call attention to a report echoing this understanding of the overlapping hypermasculine realms of business and wrestling, contending that the wwf "may look like a cartoon spectacle, but [it] is serious business. And business is good" (Leland 2000: 47). McMahon's success was traced to two factors: his paternal family instincts and his admirably ruthless skill in consolidating and dominating the wrestling business. The "twin obsessions with family and business" made McMahon "brashly ambitious," and he turned his father's regional wrestling circuit into a nationwide phenomenon during the 1980s by eschewing gentlemen's agreements to respect territorial boundaries and deploying "scorched-earth tactics" to drive competitors out of business while capitalizing on the deregulation of children's television programming under Reagan (Leland 2000: 48, 49). McMahon exploited syndicated television to spark demand for WWF wrestling instead of his competitors'—a strategy which "was risky, but this was the Reagan era. McMahon was developing a slicker, kid-friendly product" (Leland 2000: 49). The riskiness of developing the WWF through leveraged buyouts and slick advertisements that masked financial instability and questionable business practices was apparently palatable during the 1980s, in which the negative implications of a procorporate trickle-down economic and cultural agenda were masked by images of contentment and prosperity starring an affable, avuncular president. The neoconservative thrust of the apparently miraculously democratic "New Economy" presided over by Clinton—which furthered the deregulatory thrust begun under Reagan—also encouraged similar corporate risk-taking, albeit with WWF texts that were noticeably more adult oriented and less kid friendly.

McMahon's corporate success was predicated on "the workaholic template of a high-budget, high-concept Hollywood star factory," transforming the world of wrestling from "the scruffy realm of the carnival" with its regional fiefdoms into a modern (inter)national corporate state (Leland 2000: 49–50). Characterizing the obliteration of competing, locally owned wrestling circuits as a beneficial result of this individual "workaholic" effort reinforces the masculinist late-capitalist ethos suggesting that hard work and ruthlessness are primary characteristics of success—particularly if they result in excessive, expensive affairs. More important, during the consolidation process, Vince and Linda McMahon surrendered the traditional promotional line that suggested wrestling was honest sport and "repositioned their product as 'sports entertainment'"—not "as a bold move in the direction of candor, [but as] . . . a way out of an onerous tax" on pay-per-view revenues levied by state athletic commissions. This shift made wrestling "seem less alien to mainstream entertainments and advertisers, crossing into music videos and network TV" (Leland 2000: 50). Laying aside *Newsweek*'s questionable glorification of wealthy capitalists blithely exploiting tax loopholes, we find a compelling paradox at the heart of the WWF's success: removing any truth-claims by professional wrestling facilitated its ability to operate as a real economic entity and to attract advertisers, and thus increased its ability to reach a wider audience and to become a more realistic simulacrum that inspired the significant, real passion that has become increasingly elusive among disaffected young males—the WWF's target audience. In a nutshell, the ability to deal with the distinctions between real and play was articulated as a comfortably masculine expertise; if the lack of stable distinctions between the staged and the real was a deal breaker for an audience member or potential investor, that audience member or investor could be denigrated as either a feminized elitist intellectual or an obsolete consumer, lacking the social ability to understand the playful character of the WWF. Critically, the *Newsweek* article asserted that

McMahon's most cherished innovation remains his family—the on-screen version and the real. As TV's malevolent Mr. McMahon, he plays a natty corporate monster who would destroy anyone . . . in the pursuit of power. . . . The current story line has [McMahon's daughter] Stephanie and her "husband," Triple H, running the company with vindictive malice—a filial jihad that might ring a bell among students of the real McMahon saga. It is a gloriously multi-level play between what wrestlers call the work and the shoot, the staged and the real-real. And it suits the times. As Triple H says, in the post-cold-war era "there is no horror now. To the average person, the real-life enemy is now their boss" (Leland 2000: 54).

The centrality of McMahon's family to his public versus private persona —the multilevel play of his own life—highlighted the intersections of class discourses in corporate and personal life, with the latter appearing subordinated to the former. The inability to distinguish between what is staged and what is real may be considered a sign of either a feminized elitist intellectualism or a naive, premasculine lack of awareness.[6] McMahon's skill at negotiating both the staged and real realms, which has allowed him to "innovate" both his corporation and his family such that they are integrated and inseparable, offers him the opportunity to function both as savage corporate raider and as loving, doting father and husband—even while he is, within the bounds of the text, a very good CEO yet a very bad boss, father, and husband.

Given the extreme masculinist discourses circulating around the WWF and the stock market, it is no surprise that observers noted the irony of the WWFE and Martha Stewart Living Omnimedia going public on the same day, 20 October 1999. On one level, the companies and their cultural and stylistic contours are diametrically opposed: WWF programming appeals principally to viewers who are single, male, young, and in the lower- and middle-class income range, while Stewart's fare is pitched mainly toward married women, young to middle-aged, and in the middle- to upper-class income range. Stewart's products are oriented toward homemaking and responsible consumerism that optimize the use of scarce resources, while the wwf is linked with sparse or inelegant decor and irresponsible, wildly excessive consumption. Yet despite this contrast pitting "class versus crass" (Schoolman 1999: 26), news stories often asserted that both companies offered a tangible product and were worthy of investment—unlike the IPOs that fueled the then-ongoing economic expansion, principally dot-com companies with few, if any, hard assets. The *Independent* noted that while "the names may be absurd, the action choreographed and the audience very much non-U," the wwf is "a resounding financial success, thanks largely to Mr. McMahon's business acumen" (1999: 5). Moreover, the wwf's core audience of young men and children remained attractive to advertisers, and "bankers familiar with the business [were] confident that investors [would] lap up the offering regardless of their opinion of wrestling" (1999: 5; see also Schwartz and Liebowitz 1999: E01). The *Boston Globe* observed in August 1999, shortly after the IPOs for both companies were announced, that "Martha and the wrestlers are much better business propositions than many of the hot dot-com IPOs hitting Wall Street every week" (Syre and Stein 1999: D1), on the basis of their immense profits and economic backing—since wwfE was assisted in its Wall Street debut by Bear, Stearns & Co., Merrill Lynch, and Credit Suisse First Boston. The article was accompanied by a report on weak Internet stocks, which explicitly contrasted the profitability of Stewart's firm and the wwfE with the illusory profits of Internet firms.[7]

Yet this also suggests a feature of the postmodern New Economy that logically follows from both Harvey and Frank: a shift in the end point of consumption. Whereas investors formerly valued companies for their income and dividends within the Old Economy, firms became valued for what *New York Times* reporter Gretchen Morgenson labeled "freewheeling measures of worth, like revenue growth, Web site traffic, and even customer 'share of mind'," which bear no necessary relation to corporate profits or revenues. During the last years of the bull market of the 1990s, added Morgenson, this shift in valuation resulted in "equity investors [taking] on the role of financing fledgling companies—early in their development—that venture capitalists had traditionally assumed," even though historically "companies cannot go public without a track record that proved their ability to turn a profit" (2001: 1). What mattered most in the New Economy was not the revenue stream from consumers who purchased a company's product or service, but the revenue stream from investors who purchased a company's stock. Thus a firm such as the WWF, successful under the terms of the Old Economy and possessing a strong revenue stream, may have been considered less valuable because its income was capped by the collective wealth and spending capacity of its committed fans: its value was limited by traditional economic measures. A firm such as Amazon.com, on the other hand, was unsuccessful under the terms of the Old Economy but became one of the most valued entities in the New Economy for its growth potential. Its value was limited only by the wildest speculations of investors as to what it might someday be worth, and investors scrambled to buy Amazon.com stock to get in on the ground floor of this nascent New Economy. As Mary Meeker of Morgan Stanley stated, "The value of a business is its future cash flows," not its past and present performance. This may explain the inexplicable period in 2000 during which "the more a company lost, the better its stock did, while the more a company earned, the worse its stock fared" (Morgenson 2001: 1): the apotheosis of the buy low, sell high mantra. While the bursting of the stock market bubble might seem to have signaled the death knell for some features of the New Economy, even the market's metamorphosis from bull to bear may not cause this shift in the point of consumption to reverse.

Ultimately, the stock offering provided a means to perform masculinity through consumption: WWF devotees could engage with their inner fandom and express their individuality both by consuming mass-produced television texts and ancillary WWF products and by purchasing stock. Presumably lower-class fans could tap into the empowering discourses of masculine neoathleticism and high finance while maintaining their hostility toward the upper class; presumably upper-class investors could enjoy the vicarious thrills of fandom, playing an active and visible role within this hypermasculine populist drama while maintaining their hierarchical privilege.

Yet the WWF lacked a mechanism for future growth potential valued within the New Economy that would be likely to attract a critical mass of upper-class investors. Unveiling the XFL proposal in February 2000, Vince McMahon vowed to revive "old-fashioned, smash-mouth football but with cutting-edge marketing and production values" (Associated Press 2000), merging two distinct sets of masculine characteristics without the apparent drawbacks of either. The NFL had "become too conservative, too corporate with too much regulation," claimed McMahon (Associated Press

2000)—blending criticisms of mainstream culture rendered bland by its corporate-imposed homogeneity with neoconservative populist rhetoric, and replicating millennial discourses of individualist counterculture capitalism that privileges market-based ideologies. The decision of NBC to purchase $30 million worth of WWF stock and become co-owners of the XFL represented what the *New York Times* called "a mammoth injection of credibility" (Sandomir 2000: D4) both for the fledgling league and McMahon's organization, demonstrating a faith in the ability of the WWF to devise programming that attracted young male viewers, while giving the WWF the possibility of creating new revenue streams.[8] In short, the XFL enabled the WWF to offer a product quite distinct from its fabricated postmodern melodramas that could attract both its existing consumer base and, by harking back to the halcyon days of football, average middle-class U.S. football fans. Together, those assets potentially created a critical growth factor that could raise the WWFE stock's attractiveness to investors. The failure of the short-lived XFL, however, may have caused the WWF to reconsider its excursions into other athletic realms and instead concentrate on the business of professional wrestling.

CORNERING THE SQUARED CIRCLE

At the same time that the XFL fizzled, McMahon consolidated his hold on professional wrestling. In late March 2001, the WWF purchased its archrival, World Championship Wrestling (WCW), for an estimated $10–$20 million. The acquisition represented both a professional and a personal triumph by McMahon over former WCW owner, Ted Turner, who had stolen away several prominent WWF wrestlers in the previous decade. The de facto monopoly created by this purchase—though theoretically consistent with the tenets of market populism—heightened concerns that the WWF's unchallenged supremacy would result in exploitive, if not extortionist, business demands. Moreover, the suspicion of size inherent within populist discourse provoked concerns that the WWF would lose touch with the average viewer and produce an inferior product. Finally, the merger undermined both economic and athletic competition in ways that enervated the WWF's populist appeal: no longer was the WWF the edgy, upstart company run by the self-made McMahon pitted against the WCW and its multibillionaire owner; no longer did fans have the opportunity to choose to support either the WWF or the WCW (thus losing their ability to create communities and identities around their opposition to a common enemy); no longer did the wrestlers — particularly the lower-tier wrestlers — have leverage against the owners in negotiating contracts. The WWF, for all intents and purposes, had won its battle against the ninety-eight-pound weakling of the WCW.

Removing the struggle for the WWF's survival, however, also sapped the organization of a key element of its masculine appeal. Although the company retained its ability to flex its proverbial muscles, to demonstrate its overwhelming economic and physical strengths in the market and the ring, the flexing was reduced to narcissistic posturing rather than manly competition. Indeed, much of the wrestling press and many fan Web sites remarked on the WWF's arrogant posturing in the wake of the merger. Some comments even intimated that the WCW "invasion" storyline failed largely because Vince's desire to stage his victory over the WCW in the ring at the 2001 "Survivor Series" pay-per-view overrode his desire to diversify the WWF's brand and improve the company. For instance, Bruce Mitchell of the *Pro Wrestling Torch* online fanzine criticized McMahon's subversion of the Alliance storyline: "McMahon thought it more important to send a message on TV . . . than do what is best for the short-term finances of the company. Why he continues to use valuable television time to do this as revenues shrink is beyond me" (Mitchell 2001).

Eliminating competition created concern both within the television industry and among the WWF's fan base. Although cable operators were pleased by the WWF's ability to conquer the pay-per-view (PPV) market, they remained wary of its absolute market dominance,[9] which had been mitigated by the competition offered by the WCW (whose twenty pay-per-view events in 2000 produced 10 percent of all PPV revenues). With the WCW's demise, the absence of alternatives gave the television industry no leverage in negotiations with the WWF. Cable companies feared that McMahon's willingness to push the envelope with violent and sexually explicit programming would cause the WCW's more family-friendly brand of wrestling to be altered, alienating sponsors and audiences willing to embrace the WCW but not the WWF, thus narrowing the size of the overall wrestling market and potentially decreasing cable operators' profits further. The WWF reportedly grumbled about "what it perceives to be a gradual loss of marketing effort from the industry," which, if true, probably emerged out of fears that the WWF "can make PPV rate card negotiations very difficult for [cable] operators in the future" (Umstead 2001: 32).

Fans also expressed ambivalence and concern about the acquisition and its impact on the texts. Scott Keith (2001), writing in the online *Wrestling Observer Newsletter*, suggested that the WCW's demise was "a necessary evil of the proceeding," that wrestlers would "end up making more from taking their chances in a healthy WWF" than in the "bloated" contractual world of the sickly WCW, and that the WWF was and would remain a superior product. Yet other fan postings to the *Wrestling Observer Newsletter* articulated a more critical perspective. One complained that "the WWF is no longer catering to the common fan. Instead they are cornering the same market that ECW had up until very recently—the hardcore, work-rate freak, 'wrestling is sacred' fan. . . . WWF has become what ECW would have been with the unlimited pockets of a Billionaire" (Pitts 2001). Another, self-identifying as a WCW fan, contended that "the WWF was putting out a far better product" than the WCW circa 1999 but that since that time s/he had lost interest in wrestling because of the marked similarity among all the telecasts and lack of "fresh storylines and fresh faces" (Vosburgh 2001). A dip in Nielsen ratings also suggests the possibility of a populist backlash among fans concerned about the similarity of wrestling events, if trends manifest in mid-2001 provide any indication. For instance, though *Raw Is War* on TNN continued to top the cable Nielsen ratings for the week of 28 May–3 June 2001, *Smackdown* on UPN sputtered—pulling in a series-low 3.2 rating and a 6 share on 14 June 2001.

Perhaps partly to alleviate such industry and audience fears, the takeover of the WCW was worked into wrestling storylines not only as a corporate purchase but also as an act of rebellion by Shane McMahon. By having Shane purportedly steal the WCW from the despotic Vince and invade the WWF, the narrative reframed business events as a patriarchal power struggle for institutional dominance. Doing so highlighted an evidently genuine competition within WWF programming and the WWFE's corporate practices, transforming the intercorporate antagonism that pitted billionaire Turner and his cadre of soft turncoat wrestlers swiped from the WWF against the upstart millionaire McMahon and his hardscrabble, hypermasculine crew, into a struggle between the traitorous son leading an army of underdogs against his tyrannical father at the head of a giant corporation with well-paid minions (though the heel and babyface standings of the two factions were very quickly inverted when it became apparent that long-time WWF viewers were not persuaded by casting the WCW as the "face" faction). The story-line also sought to preserve the illusion of autonomous choice so critical for the maintenance of market populism within late capitalism: the appearance of intraorganizational rather than interorganizational competition obscures monopoly power and renders it more palatable to consumers, much as the appearance of competition elsewhere within the telecommunications indus-try and other sectors of the New Economy belies the accelerating concen-tration of ownership in recent years. For the WWF, CEO Linda McMahon claimed, "keeping its former rival around as a source for a family feud" and brand building would also potentially decrease the risk of organizational complacency; she added that "with a new tape library, with a new infusion of stars, with the potential of intriguing cross-brand story lines between the WWF and WCW, I think it does nothing but raise the specter of the potential of what we can do now" (Gaffney 2001: 23). Of course, the combination of a hostile response by many fans to Vince McMahon's apparent desire to crush the WCW in the ring compromised many of the potential advantages Linda McMahon had anticipated.

Ironically, the WWF's total victory seems to have cooled much of the fervor for professional wrestling, with the now-unopposed RAW regularly pulling in less than half the viewers than RAW and Nitro together had at-tracted during their head-to-head matchups during late 1990s. Similarly, the WWF has failed to enjoy a sustained and significant market boost from cornering the squared circle. Despite its monopolization of the wrestling in-dustry, WWFE share prices have remained relatively static — suggesting that audiences and investors are not necessarily mere marks and that neoconser-vative, patriarchal, and late-capitalist discourses are not too powerful to contradict or challenge. Yet the masculinist and market orientations of re-cent WWF programs and of commentary surrounding the WWF's initial pub-lic stock offering and the consolidation of the professional wrestling industry are so powerfully intertwined and mutually reinforcing as to make stepping outside the discursive realm they create rather difficult. However empower-ing WWF texts and audience participation opportunities may be on an indi-vidual level, institutional pressures constrain potentially unruly discourses, shunting fans toward a preferred position where the referee-like viewer can call 'em as he sees 'em while the actors before him or her use the distractions of irony and alleged economic growth to fix the match. Furthermore, it is crucial to note that the ratings decline coincides with the wwf's "real" break from the neoconservative and neomasculine storylines: relinquishing the position of scrappy corporate underdog undermines the populist features that drove the program's popularity, while the uncouth, hypermasculine Vince McMahon has been replaced by the genteel, feminine Linda McMahon and the corporate board as the ultimate authorities within the program's narrative (as well as on Wall Street).

Nevertheless, professional wrestling and the wwf's stock remain viable and popular, and the neoconservative and neomasculine trends that fueled the growth of the wwf's audience and incited its ipo during the 1990s do not seem to be on the wane. Although the wwf has experienced trouble with the alteration of its business model and its narrative calculus, historically it has proven particularly adept at adjusting to and capitalizing on changes within the social and industrial context. The ease with which the wwf has been able to incorporate, normalize, and naturalize neoconservative beliefs, divorcing them from their historical contexts and reproducing the same cultural hierarchies wwf texts appear to critique, suggests the necessity of continuing to examine such highly adaptive popular programming and the plethora of creative audience responses to it.

NOTES

1. The legally registered name for the World Wrestling ipo was World Wrestling Federation Entertainment, Inc., which was later shortened to World Wrestling Entertainment (wwe).

2. We are not making any claims here as to whether or not the wwf is more successful in managing audience response than other wrestling promotions have been in the past; indeed, over the course of our survey, there have been numerous instances in which the audience has rejected the wwf's attempts to mark characters as heel or face. The most notable examples may be the widespread refusal to embrace Stone Cold Steve Austin as a heel and even more pronounced rejection of Booker T., a black wcw wrestler, as a face. In other words, just because the text makes such an interpretation easier to make does not mean it's necessarily made by the audience, and the audience's social position and discourses within the broader social contexts have as much bearing on their identification as does the text's attribution of praise or scorn. We do, however, find it significant that wwf texts have adopted a much more ambivalent or open-ended structure in the late 1990s as part of an attempt to solidify and expand the organization's market base.

3. Of course, the pleasures of watching Chyna beat up a chauvinist who claims to want women "barefoot in the kitchen" in the first "wwf Good Housekeeping Match" should not be discounted—and it is certainly possible to envision a nearly infinite number of scenarios in which women other than Chyna do not need protection or are fully capable of protecting themselves. But the fact that wwf texts typically choose to use violence by men against women as the vehicle for elaborating male characters, asserting the desirability of masculine characteristics, and denigrating women is congruent with the texts' misogynist tendencies. As Sut Jhally and Jackson Katz have argued,

> While ambiguity about proper gender assignments may be the contemporary norm, in the mock-violent world of professional wrestling, masculinity and femininity are clearly defined. And while pro wrestling shares many of the values sometimes associated with elements of the political far right (among them patriarchy, opposition to homosexuality, and respect for hierarchy), many conservatives have condemned its vulgarity and sexuality. This criticism (much of it egged on by master promoters like McMahon) fuels the erroneous belief of some youngsters that somehow the wwf and wcw are alternative and rebellious. However, one of the great insights of cultural studies is that adherence to a conservative and repressive gender order can appear powerful and liberating—or rebellious—even as it assigns greater suffering to those deemed less powerful in the social order." (Jhally and Katz 2000: E1)

4. The term *screwed* is what wrestling fans used in referring to the incident at the time and how the wwf has continued to represent the event in subsequent years.

5. One charge leveled against committed fans of soap operas, sports, fantasy role-playing games, and the like is that they are immature and impotent—i.e., less than masculine. Their knowledge has either no practical economic or cultural value or a negative net value because fan activities require the personally unproductive expenditure of time or money that could go to more productive endeavors. Committed fans of the stock market, however, use their knowledge to accumulate material wealth, produce additional economic benefit, and ascend from the debased category of fan to stockholder, investor, or even venture capitalist. We suggest that the wwf's ipo offered the chance for wrestling fans to enjoy productive material as well as psychological benefits of their wrestling knowledge.

6. We use the term *premasculine* because this critical inability to distinguish between the staged and the "real-real" is typically demonstrated by males described, effectively, as suffering from arrested emotional or psychological development. Rhetorically, such figures are typically equated with immature children, effectively rendering them only potentially masculine by contemporary mainstream definitions: capable of exercising power, making money, and demonstrating at least some level of self-control and restraint.

7. Several other commentators voiced similar sentiments: the *Washington Post*, for instance, indicated that "Unlike the rash of super-hot Internet companies that have peddled their shares on the stock market, the wwf actually makes money. The company doubled its revenue for the year ended April 30 to $251 million, up from $126 million the year before. And its net income rose more than six fold, from $8.5 million to $56 million, in the same period" (Schwartz and Liebowitz 1999: E01). Similarly, several posts to the Motley Fool—an open-post Web site about stock investing—have lauded the wwf (and often McMahon in particular) for the company's ability to make money and establish itself as a stable corporate entity with excellent cash flow . . . though several have also excoriated McMahon for his greedy and self-absorbed character, which may be as much a reaction to his onscreen corporate persona as to his offscreen corporate status.

8. If the intent behind the gambit was to bolster wwfe stock, it backfired: the stock slipped after the xfl proposal was unveiled, and even nbc's investment failed to create a substantial groundswell of interest in wwfe stock. There is no direct evidence to suggest, however, that the xfl deal was intended to team the wwf brand with nbc in order to bolster the wwf's stock; most speculation on the alliance focused on nbc's desire to reach the wwf's market rather than the benefits for the wwf. Still, at least one investor was intrigued enough by the partnership to bet on the wwfe on the stock exchange: Bob Caporale, a business consultant and former owner in the failed usfl (United States Football League), confided to *Sports Illustrated* that "the day [McMahon] announced the league at a press conference—I probably shouldn't say this, but I will—I bought stock in his company, the wwf" (Montville 2001: 39).

9. According to *Cablevision* magazine, "in 2000, the wwf's 15 ppv events represented a whopping 54.5 percent of the category's $394 million revenue take. The figure is more than double the second biggest revenue generator, tvko" (Umstead 2001: 32).

REFERENCES

Ahrens, Frank. 1998. "Grappling with Good and Bad: Pro Wrestling, Adapting Its Dramas to Our Morally Ambiguous Times." *Washington Post*, 27 November, p. D01.

Associated Press. 2000. "wwf's McMahon forming xfl." espn.com Web site. 3 February, http://espn.go.com/moresports/news/2000/0203/332510.html.

Barthes, Roland. 1972 [1957]. "The World of Wrestling." In *Mythologies*. Trans. Annette Lavers. New York: Dial Press.

Clancy, Christopher. 1999. "wwfe Goes Mainstream with ipo." *O'Dwyer's PR Services Report*, December, p. 8.

"Fighting a Delusion: Wrestling's Bravado Appeals to Bullish Traders, but They Are Wrong to Believe the Bear Hug Is Dead." 1999. *Financial Times* (London), 20 September, p. 14.

Frank, Thomas. 2000. "The Rise of Market Populism: America's New Secular Religion." *Nation*, vol. 271, no. 13 (30 October): 13–19.

Furman, Phyllis. 2000. "New tv Trend Is a Guy Thing." *New York Daily News*, 17 April, p. 28.

Gaffney, John. 2001. "wwf + wcw Together 4-Ever . . . or Not." 2001. *Video Business*, 4 June, p. 23.

Gledhill, Dan. 1999. "Bankers Head for a Pinfall: The World Wrestling Federation Is Preparing to Take on Wall Street." *Independent* (London), 8 August, p. 5.

Harvey, David. 1995 [1990]. *The Condition of Postmodernity*. Cambridge, Mass.: Blackwell Publishers.

Jay, Paul, director. 1998. *Hitman Hart: Wrestling with Shadows*. Television documentary, Trimark, U.S.

Jenkins, Henry. 1997. " 'Never Trust a Snake': WWF Wrestling as Masculine Melodrama." In *Out of Bounds*, ed. Aaron Baker and Todd Boyd. Bloomington: Indiana University Press.

Jhally, Sut, and Jackson Katz. 2000. "Manhood on the Mat." *Boston Globe*, 13 February, p. E1+.

Joyrich, Lynne. 1988. "All That Television Allows: TV Melodrama, Postmodernism and Consumer Culture." *Camera Obscura* 16:129–53.

Keith, Scott. 2001. "Guest Editorial: End of WCW." *Dave Meltzer's Wrestling Observer Newsletter*. Accessed 20 March at http://www.wrestlingobserver.com/news/features/default.asp?aID=2042.

Leland, John. 2000. "Why America's Hooked on Wrestling." *Newsweek*, vol. 135, no. 6 (7 February): 46–54.

Manly, Howard. 2000. "Sportview: He's Going to the Mat. NBC's Ebersol Banking on XFL." *Boston Globe*, 4 April, p. F14.

Mitchell, Bruce. 2001. "Mitchell's Take: The Interview and the End—Paul Heyman and Vince McMahon." Posting to *Pro Wrestling Torch*. 16 November. http://www.pwtorch.com.

Montville, Leigh. 2001. "The X Factor." *Sports Illustrated*, vol. 94, no. 6 (12 February): 34–41.

Morgenson, Gretchen. 2001. "How Did They Value Stocks? Count the Absurd Ways." *New York Times*, 18 March, sec. 3, p. 1.

Pitts, Sully. 2001. "WWF drop due to ECW Emulation . . ." 16 June posting to http://www.wrestlingobserver.com/comment/.

Roberts, Johnnie L. 1999. "Wrestling for Dollars." *Newsweek*, vol. 134, no. 7 (16 August): 42.

Rosellini, Lynn. 1999. "Lords of the Ring." *U.S. News and World Report*, 17 May, pp. 52+.

Rovell, Darrell. 2001. "Stockholders, Not Fans, Are Key Now in Sports Business." ESPN.com Web site. 10 May, http://espn.go.com/otherfb/news/2001/0510/1194657.html.

Sandomir, Richard. 2000. "Tag Team Football on the Air: XFL Pins Down Deal with NBC." *New York Times*, 30 March, p. D4.

Schoolman, Judith. 1999. "Martha, WWF Live It Up: Domesticity Diva, Cable Powerhouse in Stox Debut." *New York Daily News*, 20 October, p. 26.

Schwartz, John, and Mark Liebowitz. 1999. "Stock You Can Jump On: But Look Out for a Fall." *Washington Post*, 4 August, pp. E01+.

Sorkin, Andrew Ross. 2001. "Smackdown! W.W.F. to Buy Wrestling Rival." *New York Times*, 24 March, p. C1.

Stallybrass, Peter, and Allon White. 1986. *The Politics and Poetics of Transgression.* Ithaca, N.Y.: Cornell University Press.

Syre, Steven, and Charles Stein. 1999. "A Steel-Cage Death Match on the Street." *Boston Globe*, 4 August, pp. D1+.

Umstead, R. Thomas. 2001. "WWF Is King of the Ring: Vince McMahon Now Has the Cable Industry in a Headlock." *Cablevision*, 9 April, p. 32.

Vosburgh, Dana. 2001. "Losing Interest." 23 May posting to http://www.wrestling observer.com/comment/.

HENRY JENKINS III

Afterword, Part I: Wrestling

with Theory, Grappling with Politics

n the early 1990s, my son and I went to a wrestling match at the Boston Gardens. In hindsight, many wrestling fans regard that period as one of the golden moments in the history of the World Wrestling Federation. Across a series of such arena shows, we got to see the final days of Andre the Giant, Jake "The Snake" Roberts, Jesse "The Body" Ventura, and The Ultimate Warrior; we got to see Hulk Hogan, Ric Flair, The Undertaker, and Macho Man Randy Savage in their prime; and we got to see the early days of Brett and Owen Hart, Hunter Hearst Helmsley, and Sean Michaels. On this particular evening, we were "treated" to a match between the Bushwhackers and the Beverly Brothers. I wrote about the experience in my essay "Never Trust the Snake":

> The two brothers, clad in lavender tights, hugged each other before the match, and their down-under opponents, in their big boots and work clothes, turned upon them in a flash, "queer baiting" and then "gay bashing" the Beverly Brothers. I sat there with fear and loathing as I heard thousands of men, women, and children shouting, "Faggot, faggot, faggot." I was perplexed at how such a representation could push so far and spark such an intense response. The chanting continued for five, ten minutes, as the Bushwhackers stomped their feet and waved their khaki caps with glee, determined to drive their "effeminate" opponents from the ring. The Beverly Brothers protested, pouted, and finally submitted, unable to stand firm against their tormentors. (Jenkins 1997 and in this volume)

The Bushwhackers'
perverse homosociality
was exorcised by
public performances
of homophobia.

The essay describes this incident as part of the complex negotiations which allowed the WWF to represent forms of masculine vulnerability at the price of rubbing our faces in homophobia. Almost a decade later, I look back on that moment as a glimpse of things to come, a preview of the shifts in the tone and content of the WWF this book has documented. I still remember our queasy alienation from the mob that was chanting along with the Bushwhackers, but we were not the only ones who were sitting in stony silence at ringside that night.

Wrestling had been in the background for a while. But it did not emphatically assert itself onto my consciousness until I awoke one Saturday morning a few months earlier to the gruff voices of Sergeant Slaughter and Hulk Hogan mouthing off against each other about the Gulf War. I couldn't believe what I was seeing. We were living off what I made as a starting junior faculty member, which, once my student loans were removed, amounted to a good deal less than I had been taking home as a graduate student. Our neighborhood, along the border between Cambridge and Arlington, was urban, mixed race and mostly working class, one consistent with our economic income but not our educational capital. Thanks to typical town/gown tensions, I had trouble engaging our neighbors in conversation. My son had a little bit better luck and had formed friendships with several local kids and been drawn into their circle of tastes. His mother and I experienced his growing fascination with television wrestling with some bemusement and a bit of anxiety. We joked that he was turning into a "Boston street urchin."

We weren't altogether happy with our social environment and weren't sure how much we wanted our son to fit in.

It wasn't that wrestling was alien to my upbringing. Quite the opposite! My grandmother had been a wrestling fan when I was a boy. When she had babysat for me, I watched her pound her fists on the coffee table and shout at the screen. She was horrified by the wild men from various exotic parts of the world and impassioned by the all-American boys who kept them in their place. She was a woman who had been raised in the rural South; she had simple tastes and almost no education. Across four generations, my family had moved from dirt farmer, to sheet metal worker, to construction company owner, to university professor. As a boy, I wanted to escape the taint of those "redneck" origins. My middle-class peers at school had mostly come from the North and knew little of wrestling at a time when it was still largely in the hands of regional promoters. I remember with some embarrassment overhearing some of my classmates in late elementary school making fun of the old woman who lived on their street and dried apples on her front lawn. They were talking about my grandmother. I never came to accept my grandmother in her lifetime but did come to a reconciliation with my grandfather before he died. As I got older, I came to appreciate the virtues of his working-class culture. As a boy, I saw only his lack of education. As an adult, I respected the fact that he had read, with no small difficulty, his Bible cover to cover many times.

A good deal of the backlash against wrestling has come from people like myself, southerners or midwesterners who had escaped working-class roots, often through hard struggle. They were horrified to see their own children reject middle-class tastes and celebrate what they had come to see as white-trash culture. As Annalee Newitz and Matt Wray have written, the category "white trash" arose as a way of managing some of the contradictions surrounding race and class in the American South (Newitz and Wray 1997). It was a term which allowed at least some Blacks to look down on at least some whites, and at the same time it allowed some upwardly mobile whites to separate themselves off more decisively from the culture they were trying to escape.[1]

Looking backward, writing "Never Trust a Snake" was a central part of that process of making peace with my grandmother's culture and coming to accept my son's.

Once I overcame my initial resistance, I liked going to the matches with my son. I was fascinated with the complex set of relationships between the characters. I liked shouting and booing and stomping my feet at the matches. I wanted to write an essay that conveyed the pleasure and the moral complexity of what I had seen.

Rereading the essay today, I am surprised to discover how much I had effaced my own personal experiences, my own motivations. Certainly, my own pleasure in wrestling came through in my vivid and passionate descriptions. Certainly, the essay stands out in my body of work as the one which most directly spoke to issues of class. Yet, there are things I remember which are simply not there; I had closeted the very things which drove me to write about this topic. There is, for example, no direct reference in my account of the Boston Garden incident of my son's presence—his moral support, his own feelings of discomfort—even though I was fiercely proud of his response. Nor is there really much discussion here of the degree to which he had been my expert guide. The language, the theory was mine, for better or for worse, but so many of the insights had grown out of father-son exchanges.

When Nicholas Sammond asked me to contribute an afterword, I knew that I had to engage my son more directly in the project. He was now an undergraduate studying media and creative writing at George Washington University. He had become a gifted writer and a sharp cultural critic. We had already coauthored a dialogic essay on Buffy (of the television program *Buffy the Vampire Slayer*) and the student shootings at Columbine. I wanted to make sure that he got to speak this time in his own voice.

But, our experience of wrestling had moved in different directions since the early 1990s. Somehow, wrestling lost its fascination and I found myself watching less and less. My son remained a loyal fan, sometimes watching every week, sometimes not, but always aware of developments and always ready to call something particularly remarkable to my attention. I had shut wrestling out of my thoughts and knew little about the directions it had moved in the intervening years. I could not regain the same closeness or fannish enthusiasm that had shaped the earlier essay. Yet, I have spent much of my time in recent years speaking out in public policy debates about censorship and knew that wrestling had become a target for the culture warriors, so this is the angle I want to explore here. For my son, writing an afterword has offered an opportunity to reflect on the complex ways wrestling touched his own life and to describe some of the ambivalences that have shaped fan response to the changes this book documents. He is a part of that generation of late adolescent males who grew up with the WWF. He writes as a fan; I write as a cultural theorist, but for both of us, these essays are deeply personal.

MONSTERS AND MORAL PANICS

Adopting a transhistorical and cross-cultural approach, literary critic Jeffrey Jerome Cohen has constructed a theory of the cultural work which the category of the monster performs. The monster, he suggests, "notoriously appears at times of crisis as a kind of third term that problematizes the clash of extremes" (Cohen 1996: 6). Monsters are "disturbing hybrids . . . [with] externally incoherent bodies"; they embody the contradictions and anxieties shaping a society undergoing profound change. Old modes of thinking are breaking down, and the construction of monsters represents a last-gasp effort to hold them in place. This is why wrestling is so often figured as monstrous and perverse. The WWE is a horrifying hybrid—not sports, sports entertainment; not real, not fake, but someplace in between; appealing to the "white trash" working class and the college educated alike; courting kids and appealing to adolescents on the basis of its rejection of family values; existing outside the cultural mainstream and yet a commercial success; appealing to national pride even as it shoots a bird at most American institutions; masculine as hell and melodramatic as all get out.

Cohen tells us that the monster is born from a category crisis. Thus, the undead may be considered monsters because they are liminal figures existing betwixt and between life and death. We might call wrestling the "unreal" since it stands on the border between fact and fiction. Activist David Grossman uses the "fakeness" of wrestling to justify larger claims about audience susceptibility: "People tell me, 'you can't tell me that a 6-year-old in Flint, Mich., couldn't tell the difference between fantasy and reality. . . . And I say, 'Well, you know, how many adults do you know who think professional wrestling is real?' " (quoted in Gregory 2000). In their video *Wrestling with Manhood* (2002), Sut Jhally and Jackson Katz argue that television wrestling may be the most dangerous kind of media violence because it passes itself off as real yet acknowledges no real world consequences. Referring to a moment in *Wrestling with Shadows* (2000), when Mick Foley's children become horrified after watching their father in the ring, Jackson Katz asks, "If Mick Foley's Kids can't see behind the illusion, what chance do kids have who have never been taken behind the curtain?"

One can certainly understand why this category confusion would be of concern for many of these writers. Their own literal-mindedness knows no limits. For them, to represent something is to advocate it; to advocate it is to cause it. *Wrestling with Manhood*, for example, depicts wrestling spectators as moral monsters and, at one point, compares them to the folks who watched and did nothing to stop Hitler's rise to power. (You know an argument is kaput when it resorts to the Nazi card!) The filmmakers never acknowledge what Sharon Mazer discusses in her essay in this volume—that these fans, who come to ringside in costume, mimic the catchphrases, waving signs they hope will get on camera, might see themselves as part of the performance, enacting, spoofing, taking pleasure in the imaginary roles and fantasy values on offer. The narrator explains: "Perhaps the most disturbing aspect of this is not only what's going on in the ring but the reaction of the crowd, which is wildly cheering what can only be described as a psychic and physical violation. A stadium full of seemingly normal boys and men cheering and getting off on the control, the humiliation, the degradation." Consider the rhetorical work done here by the word *seemingly*—as if the deceptiveness of the wwf extended to its audience, who are "seemingly normal" but actually ghouls and monsters. And this same literal-mindedness surfaces in the phrase "what can only be described." As far as Jhally and Katz are concerned, the wrestling spectacle can only be understood in one way, even though what has fascinated the writers in this collection is the sheer range of meanings such moments might carry.

We respond to the threat of the monster through moral panic; confronting something we don't understand and can't really classify, our normal human response is to run like hell. We can hear such panic in the words of David Walsh, the head of the National Institute for Media and the Family: "In the world of pro wrestling, it is appropriate to swear, to make obscene gestures, to engage in violent behavior, and to objectify women. This is a violent, unpredictable place where it is okay for anyone to give in to any impulse. It is a place where people are rewarded for being loud, crude and aggressive. Sexual violence, simulated sex acts, foul language, and over-the-top crudeness are the norm. And the more often kids watch this world on their TV screens, the more these attitudes and actions seem normal in the real world" (Walsh 2004a).

As Cohen suggests, the monster is a figure of transitions and boundaries. The monster calls "horrid attention to the borders that cannot — must not — be crossed" (Cohen 1996: 12). The monster is thinkable (though regretfully so), whereas what lies beyond the monster is truly unthinkable. Film critic David Denby refers to popular entertainment as "a shadow world in which our kids are breathing an awful lot of poison without knowing that there is clean air and sunshine elsewhere" (quoted in Walsh 2004b). Senator Joseph Lieberman refers to a "values vacuum in which our children learn that anything goes" (Lieberman 1997). In other words, to move into the realm of popular culture is to move into a twilight zone, a "shadow world," a "values vacuum," "a violent, unpredictable place" where rules and constraints break down. And the biggest fear of all is that the monster will cross over from that alternative reality into our own.

The monster can have no legitimate point of view. The monster has no culture, generates no meaning, and respects no values. The monster exists simply to negate the moral order. Evoking a metaphor straight out of a David Cronenberg film, Lieberman compares contemporary popular culture to "an antibody which has turned against its own immunity system" (Lieberman 1997). Former professional wrestler turned evangelist, Superstar Billy Graham, describes his visceral response to the WWE: "I didn't want this stuff coming into my house, my eyes, or my mind. It made me physically ill to my stomach" (quoted in Kennedy 2000). The WWE muddies the water, mucks up cultural hierarchies, disturbs moral oppositions, and churns up emotional reactions. No wonder critics call it cultural pollution. This is also why the WWE so often proclaims itself to be "politically incorrect," relishing its own "barbarian" status, taking pleasure in committing antisocial acts and pissing off those who would police our culture.

The moral legibility of traditional melodrama has broken down and so it has to be restored somewhere else — in our rhetorical response to such representations. Say nothing else about it, moral panic provokes ideological consensus, carves up the world into simple black-and-white categories, which seem, on the surface, so commonsensical that they are nigh on impossible to dispute. Politics makes for strange tag teams. Orthodox Jew Joseph Lieberman climbs into the ring, hand in hand, with the Christian Right, a move all the more remarkable when you consider how often both sides evoke religious language to justify their efforts to police morality. David Grossman, a military psychologist who claims to have taught marines how to kill, joins hands with the Lion and the Lamb Foundation, an organization of concerned moms who feel that violence should never be considered "child's play."[2] For some, wrestling is dangerous because it is so ruthlessly patriarchal and reactionary; for others, because it embodies moral relativism. For some, it is a symptom of a world without gatekeepers and for others, the dangers of media concentration. For most, it is frightening because it crosses class boundaries. They all agree that what we have got to do is protect our children against its seductions and temptations. After a while, the specific ideological claims get absorbed into a more generalized rhetoric of horror and disgust.

Cultural tastes and interests are a central building block of our identities; we use our consumption of popular culture to map who we are and who we are not. As Pierre Bourdieu (1987) has noted, perhaps the most powerful way to defend our tastes is through the negation of other tastes. But, the negation of a cultural form necessarily spills over into (and often intentionally taps) our hostility toward specific cultural, social, and ethnic groups who are closely associated with those forms. The concept of "law and order" surfaced in the 1960s and 1970s as a code word for racism, allowing Republicans to appeal to southern whites with a covert reassurance that they would keep disorderly Blacks in line. Similarly, at a time when it would be offensive to directly attack racial or sexual minorities, the rhetoric of "cultural pollution" functions as a code word for racism, homophobia, class war, and generational conflict. Listen to former Supreme Court nominee Robert Bork's description of a culture "slouching towards Gomorrah": "Even those of us who try to avoid the repellent aspects of popular culture know about it through a sort of peripheral vision. The rap blasts out of the car window waiting beside you at the red light; blatant sexuality, often of a perverse nature, assaults the reader in magazine advertisements" (1997: 126). Consider how differently this would read if it were Frank Sinatra or country music blasting from the car stereo or if Bork were protesting the persistence of heterosexism. If we can keep these forms of culture in line, perhaps we can also control the people who consume them. This connection was made explicit in GOP operative Mike Murphy's post-Columbine comments that "we need Goth control, not gun control" (quoted in "Verbatim" 1999).

Proponents of the cultural-pollution argument are quick to note that they have many minority supporters, and thus cannot be accused of racism. Yet, members of a minority community use culture war rhetoric to police their own borders and separate themselves from unsavory aspects of their own culture. Eric Michael Dyson (1999), for example, has mapped the tension between jazz and church music in the early twentieth century, or jazz and hip-hop in the later twentieth century. Expressions of disdain toward godless or trashy music helped to police class and generational boundaries within the African American community; jazz and later hip-hop were depicted as a threat to the goals of assimilation and upward mobility. For me, as a young man, distancing myself from wrestling had enabled me to separate my middle-class aspirations from my lumpen roots, while my son's crossing of those lines produced a certain fear that he would sink back down again. So, different groups for different reasons might share a common agenda in terms of policing cultural borders (even if they are pursuing that agenda from different cultural positions or interests).

Writers in the cultural studies tradition often characterize the culture war rhetoric as "right wing," "ultraconservative," or "reactionary." As we do so, we are constructing our own monsters, seeking to draw a sharp distinction between those "wackos" over there who want to censor our culture and nice, thoughtful liberals like ourselves who would never think of doing that kind of mischief to the Constitution. But, like most attempts to resolve the ambiguities and ambivalence surrounding the monstrous, such representations provide us with a false sense of security. To be sure, conservative Republicans were among the most visible proponents of the culture war rhetoric, as reflected in Daniel Quayle's attempt to displace concerns about the economic causes of poverty onto the breakdown of family values in *Murphy Brown*, Jerry Falwell's hysterical responses to the thought that one of the Teletubbies might be gay, or the suggestion that the ACLU might be to blame for September 11, or Pat Buchanan's commitment of the GOP to a "jihad" against those forces corrupting the American heart and mind. The initial Democratic responses to these arguments were largely negative. Much of the Democratic 1992 presidential nominating convention was devoted to ridiculing Quayle's rather narrow conception of family values and dismissing the GOP culture war rhetoric as extremist.

However, some "New Democrats" sought to take social and cultural issues "off the table," appealing to moderate Christians by claiming that

Democrats would join forces with Republicans to protect American families from "sickening" forms of popular culture. In 1985, for example, Tipper Gore (wife of then Democratic senator Albert Gore), Susan Baker (wife of Republican senator Howard Baker), and some seventeen other congressional spouses helped to form the Parents Music Resource Center. The group received financial support from Mike Love, the Beach Boys, and Joseph Coors, the owner of Coors Beer, and logistical support from Pat Robertson's 700 Club and the Religious Booksellers Convention (Chastagner 2004). Joseph Lieberman rose to political fame largely on the basis of a series of tactical alliances with cultural conservatives. For example, Lieberman serves on the advisory board of L. Brent Bozell III's Parents Television Council; stood alongside Pat Buchanan, Orrin Hatch, and Colin Powell to support an anti-Hollywood petition written by the conservative think tank Empower America; and has worked closely with David Walsh's Institute for Media and the Family in condemning the video game industry ("Lieberman Joins Watchdog Group" 1999; Statement of Senator Joe Lieberman 2001; Waldman and Green 2000). Lieberman (1997) himself described William Bennett as "my brother in arms, because we are engaged together in fighting the culture wars." He explained, "For the better part of two years, we have formed an unofficial, bipartisan partnership to coax, cajole, shout and shame the people who run the electronic media." As former WWF superstar Mick Foley notes, "whenever anyone accuses the PTC of being ultraconservative, he [Bozell] throws Joe Lieberman in their face." (Foley 2001: 467). A significantly greater number of Democrats joined the culture war following the shootings at Columbine, when, one by one, liberal senators stood up at various congressional hearings and denounced the entertainment industry for inspiring teen shooters. It is striking that both candidates on the 2000 Democratic national ticket were men who had been early Democratic backers of this cultural agenda. One lasting legacy of that election is that it will be significantly more difficult for future Democratic candidates to label that perspective as reactionary or extremist.

WHERE DO WE STAND?

In an oft-cited critique of cultural studies, Tom Frank, editor of the *Baffler*, argues, "To an undeniable degree, the official narratives of the American business community of the nineties. . . . embraced many of the same concerns as the cult studs. They shared the cult studs' oft-expressed desire to take on hierarchies, their tendency to find 'elitism' lurking behind any critique of mass culture, and their pious esteem for audience agency" (2000: 290). For Frank, this is sufficient evidence of a kind of unholy alliance between the "cult studs" and the "neo-cons." In his book *Anxious Intellects*, John Michael argues that public intellectuals construct their publics as projections of their own hopes and fears, as props in their own fantasies of social transformation.[3] If one accepts this criticism, then one must also acknowledge the opposite — that various publics construct their own visions of public intellectuals, drawing from what we write and what we say those elements that speak to their immediate needs. Thus, certain segments on the Right have appropriated aspects of cultural theory and applied them toward very different ends. To some degree, this should cause us concern, since responsible intellectuals speak out against misuses of their research. Frank poses some important critiques of the way that big business uses an empowerment rhetoric to defend itself against government regulation and deploys multiculturalism to target niche markets.

The "cult studs" might also see this commonality of rhetoric as an invitation to reexamine our own political assumptions, our tendency to stereotype rather than engage with conservative thinkers. God forbid that cultural theory might have an impact on how business or government operates! The ideas are not necessarily wrong simply because some conservatives have found them politically or intellectually useful. We need to rid ourselves of the illusion that there is a vast right-wing conspiracy, just as we need to move beyond the wrongheaded fantasy that all liberals are tireless champions of civil liberties. As cultural critics, we are part of the culture wars no matter what, and the culture wars are as much a struggle between different flavors of conservatism as they are a struggle between the Right and the Left. We are not going to really understand what the battle is all about unless we take time to read and reflect on conservative arguments. If we are going to engage in any kind of productive conversation with conservatives, we need to go into it with our eyes (and our minds) open. We need to recognize where we share agendas and where we depart. We need to be explicit about how far we can travel together and where we draw the line. As we form alliances, however, we had better be sure whom we are getting into bed with. From where I sit, there's a huge difference between the libertarian Right and cultural conservatives — even if Frank wants to lump the two groups together under the term *neo-con*.

What Frank doesn't acknowledge is that there has also been an unholy alliance between critical theory and cultural conservatism. The degree to which feminist antiporn activists formed alliances — sometimes overt, sometimes covert — with Christian conservatives has been, by now, well documented. If the empowerment rhetoric in cultural studies has made it attractive to libertarians and corporate leaders, critical studies' rhetoric of victimization, distraction, seduction, corruption, and manipulation has made it highly attractive to culture warriors. A strong strand of Puritanism underlies many critiques of media concentration, describing popular culture primarily as "bread and circuses" or "Big Fun" and then citing almost exactly the same set of exemplars of bad media content as found on the hit lists of the cultural conservatives.[4] When Todd Gitlin (2002) writes about media as an overwhelming "torrent," he taps into anxieties about the breakdown of traditional gatekeepers and the proliferation of media options which have been a central thrust of conservative critiques of popular culture. *Wrestling with Manhood* cites the Parents Television Council's claims that several children had died as a result of imitating moves seen on *Smackdown*, including claims the PTC was subsequently forced to withdraw.[5] Conservative groups are appealing to categories from the social sciences in order to translate feelings of moral outrage into a more ideologically neutral discourse. They are quite prepared to add concern about racial and sexual stereotypes or about bullying to their list of grievances against popular culture if it will enable them to draw liberals and moderates into their camp. At the same time, critical theorists are using hot-button issues and loaded examples in an effort appeal to more conservative supporters. The theorists are playing a dangerous game, since ultimately there are many more reactionaries than radicals among conservatives, and they tend to be better organized. They may simply use such research for ideological cover long enough to gain a broader base of support and then use that support to justify regulations which go well beyond those progressive critics might advocate. It is especially dangerous when certain forms of anti-intellectualism enters the critical studies vocabulary, since this helps to justify a politics based on knee-jerk affective response and thus fuels an atmosphere of moral panic. Consider, for example, these statements from *Wrestling with Manhood*:

"You don't need a Ph.D. in Cultural Studies to understand that . . ."

"We really shouldn't need studies to make the obvious point that . . ."

"We'd be naive in the extreme to think that . . ."

Such rhetoric is highly effective. It dismisses methodological debates about the validity of media effects research as "naive in the extreme"; it rejects the need for research and analysis in favor of common sense, which it defines in self-serving terms; it flattens the moral complexity of the phenomenon under discussion in order to construct a black-and-white picture of popular culture as posing an "obvious" and imminent threat; and it justifies demands to take immediate actions—to answer the public cry to "do something, even if it is wrong"—rather than to carefully consider the ramifications of rolling back long-standing commitments to free expression. Jackson and Jhally, and others in the critical studies tradition, pour kerosene onto the bonfires and then act surprised if any books get burned.

Jhally and Katz are certainly not wrong to express concern over the more reactionary elements of contemporary wrestling. However skeptical I was of their underlying argument, I found myself wishing Vince McMahon hadn't given them quite so much to work with here! We should not remain silent about the ways that popular culture circulates and perpetuates racist, sexist, or homophobic ideology or sanctions the bullying which goes on in our schools. Yet there's a difference between showing how these ideas are expressed in popular amusements and assuming that these ideas are the reason why those amusements are popular. Many of most outrageous examples Jhally and Katz reproduce in the video have already been the subject of heated debates among wrestling fans on the message boards, where flame wars erupt over when, where, and how the wwe "crosses the line." After all, one can be a fan of wrestling without fully and uncritically endorsing everything that occurs in the ring, and indeed there are times when McMahon seems to enjoy rubbing things in the noses of long-time fans, knowing full well that they will find them outrageous, just to see how much they will take before they defect. One can be concerned about such elements without feeling that they are necessarily representative of wrestling as a whole, or that they have the kinds of immediate social impact Jhally and Katz ascribe to them. The overwhelming majority—though certainly not all—of the offensive behavior shown in *Wrestling with Manhood* is performed by characters who, even in the context of the more morally ambiguous wwe, are unambiguously marked as *heels*; these actions were intended to be sufficiently outrageous to generate "heat" for their upcoming matches. The often buffoonish and boorish remarks of Jerry "the King" Lawler are treated by Jhally and Katz as if he were the moral center of the WWE; yet such comments are consistently challenged and undercut by his fellow commentators (even on the soundtrack of the documentary itself). The sensationalistic rhetoric and shocking images in *Wrestling with Manhood* are not chosen to convince the viewer through anything resembling an intellectual argument but rather by provoking an immediate emotional response. The political interpretations that are promoted may be progressive, but the tactics are reactionary.

ON POLITICAL INCORRECTNESS

We do not exhaust the topic when we describe the monstrous as a figure of moral panic; it is also a figure of desire. Cohen writes, "The same creatures who terrify and interdict can evoke potent escapist fantasies; the linking of monstrosity with the forbidden makes the monster all the more appealing as a temporary egress from constraint. . . . We distrust and loathe the monster at the same time we envy its freedom and perhaps its sublime despair" (1996: 16–17). Transgression is perhaps the WWE's most potent attraction for middle-class, suburban white kids. Katz and Jhally are right when they argue that the WWE masks some pretty reactionary class and gender politics behind claims of transgressiveness. Political incorrectness isn't a reaction against political correctness; it's a reaction against what the emerging generation was told "political correctness" was all about. It is a legacy of a previous moment in the culture wars of the past few decades. The fantasy of being politically incorrect is an ancient fantasy of being liberated from constraint, of escaping from social and moral regulation, with the traditional figure of the killjoy mapped onto the "tenured radical" rather than the ancient pedant.

The "mooks" are not the only ones who take perverse pleasure in these transgressions. Katz and Jhally use the sensational elements of the program in their video for more or less the same reasons that Vince McMahon does — to shock, to titillate, to outrage, to build "heat." The moral reformers as a group seem to take special pleasure in searching out and recounting horror stories, in bringing to their listeners the most tawdry elements of contemporary culture and watching them squirm. Horror, shock, and outrage, after all, are kinds of pleasures—if you are into that sort of thing. This is, in part, what Nicholas Sammond in his essay means when he describes the struggle between the WWE and its social critics as "mutually constitutive." The WWE needs its critics; the critics need the WWE. Moral reformers draw a line and dare the WWE to cross it; the WWE crosses a line and dares reformers to criticize it.

Cultural conservatism produces—and tries to police—the category of the politically incorrect. As Cohen claims, "Escapist delight gives way to horror only when the monster threatens to overstep these boundaries, to destroy or deconstruct the thin walls of category and culture. When contained by geographic, generic or epistemic marginalization, the monster can function as an alter ego, as an alluring projection of (an Other) self" (1996: 16–17). And this is what makes it dangerous for cultural studies to offer a simple-minded defense of transgression. As Laura Kipnis (1992) argues in regard to *Hustler*, antihegemonic elements are not necessarily progressive in their goals or effects; members of dominant social groups often engage in fanta-sies of marginality or oppression. Doug Battema and Philip Sewell, in their essay in this volume, are right to see the adolescent content of this new po-litically incorrect culture as often profoundly reactionary in its own right, as a reassertion of the power of white males, as a "backlash against clas-sic liberalism, second-wave feminism, civil rights movements for racial mi-norities and gays/lesbians, and environmental movements." We must also guard against a simpleminded dismissal of the politically incorrect. The cate-gory contains at least some material (Bill Maher; the *Onion*; the *Daily Show*; *South Park: Bigger, Longer, and Uncut* [Parker and Stone, 1999]; and Aaron McGruder's *The Boondocks* come to mind) which poses progressive critiques of the conservative agenda. Conservative historian Gertrude Himmelfarb (1998) draws a distinction between the Victorian notion of shame, which used social stigma to uphold traditional values, and the new notion of politi-cal correctness, which seeks to transform culture. For Himmelfarb, political correctness has to be destroyed so that true morality can be restored. Some-where, along the line, that distinction has broken down: the new politically incorrect culture is just as apt to take aim at "prudes" as it is to lambaste the "femi-nazis."

This new politically incorrect mode in popular culture thus rejects con-straints which might be imposed on it from the Right or the Left. It embodies what Virginia Postrel (1988) has described as a moment of political realignment where old party labels seem to have outlived their usefulness in terms of characterizing core political impulses. On both the Left and the Right, among Democrats and Republicans, there are those who would use political power to police the contents of our culture, and hence the uncanny parallels we have found here between cultural conservatism and critical theory; on both the Left and the Right, there are also those who are suspicious of the idea that state power should limit cultural expression, and hence the uncomfortable parallels which Frank draws between laissez-faire capitalism and cultural studies.

The political figure who most fully embodies the contradictions of the current moment is none other than former wwf wrestler Jesse "The Body" Ventura, who in 1998–2002 served a term as the Reform Party governor of Minnesota. Both conservative and radical critics have cited Ventura as an example of what happens when professional wrestling spills over from the ring and into the public sphere. Trying to imagine a more progressive version of television wrestling, Jhally proclaims, "If Stone Cold was a real rebel, he would form a union against the boss—not beat him up." Yet, there is no acknowledgment that Ventura had tried to unionize the wwf at some detriment to his professional career. Instead of giving him credit, Jhally and Katz show disdain: "To those who still believe that there is no connection between popular culture and broader social and political issues, that an analysis of wrestling has nothing to teach us about where our culture is heading, we have two words of caution: Jesse Ventura" (2000). Paul Cantor uses exactly the same argument to justify his conservative critique of the wwe in the *Weekly Standard*: "If postmodern wrestling was not a forerunner of postmodern politics, why is Jesse 'The Body' Ventura now the governor of Minnesota?" (1999: 20). Ventura has plenty to teach us about contemporary politics, but it may not be what Katz and Jhally or Cantor assume.

Much as the *luchadores* have used wrestling as a platform for political activism and social critique in Latin America, Ventura draws on the populist rhetoric of professional wrestling as a basis for his own critique of the American political system. Ventura tapped a deep-rooted dissatisfaction with the options on offer from the major political parties and a growing distrust of the political system itself, presenting himself as the champion of the common man against party machines and special interests:

"I'm looking at rabid self interest hustlers and agenda-driven extremists, grinding their way deeper and deeper into our political system." (Ventura 2000: xv)

"The underhandedness, the manipulation, the wheeling and dealing I've run into from the folks who have a death grip on America's political power base is astonishing." (Ventura 2000: xxiii)

A campaign advertisement tapped popular memories of his early days in the WWF, depicting two children playing with action figures — one representing Ventura, the other Special Interest Man. Upon his election, Ventura commissioned a new action figure, one with "no strings attached." Mimicking the moral clarity of wrestling in the late 1980s, Ventura cast himself as battling "corporate bullies" and compared the political parties ("Demo-Crips and Re-Blood-licans") to street gangs (Ventura 2000: 22). As Kevin Glynn suggests, Ventura used his borrowings from tabloid culture to signal the contrast between his approach and politics as usual.[6] Like the WWE itself, Ventura sought to shock his opponents and, by doing so, provoke them to reveal their "true colors." Judging politics through entertainment values, Ventura suggests that his opponents were simply "boring" (one can almost hear the fans chanting at ringside) (Ventura 1999: 6). Nobody knew what to expect from him: "I'm big, I'm loud, and I'm not afraid to say what I think" (4).

Tapping the same reformist impulses which made Ross Perot a national political figure and which helped to fuel the crossover of Democratic voters in support of John McCain's candidacy for the Republican nomination, Ventura rejected all contributions from political PACs (political action committees) and, indeed all contributions over $50. He campaigned primarily via the Internet, which set the pattern of using the Web to mobilize voters that Howard Dean would follow in 2003–2004. While his opponents spent $4.3 million, Ventura won with a campaign budget of only $250,000. At a time when election turnout is in sharp decline, Minnesota attracted the largest voter participation of any state in the country.

Media commentators and cultural critics were so shocked by Ventura's unlikely and unexpected success that few paid any attention to his actual ideological stance. Much of the criticism of Ventura's politics seems totally off the mark, reflecting more what critics think someone who looks, acts,

Tapping his pop culture past, Jesse Ventura marketed an action
figure celebrating his new role as governor.

and talks like him might believe than anything resembling his actual positions. Voters turned to Ventura as a protest candidate, as a way of thumbing
their noses at the system, but he was also expressing something—a balance
between social libertarianism and economic conservatism—which surveys
consistently find to be the sweet spot in American politics. As Ventura summarized his views, "I'm not a Democrat. I'm not a Republican. I'm a working man with commonsense ideas and goals. . . . As the cliché says, 'I don't
want Democrats in the boardroom, and I don't want Republicans in the bed-
room'" (Ventura 1999: 12). Or elsewhere: "The extreme Right tends to focus
too much on ideology and not enough on ideas; the extreme Left tends to

focus too much on rights and not enough on responsibilities" (2000: 49). Neither of the established parties could have nominated him without alienating their core constituencies. Neither elephant nor donkey but an unsettling hybrid of the two, Ventura is proud to be called politically incorrect, yet one should think twice before dismissing him as a reactionary.

As Ventura's term came to an end, it was clear that he was neither as bad a governor as his critics feared nor as good a governor as his supporters hoped. The media was quick to jump on any and all of his more flamboyant statements, and Ventura seemed hell-bent to give them things to talk about. Some of what he said and did was truly reactionary; some of it was shockingly naive; some of it was courageous, but in the end, it all got mixed up together. He had hoped to build cross-party allegiances, but instead, seemed to get caught in the crossfire between rival partisans. Yet, however flawed Ventura may have been as a messenger, he stood for something which warrants closer consideration than the glib dismissals he has received from most academics.

Throughout this essay, I have emphasized the challenges of constructing progressive cultural theory in an age where old political categories are breaking down and where all roads seem to lead us into some kind of collaboration with the Right. Do we side with *Reason*, which shares our opposition to censorship even though we fundamentally disagree about political economy, or with the *Baffler*, which flatters our leftist sensibilities even though its rhetoric of victimization and manipulation contributes to the climate of moral panic? Can we create modes of criticism that give adequate expression to our own fears about many of the more disturbing trends in contemporary culture without fostering more witch hunts? Can we separate our own sense of moral and social outrage from the impulses motivating the moral reformers and culture warriors? Can we critique without censoring? Can we oppose without oppressing? Can we theorize in shades of gray at a time when our political rhetoric seems increasingly black and white? Can we forge a politics of temporary tactical alliances rather than one based on stable identities and ideological purity? Can we become more politically incorrect if that allows us to work outside of the boxes we've built around ourselves? If old categories of Left and Right no longer offer us a political compass, how do we determine which forms of alliances are ethically acceptable and which ones compromise our core beliefs and values? Perhaps the wwe, which refuses to make simple distinctions between faces and heels, is a better embodiment of the new political order than we'd like to imagine. Maybe we are nostalgic for the moral clarity of traditional melodrama because at least then we'd know what ground to defend and whom to fight.

NOTES

1. It's worth noting that a similar defensiveness comes into play when academics denounce middle class taste or bourgeois culture, when they themselves come from middle class and middle American roots.

2. Indeed, the name the Lion and the Lamb Foundation seems to have been intentionally chosen for its ambiguity, enabling it to appeal equally to peaceniks and conservative Christians.

3. John Michael (2000). Full disclosure dictates that I acknowledge that both Frank and Michael single me out as an example of what they see as negative trends in cultural studies.

4. See, for example, FCC (Federal Communications Commission) commissioner Thomas Kopp, who cited an increase of sexual explicitness on prime time as an example of the evils of market concentration. Or see Mark Crispin Miller (2001) for an example of writing that fuses concern about media concentration with moral outrage over the content of popular culture.

5. See Foley (2001) for a witty and convincing critique of the PTC's campaign against the WWF and its allegations of links to real-world violence.

6. Glynn is one of the few cultural critics who has offered an open-minded and generally sympathetic account of Ventura's candidacy. See Glynn (2000: 235–42).

REFERENCES

Bork, Robert. 1997. *Slouching to Gomorrah*. New York: Harper Collins.

Bourdieu, Pierre. 1987. *Distinction*. Cambridge, Mass.: Harvard University Press.

Cantor, Paul A. 1999. "Pro Wrestling and the End of History." *Weekly Standard*, 4 October, p. 20.

Chastagner, Claude. 2004. "The Parents' Music Resource Center: From Information to Censorship." 10 June, online at http://www.philagora.org/about-the-world/pmrc1.htm.

Cohen, Jeffrey Jerome. 1996. "Monster Culture (Seven Theses)." In *Monster Theory: Reading Culture*. Minneapolis: University of Minnesota Press.

Dyson, Eric Michael. 1999. *Between God and Gangsta Rap: Bearing Witness to Black Culture*. New York: Oxford University Press.

Foley, Mick. 2001. *Foley Is Good. . . . And the Real World Is Faker than Wrestling*. New York: Regan Books.

Frank, Thomas. 2000. *One Market under God: Extreme Capitalism, Market Populism, and the End of Economic Democracy*. New York: Anchor Books.

Gitlin, Todd. 2002. *Media Unlimited*. New York: Owl.

Glynn, Kevin. 2000. *Tabloid Culture: Trash Taste, Popular Power, and the Transformation of American Television*. Durham, N.C.: Duke University Press.

Gregory, Ted. 2000. "Big Game Hunting: A Former Soldier and Expert on Killing Sets His Sights on Violent Video Games." *Chicago Tribune*, 25 July http://www.killology.com/chicagotribune.htm.

Himmelfarb, Gertrude. 1998. *The De-moralization of Society: From Victorian Virtues to Modern Values*. New York: Vintage.

Jenkins, Henry. " 'Never Trust a Snake': WWF Wrestling as Masculine Melodrama." In *Out of Bounds: Sports, Media, and the Politics of American Identity*, ed. Aaron Baker and Todd Boyd. Bloomington: Indiana University Press.

Jhally, Sut, and Katz, Jackson. 2002. *Wrestling with Manhood*. VHS/DVD. Media Education Foundation.

Katz, Jackson, and Sut Jhally. 2000. "Manhood on the Mat: The Problem Is Not that Pro Wrestling Makes Boys Violent. The Real Lesson of the Wildly Popular Pseudo-sport Is More Insidious." *Boston Globe*, 13 February, E1, http://www.jacksonkatz.com/manhood.html.

Kennedy, John W. 2000. "Redeemed Bad Boys of the WWF." *Christianity Today*, 22 May, http://www.christianitytoday.com/ct/2000/006/7.70.html.

Kipnis, Laura. 1992. "Reading *Hustler*." In *Cultural Studies*, ed. Lawrence Grossberg, Cary Nelson, and Paula Treichler. New York: Routledge, Chapman, and Hall.

Lieberman, Joseph. 1997. "The Values Vacuum in American Life." University of Notre Dame Annual Liss Lecture, 11 September, http://www.senate.gov/member/ct/lieberman/releases/r110797a.html.

"Lieberman Joins Watchdog Group in Releasing Report on 'Merchandizing Mayhem.' " Year. Day Month, http://lieberman.senate.gov/press/99/09/r092399b.html.

Michael, John. 2000. *Anxious Intellects: Academics, Professionals, Public Intellectuals and Enlightenment Values*. Durham, N.C.: Duke University Press.

Miller, Mark Crispin. 2001. "What's Wrong with This Picture," *Nation*, 20 December.

Newitz, Annalee, and Matt Wray. 1997. "Introduction." In *White Trash: Race and Class in America*. New York: Routledge.

Postrel, Virginia. 1998. *The Future and Its Enemies: The Growing Conflict over Creativity, Enterprise, and Progress*. New York: Free Press.

Statement of Senator Joe Lieberman on the Parents Television Council's "Sour Family Hour." 2001. Report, 8 January http://lieberman.senate.gov/~lieberman/press/01/08/2001801553.html.

Ventura, Jesse. 1999. *I Ain't Got Time to Bleed: Reworking the Body Politic from the Bottom Up*. New York: Villard.

———. 2000. *Do I Stand Alone?: Going to the Mat against Political Pawns and Media Jackals*. New York: Pocket.

"Verbatim." 1999. *Time*, 10 May, p. 28.

Waldman, Steven, and John Green. 2000. "Can Democrats Become the Morality Party?" 17 August, Beliefnet, http://www.beliefnet.com/story/38/story_3820_1.html.

Walsh, David. 2004a. "Pro Wrestling: Adult Entertainment Marketed to Kids." National Institute of Media and the Family. 17 May, http://www.mediafamily.org/mediawise/wrestling_mw.shtml.

———. 2004b. "A Culture of Disrespect: When the Extreme Becomes the Norm." National Institute of Media and the Family. 17 May. http://www.mediafamily.org/mediawise/disrespect_mw.shtml.

Afterword, Part II: Growing up

and Growing More Risqué

W hen I was a kid in the late eighties and early nineties, wrestling seemed aimed at kids. I had Hulk Hogan vitamins, Roddy Piper ice-cream bars, Andre the Giant oatmeal cookies, a ring full of action figures, and a couple of Wrestling Buddy stuffed toys, and there was an Undertaker poster hanging on my wall. Wrestlers were cartoonish icons of social groups — selfish rich and noble poor, savage islanders, blowhard Russians, sleek Asians, virginal Irish women, and slutty Jewish girls. Announcers often called the wrestlers *superstars* to suggest they were more than athletes. They were idols. We were supposed to daydream about them in math class, trade their bubble gum cards with our friends, and even long for them to appear by our hospital beds when we were ill. We were supposed to take moral lessons from them. The weak heroes would submit to painful holds, but their losses would be avenged by the gifted few who would never quit. They would eventually vanquish evil — if only for today — and raise their hands in victory as the children's champions. Each of the major players had their own subgroup of fans. There were the Hulkamaniacs, Little Warriors and, later, Creatures of the Night. Each group had merchandising lines that allowed you to show your support. Hacksaw Jim Duggan wrestled before a sea of eight-year-olds waving foam two-by-fours. The two mustwatch shows, *Superstars of Wrestling* and *Wrestling Challenge*, were on first thing Saturday mornings alongside the cartoons, a time when we could be alone with the superstars without our parents and older siblings judging us.

When I was ten I dressed up as The Undertaker for Halloween. My mother spray-painted a tie and some gardening gloves, ripped up a dress shirt, and

Icons of Wrestling's Evolution: The Undertaker (c. 1991) represented Death itself (and not just a man in tights); Bret Hart (c. 1994), with his average-Joe name and clean-cut good looks, made wrestling "more realistic" for skeptical preteen audiences; "Stone Cold" Steve Austin (c. 1997) led wrestling into the "hardcore" era of late-night college desires; Kurt Angle, a former Olympic gold medalist, brought legitimacy back to the "sport."

drew purple bags under my eyes. I got down on one knee, holding my jack-o-lantern candy bucket skyward and threw back my head like The Man from the Darkside. Although the Undertaker was a bad guy, he was my guy. This presented a problem because I'd go home from the Boston Garden matches each month with my head hung low. The good guys always won. When The Undertaker turned good I thought it was finally his turn to get recognized, so my father and I went on a day trip to Providence, Rhode Island, to see him compete for the World Championship in a casket match against Yokozuna. The winner was the one who sealed his opponent in a pine box. It seemed obvious that the casket manufacturer would win. But when he was ambushed, was sealed in an airtight box, and "died" I ran off into the crowd in tears. Before ascending like Jesus to the rafters of the arena ("invisible" wires glistening in the stage lights) he promised he "Would not rest in peace." My dad tried to convince me that that was a promise he'd return. I stopped crying.

Even then, I was starting to question wrestling's more troublesome stories. Although my dad told me they were racist stereotypes, I secretly liked the Headshrinkers, with their wild hair and necklaces of shrunken skulls. I didn't know any Samoan kids. It was no skin off my nose. But when it came to homophobic scenes, I took it more personally. I'd been raised to believe all people were bisexual whether they realized it or not, and that homophobia was the biggest problem facing our country. I quickly caught on that the Beverly Brothers, whose very name was feminine and whose pants were bright purple, were supposed to be the gay guys. One of the early live shows I attended featured the Beverlys versus the Bushwhackers, and the Bushwhackers started harassing their opponents because they'd hugged. They led the audience in a chant of "Faggot! Faggot!" I remember my dad, red in the face, telling me to stop joining in. I was simply used to going along with whatever was being chanted. It was usually something completely innocuous like "Irwin!" or "Boring!" or "USA!" I slammed on the brakes, and the more I thought about it the more I realized what was going on around me was really screwed up. My dad said he was about ready to take us home, and though a part of me was let down (having looked forward to the event for weeks) I agreed we should go. I didn't like these people any more.

The same friend who introduced me to the WWF (World Wrestling Federation) also persuaded me to try World Championship Wrestling (WCW). The first thing I noticed about the WCW was that its matches were much faster paced than the competition's. Even more impressive, they had matches between fully developed characters on their free television broadcasts, while the WWF used that time to push one established character over a generic guy in tights. WCW was probably the better of the two wrestling leagues in every way but character development. Its characters were defined by their youth, enthusiasm, and the particular region of the American South they came from (WCW had a heavy southern flavor). They didn't have professions other than wrestling and didn't seek to represent anything but themselves.

While the WWF's Red Rooster tried to act like a rooster, WCW's Yellow Dog was just a guy with a yellow mask.

As I grew older in the mid-1990s and put my toys into storage, the WWF dropped a little of its camp. The chaste Miss Elisabeth was replaced by the tigress Sable. Although she stood by her man with all the dreamy-eyed romanticism of her predecessor, she wore leather pants and carried a whip. Her character seemed designed to harness our developing sexuality without crossing any lines. In fact, the whole company seemed to be moving in that direction. The caricatures and stereotypes were replaced by colorful, Type-A personalities defined by plausible real-world traits. A Jewish underdog, a superficial fitness guru, a southern gentleman race-car driver, and a tattooed Japanese martial artist were far easier for us increasingly cynical, image-conscious thirteen- and fourteen-year-olds to endorse. Perhaps promoters stopped targeting our parents as much (dropping the political satire), as most of us no longer needed our parents to take us to the events. The price of pay-per-views went up about the same time my allowance did, once rising as high as $50 for Wrestlemania 11. But the prices soon fell and were replaced by more frequent pay-per-views at lower costs more in line with how we spent money.

Although I saw a lot of groups of kids at the wrestling events, I never once went with friends. I was thirteen, and my parents wouldn't let me go alone because they were scared by news reports about children being kidnapped in parking lots. (Never mind that I didn't have to go through any parking lots to get there.) I insisted furiously that I was old enough and, being home-schooled, I longed for a night out on my own. But I had little success, and my friends were too poor to afford the shows anyway. My dad lost all interest. He couldn't quite explain it. He just said the novelty had worn off, and he wasn't into the new characters as much. I should have been able to see in his reaction just how much the WWF was changing. But my mom took me instead and, never having had any interest, waited at the McDonalds across the street for three hours while I sat guiltily inside. I offered to buy her a ticket, but she wouldn't accept.

A year later I discovered the Internet and rec.sport.pro-wrestling (RSPW). I was fascinated to find a world of college students and even middle-aged adults more mature than my friends. I could sit there all night reading about the independent promotions, Japanese and Mexican wrestling, backyard wrestling, shoot fighting, the past sixty or seventy years of wrestling, and Extreme Championship Wrestling. The Great Muta, Antonio Inoki, Too Cold Scorpio, Chris Benoit, Rob Van Dam, Mick Foley, Eddie Guerrero, and Tazz weren't quite the entertainers wwf stars were. But the posters spoke of them as "legends," "wonders," and "gods" (rather than superstars). (You may notice all of those people were soon after picked up by the major promotions.) I also discovered e-wrestling, an online game that allowed you to create your own superstars and take on their personae. We'd debate over e-mail, sometimes writing two or three promos a day, and resolve the contests in weekly "broadcasts" scripted by the game master. The winner was usually the wittiest and most creative poster. I took great delight in utilizing my creative writing skills to win again and again. I eventually made plans to meet one of my competitors, a twenty-three-year-old engineering major at Northeastern University. He was surprised to find out I was a kid, but we started hanging out every couple of weeks.

Through e-wrestling I also met Raven Poe, an rspw poster and high-school freshman from Omaha, Nebraska. She loved The Undertaker even more than I did, going so far as to say he was the only reason she hadn't committed suicide a couple of years before (he'd reminded her that death didn't solve all of your problems). She was a staunch conservative and the daughter of two soldiers, a total tomboy who was different from me in every way except for our cultural interests. It was amazing for me to get to know someone so different from myself, and though we'd get very heated in our political debates we talked every day and eventually agreed to meet. My sophomore year of high school my dad and I flew out to Omaha for four days, and we played video games, hung out at the mall, and watched raw. The trip was awkward and depressing, but an incredible breakthrough as it was the first romantic experience I'd ever had.

When I was a high-school upperclassman, ceo Vince McMahon turned up the heat. Sable, who'd started out in a committed relationship, developed a strange determination to go nude on the air. She advocated that it was a woman's right to show off her body, downright American. Her husband turned evil and implicitly threatened her with domestic violence. He was seen as a prude for wanting to cage his wife's sexuality and to prevent her from following up on her promises to sleep with audience members. The whole thing seemed torn from the pages of a porn magazine. (Not that the Hulkamaniacs were quite old enough to buy them yet.) As we stayed up later and woke up later the next day, the Saturday morning shows were canceled and replaced by an 11:00 PM show. In hindsight it seemed timed to begin an hour after most businesses closed and a sizable percentage of dates and outings started to wind down. The late-night shows took place in seedier venues, like a Las Vegas casino with the action spilling out onto the red carpet. Marlena once flashed her breasts for the crowd, bare back tantalizing the camera. Thus the nighttime soap opera began and wrestling's cartoonish past got The Stunner. Steve Austin transformed overnight, from a bland midcarder to a beer-guzzling, bird-shooting sensation, a redneck Lenny Bruce.

On a cross-country drive to visit colleges, my dad and I stopped in Milwaukee for the King of the Ring. I expected Jake Roberts to win because he'd recently been reborn as a Christian preacher. Obviously they were trying to appeal to their middle-American constituency. But not only did he lose in the finals; he was humiliated in a matter of seconds by a forgettable, second-string player—The Ringmaster Steve Austin. As surprised as I was by the outcome, I was literally slack jawed when Austin, in his coronation speech, informed the fallen preacher "Austin 3:16 just whupped your ass." Blasphemy and obscenity on a family show? Today I look back on the moment as a real honor. I had seen the biggest swerve in wrestling history since Hulk slammed Andre. Wrestling had really grown up.

The trouble was, I was feeling increasingly disconnected from it. I didn't like "Stone Cold." In fact, I downright hated his guts (at least insofar as one hates television characters). Mister McMahon may have represented the domineering boss, but he was also the most eloquent speaker among them. He spoke with great humanity and logic, while Stone Cold could only repeat a few clichéd phrases and drink heavily. Austin attacked people from behind and then got self-righteous when they did the same to him. Every time Mankind would be nice to him and extend a hand, Austin would try to break it. Although Vince was an old man with gray hair who had never claimed to be a wrestler, Stone Cold had to prove he could take Vince in a fight. Big accomplishment, especially when Austin was holding a gun and Vince was unarmed. For Austin, might meant right. He was the *real* coward. But it wasn't the portrayal of violence that bothered me. You saw far, far worse on other shows. It was the presumption that we would identify with Austin. Did we really see ourselves as the ones beating up on the weak?

When I turned eighteen and left home for the college dorms, bikinis,

Vince McMahon, wrestling's promoter on- and offscreen, has a wicked thought (that'll probably make him a lot of money).

sexual innuendo, and obscenities became standard in pro wrestling. Instead of selling ice-cream bars, the WWF was now merchandising books about the favorite superstars, clearly aiming their product at a grown-up audience. My fellow students, who claimed never to read for fun, asked if they could borrow my copy. The posters of WWF Divas sold at events were almost identical to the "butt floss" thong poster on my neighbor's wall. When I searched the television audience, I saw absolutely no children, a far cry from the five-year-olds with Hulkamania headbands who used to peer out from under the guard rails. But I'd never heard so much public discussion. Wrestling had become "cool" again. I was going to UC Santa Barbara, which felt 50 percent white and 50 percent Hispanic. There was, interestingly enough, a clear racial divide when it came to picking favorites. The Hispanics generally rooted for The Rock and Rikishi, the Caucasians for Stone Cold, Triple H, and Chris Benoit (today no doubt it would be Rob Van Dam — the best match for their ideals so far). Far from presenting offensive racial images, the WWF was now offering images racial minorities identified with. Everyone agreed Lita was hot, ultimately indifferent to whether she was white or Hispanic (which I still haven't decided). Four years later I got a job at a movie theater in urban Boston and became close with an African American from a violent, rundown neighborhood. His favorite had always been Booker T, and he explained to me in detail how Booker accurately reflected his worldview and fashion sense.

When it comes to wrestling I no longer think of myself exclusively as a die-hard fan. I'm also a film student, critic, and fellow storyteller and filmmaker. For several years I've been active in message-board discussions about reality television. People often remark that my posts are very "academic" in that I structure my arguments, use evidence, and make claims. In writing about popular culture, though, it's impossible for me to fully separate my insights as a fan from those as an academic and an artist. I'm no longer active in online discussions of wrestling, but I've written this essay in much the same way I write my posts—wearing my different "hats" to help me express the range of ways I interact with the wwf.

Over the years I saw wrestling evolve, even grow. Sometimes the show matched my own developing personality so well that I perceived wrestling as changing less than it did. After all, I was seeing everything else differently. I assumed I was just getting new things out of wrestling I'd previously missed. But in fact wrestling was almost following me, copying me. But there was no magic to this morphing. Although I couldn't figure out how he'd done it, I knew Vince McMahon had pulled off the grandest bait and switch in business history. We started watching a kids' show, and the next thing we know it's a striptease. But how did he do it? Such an unprecedented transformation deserves careful study.

Looking back through old videos and online databases, I've tried to trace wrestling's transition from a children's show too campy for general audiences to an erotic stunt show too disturbing for them. How did the wwf grow and change with me? I have reviewed boxes of old tapes for the missing link between my past and my present. But each is one piece of a gargantuan puzzle—just a speck on the board. The only way I can really explain this change is through my own memories. In my mind I can see things even more clearly than on the tape. I can fast-forward through years and freeze-frame instants.

The more I reflect on wrestling's sweeping changes, the more certain themes start to stand out—the moral differences that divide its characters, the role of the audience in telling the story, the relationship between fantasy and reality, and the integration of alternative styles of wrestling (ecw, foreign brands) into the mainstream (wwf). I will attempt to trace each of these changes from the time I started watching to the present, pinpointing moments along the way that reveal or add insight into this change and attempting to explain why I believe such change was deemed necessary. I'll describe how and why the wwf grew up with me.

GIVING EVIL A MAKEOVER: WRESTLING
REDEFINES ITS MORAL AGENDA

In evolving an appeal to an adult audience, the WWF needed to do away with wrestling's idealistic moral code in favor of nihilism. In the 1980s and early 1990s, loyalty was virtuous and self-interest sinful. Heroes fell from grace when they became too good for their friends. In 1992 Shawn Michaels kicked partner Marty Jannetty through the Barber Shop window because he didn't want to "carry" him anymore. In Shawn's mind, Jannetty was the sidekick who was always being kidnapped, relying on Shawn for protection from dangerous opponents. But in 1997, Michaels's reasons for separating from Diesel were far less clear. I'd tune into RAW the night after a big swerve, hoping to find out why. But heels now gave stupid answers such as "I'm tired of being good. It's thankless and weak and you people suck." I chalked it up to bad writing. But if you were an optimist you'd point to a larger, more artistic plan. Wrestling was discovering nihilism. All things being equal, if you could cheat or not it seemed more helpful to cheat. "Why limit your options?" a villain might ask.

The mainstream fans continued to boo the villains regardless of their reasons, but the WWF set out to change their minds. The Undertaker, becoming The Lord of Darkness instead of The Man from the Darkside, took on God-like powers. He kidnapped the then-virginal Stephanie McMahon, made her his Bride of Darkness, and in some way corrupted her such that she still hasn't recovered her moral character. By showing how much fun it was to be bad, the WWF seemed to encourage fans to say, "Well, it's only a TV show. What's the harm?" The fans cheered Stone Cold because he was against the Corporation, but in doing so willingly overlooked the same kinds of megalomania and rule-breaking they'd previously condemned in other characters. Far from being trustworthy, Austin told his friends, "D.T.A., you stupid punk. Don't ever trust anyone." In order for Austin to be truly free, he couldn't be bound by the chains of loyalty from week to week. Evil by its very nature defines itself in opposition to good. Austin was a rebel and Mister McMahon was the obvious foil, the conservative. The late adolescent Hulkamaniacs secretly worshipped McMahon because he gave them smut, but they booed his character for threatening to take it away.

As I've gone off to college I've met more and more people who are in love with nihilism. I suspect it's been a part of youth culture for decades, but it never seems to go out of style and remains second in popularity only to hedonism. Primarily, nihilist kids want to demonstrate their philosophical chops by waxing poetic about one's right to suicide and self-mutilation, the irrationality of worried parents, and why emotionless sex is more mature than making love. The WWE's "play hard, sport death" acrobatics, heavy metal soundtrack, and the wrestler's "Diva-swapping" sex lives seem ideally targeted at my generation of nihilists. Moralistic sermons to these deviant, relativist youths by concerned elders are paralleled by Mister McMahon's lectures to Stone Cold. Nihilism hasn't been treated explicitly and positively by most mainstream dramas. Nihilists (and would-be, soft-core nihilists) are like all other "groups" in desiring representation on television, characters they can identify with. In seeking to appeal to my age group, wrestling turned the page on Hulkamania as we knew it and whispered in the ears of rebellious youths "Right on."

FIFTY THOUSAND PEOPLE SAY YOU SUCK: INTERVIEWS GO DIALOGIC

While wrestling fans have often been described as dead-eyed zombies, they're actually the first to talk back to the television. Wrestling gives viewers unprecedented opportunities to critique a show on the air. When I buy a ticket to a live show, I'm actually buying a ticket to have a tiny speaking part. Although wrestling fans all too often go along with the opinions stressed by the commentators, when we do go against the grain our resistance tends to initiate quick creative changes. Wrestling is not a one-way monologue between the producers and the fans; it's a dialogue. A good example of this is the way wrestling interviews have changed. In the 1980s and early 1990s, interviews were personal statements. Wrestlers talked. They appeared to be standing someplace removed in space and time, like theater performers on a dark stage. A fiery desert was superimposed behind The Warrior; classic Greek ruins were used for Mister Perfect; others used a simple wicker or solid-color background. The promos were filmed for regional broadcasts, with the superstars specifically referring to the city and local arena they'd be fighting in. Sometimes they'd talk about something that had happened the last time they were in that city which had never been aired. A second set of national promos would take a much more general tone in which wrestlers would establish their characters. The Repo Man talked about the thrill of repossessing a lower-class family's car in the middle of the night. IRS sat in his office reminding everyone that 15 April was coming up and promising to audit fans. Razor Ramon ate tacos and catcalled at pretty girls in a Miami marketplace.

But in the 1990s, cable shows became dominant over syndicated broadcast shows and local promos were phased out. As the gimmicks became less colorful and less focused on demographic groups, so too did character-exposition promos become uncommon. My favorite promos—in which Mankind sat in the fetal position in his mother's basement, haunting piano music in the background, telling us how cruel the world was—were unfortunately among the last. More often, the interviews would take place in an interview room backstage. Todd Pettengill, a scrawny twenty-something with a background hosting a prank-call radio show in upstate New York, would ask wrestlers to comment as they were "on their way" to a match. Since he was supposed to be a sports interviewer, he kept the focus on the action. Although the new style made them seem more like athletes, I never had a clear image of where these new characters came from. They were actually less real to me because they were still too theatrical to be human but now too displaced from any cultural identity to carry moral or political weight.

Today interviews either occur in the ring or in a more messy, backstage area. The interviews themselves are equally focused on threatening one's opponent. But in order to recapture a hint of location-based audience identification, storylines often take place outside the arena. Brawlers Farooq and Bradshaw once had a recurring subplot involving a local bar they loved. Every time the WWF taped in that city, they'd shoot a segment at the bar in which the wrestlers would smoke cigars, drink whiskey, and start fistfights. Another time, The Undertaker kidnapped someone and took him to a funeral parlor where he planned to murder the individual. No doubt this became more possible as the WWF's overall budget increased. By using preexisting locations, the WWF grounds their characters in our "real world."

On the other hand, the rhetorical style of wrestling interviews hasn't changed that much since I started watching. Interviews have always been built around a few familiar catchphrases, usually with a punch line or punctuating comment at the end. Either they take the form of a rhetorical question such as Booker T's "Can you dig that, sucka?"; a promise such as The Undertaker's "You will rest . . . in peace"; or even an exclamation such as The Legion of Doom's "Oh what a rush!" But the emphasis has changed from the early 1990s—when rambling monologues were underscored by a catch-phrase—to today, when three or four catchphrases sandwich a new joke. The appeal today comes from anticipating the refrain.

Arguably, the kinds of audience interaction in today's promos caught on as a result of the fans' organic responses to the show rather than the pro-ducer's attempts to rally support for changes in their product. Wrestlers have always played to the crowd to get cheers, holding their arms up in victory or pointing to the balcony. But what they started getting were chants. Around 1993, on an episode of *Monday Night RAW*, there was a crowd uprising that became legendary among RSPW posters. Doink the Clown, who started off as a villain, had gone sickeningly, patronizingly clean. Fans revolted by the dozens, and shouted "Kill the clown! Kill the clown!" More and more people joined in until I, as a viewer at home, could clearly hear them. Online, the hardcore fans were crowing about this as a victory for free speech over cor-porate brainwashing. Looking back, you can start to see how powerful the Internet was in changing fandom. In the early 1980s, I'm not sure you could have gotten enough strangers together in one section of the crowd to create such a clamor against the grain of the show. The crowd had always been in-tensely moralistic and easily led by producer suggestion, seeing themselves as aiding the WWE in telling the story of good versus evil (not defining good and evil for themselves, as would have been helpful in the Bushwhackers ha-rassment of the Beverly Brothers). They would even chant "USA!" for Bret Hart, who's from Canada, when he was fighting an opponent who really was from the "USA!" because they put so little thought into it. Casual fans did not intellectualize the potential for a dynamic between producers and con-sumers. They saw those who did "talk back" critically as being radicals. I remember cheering for The Million Dollar Man over El Matador very early on, when a stranger old enough to be my mother turned around, indig-nantly, and snarled, "What's your problem? Don't you know he's the bad guy?" I was just a shy kid, and she made me really uncomfortable. But I kept cheering for the one I wanted. The only way we'd eventually establish a more substantive, nuanced dynamic between fans and consumers was if individual dissenters spoke up and inspired others to join them.

If you read the wrestlers' official books, they'll say straight up that char-acters often turn good or bad to ride the building wave of public opinion. At the "RAW Tenth Anniversary Special," The Rock gave one of the worst inter-views of his career and two fans began roaring "Rocky sucks!" right behind the cameras. When I attended the Royal Rumble a few weeks later, hundreds were chanting it even though The Rock wasn't on the card. When he came back, he was a villain. If this were an isolated incident I'd say it was a coincidence, but it happens all the time. Rather than media-jamming, the fans were collectively voting "yay" or "nay," "face" or "heel." But the public can be persuaded: in a fight with The Million Dollar Man, Jake "the Snake" literally bought people's votes by throwing fistfuls of real money into the crowd. The Nation of Domination held one arm up at a ninety-degree angle, imitating the gestures of the Nation of Islam, and fans mirrored them shouting "We are the Nation of Domination!" Even though they were the bad guys, the desire to participate in such a powerful gesture of support was irresistible. The Rock did one better by playing call-and-response games with the crowd. He always used to end his promos with "If you smell what The Rock is cooking." But fans wanted to say it with him. So The Rock started pausing between "smell" and "what," and the fans would jump ahead of him, then realize he hadn't finished, and they would wait; he'd finish, and they'd try to catch up. It was a little game they played—a commercially friendly harness for their chanting. Once again Vince had seen where the crowd was going, run around to the front, and waved his hands like he was leading the parade.

"I WON'T WATCH WRESTLING; IT'S TOO REAL": MARKETING REALITY

The first time I connected to the Internet, I believed I could find the answer to any earthly question, that it was like Ziggy on the TV show *Quantum Leap*, the holographic librarian in *The Time Machine*, or *A.I.*'s Dr. Know. When I used Webcrawler, an early search engine, I typed in questions, not keywords. "Where can I find old wrestling matches?" Only through trial and error did I find that the Internet was not, in fact, unlimited in its resources. It was dependent on what people knew and what they were willing to share. While at first wrestling's high-profile fans seemed like ancient wise men, able to answer any questions I had, I soon saw the limitations of even their knowledge. At times they seemed clearly connected to the wwf, full of information about the business and its rich history, and at other times they were just as much in the dark as I was. One morning in 1995 the Syracuse press reported that Shawn Michaels had been severely beaten by drunken strangers in a parking lot outside a local bar. The fans were uncertain whether this could be true: Shawn was often jumped on the show; maybe it was an angle. When Jim Ross opened RAW the next night by describing the incident, I was resolved that the news report really had given false information for a bribe. The WWF was a fictional show and rarely brought up the performers' lives on the show. When Shawn reached for his temple and collapsed in the ring that night, I jumped off the couch and knelt in front of the TV. Had he really had a stroke? This was live television after all, and it *had* been in the newspaper. The newspaper didn't lie. Worried I ran to my dad's office (our only connection to the Internet at that time). I assumed the *Wrestling Torch* or *Observer* would know if there had been trouble. But while everyone had a theory, no one had definitive information.

Shawn's collapse was one of the most vivid milestones in the WWF's evolution from pure fantasy to structured reality. I've always heard the story that in the early to mid-1980s, Glenn Jacobs (the actor who today portrays Kane) became angry when an interviewer asked him whether wrestling was fake or not. Jacobs physically attacked him. "Does it feel fake to you?" he asked. At the time fans weren't sure whether the journalist had been in on the angle. (In fact he hadn't). Fans were even more confused (for years in fact) when comedian Andy Kaufman and wrestler Jerry Lawler, two guests on *Late Night With David Letterman*, got into a brawl on the show. Because the fight took place on a nonfiction show not owned by the WWF, most watching believed something had gone terribly wrong. But when Kaufman began wrestling soon thereafter and feuded with Lawler, it complicated that theory. (Today everyone admits their feud was an act from the beginning but that Letterman wasn't in on it.) Both were before my time, but I remember vividly one of the earliest broadcasts I saw, in which Earthquake brought a bag containing Jake "the Snake" Roberts's python, Damian, into the ring. Earthquake was a huge, fat man, and while Jake was tied up in the ropes he squashed Damian with all his weight. The station cut away to a "technical difficulties" message. I turned to my friend, appalled. "I thought this was fake?" I was convinced that the network wouldn't cooperate in reporting technical difficulties unless something violent had actually happened. It didn't occur to me as a kid that the show was taped and that the network would have reviewed the material in advance. It worked almost as well as Orson Welles's legendary "War of the Worlds" broadcast. The snake had never been in the bag.

"Falsified reality" wasn't a common occurrence in wrestling. It was a trick pulled out of the bag once every couple of years that relied heavily on un-initiated, young fans to experience each shock anew. Like so many fictional serials, the WWF depended on withholding upcoming results from fans (who would have to tune in to find out). But as the Internet grew and grew, it became harder for the WWF to keep a secret (and thus to fool anyone). Initially, I think a lot of the leaks came from those peripheral to the WWF. I once met a woman who claimed to have slept with one of the wrestlers after a local house show. She'd flirtatiously persuaded ringside security to take her backstage and had become engaged in conversation with one of the guys. She'd asked him a lot of questions, and he'd told her more than he should. Ringside security guards sometimes overheard stuff backstage. They were then passing that information on to everyone who would listen, and it was spreading throughout the crowd in a game of telephone. Online fans were always very quiet about their sources. But wrestling's so-called dirt sheets were working at cross-purposes with the WWF's creative department. The WWF had a problem, and in it they found a very creative solution. They beat the fans at their own game by revealing more detailed, timely, and de-pendable inside information (for a price). The "Ross Report" on WWE.com seemed modeled after fan dirt sheets, dishing about backstage politics, up-coming storylines, and injuries. The only difference was in Ross's case, you had reason to believe he knew what he was talking about. Writers used real-life storylines as ratings draws, encouraging fans to tune in for the latest dirt. All the stars released confessional books revealing trade secrets. These new commercial texts built off of the already-strong fan enterprise of behind the scenes reporting, but they reaped the profits for the company.

In 2000 Foley released his autobiography, *Have A Nice Day* (and sub-sequently his more political *Foley Is Good*). I had the hardest time finding a copy, because the bookstores didn't order enough. I assumed (and still do) that there was something of an assumption that wrestling fans didn't, wouldn't, and couldn't read. But despite this lack of availability, the book made the *New York Times* best-seller list in just its second week. Even on Christmas morning when I was bombarded with other luxuries, I read chap-ter after chapter. The strong, personal authorial voice and weaving of re-latable anecdotes with completely bizarre stories of the wrestling business impressed me as a young writer. But even more important, the vivid, step-by-step, behind-the-scenes account of Foley's career changed the way I saw the wrestling business (nine years into my relationship with it). Most of the in-ring performers took on secondary, offstage personas. When I watched RAW, I'd find myself more captivated by the implied real-life dynamics — rivalries between the actors, egotistical behavior, reputations being made or broken — than by the televised feuds. I'd try to imagine the backroom deals and grow heated over the hirings and firings.

Perhaps the most important shift in wrestling since I started watching is the inclusion of reality in a previously fictional show. Like so many of my generation, I was made fun of at school by seventh-grade peers who wanted to inform me that wrestling was fake and call me an idiot for falling for the act. But I knew very well wrestling was fake; I just didn't care. "Jurassic Park's fake too, but you're wearing the T-shirt!" I'd shout back. "Don't you know the dinosaurs are just special effects?" Today I'd give them a different answer. "Wrestling is real." Or more accurately, a lot of its drama stems from the semicontrolled, semiscripted exhibition of real-life transgressions. Perhaps few things in this world remain taboo, but Stephanie McMahon's wrestling another woman in a paddle-on-a-pole match written by her own father might just violate all that remain. If you didn't know about the actress's familial relationship with the executive producer, the scene wouldn't be nearly so shocking. Similarly, I found it surreal to watch Vince McMahon throw his son off a fifteen-foot scaffold at Wrestlemania. While in another context, this could be considered domestic violence, here it's entertainment. I felt uncomfortable (as I was intended to) watching Goldust and his real-life wife talk about their on-screen divorce (knowing they were going through a period of separation themselves). Was the pain they expressed onscreen real? This added emotional weight was very intense and at best a guilty pleasure. At worst it was painful to watch. Every week Vince crossed a line you thought he would never cross, and then the next week he found a new line and smashed it all to hell. The wwf had become more analogous to a semiscripted reality series than to a network drama. It was as though Vince were out to persuade everyone who'd once refused to watch wrestling because it was too fake to now refuse to watch because it was too real. Just when nonviewers found a new reason to scorn the wwf, that's when wrestling came back into the mainstream and buy rates skyrocketed.

In blurring the line between fiction and reality, however, Vince necessitated further change in the types of characters he portrayed. One could hardly mistake classic grapplers such as Xanta Claws, Tugboat, Mantaur,

Bastion Booger, Skinner, Max Moon, Damian Demento, Zeus, The Berzerker, Waylon Mercy, Dean Douglas, The Gobbledy Gooker, or Big Bully Busick for real people. Bret Hart and Shawn Michaels were the first characters to get tapped by Vince's magic wand and become "real live boys" instead of wooden puppets. It helped that they'd always had simple gimmicks. Shawn was a garage band guitarist; Bret was an ice-cool Canadian. In order to open viewers' hearts, Vince introduced Bret's parents as fans, cutting to shots of the teary-eyed applauders during his big matches (a staple of professional sports broadcasting). When Bret's archrival, Jerry "The King" Lawler, got on the microphone and blasted Bret's parents, making them beg for their son's protection, the drama took on weight. By threatening audience members, Lawler was crossing an invisible line between the stage and the crowd. How could you root for a one-dimensional caricature like The Warlord over a man with a crying mother?

Shawn Michaels toned his rock-star image way down and began talking about his emotions ("I've finally fulfilled my boyhood dream") more like a real athlete. I remember attending a television taping at which he relinquished the world title, saying "I've lost my smile." He admitted to crying a lot lately and said until he found his passion, he couldn't compete. Vulnerable heroes? Emotions before championships? It was unreal. But the fans went wild. Once you had two human characters it was easier to add a third, a fourth, a fifth. Fatu, once a racist caricature, spoke out about making a difference in his impoverished community (suddenly the bad streets of San Francisco instead of the Isle of Tonga). The Undertaker dropped the supernatural stuff. Sergeant Slaughter, an American traitor during the Gulf War, repented mournfully for his betrayal and read books to American schoolchildren. New characters, for the most part, had simpler gimmicks to begin with. Diesel was just a blues-and-leather-loving truck driver. The next phase was dropping their original names and calling them by the actor's names. Goldust became Dustin Runnels. Mankind became Mick Foley. Even those who didn't go by their real names, such as Steve Austin, went by names that sounded real. But by then we were already used to the more human characters, so it felt like a formality. Mankind had already written a book detailing his college sex life, marriage, and fatherhood by the time he formally became Mick Foley. Because the transition occurred half a character at a time over five years, it felt seamless.

HOW TO RUN A THIRD PARTY CAMPAIGN:
EXTREME WRESTLING

Not everyone was satisfied with these changes, though, and the ECW (Extreme Championship Wrestling) was the ultimate third-party candidate to challenge the WWF's and WCW's bipartisan reign. Around the time it showed up, my relationship to wrestling was changing again, when I brought it into the classroom. In high school I did my senior thesis on Jesse "The Body" Ventura's campaign for the Minnesota governor's office, analyzing his speeches, debates, and talk show appearances and his use of the Internet in reaching younger voters. I argued that the presentational skills he learned in wrestling—how to work a crowd, how to build a promo up to its crescendo, and how to connect with the Hulkamaniac generation—made him the ideal third-party candidate. In writing that report on Ventura's run for governor as a member of the Reform Party, I learned a few things about the strategies such candidates draw on. Ventura found an audience that wasn't tapped out—recently eligible, young voters. He appealed to them by breaking the formalities that made big-two politicians so unappealing—he spoke off the cuff and didn't pull any punches. He used controversy to make headlines, allowing some to view him as a comic spectacle if it ensured others would come across him at all. And most important, he used the Internet as a form of free advertising when funding made television competition impossible. ECW would use all of these methods—targeting adults patronized by their children's wrestling, sucking them in with uninhibited violence and vulgarity that offered them an "extreme" alternative to the mainstream. While the WWF spent millions on television advertising, ECW got the word out online.

But savvy as the young ECW crew may have been, the WWF, an establishment which had long controlled the wrestling world, would provide an almost insurmountable obstacle to their success. Vince McMahon ate third-party competitors for lunch. He built his company by buying local independent wrestling groups and driving others out of business. On the one hand, he united the territories behind a common set of characters and assembled a mass of star talent like never before. On the other, he did away with the intimacy of localization in favor of a one-size-fits-all national product, severing long-standing state traditions and virtually monopolizing audience choices.

ECW would have to avoid making the mistakes that rendered helpless the few remaining independent promotions if they wanted to compete with

Vince's corporate assassins. In reading wrestling news boards, I've sometimes run across stories about the regional leagues' desperate tactics. They'd
promote matches appearing to feature big-name WWF stars, but when you
showed up, they'd actually be imposters dressed like the big names. Other
times they'd promoted midgets wearing mini-sized WWF costumes. Even
WCW, which prided itself on being the WWF's biggest national competitor, restaged a lot of the WWF's most famous feuds (Hulk Hogan vs. Randy
Savage, Savage vs. Ric Flair, Hogan vs. The Giant, and so on). I remember how outraged I was when they initially introduced newcomer The Giant
as the son of WWF legend Andre the Giant just after Andre's death. Not
only was it in poor taste; it was a witless ploy to leech off of the WWF's past
rather than developing its own voice. Perhaps WCW's most mocked character of all time, The Renegade, was a blatant rip-off of The Ultimate Warrior.
He'd race out in his spray-painted body suits with the tassels on the sleeves,
shake the ropes, gorilla-press slam his opponents, rock them with clothes-
lines, and finish them with the big splash (just like the Warrior). Instead of
being Pepsi to the WWF's Coke, WCW was becoming store-brand cereal to
the WWF's Kellogg's, repackaging stale excess. Consequently, they had a hard
time catching up. But then came ECW.

In January 1998 my father and I took the MBTA out to Wonderland, a
dog-racing track an immeasurable mental distance from Boston. The security guards didn't even know there was supposed to be a wrestling event that
night. Finally we found a secondary lobby where a thousand fat, middle-
aged bleacher bums and bachelor-party groups were drinking ale by the gal-
lon. When the show began, we screamed until we could scream no more:
"E-C-W! E-C-W! E-C-W!" I got stomped on, slammed into from both sides,
and generally caught in a human tidal wave. My dad sat awkwardly in the
back. Tommy Dreamer and Shane Douglas tumbled over the barrier, brawling so close to me I could feel Dreamer's breath on my neck. I pressed, fright-
ened, against my chair. But like the world's most vivid 3-D movie, the action
stopped an inch in front of me without making contact. Francine's tiny cotton shorts were plastered to her sweaty, stripper butt. She was so close,
someone could have reached out and touched her. But no one crossed that
line. During the main event, Raven and The Sandman took foreign objects
from audience members—VCRs, jack-o'-lanterns, and piñatas. The Sandman brought a pumpkin down over Raven's back and it exploded, spraying
innards everywhere. At the time I was as much relieved to have made it out

alive as I was exhilarated by an excellent show. If it still existed today, I would love ECW and come back month after month. This was the wild frontier of wrestling.

The ECW was faced with many of the same challenges in catching the WWF and WCW that Arena Football and other alternative sports leagues have had in competing with established brands. All of the big-name talents were in the "Big Two." ECW could only hire Vince's leftovers—unproven young hands and washed up veterans. It was so desperate that it had Mikey Whipwreck, the scrawny kid it had hired to sweep trash out of the ring, don the trunks. If ECW did succeed in making someone a star, the WWF had the money and fame to sign them come the end of their ECW contract (or to pay their legal fees if they wanted to break contract). Since the WWF already aired five hours a week, and WCW about four more, few viewers had time to follow any more. Worst of all, ECW had only a tiny arena—a converted bingo hall in Philadelphia—for ticket revenue, and they aired in only a small handful of eastern seaboard markets. While other independent leagues and even the WCW competed hopelessly with the WWF for the same demographic, ECW found the blind spot in the WWF's rearview window—grown-up audiences. There were a lot of adults out there who would enjoy the primal release of live wrestling and the continuing saga of serialized wrestling if only they had their own space where they weren't crowded by preteens and patronized by "young" storylines. But the question remained: How were they going to reach those audiences?

I first read about the ECW on rec.sport.pro-wrestling. There, extreme wrestling had become an alternative chic. The group's so-called hardcore fans touted the ECW's "hardcore" wrestlers as being of vastly superior quality to the mainstream product. They criticized the WWF's oft reused, contrived storylines, embarrassing ratings ploys, and bland heroes. To some degree this so-called aesthetic revolt was all posturing, a way for a self-selected few to separate themselves from the crowd as the newsgroup's too-cool-for-the-mainstream elite. But ECW really spoke to college- and middle-aged guys a few years ahead of the Hulkamania generation. Japanese wrestling, more focused on athleticism than melodrama, was also seen as "pure" and possessing "integrity." Pennsylvania-area fans sold tapes of ECW television to those of us in the other forty-nine states. I can only imagine how much money they would have made if eBay had existed at the time. The live cards began touring the eastern seaboard, going to a few more cities each go-round. The shows were initially so unpublicized that I wonder still how high a percentage were made up of RSPW members and their friends. Eventually the television show became syndicated in my area (and an increasing spate of others).

Although it was sold in 2001, ECW clearly had a huge impact on the WWF's long-term evolution. Its high-impact, fast-paced, stunt- and weapon-oriented style has come to dominate WWF action. Its shock and titillation plotlines and frank sexuality are the meat of today's wrestling. ECW founder and guru Paul Heyman has been a force for the WWF, both on- and off-screen, serving as a manager, commentator, and booker. The WWF has signed ECW talent Steve Austin, Mick Foley, the Dudley Boys, Rob Van Dam, Chris Benoit, Rhyno, Tazz, and Lance Storm (among others). Even the little details have been picked up (Stone Cold's over-the-head beer pouring is identical to The Sandman's old routine; Tables, Ladders and Chairs matches now steal the show at Wrestlemania; and Stacey Keibler's trademark shorts look suspiciously like Francine's). ECW started the tradition of using radio-aired songs by big-name bands as wrestlers' theme music instead of synthesized originals. There's a male-dominant, sadistic sex fantasy to the whole thing. Both federations return often to images of men brutalizing damsels in distress. Sometimes the women are villainous and generally punished to the fullest extent of the heroes' ability. Sometimes they're fan favorites, and someone at least comes to their aid (before or after the abuse), only to be thanked with a kiss. I don't always get why some women are "good" and others "evil." It has nothing to do with their purity nor with their outspokenness. Molly Holly is branded villainous because she's got a so-called big butt (in fact it's smaller than Trish Stratus's, and it was Trish who branded her "fat"). But the audience seems to take equal pleasure in seeing a fair maiden slain as seeing an evil hussy "taken to the whipping shed."

As a viewer it's plain to me where Vince McMahon drew a tremendous amount of his inspiration and out-and-out stolen ideas from in building the current WWF. ECW provided him with a model for how adult wrestling fans would behave, what they'd buy, and what morals they'd want wrestlers to embody. When the Hulkamaniacs grew up, he knew just how to keep their interest. I just find it ironic that while other independent federations needed to imitate the WWF, the WWF imitated ECW. If this is the story of the WWF's often rocky romance with its fans, then ECW played the part of a mistress, luring fans away and forcing the WWF to reevaluate its advances toward the fans to better suit their desires.

WHEN DO YOU TURN OFF A RED SOX GAME?
FAN COMMITMENT

Although you may love a television show, you don't necessarily like it. I've grown up a fan of the WWF. I continue to be a fan, and it's hard to picture a time when I wouldn't know or care what was going on in wrestling. When you grow up with something, it becomes comfortable. Most good bookstores have nearly a shelf full of memoirs and retrospectives about the Boston Red Sox and New York Yankees of days gone by, written by people who grew up fans. No passage of time seems to fully distract Bronx and Boston fans from their deeply embedded allegiances. I wasn't a "slugger" or a "champ." I was a Creature of the Night. But like the Red Sox of Babe Ruth's day, the WWF of my childhood has long passed. For better or for worse, wrestling is a different game now. Just as Red Sox fans might feel a dull ache watching player salaries balloon exponentially, so do I feel disappointed whenever the WWF pulls a particularly egregious shock-jock stunt. Some moments — Eric Bischoff's hiring newcomers Rosie and Jamal to brutalize feminists and old women and violently prevent a gay wedding, Triple H's raping the rotting corpse of his opponent's high-school sweetheart, the theft of the Big Show's father's body during the funeral — made me feel ashamed of the WWF. For a brief window of time, I felt comfortable telling anyone and everyone I was a fan. But now I'd rather keep wrestling at more of a distance. When you complain about a television show, the classic response is "if you don't like it, click the off button." But what if you still care about the show and feel all the more outraged because you can see the turmoil it's going through? Red Sox fans emotionally ravage themselves season after season, always hoping against hope that this year their team will finally win the big one, and always coming up disappointed. An outsider would wonder why they don't give up and go do something more fun. It's just a game; why worry about it? It's true: at the end of the day wrestling is just a show, and you've got to put it aside and say, "Okay, now it's time for something else." You can't let it bother you too much. But I've moved eight times in my life. I don't have any friendships that go back more than four years. Many people need some sort of stability in their lives, a relationship with something they don't break, even when the going gets tough.

There's a lot I still like about wrestling. The matches themselves are better than ever. I feel burned to this day that I agreed to stand in line and buy my buddies drinks while attending the match Kurt Angle would call the best of his career to date and one of the best in wrestling history (his 2003 Royal Rumble contest against Chris Benoit). Mick Foley's matches with Triple H (especially his final Hell in the Cell) are the most breathtaking I've ever witnessed. Vince McMahon has become a better mic performer than any talent he's ever employed. There were certainly aspects of wrestling that bothered me way back in the very beginning. The Bushwhackers urging the crowd to chant "faggot" was very screwed up. As great a showman as he was, Kamala was also a broad racial stereotype, and it always made me uneasy. Roddy Piper's stripping Goldust down to a lacy teddy and beating him in homophobic rage had me red-in-the-face pissed.

And I'll be honest. As liberal, modern, and sensitive as I try to be, there are times I enjoy the WWF's sadomasochistic play. There's a healthy pleasure in exploring one's darkest fears. That's why we enjoy horror movies. It's therapeutic to blur psychological pleasure and pain because they're similarly passionate and stimulate some of the same brain chemicals. I'm told relationships are about give and take. Wrestling, as a fantasy, takes this to an extreme; for example, Jeff Hardy doesn't just take out the trash for Lita, he saves her from a beating; and Bubba Ray Dudley gains not moral power but physical power in asserting himself over Stephanie. I can explore in fantasy scenarios that would really hurt me if they happened in real life. But because I can turn off the TV or open my eyes and the images disappear every time, I feel safe returning to those fantasies.

I'll fully defend someone's right as an artist to tell in fiction any scenario they want without assuming that they'd want the scenario to happen in their real world. I'm all about the right of the reader or viewer to enjoy the material in the same, hypothetical sense. The entire point of wrestling, and of sadomasochism, lies in the suspension of disbelief—in edging up to something truly outrageous and flirting with the danger of it without seriously hurting anyone. I'm not offended by the same images that confound the Parents Television Council, because I understand they're just images.

But just as people took the WWF literally before—cheering and booing whomever they were told to, without question—I'm concerned that a small minority in the audience hasn't fully grasped this increasingly fine line between the play and the real. They might ask if, as Mick Foley says, wrestling causes the actors actual pain and injury, then isn't driving a woman through a table "real"? And if it's okay to hurt women in wrestling, why isn't it okay to hurt them in the home? These people would be idiots (with root causes no doubt very separate from the WWF), but I meet idiots every day. I don't believe we can or should censor wrestling to keep it from being misappropriated by a few sickos to suit their own agendas. That would bring art back to its lowest (and safest) common denominator, removing any meaning or nuance from it. Ultimately I think that the WWF does not cause a person to behave violently. Rather, a person predisposed to violence might be drawn to the WWF for his or her own reasons. Wrestling's storylines are sardonic and irreverent. But an unbalanced person might read the episodes very literally and identify sympathetically with what he or she sees as a radical and realistic agenda. Such a deranged individual would not have the power to differentiate between tongue-in-cheek and more serious political ideas. Nobody of sound mind and judgment could make such a mistake. Wrestling's not unclear. The WWF is extremely broad and farcical. So, rather than blaming wrestling for inspiring antisocial behavior, I would view an individual negatively influenced by it as mentally ill, and see his or her skewed view of wrestling as a symptom of that illness.

But it's true that the more "extreme" the WWF becomes, the more uncomfortable it makes me. It seems that Vince is begging to be misunderstood and testing the "any press is good press" theory to its boiling point. How can this be the same show I woke up to twelve years ago? Am I born a wrestling fan preordained to die a wrestling fan as some Sox fans seem to be? Or can I divorce my childhood fantasies? Can't two lovers just grow apart?

The WWF grew more risqué as I grew older, but I think it has actually been more mature at other points in its history. The WWF seems to define growing up as the opposite of staying innocent — saying that the more cynical you are, the older you'll look. But that's so very high school (and not in a good way). Around the time I moved into the freshman dorms, my friends rediscovered early 1980s Nintendo games, Scooby-Doo, and superheroes. They weren't afraid of being teased anymore. Maybe one day wrestling too will decide that truly growing up means being more narratively sophisticated but as sweet and approachable as ever. I'll gladly welcome them to that stage of maturity. After all, their fans are already leading the way. At Wrestlemania 18, Hulk Hogan returned after a nine-year absence, taking on The Rock in a generational clash of "classic" versus "contemporary." Hogan's reception reached higher decibels as the Hulkamaniacs, now young professionals, pulled their fifth-grade Halloween costumes out of storage for one last flag-waving hoorah. Stone Cold Steve Austin had originally been proposed as Hogan's opponent but reportedly declined because he feared he, too, would be booed.

The fans' choice of Hogan over The Rock signifies the end of an era. The WWF, which has stayed on top precisely by following the trends of fan opinion, will be staying true to form if they swing their momentum in favor of less cynical competitors. Looking around at my generation—or at least the members I have close at hand to study—there's a gradual trend away from the vocal negativity that defined the nineties. Students have rallied en masse against the war with Iraq, no longer afraid to care about something. Some would say we're following a ripple effect out from 9/11, a blow said to have softened our shells. But at the campus's 2000 election party, dozens of people wept openly when Bush was declared the winner. I'm not trying to whale on Bush. You see it in art too. The songs that have done well at the Grammies lately have been more soulful and romantic than those that did well five years ago. Melodrama is coming back in literature. My writing professor says authors are less and less often speaking with imaginary quotes around their emotional "statements," feeling less need to apologize for caring. A few years ago, I wondered how wrestling would ever top Stone Cold when he was already so extreme. But now I joke that Austin's rowdy beer guzzling will be replaced by Rob Van Dam's mellow pot high. Wrestling fans aren't getting younger, and they won't necessarily lose interest in sex, drugs, and rock and roll. But a thirty-five-year-old may relate to those experiences differently from twenty-year-olds. If the WWF is to continue following the pull of our generation and to continue serving our needs and interests, it will eventually have to drop a little of the "WWF Attitude" and relate to us as adults.

In writing this piece, I've realized they already are. Shawn Michaels, who was perhaps the last mainstay of classic wrestling, returned to increased ratings. But fans aren't living in the past. Just as new wrestlers were introduced around 1996 to promote a simpler, less campy WWF, so too are today's new characters being brought up "clean cut." Kurt Angle, the most popular journeyman today, is a milk-drinking, weeping Goody Two-shoes. Rob Van Dam, Chris Benoit, Booker T, and Brock Lesnar, the other leaders of wrestling's new generation of stars, have all led less controversial careers than their predecessors. After Angle suffered a near career-ending neck injury, reports suggested Vince was slowly toning down his "extreme" wrestling to prevent further tragedies (within the past couple of years, Stone Cold, Shawn Michaels, Kevin Nash, Chris Benoit, and Lita have also spent close to a year on the shelf with in-ring injuries). Other reports indicate that size will again play a significant factor, as "big men" will be favored (as was the case in the mid-1980s). Both of these trends would require a significant shift in the way wrestling tells stories and the way it appeals to fans. If wrestling is moving away from the extreme, then it must find a new ideal. By the time this appears in publication, I suspect the WWF will have evolved to reflect that new view such that this piece will be more a capsule of a moment in wrestling's past than a reflection of its current state. Wrestling's constant dynamic with the fans, its determination to grow and change with us and in response to our demands, is integral to its survival in the mainstream. Even though they've dropped the archetypes and political satires of the 1980s the WWF is still nothing if not socially relevant and contemporary, playing off of our moods and artistic trends as a generation. I look forward to welcoming them into the mature world of the Hulkamaniacs' thirties. But for right now I'm enjoying watching wrestling's growing pains and its struggle to define and assert itself. Well, sort of "enjoying."

GLOSSARY

card: A wrestling event or a lineup of matches

count-outs: A referee's count to ten while a wrestler is out of the ring or otherwise incapacitated

face: From "babyface"; a good guy

figure-four leglock: A submission hold involving complex intertwining of the legs

gorilla-press slam: A wrestler lifts his or her opponent over his or her head and then slams the opponent to the mat

heel: A bad guy

jobbers: Relatively unknown but reliable wrestlers who help to make more established wrestlers look good

kayfabe: Maintaining a fictional storyline, or the illusion that professional wrestling is a genuine contest

mark: A wrestling fan

mid-carder: A journeyman or a semi-popular wrestler

pankratiast: A classical Greek "no-holds-barred" wrestler

pile driver: A wrestler turns his or her opponent upside down and then drops to the knees or a sitting position, driving the opponent to the mat

pinfall: Being pinned by another wrestler

powerbomb: A wrestler puts his or her head between an opponent's legs, lifts them in the air, and then slams them into the mat

roll-up: Rolling an opponent back on the mat so that his or her legs are above the head

rudo: A rude guy, a heel

shoot: An unscripted moment in a match

smart mark: A wrestling fan who is in on, or believes to be in on, what is real and what is staged in wrestling

suplex: A take-down move

tecnico: Literally, a technician; a face

work: An apparently spontaneous moment in a match that is actually scripted

CONTRIBUTORS

Roland Barthes (1915–1980) was a French social and literary critic whose writings on semiotics were fundamental to the rise of structuralist critical analysis in the twentieth century.

Douglas Battema is Assistant Professor of Communications at Western New England College.

Susan Clerc has a PhD in American Culture Studies at Bowling Green State University. She also holds a law degree and a Masters in Library Science. Dr. Clerc is currently employed at Southern Connecticut State University.

Laurence de Garis is Associate Professor of Sport Management at James Madison University in Harrisonburg, Virginia.

Henry Jenkins III is Director of the Comparative Media Department at the Massachusetts Institute of Technology.

Henry Jenkins IV is an undergraduate at George Washington University.

Heather Levi is Assistant Professor of Anthropology at Lake Forest College.

Sharon Mazer is Head of the Department of Theatre and Film Studies at the University of Canterbury, Christchurch, New Zealand.

Carlos Monsiváis is an essayist, satirist, and novelist. Mr. Monsiváis has contributed to Mexican journals such as *Excelsior* and *Siempre*, and he currently writes for *El Financiero* and *La Jornada*.

Lucia Rahilly is a graduate student in Cinema Studies at New York University.

Catherine Salmon is Assistant Professor in the Psychology Department at the University of Redlands.

Nicholas Sammond is Assistant Professor of Media Studies at Hobart and William Smith Colleges.

Phillip Serrato is Assistant Professor of English at Fullerton College.

Philip Sewell is a PhD candidate in Communication Arts at the University of Wisconsin–Madison.

INDEX

camel clutch (de a caballo) hold, 115

Canto, Eduardo, 88

Cantor, Paul, 310

Caporale, Bob, 292 n.8

Caras, Cien, 114

Cárdenas, Lázaro, 119

Cardona, Ray: *El Enmascarado de Plata*, 92

cards, 197, 343

carnivalesque tradition, 36

Casas, Negro, 113–16

Casas, Pepe, 113, 116

Castellanos, Dionico ("Psichosis"), 245–46, 248

Castrol, 266

cauliflower ear, 203

CBS network, 141–42, 160–61 n.15, 160 n.14

censorship, 340

chain wrestling, 208

Championship Wrestling, 242

champion titles, 34–35, 40–41

Charteris, Leslie, 88–89

cheating, 42

Chicano Movement, 237, 241

Children Now, 145

choreography/scripting, 210–11, 219, 265

Christian Right, 301–2

Chuck and Billy, 7, 10–11

church music, 303

Chyna. *See* Laurer, Joanie

citizenship and consumption, 17

civilizing process, 36–38

Clancy, Christopher, 279

class: in masculine melodrama, 58–60, 64, 237; in the popular performance tradition, 153–55; and television's history, 136, 137–40

Clinton, Bill, 264, 282

Coe, Andy, 126 n.2

Cohen, Jeffrey Jerome, 299, 301, 308, 309

Cole, Michael, 133, 271

Columbine shootings (1999), 304

combat plays, 102, 103–4, 105

Comisión de Lucha Libre (Mexico), 107, 127–28 n.8, 129 n.18

Conan the Barbarian, 110

consumption: improvement/redemption via, 155–56; interest groups based on, 143–44; as social action, 143–45, 160–61 n.15

Coors, Joseph, 304

cosmetic surgery, 266

"El costo de la vida" (Guerra), 115

Cota, "Mocho," 96

count-outs, 343

court society, 38

Credit Suisse First Boston, 284

crime dramas, 138, 160 n.9, 160 n.12, 162 n.22

critical theory and cultural conservatism, 305–7, 313

Cronenberg, David, 301

Crow's Wrestling Babes site, 174

cruiserweights, 246, 248

Cruz, José G.: El Santo graphic novels, 92–93

crying, as internalized emotion, 39

Crystal Palace, 224

CSI, 155

culture: critical theory and cultural conservatism, 305–7, 313; cult studs vs. neo-cons, 304–5; and identity, 302; politics of, 15–17, 299–306, 314 n.4

cutting, pre-match, 224, 230 n.8

Daily Show, 309

Dallas, 274

Damiancito, 114

dancer gimmick, 208

danza del tigre (tiger dance), 103–4, 118

de a caballo (camel clutch) hold, 115

Dean, Howard, 311

de Certeau, Michel, 176

dedazo (the big finger), 118

defeat, spectacle of, 26–27, 28, 192

de Garis, Laurence ("Larry Brisco"; "Pro-

fairness, 29–30, 70–71. *See also* the real vs. the fake

fakery. *See* the real vs. the fake

Falwell, Jerry, 3, 303

family, psychiatrization of, 222, 229 n.5

family values, 136, 140–42, 154

fans: commitment of, 338–42; as desiring the real, 82–83, 201; expertise/sophistication of, 75–80, 81–82; interaction with promos, 326, 328–29; loss of, 209; pace of matches influenced by, 72, 207; vs. promoters, 79; racial/ethnic divide among, 323; rushing the ring by, 81–82; and stock in WWE, 278–79, 285, 291 n.5; ties to wrestlers as dependent on fakery, 67–68, 71–72, 79; on the WWE-WCW merger, 287–89. *See also* female fan Web sites; media fandom

Fantasy Universe, 175

Farooq (Ron Simmons), 327

Fatu, Rikishi (Solofa Fatu), 173, 333

feelings: crying as internalized emotion, 39; emotional display/release in masculine melodrama, 35–36, 50, 52, 63–64; emotional restraint as marker of social integration, 36–37; gendered display of, 38–39; s/m and emotional expression/experience, 216–17, 221; in sports, 36–39

Felino, 113

female fan Web sites, 167–89; AU (alternate universe) stories on, 183, 184–87, 188; caption contests and commentary, 173–74; female wrestling fans vs. media fans generally, 188–89; fiction on, 167–68, 175–87; h/c (hurt comfort) stories on, 182–84; Hunk/Stud of the Week contests, 173; Mary Sue stories on, 176–79, 186; picture galleries on, 167–68, 170–75, 188; slash stories on, 11, 179–87; tag team pages, 172; and women's enjoyment of/desire for hunks, 168,

187–88; and wrestlers' need of female fans, 168–69

femininity, as passive/consuming, 13, 262–63

feminism, 270–71, 306

La fiesta de los tastoanes, 103, 127 n.6

Fight Club, 228

figure-four leglock, 343

figure skating, 200

Filthy Animals, 251, 253–56

Financial Times (London), 279, 280–81

Fiske, John, 36, 168, 174, 176, 181

Flair, Ric, 41, 50, 53, 58, 182, 189 n.1, 250–51

Flame, 176

Flynt, Larry, 63–64

Foley, Mick ("Cactus Jack"; "Dude Love"; "Mankind"): documentary on, 220–23, 299–300; female fans of, 168–69; *Have a Nice Day*, 229 n.3, 330–31; on Lieberman, 304; personae performed by, 5; promo of, 327; "real" phase of, 333; reputation for absorbing pain, 11; and Triple H, 339

football, 40

forearm smash, 27–28

formalism, excess of, 28

Foucault, Michel, 214, 224–25, 229 n.5, 230 nn.10–11

foul play, signs of, 29–30

Fox, Vicente, 118

FOX network, 141, 143

frame grabs, 170, 173–74, 343

Francine, 335, 337

Frank, Thomas, 276–78, 304–6, 310, 314 n.3

Frankie, 84

Freedman, Jim, 238

French melodrama, 57

French wrestling, 30

Friends, 155

Fulton, Charlie, 202

Funk, Terry, 222–23

Funk family, 197, 222

Furman, Phyllis, 260

headlocks, 203–4

Headshrinkers, 319

Heart Break Kid. *See* Michaels, Shawn

heat, producing, 148

heels (villains), 207, 264, 270–71, 290–91 n.2, 325–26, 343. *See also* heroes vs. villains

Heenan, Bobby ("the Brain"), 43, 59, 236, 239–40

Heilman, Robert, 46

Hellfire's Hot Men of Wrestling, 173–74

Hellfire's Rock Gallery, 171

Helmsley, Hunter Hearst ("Triple H"), 7, 133, 150, 172, 181–82, 271, 338–39

Henaff, Marcel, 224

Henderson, Mort ("the Masked Marvel"), 99

Henricks, Thomas, 193

Henry, Mark ("Sexual Chocolate"), 268

Herman, Pee Wee, 201

heroes vs. villains, 205, 207, 218–19, 264, 328–29. *See also* babyfaces; faces; heels

Hewlette, Elizabeth, 48, 53

Heyman, Paul, 337

high spots, 204–5

Hijo del Santo (Son of El Santo), 97, 98, 113–16, 128 n.12, 129 n.16

Hillbilly Cousin Luke (Gene Petit), 197

Hillbilly Jim, 58

Himmelfarb, Gertrude, 309

hip-hop, 147, 258 n.7, 303

the Hitman. *See* Hart, Bret

Hitman Hart (Jay), 11, 218–19

Hogan, Hulk: career pushed by Vince McMahon, 242; and Gulf War restaging, 61–62; initiation into wrestling, 197; and Sid Justice, 41, 46; as martyred hero, 51; and the NWO, 247–48; popularity of, 340–41; and The Rock, 340–41; and Sgt. Slaughter, 44, 61; theme song of, 49; WWE title held by, 61

hold, definition of, 27, 223–24. *See also individual holds*

Holly Brothers, 133

homophobia, 302, 303, 319, 339

homosocial bonding, 53–54, 62–63, 65 n.4, 262, 295–96. *See also* slash stories

honor, 113–16, 125

the Honor Roll, 208–9

Huerta, Rodolfo Guzmán ("El Santo"): anonymity of, 101–2, 126–27 n.3, 128 n.9; background/wrestling career of, 88–92, 101; in comics and movies, 92–94, 96, 101–2, 126–27 n.3; de a caballo hold of, 115; death of, 91, 96–97, 122, 129 n.20; lucha libre popularized by, 15; mask of, 101–2, 116; retirement of, 96, 129 n.20; unmasking of, 96

Hustler, 63–64, 309

icons, wrestlers as, 317–19

Independent (London), 280, 284

indies (independents), 198, 334–35

injury/bleeding, 80–81, 83, 211, 224, 229–30 n.7, 230 n.8, 341–42

Institute for Media and the Family, 304

Intercontinental champion belt, 34, 45

interest groups, 143–44

Internet: companies on, 283–85, 291–92 n.7; images appropriated on, 170; limitations of knowledge on, 329; political campaigning on, 311, 334. *See also* female fan Web sites

interviews, dialogic, 326–29

invincible victims, 50–51

IPO. *See* WWE: stock of

I Remember Gorgeous George (Jolley), 69

the Iron Sheik (Ali Vazari), 73, 86 n.2, 267

irony, 263–64

IRS (Irwin R. Schyster), 41, 58, 327

Jacobs, Glen, 330

Jacobs, Glen (Kane): female fans of, 177; vs. Jericho feud, 169; journalist attacked by, 330; and Michaels, 169; and

masculinity (*continued*)

forms of, 255–56, 271–72; male-oriented
TV programming's excesses, 260–61,
266; politics of, 13–15; racist/sexist,
13–14, 270–71; and stereotypes, 261,
264–65, 267–75; and the stock market,
275–86, 290, 291–92 nn.5–8; and textual
deconstruction, 264–67. *See also* Latino
wrestlers; melodrama, masculine

Masked Marvel (Mort Henderson, among
others), 99, 101

masks: and character vs. wrestler vs.
script, 105–6, 109–10; circulation of, 14,
116–19; collections of, 110, 128 n.12; on
comic book heroes, 101, 126 n.2; empowerment via, 104–5, 123, 125–26; as
fetish, 107–8; history of, 99–102, 125, 126
n.2; as honor, 113–16, 125; and identity,
104; as an inalienable possession, 116;
in indigenous Mexican culture, 98–99,
102–5, 125–26, 127 n.4; inheritance of
designs, 112, 116, 128 n.13; and kinship,
112; in lucha libre, generally, 98–102,
105–6, 125–26; metarules of, 106–7,
108, 127–28 nn.8–10; in pastorelas, 103;
performance rules of, 106, 107–13; unmasking, 108–10, 111, 112, 118, 123, 126;
value of, 110, 112–13; and visitation, 104,
127 n.7; women's use of, 110, 112

masochistic paradigm, 225–26

mass middle class, 138–39

Mathers, Marshall ("Eminem"), 148

Matsuda, Hiro, 197

Mazaud, Armand, 25, 26

Mazer, Sharon, 5, 10, 201, 207, 246, 255–56

McCain, John, 311

McCarthy, Anna, 147, 155

McGruder, Aaron, 309

McMahon, Linda, 150, 151, 274, 282, 289

McMahon, Shane, 133, 149, 184, 186,
274–75, 288–89

McMahon, Stephanie, 150, 269–70, 274–75,
325, 332

McMahon, Vince, 323; and Austin, 273,
322, 325–26; as a businessman and WWE
character, 6–7, 279–80, 281–84, 334;
divorce announcement by, 150, 151; as
entrepreneur vs. coward, 273–74; as
exploitive, 67–68; and fans, 149–50;
Bret Hart double-crossed by, 218–19,
272–73, 291 n.4; and Chris Jericho, 271–
72; and Latino wrestlers, 256–57 (*see
also* Latino wrestlers); on legitimacy
of wrestling as a sport, 197; mic talent
of, 339; pre-match cutting by, 230 n.8;
reality vs. fiction blurred by, 332–33 (*see
also* the real vs. the fake); response to
criticism, 148–49; speaking style of, 322;
"sports entertainment" coined by, 4; on
stereotypes, 268; Stossel's attack on, 73;
and Triple H, 133; on violence on TV,
155; white wrestlers' careers pushed by,
242; as WWE owner, 12, 132, 256; on the
XFL, 285–86. *See also* WWE

McMahon family, 150, 151, 213–16, 272–75,
283. *See also individual family members*

McNeeley, Peter, 81, 86 n.4

media effects, 145–46, 161–62 n.16, 306–7

media fandom, 168, 178–79, 182–83, 186,
188–89. *See also* fans; female fan Web
sites

Media Watch, 145

Meeker, Mary, 285

melodrama, masculine, 33–64; bastards,
33–34, 46–50; of champion titles, 34–35,
40–41; class antagonisms in, 58–60, 64,
237; emotional display/release in, 50, 52,
63–64; and feelings in sports, 36–39; vs.
feminine melodrama, 35, 64 n.2, 262;
and football, 40; homosocial bonding
in, 53–54, 62–63, 65 n.4, 262, 295–96;
individual matches vs. ongoing narratives, 34–35; invincible victims in, 50–51;
jingoistic nationalism in, 60–64; and
masculine emotion, 35–36; might makes
right in, 41–42, 64, 270; populism in,

56–60, 62–64, 262–63; remaking sports via wrestling, 40–41; romance in, 52–56; soliloquies in, 48–49; suffering heroes, 33–34; theatricality vs. pseudorealism of, 51–52; wrestlers as body doubles, 42–46; wrestling as a morality play, 33–34, 40–41, 49–50. *See also* Barthes, Roland: on spectacle; slash stories

Meltzer, Dave, 278

men, emotional display by, 38–39. *See also* feelings

Men Behaving Badly, 260

Men in Pink and Black, 173

Mercado, Victor, 242

Mercy, Waylon, 332–33

Merrill Lynch, 284

mestizos, 105

Mexican Revolution (1910–17), 105

Mexico: housing in, 120–22; masked performances in, 14–15; masks in indigenous culture of, 98–99, 102–5, 125–26, 127 n.4; politics of, 118–25, 129 n.19; professional wrestling in, 89. *See also* lucha libre

Mexico City earthquake (1985), 120, 128 n.14

Michael, John, 305, 314 n.3

Michaels, Shawn ("Heart Break Kid"): accused of being gay, 169–70; collapse following head injuries, 80–81, 329–30; and Diesel, 182, 325; emotional displays by, 333; injuries to, 341–42; and Jannetty, 44–45, 325; and Kane, 169; in *Playgirl* and *RAW Magazine*, 169–70; popularity of, 169, 341; "real" phase of, 333; and Sherri, 53; Web sites dedicated to, 172

mid-carders, 343

Middle Ages, 37

middle class, 138–41, 160 n.9, 160 n.12, 297, 314 n.1. *See also* class

might makes right, 41–42, 64, 205–6, 270

Miller, Mark Crispin, 314 n.4

Miller, Toby, 228

Million Dollar belt, 34

Million Dollar Man. *See* Dibiase, Ted

minis, 114, 128 n.15, 335

Mitchell, Bruce, 287

the Model (Rick Martel), 44, 58

Molly Holly, 337

Monday Night Football, 260

Monday Night RAW, 76, 77, 328

monolithic white masculinity, 233–35, 242–48, 255

Monsiváis, Carlos, 124

monsters, 299–301, 303, 308, 309

Montrealers, 60

mook culture, 152, 153, 154–55, 308

Moon, Max, 332–33

moral agenda of wrestling, 325–26

Morales, Pedro: career decline of, 241–42, 243; ethnic neutrality of, 239; popularity of, 235–36, 237, 239; positive portrayals of, 234; racism toward, 239–40; and Sgt. Slaughter, 238; as underdog, 245; working-class status of, 237–38

moral panics, 300–304, 306–7, 308

Morgenson, Gretchen, 284, 285

Moros y Cristianos (Moors and Christians), 103, 105

Mould, Bob, 229

the Mountie, 43, 44, 46

Moustache (Kuzchenko), 30

movies: about wrestling, 101, 137–38; crime represented in, 162 n.19; violence/sexuality in, 3

MTV, 144

Mujer Maravilla, 121

Muraco, Don, 236, 243

Murphy, Dan, 244–45

Murphy, Mike, 302

Murphy Brown, 141, 303

muscle bodies, 224

Mustafa, Col., 61

Mysterio, Rey, Jr., 232, 233, 244–48, 251

by, 50; and Jake the Snake, 48, 51, 52, 53

Scaia, Rick, 175

Schultz, David ("Dr. D."), 69, 73, 74, 242

Schwarzenegger, Arnold, 3

Schyster, Irwin R. ("IRS"), 41, 58, 327

Scorpio, 108–9

scripting/choreography, 210–11, 219, 265

Sedgwich, Eve, 54

Seiter, Ellen, 18

self-nomination, 48–49

Sensational Sherrie, 45, 46, 47, 53

The Sentinel, 179

September 11 attacks (2001), 303, 341

serial fiction, as feminine vs. masculine, 35

Serling, Rod: *Requiem for a Heavyweight*, 137–38, 159 n.4

700 Club, 304

Sexual Chocolate (Mark Henry), 268

sexuality, 65 n.4, 225, 230 n.12. *See also* s/m narrative; wrestling, professional: violence/sexuality in

shame vs. political correctness, 309

Sharpe, Iron Mike, 242

Shires, Roy, 197

the Shoeshine Boy (Ben Lagerstrom), 76–78

shoot, 200, 343. *See also* work

signs, 24–26, 29–30, 31–32

Simmons, Ron ("Farooq"), 327

Simon, Larry ("the Great Malenko"), 200–201

The Simpsons, 141, 149

sincerity, excess of, 28

sitcoms, 138, 139, 159–60 n.8, 162 n.22

size, importance of. *See* monolithic white masculinity

Skinner, 332–33

slash stories, 11, 179–87

Slaughter, Sgt.: and Gulf War restaging, 61–62; and Hulk Hogan, 44, 61; and the Iron Sheik, 267; and Morales, 238;

on the Nasty Boys, 60; "real" phase of, 333

Smackdown, 132–58; adolescent appeal of, 135–36, 142, 146–47, 156–57, 159 n.2; criticism/impropriety of, 134–35, 146–47, 148–49, 154–55; family excesses of, 142–43, 148, 149–50, 151, 152; popularity of, 132, 152, 288; programming patterns of, 132; PTC criticism of, 306; Thanksgiving dinner staged by, 132–33; violence/sex on, 155–56. *See also* wrestling, professional: and television's history

smart marks (fans), 75, 343

Smash 'N Slam action figures, 232–33, 257 nn.1–2

Smith, R. J., 142–43, 152, 156, 157

Smith, William Kennedy, 51

s/m (sadomasochistic) narrative, 11, 213–29; as askesis, 225; and Blaustein's *Beyond the Mat*, 220–23, 226, 230 n.8; and "butch" performance, 227–28; and deconstructing the discursive body, 224–25; and emotional expression/experience, 216–17, 221; and family stability, 215–16; of female characters, 226–27; and good vs. evil, 221, 226; Bret Hart's family life vs. his violence, 219–20; of live events, 223; McMahon family *Wrestlemania* battle, 213–16; and Vince McMahon's double-cross of Bret Hart, 218–19; and melodrama, 218–19; and pain vs. sexual pleasure, 228–29; political implications of, 225; as therapeutic, 339; and truth, disclosure of, 222, 226

Smoking Gunns, 80

Snuka, Jimmy, 207

soccer, 40

Solar II, 108–9

soliloquies, 48–49

Sophocles: *Oedipus*, 2

Sopp, Monty, 7

South Park, 309

theme songs, 49, 337

Thorburn, David, 64 n.2, 171

Timberg, Richard, 170–71

title competitions, 34–35, 40–41

Titus, 260

Toy Biz, 232–33

training, 197–98

traveling shows, 224

Triple H. *See* Helmsley, Hunter Hearst

Tucker, C. Dolores, 146

Tugboat, 332–33

Turner, Ted, 286–87

20/20 (Stossel), 69, 72–75, 86 n.2

Twin Towers, 83

Tygress, 254

Ultimate Warrior, 47–48, 65 n.4, 295

Umstead, R. Thomas, 287–88

The Undertaker. *See* Calloway, Mark

"The Undertaker's Brides," 177–78

Union of People You OUght to ReSpect (UP YOURS), 274

University of Canterbury (Christchurch, New Zealand), 85

Unpredictable Johnny Rodz School of Professional Wrestling (Gleason's Arena, Brooklyn, N.Y.), 71, 86 n.1, 198

UPN network, 141, 143

upward mobility, 45

UP YOURS (Union of People You OUght to ReSpect), 274

Urban Wrestling Federation (UWF), 258 n.7

Valentine, Greg ("The Hammer"), 242–43

Valiant, Handsome Jimmy, 239–40

Valiant, Johnny (Tom Sullivan), 196, 197

Van Dam, Rob, 341

Van Zoonen, Liesbet, 170, 175

variety TV, 138

Vasquez, Francisco, 242

vaudeville, 1, 2, 3, 12, 153, 157

Vazari, Ali ("the Iron Sheik"), 73, 86 n.2, 267

Velázquez, Jesús ("El Murciélago el Veláz-quez"), 88, 101

Veloz, Ciclón, 90

Venis, Val, 8–9

Ventura, Jesse ("The Body"), 239–40, 295, 310–13, 314 n.6, 334

video games, 304

Vignola, Jo, 30

villains. *See* bastard character; heels

violence inspired by wrestling, 339–40

Virgil, 54, 58, 59–60

Virgin of Guadalupe, 115

Viscious, Sid, 244

voices, 50

Volkoff, Nickolai, 61, 207

Vosburgh, Dana, 288

Walkerdine, Valerie, 41–42

Walsh, David, 300–301

Walters, Barbara, 73, 74–75

Waltman, Sean, 172

Warner, William, 184

"War of the Worlds" (Welles), 330

Washington Post, 149

WBF (World Bodybuilding Federation), 194

WB network, 141

WCW (World Championship Wrestling), 6, 143, 162 n.17, 245–46, 250, 286–90, 319–20

Web sites. *See* female fan Web sites; male fan Web sites; RSPW

Weiner, Annette, 116

Welles, Orson: "War of the Worlds," 330

westerns, 138, 160 n.9

Whipwreck, Mikey, 336

White, Allon, 154, 265

white trash, 297

Will and Grace, 155

Williams, Frank, 242

Wilson, Melissa, 177

women: as an audience segment, 135, 159 n.2, 167; emotional display by, 38–39; good vs. evil, 337; marketing aimed at, 139; opportunities to look at men, 170; violence toward, 270–71, 291 n.3; voyeuristic treatment of, 269–70. *See also* female fan Web sites

work, 5, 343

working, 199–200

working class. *See* class

working the crowd, 200

working working light/snug/solid/stiff, 203, 211–12 n.2

World Bodybuilding Federation (WBF), 194

World Championship Wrestling. *See* WCW

World's Fairs, 224

World Wildlife Federation, 158 n.1

World Wrestling Entertainment. *See* WWE

World Wrestling Federation. *See* WWE

Wray, Matt, 297

Wrestlemania, 45–46, 211 n.1

Wrestlemania X-Seven, 213

wrestling, amateur, 23

wrestling, professional: backlash against, 296–97; the body of the wrestler, 1, 4, 7–8, 20 n.2, 25–26; vs. boxing, 24, 30, 193, 211 n.1; as business, 5, 12–13; careers in, 199–200; and consumption, 136, 138–40; vs. conventional sports, 4, 36–41, 192–95, 282; criticism of, 2–3, 6, 133, 134–36, 153; as cultural critique, 217–18; as drama, 193–94; emotionalism of, 3–4; family excesses of, 142–43; fans' influence on, 16–17; vs. figure skating, 200; French, 30; gendered power relations celebrated by, 3; gestures/signs in, 24–26, 31–32; as Good vs. Evil, 29–30, 31–32; vs. judo, 24, 28, 30; lineage as a popular art form, 1–2; logic of (*see* logic of professional wrestling); maturing of, 340–41; Mexican (*see* lucha libre); moral agenda of,

325–26; as a morality play, 69–70; oppression/subjugation/objectification performed by, 18–19; personae of wrestlers, 5; and the politics of culture, 15–17; and the politics of masculinity, 13–15, 42–43, 56–60, 62–63, 260–62, 266–67, 270–75, 278–86; and popular performance tradition, 153–58; as resistant/regressive, 158; revenues for, 194–95, 286; as satire/play, 18–20; sexual metaphors for, 206; as spectacle, 23–24, 26–28, 30–33, 40, 174 (*see also* melodrama, masculine); as a sport, 193–94; as sports entertainment, 223, 229–30 n.7, 282; tag team partnership in (*see* tag teams); and television's history, 134–40, 159–60 nn.6–8, 159 n.3, 160 nn.11–12; violence inspired by, 339–40; violence/sexuality in, 3–4, 6, 155, 321–24; and the wrestler as a basic sign, 6–7; wrestling as play/sex, 10–11. See also ECW; *RAW*; the real vs. the fake; *Smackdown*; WCW; WWE

Wrestling_hunks mailing list, 168

Wrestling Observer Newsletter, 288

wrestling schools, 197–98

Wrestling's Main Event, 236

Wrestling with Manhood (Jhally and Katz), 299–300, 306–8, 310

Wrestling with Shadows, 272, 299–300

WWE (World Wrestling Entertainment, Inc.; *formerly* World Wrestling Federation): audiences for, 36, 135–36, 143, 159 n.2, 260, 283–84; consolidation of the industry by, 12–13; control of televised pro wrestling by, 5–6; criticism of, 16; vs. ECW, 334–37; fans' influence on, 16–17; masculine mythology foregrounded by, 39; name change of, 158 n.1, 290 n.1; oppression/subjugation/objectification performed by, 18–19; popularity of, 143, 152, 210, 260, 289–90; PTC's lawsuit against, 146, 164 n.18; revenues for, 194,

286, 292 n.9; sports entertainment as focus of, 194; stock of, 275–76, 278–80, 285–86, 290, 291–92 nn.7–8, 291 n.5; travel by wrestlers, 20 n.3; venues for, 20 n.3; WCW bought by, 6, 286–90; weekly broadcasts by, 35. *See also* melodrama, masculine; *RAW*; *Smackdown*; *and individual wrestlers*

WWE.com, 331

WWF. *See* WWE

WWF World Champion belt, 34

Wynn, Ed, 137

Wynn, Keenan, 137

Xanta Claws, 332–33

xenophobia, 60–61

The X Files, 168

XFL (Extreme Football League), 12–13, 194, 262, 285–86, 292 n.8

X-pac Angel, 172, 180–81, 183

Xtreme Football League. *See* XFL

Yerpazian, 30

Yokozuna, 60, 318–19

"Your Online Search Engine for Professional Wrestling Websites," 174

Zabludovsky, Jacobo, 96

Zengota, Eric, 193

Zeus, 332–33